The New Historicism

The
New Historicism

Edited by H. ARAM VEESER

Routledge

New York   London

Published in 1989 by

Routledge
An imprint of Routledge, Chapman and Hall, Inc.
29 West 35 Street
New York, NY 10001

Published in Great Britain by

Routledge
11 New Fetter Lane
London EC4P 4EE

Copyright © 1989 by Routledge, Chapman and Hall, Inc.

Printed in the United States of America

Library of Congress Cataloging-in-Publication Data

The New Historicism / [edited by] Harold Veeser.
    p.   cm.
  ISBN 0-415-90069-7 : ISBN 0-415-90070-0 (pbk.)
  1. Historicism. I. Veeser, Harold, 1950– .
D16.9.N38 1988
901—dc19   88-20935
                              CIP

British Library Cataloguing in Publication Data

The New historicism
  1. Literature. criticism. Implications
of literary historiology
I. Veeser, Harold,
801'.95

  ISBN 0-415-90069-7
  ISBN 0-415-90070-0 Pbk

Contents

Contents

Acknowledgments

Completing a book of this magnitude requires the sustained, collective engagement of many people. Several of the contributors came to the project by way of two Modern Language Association special sessions that I organized: "The New Historicism: Political Commitment and the Postmodern Critic" (1986), with Gayatri Spivak, Richard Terdiman, Elizabeth Fox-Genovese, and Dominick LaCapra; and "Professionalism, Political Commitment, and the North American Critic" (1985), with Steven Mailloux, Paul Bove, Gerald Graff, Donald Pease, and Stanley Fish. Terence Hawkes, the editor of Routledge's New Accents series—and a prominent but skeptical cultural materialist in his own right—gave me early encouragement and guidance. William Germano, our editor at Routledge, took up the project, provided erudition and energy, and brought the volume to fruition.

Eighteen of the essays included here are appearing in print for the first time. Three essays or parts thereof have been published elsewhere: "Towards a Poetics of Culture," *Southern Review* (Australia) 20 (1987), 3–5; "The Struggle for the Cultural Heritage: Christina Stead Refunctions Charles Dickens and Mark Twain," *Cultural Critique* 2 (1985–6), 171–89; and "Foucault's Legacy: A New Historicism?" in Frank Lentricchia, *Ariel and the Police: Michel Foucault, William James, Wallace Stevens* (Madison: University of Wisconsin Press, 1988), 86–102. I wish to thank the publishers and editors who granted me their permission to reprint these essays.

I owe my own intellectual formation to, among others, Edward W. Said, Gayatri Spivak, Cyrus Veeser, Stephen Greenblatt, and Stanley Fish—though I am certain that the latter, at least, would disagree with almost everything I have said in my introduction. Finally, I have received important suggestions, encouragement, support and criticism from James Lee Burke, Janice Cryer, Sarah Daugherty, Albert Goldbarth, Daniel Javitch, Cassie Kircher, Ellen Messer–Davidow, Charlene Roesner, Peter Rose, Cheryl Shell, Paul Smith, Edward Tayler, and Peter Zoller, who have given of themselves with exceptional generosity. The Wichita State University has been a stimulating and supportive place to work.

Introduction

H. Aram Veeser

"I began with the desire to speak with the dead."[1]

Thus begins a book recently published by the first scholar to name as "a new historicism" the emerging emphasis in literary and American cultural studies. Although he now prefers the phrase "poetics of culture," for reasons explained in his essay in this volume, this sentence manages—brief as it is— to capture a good part of the New Historicism's appeal. Personal, even auto- biographical, the sentence challenges the norm of disembodied objectivity to which humanists have increasingly aspired. Far from invisible, this writer's desires and interests openly preside: the investigative project proceeds from an unabashed passion. Nor is that passion bland or banal.

Conventional scholars—entrenched, self-absorbed, protective of guild loyalties and turf, specialized in the worst senses—have repaired to their disciplinary enclaves and committed a classic *trahison des clercs*. As the first successful counterattack in decades against this profoundly anti-intellectual ethos, the New Historicism has given scholars new opportunities to cross the boundaries separating history, anthropology, art, politics, literature, and economics. It has struck down the doctrine of noninterference that forbade humanists to intrude on questions of politics, power, indeed on all matters that deeply affect people's practical lives—matters best left, prevailing wis- dom went, to experts who could be trusted to preserve order and stability in "our" global and intellectual domains.

New Historicism threatens this quasi-monastic order. In response, the platoons of traditionalists have predictably rushed to their guns. Announcing a state of emergency, institutional guardians over literature and the humani- ties have denounced the "new historicism" they consider hostile to Great Books and American values. Former Secretary of Education William Bennett struck first with his landmark address, "To Reclaim a Legacy" (*American Educator* 21 [1985]), and new traditionalists—including Allan Bloom, Ger- trude Himmelfarb, E. D. Hirsh and others—lent covering fire. When women, ethnic minorities, and radicals at Stanford claimed their part of the cultural inheritance, Bennett carried the attack to Palo Alto. Meanwhile, however, from the opposite side of the academic-ideological divide, J. Hillis Miller, then-president of the largest professional organization of English professors, decried the "turn away from theory toward history," and the journal *PMLA* published Edward Pechter's charge that "the specter of a new historicism— a kind of 'Marxist criticism' " is haunting the humanistic disciplines: the New Historicism put even liberals on red alert.

Accusations of canon-bashing and "the lunge toward barbarism," reiterated in *The Wall Street Journal, NYRB,* the *New York Times, Newsweek,* and *Harper's,* have projected a New Historicism unambiguously Left in its goals, subversive in its critique, and destructive in its impact. Big-ticket defense systems make costly mistakes, however. Contrary to middlebrow conservatives, some contributors to this volume contend that New Historicism is itself a conservative trend. Leftists are alarmed, for example, at the New Historicists' reluctance to speak of facts. Progressives can accept, for example, one New Historicist's fabrication of a fictitious Oxbridge graduate's British Honduras diary as an illuminating way to open his study of Colonial encounters in *The Tempest* (Malcolm Evans, *Signifying Nothing* [Athens, Georgia: University of Georgia Press, 1986]). But cannot such methods, they ask, at the same time justify specious propaganda masquerading as scholarship, such as Joan Peters' *From Time Immemorial,* where fabricated data "proves" that Palestinians are a "fairy tale"? Or Clifford Irving's biography of Howard Hughes? Or French neofascist tomes revealing that the Jewish Holocaust never occurred? Contributor Hayden White concedes that the New Historicism leaves intact no theoretical basis on which to call to account even the most spurious historical revisions.

Whereas these critics worry that New Historicism may incapacitate the scholarly armature of proof and evidence, others on the left distrust the culturalism and textualism that New Historicism seems to nourish. "Right New Historicists," in Gerald Graff's phrase, unwittingly join Bennett in idolizing community norms. Even oppositional New Historicists use the critical methods they question and so, Terdiman, Spivak, and Pecora suggest, replicate the authority they suspect. Contributor Frank Lentricchia avers that they revive liberalism and the postromantic sentimentalization of the arts. These conflicting readings prove if nothing else that far from a hostile united front or a single politics, "the New Historicism" remains a phrase without an adequate referent. Like other such phrases—from Action Painting to New Model Army—the rubric offers a site that many parties contend to appropriate.

This collection reflects that heterogeneity and contention. Although Stephen Greenblatt, Louis Montrose, and Catherine Gallagher are recognized practitioners of New Historicism, others in the book would locate themselves outside the group. The volume was not designed as a formal debate, but frequent encounters allowed many contributors to respond to each other's work, lending unusual coherence to the collection as a whole. The contributors traverse the spectrum of cultural critique and highlight the internal fractures that make current academic cultural criticism so intriguingly various. Contrary to the Bennett-Pechter Red scare, New Historicism is as much a reaction against Marxism as a continuation of it. Avowed New Historicist Gallagher ruffles graying New Leftists by arguing that good criticism embodies no necessary politics, but is constitutively driven by fierce debate and contest. Far from a single projectile hurled against Western civilization, New Historicism has a portmanteau quality. It brackets together literature, ethnography, anthropology, art history, and other disciplines and sciences, hard and soft. It scrutinizes the barbaric acts that sometimes underwrite high cultural purposes and asks that we not blink away our complicity. At the same time, it encourages us to admire the sheer intricacy and unavoidability of exchanges between culture and power. Its politics, its novelty, its historicality, its relationship to other prevailing ideologies all remain open questions. The present volume offers no definitive answers to these questions, but rather establishes the range and urgency of New Historicist inquiry.

A newcomer to New Historicism might feel reassured that, for all its heterogeneity, key assumptions continually reappear and bind together the avowed practitioners and even some of their critics: these assumptions are as follows:

1.   that every expressive act is embedded in a network of material practices;
2.   that every act of unmasking, critique, and opposition uses the tools it condemns and risks falling prey to the practice it exposes;
3.   that literary and non-literary "texts" circulate inseparably;
4.   that no discourse, imaginative or archival, gives access to unchanging truths nor expresses inalterable human nature;
5.   finally, as emerges powerfully in this volume, that a critical method and a language adequate to describe culture under capitalism participate in the economy they describe.

The New Historicists combat empty formalism by pulling historical considerations to the center stage of literary analysis. Following Clifford Geertz, Victor Turner, and other cultural anthropologists, New Historicists have evolved a method of describing culture in action. Taking their cue from Geertz's method of "thick description" they seize upon an event or anecdote—colonist John Rolfe's conversation with Pocahontas' father, a note found among Nietzsche's papers to the effect that "I have lost my umbrella"—and re-read it in such a way as to reveal through the analysis of tiny particulars the behavioral codes, logics, and motive forces controlling a whole society.

Suspicious of any criticism predetermined by a Marxist or liberal grid,

New Historicists eschew overarching hypothetical constructs in favor of surprising coincidences. The essays in this book are less concerned to project long-range trajectories than to note bizarre overlappings: of window-smashing Suffragette street actions and the "hobble skirt" presented by the Parisian fashions house of Worth (Jane Marcus); of Arthur Schlesinger's expansive New Frontier rhetoric and explosive anti-war and inner-city riots (Jon Klancher); of the end of an asphalt road and the beginning of Yosemite's regulated, policed terrain, its "wilderness" (Greenblatt); of a seventeenth-century hermaphrodite's criminal trial, Shakespeare's *Twelfth Night,* and leather and rubber gloves (Joel Fineman); of an ancient Roman tax bracket and the track-system in modern high schools (Richard Terdiman); of Charles Dickens, partriarchy, and literary incest in a popular '40s novel (Jonathan Arac); of Balinese gambling customs, mass political murder, and the C.I.A. (Vince Pecora); of Zuni tribesman eating offal and scatology in writings by Sir Thomas More and Luther; of Mailer's *The Executioner's Song* and a stabbing death in New Orleans; of anodized aluminum plaques depicting waterfalls posted beside a primordial "unspoiled" cascade. Such examples support one contributor's charge that New Historicists perform amazing contortions in order to avoid causal, deterministic equations.

The motives are clear. By forsaking what it sees as an outmoded vocabulary of allusion, symbolization, allegory, and mimesis, New Historicism seeks less limiting means to expose the manifold ways culture and society affect each other. The central difficulty with these terms lies in the way they distinguish literary text and history as foreground and background: criticism bound to such metaphors narrows its concern to the devices by means of which literature reflects or refracts its contexts. New Historicism renegotiates these relationships between texts and other signifying practices, going so far (Terence Hawkes has observed) as to dissolve "literature" back into the historical complex that academic criticism has traditionally held at arm's length.[2] It retains at the same time, those methods and materials that gave old fashioned literary study its immense interpretive authority.

Is any of this really new? New Historicists have conducted truly novel parlays with the past. Their efforts evoke unsuspected borrowings and lendings among activities, institutions, and archives—metaphors, ceremonies, dances, emblems, items of clothing, popular stories—previously held to be independent and unrelated. As Brook Thomas's contribution reminds us, one can find as many sorts of "new" history as one can find historians, and an introduction is no place to summarize them all. But in the most general terms, New Historicists argue that earlier literary historiographers tended to use totalizing or atomizing methods—a Tillyard might read one Shakespearean speech as exemplifying views embraced by every Elizabethan, a Lukács might read the demise of feudalism in the death of Hamlet. Or, alternatively, a Frances Yates might minutely disclose the occult number symbolism in an

Elizabethan tournament plan, or the influence of Giodano Bruno on George Chapman. New Historicism sets aside the potted history of ideas, the Marxist *grand récit,* the theory of economic stages, the lock-picking analysis *à clef,* and the study of authorial influence. By discarding what they view as mono-logic and myopic historiography, by demonstrating that social and cultural events commingle messily, by rigorously exposing the innumerable trade-offs, the competing bids and exchanges of culture, New Historicists can make a valid claim to have established new ways of studying history and a new awareness of how history and culture define each other.

The arrival of a new poetics of culture was neither unscheduled nor unwelcome. Stephen Orgel, Roy Strong, and D. J. Gordon, whose studies of Renaissance texts showed connections between cultural codes and political power, were doing New Historicism before anyone thought to give it a name, and the still earlier Warburg-Courtauld Institute in England had influenced these pioneers. But the New Historicism surfaced as an identifiable tendency in academic literary and cultural criticism a scant ten years ago with Green-blatt's English Institute Essay, "Improvisation and Power," Montrose's path-breaking studies of power and Renaissance poetry, and a spate of articles and MLA sessions centering on ideology and English Renaissance texts. Greenblatt's own *Renaissance Self-Fashioning* (1980) and the journal *Repre-sentations* founded by Gallagher, Walter Benn Michaels, Greenblatt, and others consolidated the New Historicism, not as a doctrine but as a set of themes, preoccupations, and attitudes. Even the rubric "New Historicism" came belatedly, coined in an aside in Greenblatt's introduction to a special issue of *Genre* in 1982.

In a decade the New Historicism has mustered able cadres across several periods and disciplines and produced a substantial body of publications but it has been Renaissance scholars who have evolved the fundamental themes and concerns. These have included the idea that autonomous self and text are mere holograms, effects that intersecting institutions produce; that selves and texts are defined by their relation to hostile others (despised and feared Indians, Jews, Blacks) and disciplinary power (the King, Religion, Masculin-ity); that critics hoping to unlock the worship of culture should be less concerned to construct a holistic master story of large-scale structural ele-ments directing a whole society than to perform a differential analysis of the local conflicts engendered in individual authors and local discourses.[3] Subsequently New Historicism has enlarged its range beyond the Renais-sance to regions as far afield as the American Renaissance, British Romanti-cism, Victorian Studies, and Latin American Literature, so that today no bastion of literary scholarship has managed to exclude New Historicism.

It seems a propitious time to bring forward a volume that assesses the state of the art in the New Historicism. For while New Historicists have made critical self-scrutiny their sine qua non, there has been no systematic discussion of the methodology and implications of the tendency. Its sheer success has made the task difficult, since the volume and variety of the work done and the blurred boundaries of the concept makes a fully representative selection impossible. Given the purpose of this book—to define, illustrate, and raise questions about New Historicism—it seemed a sound idea to explore limits and differences.

Circulation, negotiation, exchange—these and other marketplace metaphors characterize New Historicists' working vocabulary, as if to suggest the ways capitalism envelops not just the text but also the critic. By making that entanglement their premise, Catherine Gallagher suggests that New Historicists echo the edgiest, uneasiest Marxist voices—those of Benjamin, Adorno, and others who sense the difficulty of liberating themselves, much less humankind. In Greenblatt's words, "Society's dominant currencies, money and prestige, are invariably involved." So insistently do New Historicists spotlight their own compromised motives—Montrose enacts one such exemplary confession below—that they become targets of Frank Lentricchia's charge that such *mea culpas* have become ritual gestures.

The moment of exchange fascinates the New Historicists. Circulation involves not just money and knowledge but also, for New Historicists, prestige—the "possession" of social assets as evanescent as taste in home furnishings or as enduring as masculinity. Their point is that such social advantages circulate as a form of material currency that tends to go unnoticed because it cannot be crudely translated into liquid assets. One New Historicists study of *As You Like It* shows that Rosalind profits by exchanging gender-roles. While such transactions are most visible in literature, the New Historicist point is that such exchanges happen all the time. Everyone's sexual identity, not just Rosalind's, remains in ceaseless upheaval, but our society rewards those who choose one gender or other. Symbolic capital accrues in the ruses used to enhance one's social standing in the marriage mart, or in the symbolic meal given in the mason's honor when a house is built—a bonus disguised as a gift. All such practices have cash equivalents and aim, even if unconsciously, at material advantages.

For Greenblatt the critic's role is to dismantle the dichotomy of the economic and the non-economic, to show that the most purportedly disinterested and self-sacrificing practices, including art, aim to maximize material or symbolic profit. Such a critic would not conduct symptomatic readings— so called for their focus on traces, margins, things left unsaid, and other telltale signs of all that a text represses. The New Historicist rarely practices criticism as a physician, as though, after the manner of Macherey, Althusser, or Eagleton, one could diagnose the absences or self-deception "in" a text. (Gayatri Spivak argues below that critics should regard texts as their accomplices, not as their patients.)

Rather the New Historicist will try to discover how the traces of social circulation are effaced. The degree to which a text successfully erases its practical social function matches the degree to which it secures autonomy as a poetic, purely cultural, unmarketable object; on its ability to sustain this illusion depends its privileged status in a zone that supposedly supersedes market values.

By challenging this traditional aesthetic claim and showing that symbolic exchanges have cash value, New Historicists also challenge the assumptions that help to compartmentalize the disciplines. Often cited as exemplary New Historicism is Montrose's early paper, " 'The Place of a Brother' in *As You Like It*: Social Process and Comic Form" (in *Shakespeare Quarterly* 32 [1981], 28-54). This study entails evidence taken from the literary and autobiographical subgenre of "advice to a son"; a social historian's data on the endowments, inheritances, and marriage patterns of younger brothers; the rites of pastoral sequestration and initiation performed by tribal adolescents, as reported by ethnographers and anthropologists: all these may be summoned to contextualize the Shakespearean comedy. A seemingly fixed social given like masculinity reemerges as a tenuous value that its possessors must unendingly strive to keep in place. The enduring condition of gender becomes the volatile act of gendering.

In this way, New Historicists muddy the formal walkways that criticism has up to now generally followed. They refuse to apportion the discussion of character, language, and theme to literary scholars, of primitive customs to anthropologists, of demographic patterns to social historians. By redistributing this disciplinary legacy, New Historicists threaten all defenders of linear chronology and progressive history, whether Marxists or Whig optimists. Those who would jealously enclose their private gardens against communal interference may well lock arms against a criticism that mingles disparate periods and upsets the calculus of Left and Right politics.

As the tenor of debate in this volume amply demonstrates, crisis not consensus surrounds the New Historicist project. Instead of condensing into the latest academic orthodoxy, as in 1986 Montrose feared it might, New Historicism has been kept off-balance by internal stresses, and has had to plunge ahead just to keep itself erect.[4] Few of the feminist, Marxist, Third World, and cultural materialist critics included here would accept, for example, the New Historicist account of the way symbolic capital circulates. From Richard Terdiman's Marxist point of view, it is important to give the concept of "circulation" a class reference: the privileged classes guard their symbolic capital as jealously as they manage their pelf. Marxist-feminist Judith Newton acidly notes that New Historicists often counterfeit earlier feminist ideas and claim them as their own. The pragmatist with a politics, Frank Lentricchia, charges that New Historicists not only fail to show how traces of social circulation are effaced by art, but also place art over against the degraded marketplace of life. For Spivak, coming from her Third World, feminist, Marxist, and deconstructionist background, culture and criticism circulate too peaceably already; instead they should interrupt and push each other to crisis. Graff contends that Right New Historicists border on installing a new complacency, and Pecora argues that "thick description" screens off the world and halts intellectual traffic.

But the contributors can speak for themselves. Their essays cut a wide swath from thick description to severe pragmatism through far-ranging cultural critique. Readers should be pleased to find that the contributors to this book have written in accessible language, clearly summarizing the issues raised by New Historicism and explaining the debates within and around it. Though the volume leaves questions still open about the novelty of New Historicism, about its politics, influences, and relationship to competing methods and ideologies, it offers provisional and suggestive answers. At the very least, critics should now have to pause before they dismiss New Historicist inquiry as the latest lunge toward barbarism.

Notes

1.   Stephen Greenblatt, *Shakespearean Negotiations: The Circulation of Social Energy in Renaissance England* (Berkeley and Los Angeles: The University of California Press, 1988), 1.

2.   Terence Hawkes, "Uses and Abuses of the Bard," *Times Literary Supplement* (10 April 1987), 391–93.

3.   See *Shakespearean Negotiations*, "The Circulation of Social Energy," 1–20.

4.   It is instructive to compare Montrose, "Renaissance Literary Studies and the Subject of History," (*English Literary Renaissance* 16:1 [Winter 1986], 5–12) with Montrose's essay in this volume.

1

Towards a Poetics of Culture

Stephen Greenblatt

I feel in a somewhat false position, which is not a particularly promising way to begin, and I might as well explain why.[1] My own work has always been done with a sense of just having to go about and do it, without establishing first exactly what my theoretical position is. A few years ago I was asked by *Genre* to edit a selection of Renaissance essays, and I said OK. I collected a bunch of essays and then, out of a kind of desperation to get the introduction done, I wrote that the essays represented something I called a "new historicism." I've never been very good at making up advertising phrases of this kind; for reasons that I would be quite interested in exploring at some point, the name stuck much more than other names I'd very carefully tried to invent over the years. In fact I have heard—in the last year or so— quite a lot of talk about the "new historicism" (which for some reason in Australia is called Neohistoricism); there are articles about it, attacks on it, references to it in dissertations: the whole thing makes me quite giddy with amazement. In any case, as part of this peculiar phenomenon I have been asked to say something of a theoretical kind about the work I'm doing. So I shall try if not to define the new historicism, at least to situate it as a practice—a practice rather than a doctrine, since as far as I can tell (and I should be the one to know) it's no doctrine at all.

One of the peculiar characteristics of the "new historicism" in literary studies is precisely how unresolved and in some ways disingenuous it has been—I have been—about the relation to literary theory. On the one hand it seems to me that an openness to the theoretical ferment of the last few years is precisely what distinguishes the new historicism from the positivist historical scholarship of the early twentieth century. Certainly, the presence of Michel Foucault on the Berkeley campus for extended visits during the last five or six years of his life, and more generally the influence in America of European (and especially French) anthropological and social theorists, has helped to shape my own literary critical practice. On the other hand the historicist critics have on the whole been unwilling to enroll themselves in one or the other of the dominant theoretical camps.

I want to speculate on why this should be so by trying to situate myself in relation to Marxism on the one hand, and poststructuralism on the other. In the 1970s I used to teach courses with names like "Marxist Aesthetics" on the Berkeley campus. This came to an inglorious end when I was giving such a course—it must have been the mid-1970s—and I remember a student getting very angry with me. Now it's true that I tended to like those Marxist figures who were troubled in relation to Marxism—Walter Benjamin, the early rather than the later Lukács, and so forth—and I remember someone finally got up and screamed out in class "You're either a Bolshevik or a Menshevik—make up your fucking mind," and then slammed the door. It was a little unsettling, but I thought about it afterwards and realized that I wasn't sure whether I was a Menshevik, but I certainly wasn't a Bolshevik. After that I started to teach courses with names like "Cultural Poetics." It's true that I'm still more uneasy with a politics and a literary perspective that is untouched by Marxist throught, but that doesn't lead me to endorse propositions or embrace a particular philosophy, politics or rhetoric, *faute de mieux*.

Thus the crucial identifying gestures made by the most distinguished American Marxist aesthetic theorist, Fredric Jameson, seem to me highly problematic. Let us take, for example, the following eloquent passage from *The Political Unconscious:*

> the convenient working distinction between cultural texts that are social and political and those that are not becomes something worse than an error: namely, a symptom and a reinforcement of the reification and privatization of contemporary life. Such a distinction reconfirms that structural, experiential, and conceptual gap between the public and the private, between the social and the psychological, or the political and the poetic, between history or society and the "individual," which—the tendential law of social life under capitalism—maims our existence as individual subjects and paralyzes our thinking about time and change just as surely as it alienates us from our speech itself.[2]

A working distinction between cultural texts that are social and political and those that are not—that is, an aesthetic domain that is in some way marked off from the discursive institutions that are operative elsewhere in a culture—becomes for Jameson a malignant symptom of "privatization." Why should the "private" immediately enter into this distinction at all? Does the term refer to private property, that is, to the ownership of the means of production and the regulation of the mode of consumption? If so, what is the historical relation between this mode of economic organization and a working distinction between the political and the poetic? It would seem that in print, let alone in the electronic media, private ownership has led not to "privatization" but to the drastic communalization of all discourse, the constitution of an ever larger mass audience, the organization of a commercial sphere unimagined and certainly unattained by the comparatively modest attempts in pre-capitalist societies to organize public discourse. Moreover, is it not possible to have a communal sphere of art that is distinct from other communal spheres? Is this communal differentiation, sanctioned by the laws of property, not the dominant practice in capitalist society, manifestly in the film and television industries, but also, since the invention of movable type, in the production of poems and novels as well? Would we really find it less alienating to have no distinction at all between the political and the poetic— the situation, let us say, during China's Cultural Revolution? Or, for that matter, do we find it notably liberating to have our own country governed by a film actor who is either cunningly or pathologically indifferent to the traditional differentiation between fantasy and reality?

For *The Political Unconscious* any demarcation of the aesthetic must be aligned with the private which is in turn aligned with the psychological, the poetic, and the individual, as distinct from the public, the social, and the political. All of these interlocking distinctions, none of which seems to me philosophically or even historically bound up with the original "working distinction," are then laid at the door of capitalism with its power to "maim" and "paralyze" us as "individual subjects." Though we may find a differentiation between cultural discourses that are artistic and cultural discourses that are social or political well before the European seventeenth century, and in cultures that seem far removed from the capitalist mode of production, Jameson insists that somehow the perpetrator and agent of the alleged maiming is capitalism. A shadowy opposition is assumed between the "individual" (bad) and the "individual subject" (good); indeed the maiming of the latter creates the former.

The whole passage has the resonance of an allegory of the fall of man: once we were whole, agile, integrated; we were individual subjects but not individuals, we had no psychology distinct from the shared life of the society; politics and poetry were one. Then capitalism arose and shattered this luminous, benign totality. The myth echoes throughout Jameson's book, though by the close it has been eschatologically reoriented so that the totality lies not in a past revealed to have always already fallen but in the classless future. A philosophical claim then appeals to an absent empirical event. And literature is invoked at once as the dark token of fallenness and the shimmering emblem of the absent transfiguration.

But, of course, poststructuralism has raised serious questions about such a vision, challenging both its underlying oppositions and the primal organic unity that it posits as either paradisal origin or utopian, eschatalogical end.[3] This challenge has already greatly modified, though by no means simply displaced, Marxist discourse. I could exemplify this complex interaction between Marxism and poststructuralism by discussing Jameson's own most recent work in which he finds himself, from the perspective of postmodernism, deploring the loss of those "working distinctions" that at least enabled the left to identify its enemies and articulate a radical program.[4] But to avoid confusions, I want to focus instead on the work of Jean-François Lyotard. Here, as in *The Political Unconscious,* the distinction between discursive fields is once again at stake: for Lyotard the existence of proper names makes possible

> the co-existence of those worlds that Kant calls fields, territories, and domains— those worlds which of course present the same object, but which also make that object the stakes of heterogenous (or incommensurable) expectations in universes of phrases, none of which can be transformed into any other.[5]

Lyotard's model for these differentiated discourses is the existence of proper names. But now it is the role of capitalism not to demarcate discursive domains but, quite the opposite, to make such domains untenable. "Capital is that which wants a single language and a single network, and it never stops trying to present them" (p. 55). Lyotard's principal exhibit of this attempt by capital to institute a single language—what Bakhtin would call monologism—is Faurisson's denial of the Holocaust, and behind this denial, the Nazis' attempt to obliterate the existence of millions of Jews and other undesirables, an attempt Lyotard characterizes as the will "to strike from history and from the map entire worlds of names."

The problem with this account is that the Nazis did not seem particularly interested in exterminating names along with the persons who possessed those names; on the contrary, they kept, in so far as was compatible with a campaign of mass murder, remarkably full records, and they looked forward to a time in which they could share their accomplishment with a grateful world by establishing a museum dedicated to the culture of the wretches they had destroyed. The Faurisson affair is at bottom not an epistemological dilemma, as Lyotard claims, but an attempt to wish away evidence that is both substantial and verifiable. The issue is not an Epicurean paradox—"if death is there, you are not there; if you are there, death is not there; hence it is impossible for you to prove that death is there"—but a historical problem: what is the evidence of mass murder? How reliable is this evidence? Are there convincing grounds for denying or doubting the documented events? And if there are not such grounds, how may we interpret the motives of those who seek to cast doubt upon the historical record?

There is a further problem in Lyotard's use of the Faurisson affair as an instance of capitalist hostility to names: the conflation of Fascist apologetics and capitalism would seem to be itself an instance of monologism, since it suppresses all the aspects of capitalism that are wedded to the generation and inscription of individual identities and to the demarcation of boundaries separating those identities. We may argue, of course, that the capitalist insistence upon individuality is fraudulent, but is is difficult, I think, to keep the principle of endlessly proliferated, irreducible individuality separate from the market place version against which it is set. For it is capitalism, as Marx suggested, that mounts the West's most powerful and sustained assault upon collective, communal values and identities. And it is in the market place and in the state apparatus linked to the circulation and accumulation of capital that names themselves are forged. Proper names, as distinct from common names, seem less the victims than the products of property—they are bound up not only with the property one has in oneself, that is, with the theory of possessive individualism, but quite literally with the property one possesses, for proper names are insisted upon in the early modern period precisely in order to register them in the official documents that enable the state to calculate and tax personal property.[6]

The difference between Jameson's capitalism, the perpetrator of separate discursive domains, the agent of privacy, psychology, and the individual, and Lyotard's capitalism, the enemy of such domains and the destroyer of privacy, psychology, and the individual, may in part be traced to a difference between the Marxist and poststructuralist projects. Jameson, seeking to expose the fallaciousness of a separate artistic sphere and to celebrate the materialist integration of all discourses, finds capitalism at the root of the false differentiation; Lyotard, seeking to celebrate the differentiation of all discourses and to expose the fallaciousness of monological unity, finds capitalism at the root of the false integration. History functions in both cases as a convenient anecdotal ornament upon a theoretical structure, and capitalism appears not as a complex social and economic development in the West but as a malign philosophical principle.[7]

I propose that the general question addressed by Jameson and Lyotard—what is the historical relation between art and society or between one institutionally demarcated discursive practice and another?—does not lend itself to a single, theoretically satisfactory answer of the kind that Jameson and Lyotard are trying to provide. Or rather theoretical satisfaction here seems to depend upon a utopian vision that collapses the contradictions of history into a moral imperative. The problem is not simply the incompatibility of two theories—Marxist and poststructuralist—with one another, but the inability of either of the theories to come to terms with the apparently contradictory historical effects of capitalism. In principle, of course, both Marxism and poststructuralism seize upon contradictions: for the former they are signs of repressed class conflicts, for the latter they disclose hidden cracks in the spurious certainties of logocentrism. But in practice Jameson treats capitalism as the agent of repressive differentiation, while Lyotard treats it as the agent of monological totalization. And this effacement of contradiction is not the consequence of an accidental lapse but rather the logical outcome of theory's search for the obstacle that blocks the realization of its eschatological vision.

If capitalism is invoked not as a unitary demonic principle, but as a complex historical movement in a world without paradisal origins or chiliastic expectations, then an inquiry into the relation between art and society in capitalist cultures must address both the formation of the working distinction upon which Jameson remarks and the totalizing impulse upon which Lyotard remarks. For capitalism has characteristically generated neither regimes in which all discourses seem coordinated, nor regimes in which they seem radically isolated or discontinuous, but regimes in which the drive towards differentiation and the drive towards monological organization operate simultaneously, or at least oscillate so rapidly as to create the impression of simultaneity.

In a brilliant paper that received unusual attention, elicited a response from a White House speech-writer, and most recently generated a segment on CBS's "Sixty Minutes," the political scientist and historian Michael Rogin recently observed the number of times President Reagan has, at critical moments in his career, quoted lines from his own or other popular films. The President is a man, Rogin remarks, "whose most spontaneous moments— ('Where do we find such men?' about the American D-Day dead; 'I am paying for this microphone, Mr. Green,' during the 1980 New Hampshire primary debate)—are not only preserved and projected on film, but also turn out to be lines from old movies."[8] To a remarkable extent, Ronald Reagan, who made his final Hollywood film, *The Killers* in 1964, continues to live within the movies; he has been shaped by them, draws much of his cold war rhetoric from them, and cannot or will not distinguish between them and an external reality. Indeed his political career has depended upon an ability to project himself and his mass audience into a realm in which there is no distinction between simulation and reality.

The response from Anthony Dolan, a White House speech-writer who was asked to comment on Rogin's paper, was highly revealing. "What he's really saying," Dolan suggested, "is that all of us are deeply affected by a uniquely American art form: the movies."[9] Rogin had in fact argued that the presidential character "was produced from the convergence of two sets of substitutions which generated Cold War countersubversion in the 1940s and underlie its 1980s revival—the political replacement of Nazism by Communism, from which the national security state was born; and the psychological shift from an embodied self to its simulacrum on film." Both the political and the psychological substitution were intimately bound up with Ronald Reagan's career in the movies. Dolan in response rewrites Rogin's thesis into a celebration of the power of "a uniquely American art form" to shape "all of us." Movies, Dolan told the *New York Times* reporter, "heighten reality rather than lessen it."

Such a statement appears to welcome the collapse of the working distinction between the aesthetic and the real; the aesthetic is not an alternative realm but a way of intensifying the single realm we all inhabit. But then the spokesman went on to assert that the President "usually credits the films whose lines he uses." That is, at the moment of appropriation, the President acknowledges that he is borrowing from the aesthetic and hence acknowledges the existence of a working distinction. In so doing he respects and even calls attention to the difference between his own presidential discourse and the fictions in which he himself at one time took part; they are differences upon which his own transition from actor to politician in part depends, and they are the signs of the legal and economic system that he represents. For the capitalist aesthetic demands acknowledgments—hence the various marks of property rights that are flashed on the screen or inscribed in a text—and the political arena insists that it is not a fiction. That without acknowledgment the President delivers speeches written by Anthony Dolan or others does not appear to concern anyone; this has long been the standard operating procedure of American politicians. But it would concern people if the President recited speeches that were lifted without acknowledgment from old movies. He would then seem not to know the difference between fantasy and reality. And that might be alarming.

The White House, of course, was not responding to a theoretical problem, but to the implication that somehow the President did not fully recognize that he was quoting, or alternatively that he did realize it and chose to repress the fact in order to make a more powerful impression. In one version he is a kind of sleepwalker, in the other a plagiarist. To avoid these implications the White House spokesman needed in effect to invoke a difference that he had himself a moment before undermined.

The spokesman's remarks were hasty and *ad hoc,* but it did not take reflection to reproduce the complex dialectic of differentiation and identity that those remarks articulate. That dialectic is powerful precisely because it is by now virtually thoughtless; it takes a substantial intellectual effort to *separate* the boundaries of art from the subversion of those boundaries, an effort such as that exemplified in the work of Jameson or Lyotard. But the effect of such an effort is to remove itself from the very phenomenon it had proposed to analyze, namely, the relation between art and surrounding discourses in capitalist culture. For the effortless invocation of two apparently contradictory accounts of art is characteristic of American capitalism in the late twentieth century and an outcome of long-term tendencies in the relationship of art and capital; in the same moment a working distinction between the aesthetic and the real is established and abrogated.

We could argue, following Jameson, that the establishment of the distinction is the principal effect, with a view towards alienating us from our own imaginations by isolating fantasies in a private, apolitical realm. Or we could argue, following Lyotard, that the abrogation of the distinction is the principal effect, with a view towards effacing or evading differences by establishing a single, monolithic ideological structure. But if we are asked to choose between these alternatives, we will be drawn away from an analysis of the relation between capitalism and aesthetic production. For from the sixteenth century, when the effects for art of joint-stock company organization first began to be felt, to the present, capitalism has produced a powerful and effective oscillation between the establishment of distinct discursive domains and the collapse of those domains into one another. It is this restless oscillation rather than the securing of a particular fixed position that constitutes the distinct power of capitalism. The individual elements—a range of discontinuous discourses on the one hand, the monological unification of all discourses on the other—may be found fully articulated in other economic and social systems; only capitalism has managed to generate a dizzying, seemingly inexhaustible circulation between the two.

My use of the term *circulation* here is influenced by the work of Jacques Derrida, but sensitivity to the practical strategies of negotiation and exchange depends less upon poststructuralist theory than upon the circulatory rhythms of American politics. And the crucial point is that it is not politics alone but the whole structure of production and consumption—the systematic organization of ordinary life and consciousness—that generates the pattern of boundary making and breaking, the oscillation between demarcated objects and monological totality, that I have sketched. If we restrict our focus to the zone of political institutions, we can easily fall into the illusion that everything depends upon the unique talents—if that is the word—of Ronald Reagan, that he alone has managed to generate the enormously effective shuttling between massive, universalizing fantasies and centerlessness that characterizes his administration. This illusion leads in turn to what John Carlos Rowe has called the humanist trivialization of power, a trivialization that finds its local political expression in the belief that the fantasmatics of current American politics are the product of a single man and will pass with him. On the contrary, Ronald Reagan is manifestly the product of a larger and more durable American structure—not only a structure of power, ideological extremism and militarism, but of pleasure, recreation, and interest, a structure that shapes the spaces we construct for ourselves, the way we present "the news," the fantasies we daily consume on television or in the movies, the entertainments that we characteristically make and take.

I am suggesting then that the oscillation between totalization and difference, uniformity and the diversity of names, unitary truth and a proliferation of distinct entities—in short between Lyotard's capitalism and Jameson's—is built into the poetics of everyday behavior in America.[10] Let us consider, for example, not the President's Hollywood career but a far more innocent California pastime, a trip to Yosemite National Park. One of the most popular walks at Yosemite is the Nevada Falls Trail. So popular, indeed, is this walk that the Park Service has had to pave the first miles of the trail in order to keep them from being dug into trenches by the heavy traffic. At a certain point the asphalt stops, and you encounter a sign that tells you that you are entering the wilderness. You have passed then from the National Forests that surround the park—forests that serve principally as state-subsidized nurseries for large timber companies and hence are not visibly distinguishable from the tracts of privately owned forest with which they are contiguous—to the park itself, marked by the payment of admission to the uniformed ranger at the entrance kiosk, and finally to a third and privileged zone of publicly demarcated Nature. This zone, called the wilderness, is marked by the abrupt termination of the asphalt and by a sign that lists the rules of behavior that you must now observe: no dogs, no littering, no fires, no camping without a permit, and so forth. The wilderness then is signaled by an intensification of the rules, an intensification that serves as the condition of an escape from the asphalt.

You can continue on this trail then until you reach a steep cliff on to which the guardians of the wilderness have thoughtfully bolted a cast-iron stairway. The stairway leads to a bridge that spans a rushing torrent, and from the middle of the bridge you are rewarded with a splendid view of Nevada Falls. On the railing that keeps you from falling to your death as you enjoy your vision of the wilderness, there are signs—information about the dimensions of the falls, warnings against attempting to climb the treacherous, mist-slickened rocks, trail markers for those who wish to walk further—and an anodyzed aluminium plaque on which are inscribed inspirational, vaguely Wordsworthian sentiments by the California environmentalist John Muir. The passage, as best I can recall, assures you that in years to come you will treasure the image you have before you. And next to these words, also etched into the aluminium, is precisely an image: a photograph of Nevada Falls taken from the very spot on which you stand.

The pleasure of this moment—beyond the pleasure of the mountain air and the waterfall and the great boulders and the deep forest of Lodgepole and Jeffrey pine—arises from the unusually candid glimpse of the process of circulation that shapes the whole experience of the park. The wilderness is at once secured and obliterated by the official gestures that establish its boundaries; the natural is set over against the artificial through means that render such an opposition meaningless. The eye passes from the "natural" image of the waterfall to the aluminium image, as if to secure a difference (for why else bother to go to the park at all? Why not simply look at a book of pictures?), even as that difference is effaced. The effacement is by no means complete—on the contrary, parks like Yosemite are one of the ways in which the distinction between nature and artifice is constituted in our society—and yet the Park Service's plaque on the Nevada Falls bridge conveniently calls attention to the interpenetration of nature and artifice that makes the distinction possible.

What is missing from this exemplary fable of capitalist aesthetics is the question of property relations, since the National Parks exist precisely to suspend or marginalize that question through the ideology of protected public space. Everyone owns the parks. That ideology is somewhat bruised by the actual development of a park like Yosemite, with its expensive hotel, a restaurant that has a dress code, fancy gift shops and the like, but it is not entirely emptied out; even the administration of the right-wing Secretary of the Interior James Watt stopped short of permitting a private golf course to be constructed on park grounds, and there was public outrage when a television production company that had contracted to film a series in Yosemite decided to paint the rocks to make them look more realistic. What we need is an example that combines recreation or entertainment, aesthetics, the public sphere, and private property. The example most compelling to a literary critic like myself is not a political career or a national park but a novel.

In 1976, a convict named Gary Gilmore was released from a federal penitentiary and moved to Provo, Utah. Several months later, he robbed and killed two men, was arrested for the crimes, and convicted of murder. The case became famous when Gilmore demanded that he be executed—a punishment that had not been inflicted in America for some years, due to legal protections—and, over the strenuous objections of the American Civil Liberties Union and the National Association for the Advancement of Colored People, had his way. The legal maneuvers and the eventual firing-squad execution became national media events. Well before the denouement the proceedings had come to the attention of Norman Mailer and his publisher Warner Books which is, as it announces on its title pages, "a Warner Communications Company." Mailer's research assistant, Jere Herzenberg, and a hack writer and interviewer, Lawrence Schiller, conducted extensive interviews and acquired documents, records of court proceedings, and personal papers such as the intimate letters between Gilmore and his girlfriend. Some of these materials were in the public domain but many of them were not; they were purchased, and the details of the purchases themselves become part of the materials that were reworked by Mailer into *The Executioner's Song*,[11] a "true life novel" as it is called, that brilliantly combines documentary realism with Mailer's characteristic romance themes. The novel was a critical and popular success—a success signaled not only by the sheaves of admiring reviews but by the Universal Product Code printed on its paperback book cover. It was subsequently made into an NBC-TV mini-series where on successive evenings it helped to sell cars, soap powder, and deodorant.

Mailer's book had further, and less predictable, ramifications. While he was working on *The Executioner's Song,* there was an article on Mailer in *People* magazine. The article caught the attention of a convict named Jack H. Abbott who wrote to offer him first-hand instruction on the conditions of prison life. An exchange of letters began, and Mailer grew increasingly impressed not only with their detailed information but with what he calls their "literary measure." The letters were cut and arranged by a Random House editor, Erroll McDonald, and appeared as a book called *In the Belly of the Beast*. This book too was widely acclaimed and contributed, with Mailer's help, to win a parole for its author.

"As I am writing these words," Mailer wrote in the Introduction to Abbott's book, "it looks like Abbott will be released on parole this summer. It is certainly the time for him to get out."[12] "I have never come into bodily contact with another human being in almost twenty years," wrote Abbott in his book, "except in combat; in acts of struggle, of violence" (63). Shortly after his release, Abbott, now a celebrity, approached a waiter in an all-night restaurant and asked to use the men's room. The waiter—Richard Adan, an aspiring actor and playwright—told Abbott that the restaurant had no men's room and asked him to step outside. When Adan followed him on to the sidewalk, Abbott, apparently thinking that he was being challenged, stabbed Adan in the heart with a kitchen knife. Abbott was arrested and convicted once again of murder. The events have themselves been made into a play, also called *In the Belly of the Beast*, that recently opened to very favorable reviews.

Literary criticism has a familiar set of terms for the relationship between a work of art and the historical events to which it refers: we speak of allusion, symbolization, allegorization, representation, and above all mimesis. Each of these terms has a rich history and is virtually indispensable, and yet they all seem curiously inadequate to the cultural phenomenon which Mailer's book and Abbott's and the television series and the play constitute. And their inadequacy extends to aspects not only of contemporary culture but of the culture of the past. We need to develop terms to describe the ways in which material—here official documents, private papers, newspaper clippings, and so forth—is transferred from one discursive sphere to another and becomes aesthetic property. It would, I think, be a mistake to regard this process as uni-directional—from social discourse to aesthetic discourse—not only because the aesthetic discourse in this case is so entirely bound up with capitalist venture but because the social discourse is already charged with aesthetic energies. Not only was Gilmore explicitly and powerfully moved by the film version of *One Flew Over the Cuckoo's Nest*, but his entire pattern of behavior seems to have been shaped by the characteristic representations of American popular fiction, including Mailer's own.

Michael Baxandall has argued recently that "art and society are analytical concepts from two different kinds of categorization of human experience . . . unhomologous systematic constructions put upon interpenetrating subject-matters." In consequence, he suggests, any attempt to relate the two must first "modify one of the terms till it matches the other, but keeping note of what modification has been necessary since this is a necessary part of one's information."[13] It is imperative that we acknowledge the modification and find a way to measure its degree, for it is only in such measurements that we can hope to chart the relationship between art and society. Such an admonition is important—methodological self-consciousness is one of the distinguishing marks of the new historicism in cultural studies as opposed to a historicism based upon faith in the transparency of signs and interpretative procedures—but it must be supplemented by an understanding that the work of art is not itself a pure flame that lies at the source of our speculations. Rather the work of art is itself the product of a set of manipulations, some of them our own (most striking in the case of works that were not originally conceived as "art" at all but rather as something else—votive objects, propaganda, prayer, and so on), many others undertaken in the construction of the original work. That is, the work of art is the product of a negotiation between a creator or class of creators, equipped with a complex, communally shared repertoire of conventions, and the institutions and practices of society. In order to achieve the negotiation, artists need to create a currency that is valid for a meaningful, mutually profitable exchange. It is important to emphasize that the process involves not simply appropriation but exchange, since the existence of art always implies a return, a return normally measured in pleasure and interest. I should add that the society's dominant currencies, money and prestige, are invariably involved, but I am here using the term "currency" metaphorically to designate the systematic adjustments, symbolizations and lines of credit necessary to enable an exchange to take place. The terms "currency" and "negotiation" are the signs of our manipulation and adjustment of the relative systems.

Much recent theoretical work must, I think, be understood in the context of a search for a new set of terms to understand the cultural phenomenon that I have tried to describe. Hence, for example, Wolfgang Iser writes of the creation of the aesthetic dimension through the "dynamic oscillation" between two discourses; the East German Marxist Robert Weimann argues that

> the process of making certain things one's own becomes inseparable from making other things (and persons) alien, so that the act of appropriation must be seen always already to involve not only self-projection and assimilation but alienation through reification and expropriation. . . .

Anthony Giddons proposes that we substitute a concept of textual distanciation for that of the autonomy of the text, so that we can fruitfully grasp the "recursive character" of social life and of language.[14] Each of these formulations—and, of course, there are significant differences among them—pulls away from a stable, mimetic theory of art and attempts to construct in its stead an interpretative model that will more adequately account for the unsettling circulation of materials and discourses that is, I have argued, the heart of modern aesthetic practice. It is in response to this practice that contemporary theory must situate itself: not outside interpretation, but in the hidden places of negotiation and exchange.

Notes

1. This is the text of a lecture given at the University of Western Australia on 4 September 1986. A slightly different version appears in Murrary Krieger, ed., *The Aims of Representation* (New York: Columbia Univ. Press. 1987).

2. Fredric Jameson, *The Political Unconscious: Narrative as a Socially Symbolic Act* (Ithaca: Cornell Univ. Press. 1981) p. 20.

3. See Mark Poster, "Foucault, Poststructuralism, and the Mode of Information," in *The Aims of Representation.*

4. Jameson himself does not directly account for the sudden reversal in his thinking; he suggests rather that it is not his thinking that has changed but capitalism itself. Following Ernest Mandel, he suggests that we have moved into late capitalism, and in this state cultural production and consumption operate by wholly different rules. In the cultural logic of postmodernism, the working distinctions Jameson earlier found paralyzing and malignant have in fact vanished, giving way to an organization of discourse and perception that is at once dreadful and visionary. Dreadful because the new postmodern condition has obliterated all the place markers—inside and outside, culture and society, orthodoxy and subversion—that made it possible to map the world and hence mount a critique of its power structures. Visionary because this new multi-national world, a world with intensities rather than emotions, elaborated surfaces rather than hidden depths, random, unreadable signs rather than signifiers, intimates a utopian release from the traditional nightmare of traditional history. The doubleness of the postmodern is perfectly figured for Jameson by contemporary architecture, most perfectly by the Bonaventura Hotel in Los Angeles.
    The rapidity of the shift between modern and postmodern charted in Jameson's shift from *The Political Unconscious* (1981) to "Postmodernism, or the Cultural Logic of Late Capitalism," *New Left Review*, No. 146 (July–Aug. 1984), pp. 53–93, is, to say the least, startling.

5. J. F. Lyotard, "Judiciousness in Dispute or, Kant after Marx," in *The Aims of Representation, p.* 37.

6. See, for example, William E. Tate, *The Parish Chest: A Study in the Records of Parochial Administration in England* (Cambridge: Cambridge Univ. Press, 1946).

7. Alternatively, of course, we can argue, as Jameson in effect does, that there are two capitalisms. The older, industrial capitalism was the agent of distinctions; the new, late capitalism is the effacer of distinctions. The detection of one tendency or the other in the phase of capitalism where it does not theoretically belong can be explained by invoking the distinction between residual and emergent. I find this scholastic saving of the theory infinitely depressing.

8. Michael Rogin, *"Ronald Reagan,"The Movie and Other Episodes in Political Demonology* (Berkeley: University of California Press, 1988).

9. Quoted by reporter Michael Tolchin in the *New York Times* account of Rogin's paper, headlined "How Reagan Always Gets the Best Lines," *New York Times,* 9 Sept. 1985, p. 10.

10.   I borrow the phrase "the poetics of everyday behavior" from Iurii M. Lotman. See his essay in *The Semiotics of Russian Cultural History,* ed. A. D. Nakhimovsky and A. S. Nakhimovsky (Cornell: Cornell Univ. Press, 1985).

11.   Norman Mailer, *The Executioner's Song* (New York: Warner Books, 1979).

12.   Introduction to Jack Henry Abbott, *In the Belly of the Beast: Letters from Prison* (New York: Random House, 1981), p. xviii.

13.   Michael Baxandall. "Art, Society, and the Bouger Principle," *Representations,* 12 (1985), 40–41.

14.   All in *The Aims of Representation.*

2

Professing the Renaissance:
The Poetics and Politics of Culture

Louis A. Montrose

There has recently emerged within Renaissance studies, as in Anglo-American literary studies generally, a renewed concern with the historical, social, and political conditions and consequences of literary production and reproduction: The writing and reading of texts, as well as the processes by which they are circulated and categorized, analyzed and taught, are being reconstrued as historically determined and determining modes of cultural work; apparently autonomous aesthetic and academic issues are being reunderstood as inextricably though complexly linked to other discourses and practices—such linkages constituting the social networks within which individual subjectivities and collective structures are mutually and continuously shaped. This general reorientation is the unhappy subject of J. Hillis Miller's 1986 Presidential Address to the Modern Language Association. In that address, Miller noted with some dismay—and with some hyperbole—that "literary study in the past few years has undergone a sudden, almost universal turn away from theory in the sense of an orientation toward language as such and has made a corresponding turn toward history, culture, society, politics, institutions, class and gender conditions, the social context, the material base."[1] By such a formulation, Miller polarizes the linguistic and the social. However, the prevailing tendency across cultural studies is to emphasize their reciprocity and mutual constitution: On the one hand, the social is understood to be discursively constructed; and on the other, language-use is understood to be always and necessarily dialogical, to be socially and materially determined and constrained.

Miller's categorical opposition of "reading" to cultural critique, of "theory" to the discourses of "history, culture, society, politics, institutions, class and gender" seems to me not only to oversimplify both sets of terms but also to suppress their points of contact and compatibility. The propositions and operations of deconstructive reading may be employed as powerful tools of ideological analysis. Derrida himself has recently suggested that, at least in his own work and in the context of European cultural politics, they have always been so: He writes that "deconstructive readings and writings are concerned not only with . . . discourses, with conceptual and semantic contents. . . . Deconstructive practices are also and first of all political and institutional practices."[2] The notorious Derridean aphorism, *"il n'ya pas de hors-text,"* may be invoked to abèt an escape from the determinate necessities of history, a self-abandonment to the indeterminate pleasures of the text; however, it may also be construed as an insistence upon the ideological force of discourse in general and of those discourses in particular which reduce the work of discourse to the mere reflection of an ontologically prior, essential or empirical reality.

The multiplicity of unstable, variously conjoined and conflicting discourses that may be said to inhabit the field of post-structuralist theory have in common the problematization of those processes by which meaning is produced and grounded, and a heightened (though, of course, necessarily limited) reflexivity concerning their own assumptions and constraints, their methods and their motives. Miller wholly identifies "theory" with domesticated, politically eviscerated varieties of Deconstruction, which he privileges ethically and epistemologically in relation to what he scorns as "ideology"— that impassioned and delusional condition which "the critics and antagonists of deconstruction on the so-called left and so-called right" (289) are said to share. Although his polemic indiscriminately though not unintentionally lumps them with the academy's intellectually and politically reactionary forces, the various modes of sociopolitical and historical criticism have not only been challenged and influenced by the theoretical developments of the past two decades but have also been vitally engaged in their definition and direction. And one such direction is the understanding that "theory" does not reside serenely above "ideology" but rather is mired within it. Representations of the world in written discourse are engaged in constructing the world, in shaping the modalities of social reality, and in accommodating their writers, performers, readers, and audiences to multiple and shifting subject positions within the world they both constitute and inhabit. Traditionally, "ideology" has referred to the system of ideas, values, and beliefs common to any social group; in recent years, this vexed but indispensable term has in its most general sense come to be associated with the processes by which social subjects are formed, re-formed and enabled to perform as conscious agents in an apparently meaningful world.[3] In such terms, our professional practice, like our subject matter, is a production of ideology: By this I mean not merely that it bears the traces of the professor's values, beliefs, and experiences—his or her socially constructed subjectivity—but also that it actively instantiates those values, beliefs and experiences. From this perspective, any claim for what Miller calls an "orientation to language *as such*" (my italics) is itself—always already—an orientation to language that is being produced from a position *within* "history, culture, society, politics, institutions, class and gender conditions."

As if to reinforce Miller's sense of a general crisis in literary studies with the arraignment of an egregious example, the issue of *PMLA* which opens with his Presidential Address immediately continues with an article on the "politicizing" of Renaissance Drama. The latter begins with the ominous warning that "A specter is haunting criticism—the specter of a new historicism."[4] Edward Pechter's parody of *The Communist Manifesto* points toward his claim that, although the label "New Historicism" embraces a variety of critical practices, at its core this project is "a kind of 'Marxist criticism' "—the latter, larger project being characterized in all its forms and variants as a view of "history and contemporary political life as determined, wholly or in essence, by struggle, contestation, power relations, *libido dominandi*" (292). It seems to me that, on this essentialist definition, such a project might be better labelled as Machiavellian or Hobbesian than as Marxist. In any event, Pechter's specter is indeed spectral, in the sense that it is largely the (mis)construction of the critic who is engaged in attacking it, and thus also in the sense that it has become an object of fascination and dread.

A couple of years ago, I attempted briefly to articulate and scrutinize some of the theoretical, methodological and political assumptions and implications of the kind of work produced since the late 1970s by those (including myself) who were then coming to be labelled as "New Historicists."[5] The focus of such work has been upon a refiguring of the socio-cultural field within which canonical Renaissance literary and dramatic works were originally produced; upon resituating them not only in relationship to other genres and modes of discourse but also in relationship to contemporaneous social institutions and non-discursive practices. Stephen Greenblatt, who is most closely identified with the label "New Historicism' in Renaissance literary studies, has himself now abandoned it in favor of "Cultural Poetics," a term he had used earlier and one which perhaps more accurately represents the critical project I have described.[6] In effect, this project reorients the axis of inter-textuality, substituting for the diachronic text of an autonomous literary history the synchronic text of a cultural system. As the conjunction of terms in its title suggests, the interests and analytical techniques of "Cultural Poetics" are at once historicist and formalist; implicit in its project, though perhaps not yet adequately articulated or theorized, is a conviction that formal and historical concerns are not opposed but rather are inseparable.

Until very recently—and perhaps even now—the dominant mode of interpretation in English Renaissance literary studies has been to combine formalist techniques of close rhetorical analysis with the elaboration of relatively self-contained histories of "ideas," or of literary genres and topoi—histories that have been abstracted from their social matrices. In addition to such literary histories, we may note two other traditional practices of "history" in Renaissance literary studies: one comprises those commentaries on political commonplaces in which the dominant ideology of Tudor-Stuart society—the unreliable machinery of socio-political legitimation—is misrecognized as a stable, coherent, and collective Elizabethan world picture, a picture discovered to be lucidly reproduced in the canonical literary works of the age; and the other, the erudite but sometimes eccentric scholarly detective work which, by treating texts as elaborate ciphers, seeks to fix the meaning of fictional characters and actions in their reference to specific historical persons and events. Though sometimes reproducing the methodological shortcomings of such older idealist and empiricist modes of historical criticism, but also often appropriating their prodigious scholarly labors to good effect, the newer historical criticism is *new* in its refusal of unproblematized distinctions between "literature" and "history," between "text" and "context"; new in resisting a prevalent tendency to posit and privilege a unified and autonomous individual—whether an Author or a Work—to be set against a social or literary background.

In the essay of mine to which I have already referred, I wrote merely of a new historical *orientation* in Renaissance literary studies, because it seemed to me that those identified with it by themselves or by others were actually quite heterogeneous in their critical practices and, for the most part, reluctant to theorize those practices. The very lack of such explicit articulations was itself symptomatic of certain eclectic and empiricist tendencies that threatened to undermine any attempt to distinguish a new historicism from an old one. It may well be that these very ambiguities rendered New Historicism less a critique of dominant critical ideology than a subject for ideological appropriation, thus contributing to its almost sudden installation as the newest academic orthodoxy, to its rapid assimilation by the "interpretive communty" of Renaissance literary studies. Certainly, some who have been identified as exemplary New Historicists now enjoy the material and symbolic tokens of academic success; and any number of New Historicist dissertations, conferences, and publications testify to a significant degree of disciplinary influence and prestige. However, it remains unclear whether or not this latest "ism," with its appeal to our commodifying cult of the "new," will have been more than another passing intellectual fancy in what Fredric Jameson would call the academic marketplace under late capitalism. "The New Historicism" has not yet begun to fade from the academic scene, nor is it quietly taking its place in the assortment of critical approaches on the interpreter's shelf. But neither has it become any clearer that "*The* New Historicism" designates any agreed upon intellectual and institutional program. There has been no coalescence of the various identifiably New Historicist practices into a systematic and authoritative paradigm for the interpretation of Renaissance texts; nor does the emergence of such a paradigm seem either likely or desirable. What we are currently witnessing is the convergence of a variety of special interests upon "New Historicism," now constituted as a terminological site of intense debate and critique, of multiple appropriations and contestations within the ideological field of Renaissance studies itself, and to some extent in other areas of the discipline.

If Edward Pechter dubiously assimilates New Historicism to Marxism on the grounds that it insists upon the omnipresence of struggle as the motor of history, some self-identified Marxist critics are actively indicting New Historicism for its evasion of both political commitment and diachronic analysis—in effect, for its failure to be genuinely *historical*; while some female and male Renaissance scholars are fruitfully combining New Historicist and Feminist concerns, others are representing these projects (and/or their practitioners) as deeply antagonistic in gender-specific terms; while some see New Historicism as one of several modes of socio-criticism engaged in constructing a theoretically informed, post-structuralist problematic of historical study, others see it as aligned with a neo-pragmatist reaction against all forms of High Theory; if some see New Historicist preoccupations with ideology and social context as threatening to traditional critical concerns and literary values, others see a New Historicist delight in anecdote, narrative and what Clifford Geertz calls "thick description" as a will to construe *all* of culture as the domain of literary criticism—a text to be perpetually interpreted, an inexhaustible collection of stories from which curiosities may be culled and cleverly retold.[7]

Inhabiting the discursive spaces traversed by the term "New Historicism" are some of the most complex, persistent, and unsettling of the problems that professors of literature attempt variously to confront or to evade: Among them, the essential or historical bases upon which "literature" is to be distinguished from other discourses; the possible configurations of relationship between cultural practices and social, political and economic processes; the consequences of post-structuralist theories of textuality for the practice of an historical or materialist criticism; the means by which subjectivity is socially constituted and constrained; the processes by which ideologies are produced and sustained, and by which they may be contested; the patterns of consonance and contradiction among the values and interests of a given individual, as these are actualized in the shifting conjunctures of various subject positions—as, for example, intellectual worker, academic professional, and gendered domestic, social, political and economic agent. My point is not that "The New Historicism" as a definable project, or the work of specific individuals identified by themselves or by others as New Historicists, can necesarily provide even provisional answers to such questions, but rather that the term "New Historicism" is currently being invoked in order to bring such issues into play and to stake out—or to hunt down—specific positions within the discursive spaces mapped by these issues.

The post-structuralist orientation to history now emerging in literary studies may be characterized chiastically, as a reciprocal concern with the historicity of texts and the textuality of history. By *the historicity of texts*, I mean
to suggest the cultural specificity, the social embedment, of all modes of
writing—not only the texts that critics study but also the texts in which we
study them. By *the textuality of history*, I mean to suggest, firstly, that we
can have no access to a full and authentic past, a lived material existence,
unmediated by the surviving textual traces of the society in question—traces
whose survival we cannot assume to be merely contingent but must rather
presume to be at least partially consequent upon complex and subtle social
processes of preservation and effacement; and secondly, that those textual
traces are themselves subject to subsequent textual mediations when they
are construed as the "documents" upon which historians ground their own
texts, called "histories." As Hayden White has forcefully reminded us, such
textual histories necessarily but always incompletely constitute in their narrative and rhetorical forms the "History" to which they offer access.[8]

In *After the New Criticism*, Frank Lentricchia links "the antihistorical
impulses of formalist theories of literary criticism" with monolithic and
teleological theories of "history."[9] I assume that among the latter belongs
not only the great code of Christian figural and eschatological history but also
the classical Marxian master-narrative that Fredric Jameson characterizes as
"history now conceived in its vastest sense of the sequence of modes of
production and the succession and destiny of the various human social
formations"; and which he projects as the "untranscendable horizon" of
interpretive activity, subsuming "apparently antagonistic or incommensurable critical operations, assigning them an undoubted sectoral validity within
itself, and thus at once cancelling and preserving them."[10] Against an unholy
alliance of unhistoricized formalisms and totalized History, Lentricchia opposes the multiplicity of "histories," history as characterized by "forces of
heterogeneity, contradiction, fragmentation, and difference." It seems to me
that the various modes of what could be called post-structuralist historical
criticism (including modes of revisionist or "post" Marxism, as well as "New
Historicism" or Cultural Poetics") can be characterized by such a shift from
History to histories.

Recent invocations of "History" (which, like "Power," is a term now in
constant danger of hypostatization) often appear as responses to—or, in
some cases, merely as positivistic retrenchments against—various structuralist and post-structuralist formalisms that have seemed, to some, to put
into question the very possibility of historical understanding and historical
experience; that have threatened to dissolve history into what Perry Anderson has recently suggested is an antinomy of objectivist determinism and
subjectivist free-play, an antinomy which allows no possibility for historical
agency on the part of individual or collective human subjects.[11] "Subject,"

a simultaneously grammatical and political term, has come into widespread use not merely as a fashionable synonym for "The Individual" but precisely in order to emphasize that individuals and the very concept of "The Individual" are historically constituted in language and society. The freely self-creating and world-creating Individual of so-called bourgeois humanism is—at least, in theory—now defunct. Against the beleaguered category of the historical agent, contending armies of Theory now oppose the specters of structural determinism and post-structural contingency (the latter tartly characterized by Anderson as "subjectivism without a subject" [*In the Tracks of Historical Materialism*, 54]): We behold, on the one hand, the implacable code, and on the other, the slippery signifier—the contemporary equivalents of Predestination and Fortune. Anderson remarks that the "one master-problem around which *all* contenders have revolved" on the battlefield of contemporary social theory is "the nature of the relationships between structure and subject in human history and society" (33). (Variations on this problem might juxtapose system, totality, or hegemony, on the one hand, to strategy, practice, or agency, on the other.) I believe that we should resist the inevitably reductive tendency to constitute such terms as binary oppositions, instead construing them as mutually constitutive *processes*. We might then entertain the propositions that the interdependent processes of subjectification and structuration are both ineluctably social and historical; that social systems are produced and reproduced in the interactive social practices of individuals and groups; that collective structures may enable as well as constrain individual agency; that the possibilities and patterns for action are always socially and historically situated, always limited and limiting; and that there is no necessary relationship between the intentions of actors and the outcomes of their actions. Thus, my invocation of the term "Subject" is meant to suggest an equivocal process of *subjectification*: on the one hand, shaping individuals as loci of consciousness and initiators of action—endowing them with *subjectivity* and with the capacity for agency; and, on the other hand, positioning, motivating, and constraining them within—*subjecting them to*—social networks and cultural codes that ultimately exceed their comprehension or control.[12]

As has been noted by Jonathan Dollimore and Alan Sinfield, among others, a version of this subject/structure problematic is apparent within the new historical orientation to Renaissance studies: On one side are those who emphasize the possibilities for effective *contestation* or *subversion* of the dominant ideology—that is, for the agency of subjects; on the other side are those who emphasize the hegemonic capacity of the Tudor-Stuart state, as personified in the monarch, to *contain* apparently subversive gestures, or even to *produce* them in order to contain them—the latter capacity marking "the very condition of power."[13] One can readily see that such a theoretical position concerning the operations of ideology might be suspect not only to those who cherish liberal Humanist ideals of individual self-determination but also to those cultural critics who have so strong a stake in making their own discursive practice a direct intervention in the process of ideological reproduction.

I am concerned that the terms in which the problem of ideology has been posed and is now circulating in Renaissance literary studies—namely as an opposition between "containment" and subversion"—are so reductive, polarized, and undynamic as to be of little or no conceptual value. A closed and static, singular and homogeneous notion of ideology must be succeeded by one that is heterogeneous and unstable, permeable and processual. It must be emphasized that an ideological dominance is qualified by the specific conjunctures of professional, class, and personal interests of individual cultural producers (such as poets and playwrights); by the specific though multiple social positionalities of the spectators, auditors and readers who variously consume cultural productions; and by the relative autonomy—the specific properties, possibilities and limitations—of the cultural medium being worked. In other words, sufficient allowance must be made for the manifold mediations involved in the production, reproduction and appropriation of an ideological dominance: for the collective and individual agency of the state's subjects, and for the specific character and conventions of the representational forms (genres or rhetorical figures, for example) that they employ.[14]

In this sense, all texts are ideologically marked, howsoever multivalent or inconsistent that inscription may be. If, on the one hand, ideology can be said to exist only as it is instantiated in particular cultural forms and practices, including those categorized as "literature," then on the other hand, the ideological status of any given "literary work" is necessarily overdetermined and unstable. If, for example, I characterize *The Faerie Queene* or *Hamlet* as a "complex" text, I am not reverting to the essentialist terms of New Critical aesthetics; rather, I am describing the text's status as a discourse produced and appropriated within history and within a history of other productions and appropriations. In such a textual space, so many cultural codes converge and interact that ideological coherence and stability are scarcely possible. In *Marxism and Literature,* Raymond Williams has helpfully construed ideology in dynamic and dialogical terms, emphasizing "interrelations between movements and tendencies both within and beyond a specific and effective dominance" (121). Williams has in mind the existence, at any point in time, of residual and emergent, oppositional and alternative values, meanings and practices. The shifting conjunctures of such "movements and tendencies" may create conceptual sites within the ideological field from which the dominant can be contested, and against which it must be continuously redefined and redefended. In its emphasis on a dynamic, temporal model of culture and ideology—a ceaseless jostling among dominant and subordinate positions, a ceaseless interplay of continuity and change—such a perspective opens both the *object* and the *practice* of cultural poetics to history.

"The Historicity of Texts and the Textuality of History": If such chiastic formulations are in fashion now, when the concept of referentiality has become so vexed, it may be because they figure forth from within discourse itself the model of a dynamic, unstable, and reciprocal relationship between the discursive and material domains.[15] This refiguring of the relationship between the verbal and the social, between the text and the world, involves a re-problematization or wholesale rejection of some prevalent alternative conceptions of literature: As an automomous aesthetic order that transcends the shifting pressure and particularity of material needs and interests; as a collection of inert discursive records of "real events"; as a superstructural reflexion of an economic base. Current practices emphasize both the *relative* autonomy of specific discourses and their capacity to impact upon the social formation, to make things happen by shaping the subjectivities of social beings. Thus, to speak of the social production of "literature" or of any particular text is to signify not only that it is socially produced but also that it is socially productive—that it is the product of work and that it performs work in the process of being written, enacted, or read. Recent theories of textuality have argued persuasively that the referent of a linguistic sign cannot be fixed; that the meaning of a text cannot be stabilized. At the same time, writing and reading are always historically and socially determinate events, performed *in* the world and *upon* the world by gendered individual and collective human agents. We may simultaneously acknowledge the theoretical indeterminacy of the signifying process and the historical specificity of discursive practices—acts of speaking, writing, and interpreting. The project of a new socio historical criticism is, then, to analyze the interplay of culture-specific discursive practices—mindful that it, too, is such a practice and so participates in the interplay it seeks to analyze. By such means, versions of the Real, of History, are instantiated, deployed reproduced; and by such means, they may also be appropriated, contested, transformed.

Integral to such a collective project of historical criticism must be a realization and acknowledgement that our analyses and our understandings necessarily proceed from our own historically, socially and institutionally shaped vantage points; that the histories we reconstruct are the textual constructs of critics who are, ourselves, historical subjects. If scholarship actively constructs and delimits its object of study, and if the scholar is historically positioned vis-à-vis that object, it follows that the quest of an older historical criticism to recover meanings that are in any final or absolute sense authentic, correct, and complete is illusory. Thus, the practice of a new historical criticism invites rhetorical strategies by which to foreground the constitutive acts of textuality that traditional modes of literary history efface or misrecognize. It also necessitates efforts to historicize the present as well as the past, and to historicize the dialectic between them—those reciprocal historical pressures by which the past has shaped the present and the present reshapes the past. In brief, to speak today of an historical criticism must be to recognize that not only the poet but also the critic exists in history; that the texts of each are inscriptions of history; and that our comprehension, representation, interpretation of the texts of the past always proceeds by a mixture of estrangement and appropriation, as a reciprocal conditioning of the Renaissance text and our text of Renaissance.[16] Such a critical practice constitutes a continuous dialogue between a *poetics* and a *politics* of culture.

A gentle/manly—that is, benignly patriarchal—Anglo-Saxon, Protestant, Humanist ethos remains still today deeply ingrained in "the interpretive community" of English Renaissance studies, not only in Britain but also in The United States and Canada. The majority of critical books and articles that have long continued to form its essential bibliography are characterized by the celebration of an apparently continuous tradition of religious, social and aesthetic values shared by sixteenth-century poets and twentieth-century critics, and/or by romantic and reactionary idealizations of a Renaissance England at once ebullient and ordered. Such representations are at variance with surviving documentary evidence of Elizabethan religious, economic, social and domestic violence, instability, and heterodoxy. To isolate a transhistorical aesthetic domain from didactic and instrumental categories of culture, to separate a literary canon from historical, political and philosophical discourses, are operations which appear to be conceptually alien to most sixteenth and seventeenth century writing. Nevertheless, subsequent practices of literary criticism have selected out certain poetic and dramatic texts and canonized them as Renaissance Literature; so constituted, they are studied in the context of literary history or a cultural tradition. In such contexts, they are valued as enduring reflections of the subjectivities of their creators, or as exemplary instances of a distinctively aesthetic mode of perception; as compelling embodiments of timeless and universal truths; or, at the least, as abiding monuments to the liberal spirit of Judeo-Christian, Anglo-American civilization.

In various combinations and with varying degrees of consistency and success, the intellectual forces identifiable as New Historicism or Cultural Poetics, Cultural Materialism, Feminism, and revisionist forms of Marxism and Psychoanalysis, have been engaged in redrawing the boundaries and restructuring the content of Renaissance studies during the past decade. Such forces have in common a concern at once to affirm and to render problematic the connections between literary and other discourses, the dialectic between the text and the world. The enabling conditions of these relatively recent, uneven and inconsistent challenges to the dominant paradigm are various in their sources and complex in their interactions; I shall merely suggest three factors that are of both general and personal relevance. First, there has been taking place for some time, an opening of the profession of English literature to scholars whose gender or ethnicity, whose religious or class origins, whose political allegiances or sexual preferences (or some combination of these) complicates their actual or imaginative participation in the cultural and ideological tradition enshrined in the works which they study and teach. Experiences of historical and cultural exclusion or otherness may, of course, provoke a compensatory embrace of the dominant culture, a desire for acceptance and assimilation; but they may also provoke ambivalent or even contestatory attitudes, and provide vantage points for the appropriation and critique not only of Renaissance texts but also of the interpretive norms of Renaissance studies. Second, the reorientation in the field under way since at least the beginning of the 1980s is largely the work of scholars who were students during the turbulent '60s, and who have responded to the radically altered socio-political climate of the current decade—and, perhaps, to their own discomfortable comfort within its academic establishment—with intellectual work that is explicitly sociopolitical in its manifest historical content, although not always such in its own historical positioning. Third, the modes of Renaissance criticism to which I have referred have variously reacted against and contributed to the intellectual ferment of the past two decades—a ferment, summed up in the word "Theory," that has challenged the assumptions and procedures of normative discourses in several academic disciplines and has shaken the foundations of literary studies.[17]

There is another, complementary perspective from which to view the recent revival of interest in questions of history in literary studies in The United States: namely, as a compensation for that acceleration in the forgetting of history which seems to characterize an increasingly technocratic and commodified academy and society. Many of those who profess the Humanities in American universities see themselves and their calling as marginalized within a system of higher education increasingly geared to the provision of highly specialized technological and pre-professional training; within an academic institution that encourages industrial and military applications in scientific research, and that promotes scientistic quantification in the study of society and culture; within an intellectual community ever more closely bound to the interests of the circumambient political and commercial establishments and to the workings of a multi-national corporate economy. To the painfully dismissive expression, "Oh, that's academic," we must add another, more pernicious: "Oh, that's history." A primary task for the teacher of a new historical criticism must be to disabuse students of the notion that history is what's over and done with; to bring them to understand that they themselves live *in* history, and that they *live* history.

In its anti-reflectionism, its shift of emphasis from the formal analysis of verbal *artifacts* to the ideological analysis of discursive *practices*, its refusal to observe strict and fixed boundaries between "literary" and other texts (sometimes including the critic's own), the emergent social/political/historical orientation in literary studies is pervasively concerned with writing, reading and teaching as modes of *action*. I do not believe that the intellectual and social seriousness of our concerns with the instrumentality of cultural work are undermined by seeing them as partially impelled by a questioning of our very capacity for action—by a nagging sense of professional, institutional, and politcal powerlessness or irrelevance. I am not suggesting that such academic work is nothing more than a psychological compensation for social inactivity and political quiescence, although I agree that it can all too easily become so. Critical research and teaching in the Humanities may be either a merely academic displacement or a genuine academic instantiation of oppositional social and political praxis.

In the United States, it is Feminism and the Women's Movement which in recent years have provided the most powerful infusions of intellectual and social energy into the practices of cultural critique, both written and lived.[18] In Renaissance studies, as across the discipline of criticism, feminist theory and practice have called attention to the discursive construction of gender and of social and domestic relations generally; and this in turn has fore-grounded the differential subject positions from which readers read, and into which they are maneuvered during the process of reading. By articulating the ways in which women's voices are marginalized, suppressed or ventrilo-quized in Renaissance literary and dramatic works—and in previous com-mentaries upon those works—and by the scholarly recovery of extant texts written by Renaissance women, they have put into question liberal-humanist claims that the traditional literary canon and the canon of traditional critical readings embody an essential and inclusive range of human experience and expression; by seeking openly and collectively to connect the spheres of critical practice, academic policy, and socio-political activity, they have at once demystified claims that scholarship and the academy stand apart from or above the interests, biases, and struggles of material existence, and have provided a model for the integration of intellectual, professional and social commitments.[19]

In marked contrast to Feminist practices, there has been a tendency in much New Historicist work produced by American male academics to dis-place and contain its own cultural politics by at once foregrounding relations of power and confining them to the English past that is presently under study. Complex geographical, social, ethnic, and institutional factors are at work in producing this emphasis upon historical and cultural discontinuities, upon the fascinating Otherness of the Renaissance. In Britain—where class barriers remain more clearly articulated than in the United States; where, too, radical politics and radical discourses enjoy stronger tradition; and where the coercive pressure of the state upon educational institutions and practices is now conspicuously direct and intense—there has been a polemical emphasis by so-called Cultural Materialist critics upon the uses to which an historical *present* puts its versions of the English past, upon the history of ideological appropriations of the Renaissance. The characteristic concern of such work is with the processes by which the canon of English Renaissance Authors and Works incorporated into English culture and the British educational system has helped to forge and perpetuate a dominant ideology.[20] In Britain, for obvious reasons, the field of English studies—and, quintessentially, the study and performance of Shakespeare, the National Poet—readily becomes the site of a struggle over the definition of national problems and priorities, a struggle to shape and reshape national identity and collective consciousness.

In the United States—with its ethnic and social diversity, its lack of both a clearly articulated class structure and a strong tradition of radical politics and culture, its immensely complex and decentralized cultural and educational institutions, and its relatively large, prosperous and secure professoriate—the presence and direction of such ideological processes are perhaps less easily discernible, and sometimes less comfortably acknowledged; nevertheless, it would be willfully naive to deny their existence. Indeed, the study of the Humanities, and specifically of Shakespeare, may be prescribed precisely to counter the perceived threat to Anglo-Saxon hegemony by forces of cultural and ethnic diversity in the United States. Consider the following agenda:

> Fortunately, about the time the forces of immigration became a menace to the preservation of our long-established English civilization, there was initiated throughout the country a system of free and compulsory education for youth. In a spirit of efficiency, that education was made stereotyped in form; and in a spirit of democracy, every child was forced by law to submit to its discipline. . . . In our fixed plan of elementary schooling, [Shakespeare] was made the cornerstone of cultural discipline. . . . Shakespeare was made the chief object of . . . study and veneration.

The speaker was the distinguished American Shakespeare scholar, Joseph Quincy Adams; the occasion, the opening of The Folger Shakespeare Library in Washington, D.C.; the year, 1932.[21] The rhetoric is in conformity with changed political realities but there is continuity in the agenda of a latter-day humanist's report "on the State of Learning in the Humanities in Higher Education":

> American higher education today serves far more people and many more purposes than it did a century ago. Its increased accessibility to women, racial and

ethnic minorities, recent immigrants, and students of limited means is a positive accomplishment of which our nation is rightly proud. As higher education broadened, the curriculum became more sensitive to the long-overlooked cultural achievements of many groups. . . . This too is a good thing. But our eagerness to assert the virtues of pluralism should not allow us to sacrifice the principle that formerly lent substance and continuity to the curriculum, namely that each college and university should recognize and accept its vital role as conveyor of the accumulated wisdom of our civilization. . . . Ideas descended directly from great epochs of Western civilization . . . are the glue that binds together our pluralistic nation. . . . We as Americans—whether black or white, Asian or Hispanic, rich or poor—share these beliefs.

The year was 1984; the writer, William Bennett, then the Director of The National Endowment for the Humanities, and subsequently the United States Secretary of Education.[22]

Bennett's text repeatedly expressed alarm that "sometimes the humanities are used as if they were the handmaiden of ideology, subordinated to particular prejudices and valued or rejected on the basis of their relation to a certain social stance" (10). Of course, Bennett himself values the humanities "on the basis of their relation to a certain social stance"—namely, their role in the reproduction of the dominant socio-cultural order through the neutralization of difference, the containment of alternative and contestatory values and interests, such as those of feminists, ethnic minorities, and the economically disadvantaged. Bennett reserves the term "ideology" for the disapprobation of other people's "social stances"; nevertheless, his own report is in just this sense "ideological" through and through. In his case, however, the "social stance" has been rendered objective and disinterested, self-evident and incontrovertible: it is "a clear vision of what is worth knowing and what is important in our heritage that all educated persons should know" (7). Like the legislative and judicial agendas of the Reagan administration, the sermons of television evangelists and the bestsellers of neoconservative professors, Bennett's campaign for curricular reform plays upon a widespread anxiety about the perceived demise of "tráditional values" beginning in the permissive 1960s; and it does so in order to attack all forms of cultural interpretation which draw attention to differential and contestatory perspectives of history, politics, class, race and gender.

At the close of his recent polemic, *The Closing of the American Mind*, Allan Bloom avers that "men live more truly and fully in reading Plato and Shakespeare than at any other time, because then they are participating in essential being and are forgetting their accidental lives."[23] In discussing the sexual politics of Shakespeare's comedies, Bloom sympathizes with the position of enlightened patriarchalism that is repeatedly expressed in Elizabethan and Jacobean tracts concerning the ordering of the domestic economy and the intrinsic differences between the sexes. He writes that,

In order to assure the proper ordering of things, the transvestite women in Shakespeare, like Portia and Rosalind, are forced to masquerade as men because the real men are inadequate and need to be corrected. . . . The family is a sort of miniature body politic in which the husband's will is the will of the whole. The woman can influence the husband's will, and it is supposed to be informed by the love of the wife and children.

Now all of this has simply disintegrated. It does not exist, nor is it considered good that it should. But nothing certain has taken its place. (126–27)

In the following pages, Bloom puts the blame for our present social, ethical and academic confusion and crisis upon Feminism, which has destabilized marriage and the family, and fragmented the lives of both women and men. If then, according to Bloom, when they are reading Shakespeare, "*men . . . are participating in essential being and are forgetting their accidental lives*" (my italics), an enabling cause of that privileged male access to the Real would seem to be the assurance that Shakespeare's women know their places.

Invoking Professor Bloom's critique of American higher education, the leading editorial in a recent Sunday edition of my local newspaper, *The San Diego Union*, described ongoing efforts by "ethnic minorities and leftist faculty members" at "prestigious universities around the country" to abandon wholesale "the intellectual heritage of Western Civilization"—a "curriculum revolution" tantamount to "cultural suicide," "a lunge toward barbarism" here compared to the Nazi book-burnings.[24] Invoking Secretary Bennett's denunciations of "faculty trashing of Plato and Shakespeare," the editorial observes that, "When immortal literature is studied, it is often perverted." Thus, Shakespeare is used "as a means of showing how 17th-century society mistreated women, the working class, and minorities. The academics dress up such gross misinterpretation of deathless prose by terming it 'New Historicism'." Those so-called "leftist scholars" whose concerns are vulgarized and attacked in such texts as these will nevertheless dismiss or ignore them at their own risk, and to their own loss. For whatever other responses they may provoke, such discourses provide confirmation that the university is perceived to be a site for the contestation as well as for the reproduction of ideological dominants; that there is something immediately important at stake in our reading and teaching of Shakespeare; and that, if we suddenly discover ourselves to be not marginal but rather in positions of cultural and institutional power, we are also now compelled to choose if, when and how to employ that power.

In pointing to the all too obvious mystifications of special interests in the texts of Bennett and Bloom, I do not mean to imply (as Bennett does) that ideology is the name for other people's values. Like any others, my own readings of Elizabethan cultural texts cannot but be partial—by which I mean incapable of offering an exhaustive description, a complete explanation; but

also, incapable of offering any description or explanation that is located at
some Archimedean point outside the history I study, in some ideal space that
transcends the coordinates of gender, ethnicity, class, age, and profession
that plot my own shifting and potentially contradictory subject positions.
As a professional reader of Renaissance texts, I have an investment—an
overdetermined investment, which will always remain at least partially ob-
scure to me—in those versions of "The Renaissance" represented and produced, discovered and invented, in the texts I call mine. By choosing to
foreground in my readings of Shakespeare or Spenser such issues as the
politics of gender, the contestation of cultural constraints, the social instrumentality of writing and playing, I am not only engaged in our necessary
and continuous re-invention of Elizabethan culture but I am also endeavoring
to make that engagement participate in the re-formation of our own.

I am compelled to temper my self-congratulation, however, by acknowledging that my professional practice as a teacher-scholar is also a vehicle for
my partly unconscious and partly calculating negotiation of disciplinary,
institutional, and societal demands and expectations; that, to the degree that
it is an inscription of cultural priorities and a medium for professional
advantage, this pursuit of knowledge and virtue is necessarily impure. I have
a complex and substantial stake in sustaining and reproducing the very
institutions whose operations I wish to call into question. (I suspect that this
may also be true of the other contributors to this volume, and of its potential
readers.) The possibility of political and institutional agency cannot be based
upon the illusion of an escape from ideology. However, the very process of
subjectively *living* the confrontations or contradictions within or among
ideologies makes it possible to experience facets of our own subjection at
shifting internal distances—to read, as in a refracted light, one fragment of
our ideological inscription by means of another. A reflexive knowledge so
partial and unstable may, nevertheless, provide subjects with a means of
empowerment as agents.

The politics of the academy extend beyond that we casually refer to as
"academic politics": the study and teaching of cultural poetics are enmeshed
in a larger cultural politics that is without disinterested parties, without
objective positions. Bennett describes the Humanities as "the best that has
been thought and written about the human condition: (15); he represents
humanists as a kind of secular priesthood, whose mission is "to protect and
transmit a legacy" (10). There are those of us who would wish to contest
such an uncritical, such a mystified view of our profession and of our
relationship to what we study; who believe our most important work as
teachers and scholars to be to interrogate the legacy that we are charged
(and paid) to transmit. It is by construing literature as an unstable and
agonistic field of verbal and social practices—rather than as the trans-histori-
cal residence of what Bennett calls "great works, ideas, and minds" (10)—

that literary criticism rearticulates itself as a site of intellectually and socially significant work in the historical present. If, by the ways in which we choose to read Renaissance texts, we bring to our students and to ourselves a sense of our own historicity, an apprehension of our own positionings within ideology, then we are at the same time demonstrating the limited but nevertheless tangible possibility of contesting the regime of power and knowledge that at once sustains us and constrains us.

Notes

1. J. Hillis Miller, "Presidential Address 1986. The Triumph of Theory, the Resistance to Reading, and the Question of the Material Base," *PMLA* 102 (1987), 281–91; p. 283.

2. Jacques Derrida, "But, beyond . . . (Open Letter to Anne McClintock and Rob Nixon)," trans. Peggy Kamuf, *Critical Inquiry* 13 (1986), 155–70; p. 168.

3. For a concise history of the term "ideology," see Raymond Williams, *Marxism and Literature* (Oxford: Oxford Univ. Press, 1977), 55–71. Of central importance for the sense of "ideology" I am using here is the essay on "Ideology and Ideological State Apprartuses" in Louis Althusser, *Lenin and Philosophy and Other Essays,* trans. Ben Brewster (New York and London: Monthly Review Press, 1971), 127–86. According to Althusser's well-known formulation, "Ideology is a 'Representation' of the Imaginary Relationship of Individuals to their Real Conditions of Existence," which "Interpellates Individuals as Subjects" (162, 170). Althusser's theories of Ideology and the Subject have provoked considerable commentary and criticism, notably for appearing to disallow human agency in the making of history. On this debate, with special reference to the anti-Althusserian polemic of E. P. Thompson, see Perry Anderson, *Arguments Within English Marxism* (London: Verso, 1980), 15–58 .
A concise clarification of relevant terms is provided in Paul Smith, *Discerning the Subject* (Minneapolis: University of Minnesota Press, 1988)—which was published too late for me to have made more use of it here:
> "The individual" will be understood here as simply the illusion of whole and coherent personal organization, or as the misleading description of the imaginary ground on which different subject-positions are colligated.
>
> And thence the commonly used term "subject" will be broken down and will be understood as the term inaccurately used to describe what is actually the series of the conglomeration of *positions*, subject-positions, provisional and not necessarily indefeasible, into which a person is called momentarily by the discourses and the world that he/she inhabits.
>
> The term "agent," by contrast, will be used to mark the idea of a form of subjectivity where, by virtue of the contradictions and disturbances in and among subject-positions, the possibility (indeed, the actuality) of resistance to ideological pressure is allowed for (even though that resistance too must be produced in an ideological context). (p. xxxv)

4. Edward Pechter, "The New Historicism and Its Discontents: Politicizing Renaissance Drama," *PLMA* 102 (1987), 292–303; p. 292.

5. Louis Montrose, "Renaissance Literary Studies and the Subject of History," *English Literary Renaissance* 16 (1986), 5–12. Much of that essay is subsumed and reworked in the present one. My thanks to Arthur Kinney, Editor of *ELR*, for permission to reprint previously published material; and to Roxanne Klein for her continuing encouragement and advice.

6. The term "new historicism" seems to have been introduced into Renaissance studies (with reference to cultural semiotics) in Michael McCanles, "The Authentic Discourse of the Renaissance," *Diacritics* 10: 1 (Spring 1980), 77–87. However, it seems to have gained currency from its use by Stephen Greenblatt in his brief, programmatic introduction to "The Forms of Power and the Power of Forms in the Renaissance," a special issue of *Genre* (15: 1–2 [1982], 1–4). Earlier, in the Introduction to *Renaissance Self-Fashioning* (Chicago: Univ. of Chicago Press, 1980), Greenblatt had called his project a "cultural poetics." He has returned to this term in the introductory chapter of his recent book, *Shakespearean Negotiations: The Circulation of Social Energy in Renaissance England* (Berkeley and Los Angeles: Univ. of California Press, 1988). Here he defines the enterprise of cultural poetics as "study of the collective making of distinct cultural practices and inquiry into the relations among these practices"; the relevant concerns are "how collective beliefs and experiences were shaped, moved from one medium to another, concentrated in manageable aesthetic form, offered for consumption [and] how the boundaries were marked between cultural practices understood to be art forms and other, contiguous, forms of expression" (5). I discuss the relevance of anthropological theory and ethnographic practice—specifically, the work of Clifford Geertz—to the study of early modern English culture in my review essay on *Renaissance Self-Fashioning*: "A Poetics of Renaissance Culture," *Criticism* 23 (1981), 349–59.

7. Two influential and generally sympathetic early surveys/critiques of New Historicist work are: Jonathan Goldberg, "The Politics of Renaissance Literature: A Review Essay," *ELH* 49 (1982), 514–42; and Jean E. Howard, "The New Historicism in Renaissance Studies," *English Literary Renaissance* 16 (1986), 13–43. A number of critiques of New Historicism from various ideological positions have subsequently been published, and more are on the way. In addition to Pechter's hostile neo-conservative essay, within English Renaissance studies these critiques include the following: from a generally neo-Marxist perspective, Walter Cohen, "Political Criticism of Shakespeare," in *Shakespeare Reproduced: The Text in History and Ideology,* ed. Jean E. Howard and Marion F. O'Connor (New York and London: Methuen, 1987), 18–46, and Don E. Wayne, "Power, Politics, and the Shakespearean Text: Recent Criticism in England and the United States," in *Shakespeare Reproduced,* 47–67; from a liberal American feminist perspective, Peter Erickson, "Rewriting the Renaissance, Rewriting Ourselves," *Shakespeare Quarterly* 38 (1987), 327–37, Lynda E. Boose, "The Family in Shakespeare Studies; or—Studies in the Family of Shakespeareans; or—The Politics of Politics," *Renaissance Quarterly* 40 (1987), 707–42, and Carol Thomas Neely, "Constructing the Subject: Feminist Practice and New Renaissance Discourses," *English Literary Renaissance* 18 (1988), 5–18; from a deconstructionist perspective, A. Leigh DeNeef, "Of Dialogues and Historicisms," *South Atlantic Quarterly* 86 (1987), 497–517. I want to record here my thanks to Alan Liu and Carolyn Porter for sharing with me their as yet unpublished studies of Renaissance New Historicism from the perspectives of English Romanticism and American studies, respectively.

In a recent essay, "Towards a Poetics of Culture," *Southern Review* (Australia) 20 (1987), 3–15, Stephen Greenblatt remarks that "one of the peculiar characteristics of the 'new historicism' in literary studies is precisely how unresolved and in some ways disingenuous it has been—I have been—about the relation to literary theory." Accordingly, the essay does not set out an explicit theoretical position but rather a demonstration of his resistance to theory: "I want to speculate on why this should be so by trying to situate myself in relation to Marxism on the one hand, and poststructuralism on the other" (3). Greenblatt goes on to situate himself as a neo-pragmatist in relation to two totalizing discourses in each of which, "history functions . . . as a convenient anecdotal ornament upon a theoretical structure." What he seems to offer in opposition to such theoretical discourses, which collapse "the contradictions of history into a moral imperative" (7), is essentially an empirical historical analysis that has not been fettered by ideology. By means of a striking personal anecdote, Greenblatt suggests that the practice of cultural poetics involves a repudiation of cultural politics. My own conviction is that their separation is no more desirable than it is possible.

8. On the constitutive discourse of the historian and the genres of history writing, see Hayden White, *Tropics of Discourse* (Baltimore: Johns Hopkins Univ. Press, 1978).

9. Frank Lentricchia, *After the New Criticism* (Chicago: Univ. of Chicago Press, 1980), xiii–xiv.

10. Fredric Jameson, *The Political Unconscious: narrative as a socially symbolic act* (Ithaca: Cornell Univ. Pres, 1981), 75, 10.

11. See the incisive Marxist critique of structuralism and post-structuralism in Perry Anderson, *In the Tracks of Historical Materialism* (Chicago: Univ. of Chicago Press, 1984), 32–55; and, for a Marxist critique of Anderson's own summary dismissal of Deconstruction, see Terry Eagleton, "Marxism, Structuralism, and Post-Structuralism," *Diacritics* 15: 4 (Winter 1985), 2–12.

12. The process of subjectification as a seemingly uncontestable process of *subjecting to* is central to much of Michel Foucault's work: See, for example, "The Subject and Power," *Critical Inquiry* 8 (1982), 777–95; and, for a Marxist critique, Peter Dews, "Power and Subjectivity in Focault," *New Left Review* no. 144 (March-April 1984), 72–95. Edward Said comments that "Foucault's imagination of power was largely within rather than against it.... His interest in domination was critical but not finally as contestatory, or as oppositional as on the surface it seems to be. This translates into the paradox that Foucault's imagination of power was by his analysis of power to reveal its injustice and cruelty, but by his theorization to let it go on more or less unchecked" ("Foucault and the Imagination of Power," in *Foucault: A Critical Reader*, ed. David Couzens Hoy [Oxford: Basil Blackwell, 1986], 149–55; p. 152).

I am indebted to the chapter, "Agency, Structure," in Anthony Giddens, *Central Problems in Social Theory* (Berkeley: University of California Press, 1979), 49–95. Also see the cogent formulation of "experience" ("a process by which, for all social beings, subjectivity is constructed"), in Teresa de Lauretis, *Alice Doesn't: Feminism, Semiotics, Cinema* (Bloomington: Indiana University Press, (1984): "Through that process one places oneself or is placed in social reality, and so perceives and comprehends as subjective (referring to, even originating in, oneself) those relations—material, economic, and interpersonal—which are in fact social and, in a larger perspective, historical. The process is continuous, its achievement unending or daily renewed. For each person, therefore, subjectivity is an ongoing construction, not a fixed point of departure or arrival from which one then interacts with the world. On the contrary, it is an effect of that interaction ... and thus it is produced not by external ideas, values, or material causes, but by one's personal, subjective engagement in the practices, discourses, and institutions that lend significance (value, meaning, and affect) to the events of the world" (159).

13. Stephen Greenblatt, "Invisible Bullets: Renaissance Authority and Its Subversion," in *Political Shakespeare*, ed. Jonathan Dollimore and Alan Sinfield (Ithaca: Cornell Univ. Press, 1985), 18–47; p. 45 (rpt. in Stephen Greenblatt, *Shakespearean Negotiations*, 21–65). This position suggests a reading of Foucault that emphasizes the discontinuity of history and the subjection of subjects; it makes no space for change or for contestation. For critiques of the "containment" position, see Dollimore's Introduction to *Political Shakespeare*, 2–17; and Alan Sinfield, "Power and Ideology: An Outline Theory and Sidney's *Arcadia*," *ELH* 52 (1985), 259–77. I have discussed these issues in more detail, with particular reference to Spenser, in "The Elizabethan Subject and the Spenserian Text," in *Literary Theory/Renaissance Texts*, ed. Patricia Parker and David Quint (Baltimore: Johns Hopkins Univ. Press, 1986), 303–40. Although without specific reference to this context of critique and debate, in the newly composed opening chapter of *Shakespearean Negotiations*, Greenblatt writes of unforeseen "turns" in his thinking:

I had tried to organize the mixed motives of Tudor and Stuart culture under the rubric *power,* but that term implied a structural unity and stability of command belied by much of what I actually knew about the exercise of authority and force in the period.

If it was important to speak of power in relation to Renaissance literature—not only as the object but as the enabling condition of representation itself—it was equally important to resist the integration of all images and expressions into a single master discourse. . . . Even those literary texts that sought most ardently to speak for a monolithic power could be shown to be the sites of institutional and ideological contestation. (pp. 2–3)

14.   Compare Pierre Bourdieu, "Symbolic Power" (trans. Richard Nice), *Critique of Anthropology* 4 (Summer 1979), 77–85: "When we insist that ideologies are always doubly determined, that they owe their most specific characteristics not only to the interests of the classes or class fractions which they express . . . but also to the specific interests of those who produce them and to the specific logic of the field of production (usually transfigured into the ideology of 'creation' and the 'creator'), we obtain the means of escaping crude reduction of ideological products to the interests of the classes they serve . . . without falling into the idealist illusion of treating ideological productions as self-sufficient and self-generating totalities amenable to pure, purely internal analysis" (81–82).

15.   Compare Fredric Jameson's counter-Deconstructinist formulation of this relationship in terms of Marxism that is itself necessarily post-structuralist:

The type of interpretation here proposed is more satisfactorily grasped as the rewriting of the literary text in such a way that the latter may itself be seen as the rewriting or restructuration of a prior historical or ideological *subtext,* it being always understood that that "subtext" is not immediately present as such, not some common-sense external reality, nor even the conventional narratives of history manuals, but rather must itself always be (re)constructed after the fact. . . . The whole paradox of what we have here called the subtext may be summed up in this, that the literary work or cultural object, as though for the first time, brings into being that very situation of which it is also, at one and the same time, a reaction. . . . History is inaccessible to us except in textual form. . . . It can be approached only way of prior (re)textualization. . . . To overemphasize the active way in which the text reorganizes its subtext (in order, presumably, to reach the triumphant conclusion that the "referent" does not exist); or on the other hand to stress the imaginary status of the symbolic act so completely as to reify its social ground, now no longer understood as a subtext but merely as some inert given that the text passively or fantasmatically "reflects"—to overstress either of these functions of the symbolic act at the expense of the other is surely to produce sheer ideology, whether it be, as in the first alternative, the ideology of structuralism, or, in the second, that of vulgar materialsm. *(The Political Unconscious,* pp. 81–81)

For another Marxist consideration of and responses to recent theoretical challenges to historical criticism, see "Text and History: Epilogue 1984" in Robert Weimann, *Structure and Society in Literary History,* expanded ed. (Baltimore: Johns Hopkins University Press, 1984), pp. 267–323.

Introductions to materialist cultural theory include Raymond Williams, *Marxism and Literature;* Raymond Williams, *Culture* (London: Fontana, 1981); Janet Wolff, *The Social Production of Art* (London: Macmillan, 1981).

16.   See the forceful critique of traditional historicist Renaissance literary criticism in Michael McCanles, "The Authentic Discourse of the Renaissance": McCanles writes that, "instead of viewing the scholar's enterprise as merely the recovery and explanation of an already constituted Renaissance text, Renaissance studies should recognize that its central task lies in

the constitution of that text through an intertextuality whereby two texts are brought together and fused: the constituted discourse of the Renaissance and the constitutive discourse of the scholar" (p. 81). For similar arguments regarding the discourse of intellectual history, see "Rethinking Intellectual History and Reading Texts," in Dominick LaCapra, *Rethinking Intellectual History* (Ithaca: Cornell Univ. Press, 1983), 23–71; and, regarding the discourse of ethnography, Roy Wagner, *The Invention of Culture*, rev. and expanded ed. (Chicago: Univ. of Chicago Press, 1981).

Wagner writes that

An anthropoligist "invents" the culture he believes himself to be studying. . . . In the act of inventing another culture, the anthropologist invents his own, and in fact he reinvents the notion of culture itself. . . .

The relation an anthropologist builds between two cultures—which, in turn, objectifies and hence "creates" those cultures for him—arises precisely from his act of "invention", his use of meanings known to him in constructing an understandable representation of his subject matter. . . .

The study of culture *is* culture (4, 9, 16).

The status of the ethnographer as participant-observer of the culture under study has been re-problematized in recent, post-structuralist anthropological theory by foregrounding matters of textuality and ideology in the writing of ethnography: See *Writing Culture: The Poetics and Politics of Ethnography*, ed. James Clifford and George E. Marcus (Berkeley and Los Angeles: Univ. of California Press, 1986). As intellectual historians and anthropologists become increasingly concerned with the cognitive and ideological import of narrative forms and rhetorical strategies, the intellectual center of gravity in the humanities and interpretive social sciences appears to be shifting toward the traditional domain of literary criticism.

17.   For more detailed discussion of some of these and other, related topics, see Walter Cohen, "Political Criticism of Shakespeare," and Don E. Wayne, "Power, Politics, and the Shakespearean Text," both in *Shakespeare Reproduced.*

18.   Like other male academics who have long been supportive of feminist agendas—in personal and social as well as intellectual and institutional contexts—at the present historical moment, I cannot comfortably arrogate to myself the title of a feminist. As Stephen Heath has recently written:

Men have a necessary relation to feminism—the point after all is that it should change them too, that it involves new ways of being women *and men* against and as an end to the reality of women's oppression—and that relation is also necessarily one of a certain exclusion—the point after all is that this is a matter *for women,* that it is their voices and actions that must determine the change and redefinition. Their voices and actions, not ours: no matter how "sincere," "sympathetic," or whatever, we are always also in a male position which brings with it all the implications of domination and appropriation, everything precisely that is being challenged, that has to be altered. . . . Which does not mean . . . that I cannot respond to and change for feminism . . . it just means that I have to realize . . . that I am not where they are and that I cannot pretend to be. ("Male Feminism," in *Men in Feminism,* ed. Alice Jardine and Paul Smith [New York and London: Methuen, 1987], 1–32; p. 1)

In different aspects of my own life, not least as a scholar and teacher but neither exclusively so, I have come to feel during the past few years what Heath calls "the impossibility of my, of men's, relation" to Feminism—by which I do not mean to suggest the futility of such a relation but rather its always suspect necessity. What I would want to emphasize here is not the impossibility but precisely the necessity for men to work in dialogue with and support of Feminism and of feminists, howsoever vexed such attempts may be. One way in which men may do this is to direct our scholarly attention to socio-historical constructions of gender and of male subjectivity, and our metacritical attention to the influences upon our intellectual and professional practices and perspectives of our own gendered subject positions. On issues such as these, Feminist theory and practice have much to teach any "New Historicism" about what it means to historicize.

19.   The following books and collections are representative of the burgeoning bibliography of relevant work in English Renaissance literary studies: *The Woman's Part: Feminist Criticism of Shakespeare,* ed. Carolyn Ruth Swift Lenz, Gayle Green, and Carol Thomas Neely (Urbana: Univ. of Illinois Press, 1980); Hilda L. Smith, *Reason's Disciples: Seventeenth-Century English Feminists* (Urbana: Univ. of Illinois Press, 1982); Lisa Jardine, *Still Harping on Daughters: Women and Drama in the Age of Shakespeare* (Brighton: Harvester Press, 1983); Linda Woodbridge, *Women and the English Renaissance* (Urbana: Univ. of Illinois Press, 1984); *English Literary Renaissance* 14: 3 (Autumn 1984) and 18: 1 (Winter 1988), two special issues on "Women in the Renaissance"; Catherine Belsey, *The Subject of Tragedy: Identity and Difference in Renaissance Drama* (London and New York: Methuen, 1985); *Silent But for the Word: Tudor Women as Patrons, Translators, and Writers of Religious Works,* ed. Margaret Patterson Hannay (Kent, Ohio: Kent State Univ. Press, 1985); *Rewriting the Renaissance: The Discourses of Sexual Difference in Early Modern Europe,* ed. Margaret W. Ferguson, Maureen Quilligan and Nancy J, Vickers (Chicago: Univ. of Chicago Press, 1986); *Women in the Middle Ages and the Renaissance: Literary and Historical Perspectives,* ed. Mary Beth Rose (Syracuse: Syracuse Univ. Press, 1985); Elaine V. Beilin, *Redeeming Eve: Women Writers of the English Renaissance* (Princeton: Princeton Univ. Press, 1987).

20.   See, for example: "Part II: Reproductions, Interventions," in *Political Shakespeare,* ed. Dollimore and Sinfield, 130-239; Simon Barker, "Images of the Sixteenth and Seventeenth Centuries as a History of the Present," in *Literature, Politics and Theory: Papers from the Essex Conference 1976–84,* ed. Francis Barker, Peter Hulme, Margaret Iversen, Diana Loxley (London and New York: Methuen, 1986), 173–89; Terence Hawkes, *That Shakespeherian Rag: Essays on a Critical Process* (London and New York: Methuen, 1986); Derek Longhurst, " 'Not for all time, but for an Age': An Approach to Shakespeare Studies," in *Re-Reading English,* ed. Peter Widdowson (London and New York: Methuen, 1982), 150–63; Alan Sinfield, "*Macbeth:* History, Ideology and Intellectuals," *Critical Quarterly* 28 (1986), 63–77.

21.   Joseph Quincy Adams, "The Folger Shakespeare Memorial Dedicated, April 23, 1932; Shakespeare and American Culture," *The Spinning Wheel* 12 (1932), as quoted in Stephen J. Brown, "The Uses of Shakespeare in America: A Study in Class Domination," in *Shakespeare, Pattern of Excelling Nature,* ed. David Bevington and Jay L. Halio (Newark: Univ. of Delaware Press, 1978), 230–38; p. 231. I owe this reference to Don Wayne.

22.   William Bennett, "To Reclaim a Legacy," *American Education* 21 (1985), 4–15; pp. 14–15. For a telling contemporaneous British analogue, see the excerpts from The Scarman Report on London's Brixton riots (1981) printed and discussed in Terence Hawkes, "Swisser-Swatter: Making a Man of English letters," in *Alternative Shakespeares,* ed. John Drakakis (London: Methuen, 1985), 26–46; pp. 44–45.

23.   Allan Bloom, *The Closing of the American Mind* (New York: Simon and Schuster, 1987), p. 380.

24.   "Barbaric Betrayal," *The San Diego Union,* Sunday, 21 February 1988. This editorial is a spin-off from an article by David Brooks that originally appeared in *The Wall Street Journal,* Tuesday, 2 February 1988, entitled "From Western Lit to Westerns as Lit." I owe these references to Susan Montrose and Annabel Patterson, respectively.

3

Marxism and The New Historicism

Catherine Gallagher

Critics of the "new historicism" have given wildly different accounts of its political implications, but they generally agree that its politics are obnoxious. Charged on the one hand with being a crude version of Marxism and on the other with being a formalist equivalent of colonialism,[1] the new historicism attracts an unusual amount of specifically political criticism for a criticism whose politics are so difficult to specify. One could, of course, simply stand back, amused, and let the countervailing charges collide and explode each other, but one might also be curious about why a phenomenon of such apparent political indeterminacy should seem such a general political irritant.

There is no mystery about why the new historicism's politics should attract speculation. Although there has been a certain amount of controversy over just what the new historicism is, what constitutes its essence and what its accidents, most of its adherents and opponents would probably agree that it entails reading literary and nonliterary texts as constituents of historical discourses that are both inside and outside of texts and that its practitioners generally posit no fixed hierarchy of cause and effect as they trace the connections among texts, discourses, power, and the constitution of subjectivity. Since these are the issues new historicists study, it's hardly surprising that they have kindled speculation about their own discursive contexts, commitments to and negotiations of power, or the constitution of their historical subjectivity. Such speculation is obviously very much in the spirit of their own inquiries and can hardly be called impertinent or irrelevant.

However, the insistence on finding a *single,* unequivocal political meaning for this critical practice, indeed in some cases on reducing it to a politics or a relation to power, is puzzling and certainly runs counter to what seem to me to be new historicism's most valuable insights: that no cultural or critical practice is simply a politics in disguise, that such practices are seldom *intrinsically* either liberatory or oppressive, that they seldom contain their politics as an essence but rather occupy particular historical situations from which they enter into various exchanges, or negotiations, with practices designated "political." The search for the new historicism's political essence can be seen as a rejection of these insights. Critics on both the right and left seem offended by this refusal to grant that literature and, by extension, criticism either ideally transcend politics or simply are politics when properly decoded.

To ask what is the intrinsic political meaning or content of the new historicism, then, is to pose the question in terms that wipe out the assumptions on which many critics who are routinely called new historicists might base a reply. Consequently, the following remarks proceed from a different question: what are the historical situations of the new historicism and how have these defined the nature of its exchanges with explicitly political discourses?

Having formulated this more congenial question, I must at once admit my inability to answer it adequately. I have neither the space nor the knowledge to identify the situations and sources of such a vast and various phenomenon; I can only write from what may seem a highly unusual perspective, that of critics who have arrived at new historicist postions via continental Marxist theory and 1960s radical politics. Marxist critics[2] have themselves called attention to this filiation by accusing new historicists of "left disillusionment." Whereas I acknowledge the "left" inspiration in the work of many new historicists, I disagree that "disillusionment" intervened between our current work and our more "optimistic" youth. I'll be arguing, on the contrary, that American radicalism of the sixties and early seventies bred just those preoccupations that have tended to separate new historicist from Marxist critics in the eighties and that the former preserve and continue, rather than react against, many of the characteristic tendencies of New Left thought. I'll be concentrating especially on new historicism's residual formalism, its problematization of representation, and its dual critique and historicization of the subject.

We should bear in mind that American left-wing literary critics had developed a strong, optimistic and politically problematic brand of formalism a generation before the New Left. In its most independent and intelligent sectors, the American left offered its children in the post-war years a politics that had already begun to transfer its hopes from the traditional agent of revolutionary change, the proletariat, to a variety of "subversive" cultural practices, the most prominent of which was aesthetic modernism. The transferral had started in the earlier belief that modernism was a support for revolutionary social change of an anti-Stalinist kind; writers such as Philip Rahv, William Phillips, Dwight Macdonald, Harold Rosenberg, and Mary McCarthy, were reacting in the 1930s against the popular front for its Stalinism, its uncritical embrace of Democratic Party politics and its sentimental, traditional cultural nationalism. The very difficulty of modernist forms, they believed, cut against the grain of American conservatism. Hence we find Harold Rosenberg, for example, trying even in the 1940s to yoke the modern working class, modernist culture, traditionless America, and his own immigrant experience into one complex of radical forces. But the joining soon became a substitution of elements whereby cultural modernism and the rootless intellectual were increasingly valued as the privileged representations of latent and repressed social contradictions.

The generation of cultural critics that came of age in the 1960s, therefore, might have inherited a belief in the political efficacy of certain aesthetic forms, for left formalism had reached a high level of sophistication before the war. If these aspiring critics had then merely read the available continental Marxist aesthetic theory in the sixties and early seventies, they might have stayed very much within this legacy. The Marxist criticism that circulated most widely in those years tended to be the work of Western Marxists, especially Lukács and members of the Frankfurt School. From these sources one might have picked up a number of different critical orientations toward the dominant culture. For example, one would probably have learned that culture as a realm differentiated itself from the social whole during the period of bourgeois ascendancy for the purpose of creating false resolutions for social contradictions. Its function, according to this account, was to create a consciousness capable of at once acknowledging these contradictions and justifying them by ascribing them to any number of supra-social causes. The Marxist literary critic committed to this model of bourgeois culture saw her job as the undoing of the false resolution, the detection in the text of the original contradiction and the formal signs of its irresolvability. She believed that identifying such signs exposed the false ideological solution, that turning the text back on its moments of instability confronted the culture with things it could not stand to acknowledge.

Alternatively, to take another influential Western Marxist commonplace from that period, she might have viewed the bourgeois work of art's imperfect attempts at harmonious resolution as expressions of utopian hopes and hence as potential incitements to subversive realizations. To be sure, the job of the critic was still the exposure of the gap between conflict and resolution, for the reader must be made to understand that only action in the social world could resolve the conflict. Nevertheless, the imperfect formal reconciliation itself became in this view more than a functional component of bourgeois ideology; it became a disfunctional moment as well, a vision of fulfillment not yet achieved and hence a disturbance of the status quo.

A third strand of continental Marxist aesthetics, that of the Brecht revival of the late sixties, probably also had an effect on this generation of critics. Brechtian aesthetics emphasized, like the other available Marxisms, the role of culture and cultural analysis in exposing ideological contradictions. Among Brechtians, moreover, a critic with close ties to American Left formalism might have felt very much at home, since, despite serious political differences, both tendencies believed in the almost magical subversive power of modernist forms. But whether pro- or anti-modernist, whether cognitive or affective in its orientation, whether concentrating on critical or creative practice, the continental Marxist aesthetics that was being circulated in this country in the late sixties and early seventies tended to confirm the left formalist's belief in a privileged realm of representation and her optimism about the efficacy of exposing ideological contradictions.

Such confirmation, however, might easily have collided with the implied cultural and aesthetic assumptions of the life one was actually living in the late sixties. For this generation of critics was not just reading Marxist aesthetic theory produced decades earlier; many of its members were also living, reading, writing and acting the political culture of the New Left. And it is to that culture, inchoate as it was, that we should look for several important departures from what had been the influential Marxist models.

First, for a variety of reasons, the New Left dispensed with what we might call a politics of substitution that relied on a hierarchy of causation to determine just what the crucial contradictions were. Most obviously, the intellectual activist herself did not claim to stand or speak for some other oppressed group. New Left activists notoriously invoked the principle of individual and group liberation in justifying rebellion instead of invoking their connection to the objective interests of a universal class. In the 1940s, Harold Rosenberg had taken pains to show that the ideological crisis informing his own immigrant experience could be traced back, not just to other conflicts, but to the one conflict that counted: class conflict. In contrast, New Left intellectuals generally avoided the implicit causal hierarchy of such analyses and their logic of substitution.

For example, in New Left rhetoric particular struggles were often joined to the general interest through a logic of decentered distribution, in which each group, in speaking for itself, spoke against a "system" that was oppressing all. This was the case at the outset of the "movement," when middle-class, white, civil rights activists learned that they could not think of themselves as representing or even as altruistically aiding black people, for altruism implied condescension. Indeed, the roots of the movement in black civil rights struggles was no doubt a strong factor obviating the rhetoric of representation for white radicals,[3] who claimed instead to be freeing themselves from racism. And the avoidance of substitutional politics only increased as group after group claimed the legitimacy of action on its own behalf.

This is not to deny the importance of such slogans as "serve the people" or the vehemence of New Left anti-middle-class sentiments. But the slogan, after all, only proves my general point: "the people" was a category designed to include oneself and anyone else content to join a decentered coalition of disaffected groups. Certainly, solidarity was as important to the radicals of the sixties as it had been to those of the thirties, but the grounds of solidarity had shifted from an identification with a designated specific class to a recognition of shared oppressions that cut across class divisions. Moreover, "serving the people" was often imagined to be a means of self-transformation, even the realization and liberation of self stifled by middle-class conventionality.

Thus, because of its sociological base in groups outside the organized traditional proletariat—its reliance on upwardly mobile sectors of racial minorities, women of all races, and college students in general—important segments of the New Left devised a profoundly anti-representational form of political activism. One no longer needed to justify her own cause by claiming that it ultimately substituted for the crucial cause, the cause of the universal class. Instead, one could believe that a number of local contests, a number of micro-contradictions, would condense into a systemic crisis, a revolutionary conjunction.

All of this has been said before, but its consequences for the budding cultural critic have generally not been remarked. First, it led to an emphasis, still very influential in "oppositional" American criticism, on indeterminant negativity. It was no longer necessary, indeed it was impossible, to specify the inverse positive valence on every group's oppositional stance toward the "system." Indeed, in certain quarters, indeterminant negativity came to be seen as superior to positive programs because less liable to cooptation. Negativity and marginality became values in themselves.

Second, but perhaps more important for the future of literary studies in general, was simply the collapse of the logic of representation itself. There was no longer a privileged realm of representation any more than there was a privileged referent. Cultural activity itself in this context began discarding its claim to separate status; lived and symbolic experience were consciously merged in guerilla theater, in happenings, in attempts to live a radical culture. Everything was equally symbolic and immanent, readable and opaque, and something (unspecified) in excess of itself.

This, rather than continental Marxist theory, was the intellectual and political experience that prepared the way for the American reception of French post-structuralist thought in left-wing circles, where it was often filtered through an increasingly attenuated Althusserianism. For some, Althusserianism became a step toward re-Marxification, for others it was a step toward the deconstructive critique of representation. In either case it reformulated the problem of the constitution of the subject, giving it a new, linguistic emphasis. When this was then supplemented by Jacques Derrida's work, a method of analysis resulted that accorded with some aspects of New Left political thought and contravened others. Specifically, although Derridean critiques also decentered a "system," collapsed the distinction between things and signs, and concentrated on the fungibility of a series of diacritical moments, they often defined the system as nothing but its diacritical moments and implied that those moments displace one another in an endless chain of signification instead of condensing in a revolutionary conjunction. What came to be called "deconstruction," then, could be used both to confirm important New Left tenets and, at the very time when the movement was losing momentum, to provide an explanation for that loss.

Many of us, however, found that we could neither renew our faith in Marxism nor convert to deconstruction, for neither seemed sufficient to explain the permutations of our own historical subjectivities and our relationship to a system of power, which we still imagined as decentered, but which we no longer viewed as easily vulnerable to its own contradictions. At this juncture, the process that had begun when the hierarchy of contradictions was abandoned, the process of rethinking the relationship between power and apparently oppositional subjectivity, became exigent. This was not so much a process of disillusionment as it was an extension of our belief in the efficacy of combining personal and political self-reflection. Was it possible, we asked, that certain forms of subjectivity that felt oppositional were really a means by which power relations were maintained? Was a politics organized by the discourse of liberation inevitably caught inside modern America's terms of power? Was it theoretically possible even to differentiate the individual subject from a system of power relationships?

This sort of self-questioning had extensive left-wing credentials, not only in the works of Louis Althusser, but also in Herbert Marcuse's highly influential repressive desublimation thesis. Such self-questioning became all the more urgent as feminist self-consciousness spread among activists. Indeed, the women's liberation movement taught us several things that are apposite here. First, it forced us to see that the more "personal" and "mundane" the issues, the more resistance to change we encountered. We could achieve what at the time seemed virtual generational consensus for abolishing the draft, winning a strike, reorganizing a university, ending the war, and passing affirmative action laws. But there was no such consensus about sharing the housework, reorganizing childcare, exposing family violence, or ending exploitative sexual relations. In the early years of the women's liberation movement, we were repeatedly told that we were siphoning off energy from significant political activities and wasting it in trivial, personal confrontations. Of course, we took such resistance, including the very rhetoric of triviality, as a token of the radical significance of our movement. Finally, we thought, we had penetrated the deepest, least questioned and most inaccessible region of social formation: the formation of ourselves as gendered subjects.

Thus we went beyond dismantling the old hierarchy of significance and began erecting a new one in which those aspects of life whose continuity was assured by their classification under the category of the trivial came to seem the most important. But this lesson had a second implication as well; by focusing attention on our gendered individuation as the deepest moment of social oppression, some of us called into question the political reliability of our own subjectivity. We effectively collapsed the self/society division and began regarding our "normal" consciousness and "natural" inclinations as profoundly untrustworthy. We, along with our erstwhile political optimism, became for ourselves the objects of a hermenuetics of suspicion. We wondered at our pre-feminist radical consciousness, which had imagined social arrangements to be relatively fragile. Could the illusion of fragility maintained by a belief that the system could not bear an exposure of its contradictions be a functioning part of its endurance? This was not the end of politics for many of us, but it was the end of a naive faith in the transparency of our own political consciousness.

The women's liberation movement had a third relevant consequence. We became fascinated with the history of gender, of how things have changed and how they don't change. The work of the Annales school and other anthropologically inspired historians gave some methodological direction in the mid-seventies, and in those years Michel Foucault's work appeared, addressing exactly the issues that preoccupied us.

These were the seed years for the new historicist work that has been appearing in the eighties. In many ways this work has maintained New Left assumption about the sources, nature, and sites of social conflict and about the issue of representation. Instead of resubscribing, as some Marxist critics have, to a historical meta-narrative of class conflict, we have tended to insist that power cannot be equated with economic or state power, that its sites of activity, and hence of resistance, are also in the micro-politics of daily life. The traditionally important economic and political agents and events have been displaced or supplemented by people and phenomena that once seemed wholly insignificant, indeed outside of history: women, criminals, the insane, sexual practices and discourses, fairs, festivals, plays of all kinds. Just as in the sixties, the effort in the eighties has been to question and destabilize the distinctions between sign systems and things, the representation and the represented, history and text.

In all of these ways, much new historicist work can be said to possess a remarkable continuity with certain cultural assumptions of the New Left. But the work has also exposed and taken off from a number of contested moments within those assumptions, especially those regarding form and ideological contradiction. Despite the critique of substitutionalist politics and the supposed de-privileging of a realm of representation during the sixties and seventies, left formalism managed to thrive. In its Althusserian form, it tended, ironically, to reestablish many former Hegelian notions about the special status of art as a displayer of ideological contradictions. The art *form*, according to Althusser and Pierre Macherery, created internal distantiations which allow us to "see" the gaps and fissures, the points of stress and incoherence, inside the dominant ideology. "Seeing" was not to be confused with "knowing"; nevertheless, Althusserian literary criticism in practice made very little of this distinction and proceeded as if form were in itself revelatory.[4] This did not entail the privileging of any particular form, but of all forms. It was against such claims for the automatic subversiveness of art, as well as parallel deconstructive claims for literature's self-referential and therefore anti-ideological rhetoricity, that many new historicists directed their critiques. Their effort was, and still is, to show that under certain historical circumstances, the display of ideological contradictions is completely consonant with the maintenance of oppressive social relations. New historicists were often bent on proving that the relationship between form and ideology was neither one of simple affirmation, in which form papers over ideological gaps, nor one of subversive negation, in which form exposes ideology and thereby helps render it powerless. The contribution of the new historicism has been to identify a third alternative in which the very antagonism between literature and ideology becomes, in specific historical environments, a powerful and socially functional mode of constructing subjectivity.

This could be seen as the final de-privileging of the realm of representation, the final blow to left formalism, and hence a further extension of a New Left tendency. But it is precisely this mode of construing the relationship between literature and ideology that other left-wing critics have found not only quietistic in its implications but also formalist[5] in its assumptions. I will treat the second of these charges first, since it seems to me undeniable. The actual procedures of many new historicist analyses are often not very different from those of left formalists. We too often take the text as a constant, the very instability of which is stable across time, so that its historical impact can be determined from an analysis of its structures and the logic of their disintegration when set against other discourses. Historical reception studies are sometimes suggested as an antidote to such formalism,[6] and, despite the fact that these often import their own epistemological naivete, they certainly deserve much more of our attention than they currently receive. However, there is no simple solution to the problem of formalism—one variant of the problem of textuality—in historical studies; we can only hope to maintain a productive tension between the textualist and historicist dimensions of our work.

The charge of quietism in response to attacks on left formalism returns us to the issue with which we began, the issue of the relationship between politics and criticism. To argue that it is inherently quietistic to deny literature an inherent politics is, first of all, to reason tautologically. Such reasoning begins with the assumption that everything has *a* politics; a denial of this assumption must also have *a* politics, no doubt reactionary. Such reasoning is impervious to evidence; the accusers need not do the difficult work of examining how critical orientations interact with specific political initiatives, even in the most immediate arena of academic politics. They need not ask, for example, what impact the new historicism has had on curricula in literature departments, whether or not it has had a role in introducing non-canonical texts into the classroom, or in making students of literature more aware of the history and significance of such phenomena as imperialism, slavery, and gender differentiation in western culture. It is my guess, although the evidence is yet to be gathered, that new historicists have been, along with Marxists and feminists, fairly active in achieving these goals, which are generally considered to be on the "left" of the academic political spectrum.

All this is oddly irrelevant to critics of the new historicism on the left, while it forms the basis of political complaints coming from the right.[7] Left-wing critics would concede that new historicists often read the right texts and ask the right questions, but they complain that such readings yield the wrong answers. Specifically, they tend to complain that new historicists fail to emphasize that the text is a site of subversive potential and that the critic's job is to activate it.[8] They imply that the new historicist, in describing how texts may create modern subjectivity by playing the literary against the ideological, somehow becomes complicit in the process described.[9] There are many versions of this argument, some more persuasive than others, but they share a dismay at the new historicist's tendency to identify precisely the things in texts that had been named subversive, destabilizing, and self-distantiating, as inscriptions of the formative moments, not the disruptions, of the liberal subject. The negativity of literary culture is not denied but is rather re-presented as a potential basis of its positivity. Such a representation seems in itself quietistic to some critics because it apparently presents culture as achieving, through its very fracturing, an inescapable totalizing control. It could thus, the argument runs, convince people of the uselessness of opposition. And it certainly discredits the left-formalist assumptions that have underwritten much of this generation's emotional investment in the study of literature.

There is no doubt, then, that those new historicists who emphasize that modern subjectivity is subtended by what we might call a sub-tension pose a challenge to the usual methods of left-wing criticism. But it does not follow that this is a reactionary or quietistic challenge to the left. Indeed, one can find no more generally agreed-upon proposition in all sectors of literary criticism than the proposition that literature shakes us up and disturbs our moral equilibrium (liberal humanism), destabilizes the subject (deconstruction), and self-distantiates ideological formations (Marxism). New historicists find the terms of this consensus fascinating, and far from imagining that it has a politics, simply point to the ways in which it can take the place of many politics. As D. A. Miller has succinctly expressed it, "even if it were true that literature exercises a destabilizing function in our culture, the current consensus that it does so does not."[10] By posing challenges to the left-wing version of this consensus, indeed by simply pointing out that there is such a consensus, new historicists on the left ask more traditional leftists to see how the "subversion hypothesis," to use Miller's words again, "tends to function within the overbearing cultural 'mythologies' that will already have appropriated it." This is not an attempt to demoralize the left, but it can be seen as an attempt to de-moralize our relationship to literature, to interrupt the moral narrative of literature's benign disruptions with which we soothe ourselves.

What is the political import of this interruption? It doesn't have *one*. Even if its political origins were wholly comprised in the history I have sketched—of course, they are not—its tendencies and potential affiliations are never fully determined. We can reasonably predict, however, that new historicism's most active interlocutors will continue to be Marxists and other "oppositional" critics, and that the effects of their debate might be to alter long-standing critical procedures. For new historicism and Marxism are nudging one another toward previously undeveloped evidenciary bases for their conclusions and away from a belief in the self-consistency or constant "difference" of the text over time that warrants deriving historical effect from formal features or "rigorous" readings.

But we probably cannot predict a happy collaboration in the future, because some new historicists will continue to resist the goal of synthesizing their historical, literary critical, and political consciousnesses into one coherent entity. The new historicist, unlike the Marxist, is under no nominal compulsion to achieve consistency. She may even insist that historical curiosity can develop independently of political concerns; there may be no political impulse whatsoever behind her desire to historicize literature. This is not to claim that the desire for historical knowledge is itself historically unplaced or "objective"; it is, rather, to insist that the impulses, norms, and standards of a discipline called history, which has achieved a high level of autonomy in the late twentieth century, are a profound part of the subjectivity of some scholars and do not in all cases require political ignition.

Moreover, even for those of us whose political and historical concerns quite clearly overlap, a perfect confluence between the two might arouse more suspicion than satisfaction, for what would such a confluence be based on but the myth of a self-consistent subject impervious to divisions of disciplinary boundaries and outside the constraints of disciplinary standards? The demands that one so often hears on the left for self-placement, for exposing the political bases of one's intellectual endeavors, for coming clean about one's political agenda, for reading and interpreting everything as a feminist or a Marxist or an anti-imperialist, for getting to and shoring up a solid political foundation for all of one's endeavors, demands often made in the name of historical self-consciousness, resound only in a historical vacuum, so deeply do they mistake the constitution of modern subjectivity.

One could retort, using the analyses of some new historicists, that this modern subject, whose supposed nonidentity often facilitates the circulation of disciplinary power, is precisely what needs to be overcome. Such a retort would temporarily reverse the positions of the interlocutors, for the people who call for a single political-historical-critical enterprise often celebrate the subversive potential of the non-identical subject, while the new historicist finds herself insisting on the very nonidentity she has so often shown to be part of disciplinary processes. In doing so, however, new historicists have not claimed that the historical experience of nonidentity is merely chimerical and can be overcome by simply dismissing it as a literary effect underneath which some essential consistency can be unearthed. In fact, it does not follow from new historicist arguments either that the subject can or should be reconstituted on an identitarian model. Rather, the effort of this criticism has been to trace the creation of modern subjectivity in the necessary failures of the effort to produce a stable subject. It is difficult to see how attempts at producing stable critical subjects on a political model will escape repeating this circuit, will not result once again in an experience of decentered helplessness.

Of course, many of the points I'm making here come from inside the Marxist tradition; Lukács, Adorno, Althusser, indeed, Marx himself all warned against subordinating theory, critique, or historical scholarship to practical political goals. New historicism confronts Marxism now partly as an amplified record of Marxism's own edgiest, uneasiest voices. Those Marxists who listen carefully may hear many of their own unanswered doubts and questions. To dismiss such challenges as the mere echoes of a reactionary defeatism would be a serious mistake.

Notes

1. For the former charge, see Edward Pechter, "The New Historicism and Its Discontents: Politicizing Renaissance Drama," *PMLA* 102 (1987), 292–303; for the latter see Carolyn Porter, "Are We Being Historical Yet?" forthcoming in *South Atlantic Quarterly*. An argument similar to but less substantial and sophisticated than Porter's is made by Marguerite Waller in "Academic Tootsie: The Denial of Difference and the Difference It Makes," *Diacritics*, 17, No. 1 (1987), 2–20. It must be noted that all of the above and most of the critics yet to be cited here focus their attacks on the work of Stephen Greenblatt. I've attempted in this article to discuss only those charges that seem to me applicable to other critics, outside the field of Renaissance literature, who are routinely called new historicists.

2. Carolyn Porter uses this term, quoting Walter Cohen's "Political Criticism of Shakespeare," in Jean E. Howard and Marion F. O'Connor, eds., *Shakespeare Reproduced: The Text in History and Ideology* (New York and London: Methuen, 1987).

3. I am grateful to Houston Baker for this suggestion.

4. Michael Sprinker has recently explicated this distinction in *Imaginary Relations: Aesthetics and Ideology in the Theory of Historical Materialism* (New York: Verso, 1987). See especially pp. 101–104 and 267–295.

5. On the issue of formalism, see Cohen, "Political Criticism."

6. Both Porter and Cohen have made this suggestion.

7. According to David Brooks of *The Wall Street Journal,* the new historicism is a left-wing plot to destroy the canon and substitute a political agenda for a loving exploration of "literary excellence": "Annabel Patterson of Duke is typical. She uses Shakespeare, she says, as a vehicle to illuminate the way 17th-century society mistreated women, the working class and minorities. This emphasis is called the New Historicism." "From Western Lit to Westerns as Lit," *The Wall Street Journal,* February 2, 1988, p. 24, cols. 3-5. And according to *Newsweek,* new historicism is one among many schools prescribing "the study of books not because of their moral or esthetic value but because they permit the professor to advance a political, often Marxist agenda." David Lehman, "Deconstructing de Man's Life: An Academic Idol Falls Into Disgrace," *Newsweek,* February 15, 1988, p. 62. Frederick Crews, to whom these sentiments are attributed in the article, has energetically repudiated them in a letter to the editor, insisting that they are Lehman's own construction. There may be a certain amount of confusion evident in these mass-media attacks, but they are, in their own way, arguably accurate about the new historicism's usual affiliations in the overall politics of the discipline.

8. See both Cohen and Waller.

9. For the argument that new historicists themselves repeat the marginalization and/or containment of disruptive elements accomplished by the discursive practices they analyze, see Porter, op. cit.; and Lynda Boose, "The Family in Shakespeare Studies; or—Studies in the Family of Shakespeareans; or—The Politics of Politics," forthcoming in *Renaissance Quarterly.*

10. D. A. Miller, *The Novel and the Police* (Berkeley: Univ. of California Press, 1987), p. xi.

4

The History of the Anecdote: Fiction and Fiction[1]

Joel Fineman

The sexual impasse exudes the fictions that rationalize the impossible within which it originates. I don't say they are imagined; like Freud, I read in them the invitation to the real that underwrites them.

(Jacques Lacan, *Television*)[2]

A letter for me! it gives me an estate of seven years' health, in which time I will make a lip at the physician. The most sovreign prescription in Galen is but empiricutic, and, to this preservative, of no better report than a horse-drench.

(William Shakespeare, Coriolanus)[3]

1

This will be an informal, not a formal, talk, because when it happens, if it happens, I give what I originally thought would be the practical illustration of what I have to say about the New Historicism—a discussion of the way Stephen Greenblatt's essay, "Fiction and Friction," anecdotally collates traditional, Galenic, gynecological medical theory with a reading of Shakespeare's *Twelfth Night,* an essay I take to exemplify the relation of what is called the New Historicism to, on the one hand, what is called literature and, on the other, what is called history—I will be speaking, for the most part, informally from notes rather than reading a paper.[4]

I say "if it happens" I speak about Greenblatt's essay because what I have to say about that essay builds on and derives from more general considerations, both formal and historical, regarding the anecdote, and so, as prefatory prolegomenon to what I want to say about Greenblatt's "Fiction and Friction," I am obliged to develop, in a general, programmatic, and schematic way, some introductory material. As a result, my presentation today will be somewhat ill-proportioned and promissory. In effect, I will be reporting on the early stages of a research project concerned both with the formal operation of the anecdote, understood as a specific literary genre, with peculiar literary properties, and also with a practical literary history of the anecdote in so far as the formal operation of the anecdote bears on the history of historiography, i.e., on the history of the writing of history. Initially, I want to argue, on formal grounds, that the anecdote, in significant ways, determines the practice of historiography, but, as can readily be imagined, such a formal argument will necessarily look to derive its evidentiary exemplifications from a practical literary history of the history of historiography. Accordingly, because what I have to say about the New Historicism only makes sense within the general context of this twofold project, formal and historical, I must spend some considerable amount of time rehearsing, sketching out, and summarizing the main lines or reasoning guiding my research. Hence the following, rather extended, set of preliminary remarks— quite extended; they will likely take up the entirety of the time I am allotted. If so, when time will tell, I plan at the end of these preliminary remarks very quickly to sketch out what it was I wanted to say about Stephen Greenblatt's essay, "Fiction and Friction," and its relation to the New Historicism, in the paper that, finally, in the event, I may not get to deliver today, a paper that is called "The History of the Anecdote: Fiction and Fiction."

When the idea of participating in this panel on the New Historicism first arose—it was as a panel on the New Historicism that this occasion was first described to me, and I am assuming this has some relation to the session's subsequently revised or further specified scope, "The Boundaries of Social History"—it was my plan to approach the topic in terms of what I will be calling the history of the anecdote, taking Thucydides's *History of the Peloponnesian War* as an exemplary text with which to illustrate the operation of the history of the anecdote, and taking Thucydides as an historically significant, because the first, example of a New Historicist. "New Historicism" is, of course, I need hardly say, a recently developed term or name, probably coined on the model of an older rubric, "The New Criticism," but perhaps also affected or inflected by left-over memories of 1950s and 1960s, maybe even earlier, philosophical discussions of history and historicism— e.g., Karl Popper on *The Poverty of Historicism* (which dates back to the thirties, but was published in the forties and was influential in the fifties), or R. G. Collingwood's *The Idea of History* (1946, but based on lectures delivered in the 1930s), or Thomas S. Kuhn's *The Structure of Scientific Revolutions*, published in 1962, which initiated, through what it had to say about the history of science, a popular debate about the scientificity of science, a debate that not only had considerable currency in the sixties and seventies but one that inspired a remarkable amount of interest outside the relatively narrow world of the philosophy of science (in many ways what Kuhn had to say about scientific paradigms and paradigmatic shifts really did, as has often been said to be mistakenly said, condition and prepare for the later, American reception of Michel Foucault).[5] Primarily designed to mark out or off a methodological and self-described interdisciplinary approach to the embedding—"embedding" being the metaphor regularly put into play— of cultural artifacts, primarily literary artifacts (what was then still called literature), within the particularity of their social context, the term, the New Historicism, was also intended to function more urgently as a rallying cry calling out for an increasingly explicit thematic concern with the historical as such in the professional practice of American academic literary criticism. In principle, therefore, because addressed to the entire field of literary studies, New Historicism was intended to sound out a very general appeal, across the disciplinary board, for an historiographic consciousness and conscience, but, in fact, for reasons the significance of which I will later want to consider, the first and central projects of the New Historicism, so-called, and understood in the restricted and restricting sense to which I have just referred, were materialized primarily in studies of the Renaissance, in studies of the English literary Renaissance in particular. We can add that the term "New Historicism" initially carried with it a somewhat polemical air, for the literary criticisms and literary histories that pronounced themselves New Historicist, and that thereby understood their own critical practices to amount to actions performed, quietly enough, in the name of history, presented themselves as overdue corrections of, or as morally and politically motivated reactions against, the formalism— more precisely and more pejoratively, the "mere formalism" (which, as such, as something merely or purely formal, was thought to be apolitical, sexist, hermetic, elitist, etc.)—that, for one good or bad reason or another, had come to be associated with everything from the kind of close, immanent textual readings said to be endemic to the New Criticism, to the scientistic, agentless, essentialist, cross-cultural typologizations said to be characteristic of what was called Structuralism, to the kinds of deconstructive, but still mandarin and still strictly textual, and therefore still formalist, and therefore still objectionable, formulations—mere formulations—identified with either the phenomenologically or the rhetorically conceived versions of what came to be called Post-Structuralism: Jacques Derrida, for example, on the one hand, Paul de Man, for example, on the other, not that these two hands did not let each other know what they were up to.

In the context of so relatively recent, datable, even dated, a derivation of the New Historicism—and here I will assume the inadequacies, both historical and intellectual, of this genealogical account, developed from the point of view of the history of ideas, of the emergence of the New Historicism as one merchandisable rubric amongst others in the not so free marketplace of academic ideas are more or less obvious—my characterization of Thucydides as the first New Historicist might seem either overcoyly playful or anachronistically misplaced, especially if we recall the quite particular institutional demographic and economic factors that effectively conditioned and enabled the New Historicism to emerge as an identifiable intellectual posture in the first place.[6] But if the New Historicism, despite its programmatic refusal to specify a methodological program for itself—its characteristic air of reporting, haplessly, the discoveries it happened serendipitously to stumble upon in the course of undirected, idle rambles through the historical archives—can be identified in this way with the specificity of a particular moment in recent American academic intellectual history—i.e., if, in addition to pronouncing its name, "The New Historicism," we can also locate for that name a very local habitation within the extended apparatus of the University—it is still the case that it is also possible to relate the specificity of the New Historicism, as a practice, however amorphous, to a far more general, but still historically specifiable, impulse towards the historical; it is possible, that is to say, to relate the New Historicism to an historical tradition of historicity or of historicizing within which it, the New Historicism, can be understood to occupy a coherent time and place. In this more general context, it makes sense, for several reasons, to turn to Thucydides, or to what goes on in the name of Thucydides, for Thucydides, quite apart from questions of his historical influence, is not only exemplary of, but also constitutive of, in an historically significant way, Western historiographic consciousness.[7]

I will not really be turning to Thucydides in any detailed, pressured way, but it is important to recall, in a very general way, that Thucydides is usually taken to be, and praised for being, the very early, if not the first, historian who takes a scientific view of history; explicitly and implicitly, he introduces, discovers, presupposes—for my purposes there is no need to decide or to determine just which—regularizing, normativizing, essentializing laws of historical causation by reference to which it becomes possible to fit particular events into the intelligible whole of a sequential, framing narrative—a whole that then becomes a pattern in accord with which one can understand an altogether different set or sequence of historical events, again on the assumption these events are also subject to or exemplary of one or another principle of nomological historical succession. For Thucydides the identification of such recurrent patterns defines the eternal usefulness of his history, or, in the famous words with which he announces and defends the novelty of his historical project, novel, in comparison, say, to the memorializing, commemorative, more or less epideictic, historiography of Herodotus: "And it may well be that the absence of the fabulous from my narrative will seem less pleasing to the ear; but whoever shall wish to have a clear view both of the events which have happened and of those which will someday, in all human probability, happen again in the same or a similar way—for these to adjudge my history profitable will be enough for me. And, indeed, it has been composed, not as a prize-essay to be heard for the moment, but as a possession for all time.[8]

A clear view of particular events which have, in fact, happened, plus a way of understanding the happening of these events through a general or generic logic of succession such that how they happened is predictably recurrent thus defines the double focus of Thucydides's history—but a double focus necessarily directed towards a single end. To the extent Thucydides's successivity is successful, his characteristic *"meta touto,"* "after this," i.e., the way Thucydides modulates within his history from one moment to another, will become the model for connecting any *touto,* any particular "this," to another, through some logic of sequential and transitional necessity that gives to every individual and singular event its representative historical significance. Only through the mutual coordination of a particular event and its genericizing narrative context—a coordination such that the particularity of the *touto,* the "this," and the generic, representative urgency of the logic of the *meta* reciprocally will call each other up—is it possible to identify or to attribute an historical significance either to a "this" or to a *meta,* for the specifically historical importance of either depends upon the way they each co-constitute or co-imply each other. We can say this more simply, in more familiar theoretical terms, by saying that Thucydides's *"meta touto,"* his "metahistory"—to use, but with a different inflection, Hayden White's carefully considered phrase—works by collating structure and genesis.[9] Thus it is, for famous example, that Thucydides can frankly admit that the versions he reports of the speeches delivered at one or another particular deliberative or forensic occasion are not verbatim records of what, in fact, was said, but are nevertheless historically representative, i.e., historically significant examples of what was called for, at the occasion, by the logic of events: "The speeches are given in the language in which, as it seemed to me, the several speakers would express, on the subjects under consideration, the sentiments most befitting the occasion, though at the same time I have adhered as closely as possible to the general sense of what was actually said."[10] The Greek here translated as "the sentiments most befitting the occasion" is *ta deonta,* i.e., "the things necessary," and, as scholars have noted, for Thucydides the reconstruction of this occasional "necessity," the necessity of the historically significant occasion, is more important than, though not necessarily at odds with, "the general sense of what was actually said"—this kind of necessity, we can add, reappears within the rhetoricity of the speeches that are reported, which develop, scholars generally agree, arguments based on probability and plausibility, likelihood, generic types and situations, etc., in accord with sophistic modes introduced to the deliberative protocols and forensic atmosphere of the Athens of Thucydides's youth.[11]

Thus understood, as representative historiography of significant historical events—of events joined together by a narrative formation, where events derive historical significance because they fit into a representative narrative account, and where the narrative account derives its historical significance because it comprehends significant historical events—familiar questions relating to such an historiographic enterprise immediately arise. On the one hand, how, in principle, does one identify an event within an historical frame, first, as an event, second, as an event that is, in fact, historically significant? These are two questions because, in principle, there are events that are not historically significant events. Correspondingly, on the other hand, how do singular events warrant or call out for the contextualizing, narrative frame within which they will individually play their collectively intelligible parts, i.e., how does one arrive, from a multiplicity of occurrences, first, at a single and coordinating story, second, at an historically significant story, for, again, there are stories that are not, as such, historically significant?

Here the question of the apparently incomplete state of Thucydides's manuscript, the way, for example, it seems to trail off at its end, and the way this fact affects a determination of just when Thucydides wrote his history acquires a more than biographical historiographic interest. In his very first paragraph, Thucydides recalls, retrospectively, that he began to write his history "at the very outset of the war" anticipating that this war would be "great and noteworthy above all the wars that had gone before."[12] Accordingly, we can, on the one hand, imagine Thucydides writing up his history as its events occurred and deriving or observing the overriding logic of their historical occurrence, the logic of their *meta*, in the course of their occurrence, guided here by his historian's foreknowledge of what would come to pass. Alternatively, on the other hand, we can imagine Thucydides writing up his history at the end of the war, when the final scheme of its unfolding had at last revealed itself to him, i.e., after the fact of its facts, and that, like the owl of Minerva at dusk, or like Hegel at the end of history, he then returns to his historiographic beginning with its concluding and historically significant end already clearly in his retrospective sight. We can no doubt reasonably presume that Thucydides did both, that he wrote his history both backwards and forwards, in retrospection and prospection, but whether he did both, or more of the one or more of the other, his biographical relation to the history he lives through foregrounds the general questions I have mentioned regarding the way events and framing context are to be related to, derived from, or thought through each other.

I mention the biographical version of this familiar problematic relating to the intersection of event and context because it repeats the terms and situation of the medical historiographic model that, it is sometimes said, is an important influence on Thucydides's conception of historiographic method and succession.[13] Here I refer to the medical writings associated with the name of Hippocrates (what will later become Stephen Greenblatt's Galen), and to the stylistic, lexical, and procedural affinities that can be identified between them and the practice of Thucydides in his history. Thus, scholars have noted that Thucydides adopts the specifically semiological language and method of the Hippocratic doctor who is concerned to interpret the signs of disease for the sake of diagnosis and prognosis; Thucydides does the same with political, military, and social facts, and does so with the same language of diagnosis, prognosis, and natural cause, *prophasis*. So too, there are stylistic affinities between Thucydides's compressed and stressedly antithetical prose style and the noticeably aphoristic manner of the Hippocratic corpus—e.g., "Life is short, Art long," to quote the famous opening of the medical treatise that goes under the name *Aphorisms*—and it is possible to show that these stylistic patterns at the level of the sentence also correspond with larger architectural patterns in Thucydides's narrative, e.g., the balanced disposition of one speech against another, and related contrapuntal symmetries and formal arrangements that serve to organize the narrative. Finally, it seems clear Thucydides conceives his history under the model of the medical case history, so that the generic frame of Thucydides's events is imagined in conformity with the organic form of an Hippocratic illness that passes through significant events, i.e, symptoms, which appear in a coherent, chronological succession—one that starts from some zero-degree of vulnerable healthiness, that then builds up, through a series of significant symptoms, to a predictable dramatic climax at a moment of required "crisis" ("crisis" being a technical medical term), after which the disease completes its predetermined and internally directed course, when the patient either dies or returns to health.

In such medical cases histories, which, in sufficient number, will generate a natural history of particular diseases, an abstract model for the integration of event within a context is straightforwardly disclosed, for it is within the frame of a natural and teleologically governed progress, passing inexorably from a beginning through a middle to an end, that the individuated, symptomatic moments of any given disease acquire their historical—in this case their medical historical—significance—in Thucydidean terms, the *logos,* or principle, of the facts, the *erga*. Thus the Hippocratic doctor, writing up a case history—of which there are many examples, e.g., in the treatise on *Epidemics*—will selectively report, for example, the acute fever of the third day, the bilious stools of the seventh, the yellow vomit of the sixteenth, the sedimented urine of the seventeenth, the crisis on the twentieth, the death or cure thereafter, and all these individuated moments, the days omitted as well as those selected, the items noticed as well as those ignored, acquire their specifically medical significance insofar as they are understood to articulate in their appearance or omission what are coherently segmented moments in the fluid and continuous unfolding of the internal logic of disease, just as their appearance is what circularly corroborates the doctor's nosological description of disease—his nomological narrative or *meta*—that turns the disease into an abstract, reified entity with its own representative, medical significance.[14] This double articulation is what allows the doctor to diagnose the disease, so that he can account for its events in terms of one medical explanation as opposed to another; this is what allows him to make, in similar cases, predictive prognoses of the course of an illness before it runs its course; and, in general, this is what allows him to believe in medical laws controlling the historical unfolding of beginning, middle, and end. For shorthand evidence of all this, especially evidence of the doctor's concern with establishing a continuous, seamless narrative of beginning, middle, and end, I quote the savvy opening of the Hippocratic treatise called *Prognostic:*

> I hold that it is an excellent thing for a physician to practice forecasting. For if he discover and declare unaided by the side of his patients the present, the past, and the future, and fill in the gaps of the account given by the sick, he will be the more believed to understand the cases, so that men will confidently entrust themselves to him for treatment. Furthermore, he will carry out the treatment best if he know beforehand from the present symptoms what will take place later. Now to restore every patient to health is impossible. To do so indeed would have been better even than forecasting the future. But as a matter of fact men do die, some owing to the severity of the disease before they summon the physician, others expiring immediately after calling him in—living one day or a little longer—before the physician by his art can combat the disease. It is necessary, therefore, to learn the natures of such disease, how much they exceed the strength of men's bodies, and to learn how to forecast them. For in this way you will justly win respect and be an able physician. For the longer time you plan to meet each emergency the greater your power to save those who have a chance of recovery, while you will be blameless if you learn and declare beforehand those who will die and those who will get better."[15]

It is here, where the logic of event and context established by the historiography of the medical case history of the aphoristic Hippocratic corpus coincides with the logic of event and context as this is developed by Thucydides, that the anecdote, a specific literary form, is important, and this because, I want to argue, the anecdote determines the destiny of a specifically historiographic integration of event and context. The anecdote, let us provisionally remark, as the narration of a singular event, is the literary form or genre that uniquely refers to the real. This is not as trivial an observation as might at first appear. It reminds us, on the one hand, that the anecdote has something literary about it, for there are, of course, other and non-literary ways to make reference to the real—through direct description, ostention, definition, etc.—that are not anecdotal. On the other hand, it reminds us also that there is something about the anecdote that exceeds its literary status, and this excess is precisely that which gives the anecdote its pointed, referential access to the real; a summary, for example, of some portion of a novel, however brief and pointed, is, again, not something anecdotal. These two features, therefore, taken together—i.e., first, that the anecdote has something literary about it, but, second, that the anecdote, however literary, is nevertheless directly pointed towards or rooted in the real—allow us to think of the anecdote, given its formal if not its actual brevity, as a *historeme,* i.e., as the smallest minimal unit of the historiographic fact. And the question that the anecdote thus poses is how, compact of both literature and reference, the anecdote possesses its peculiar and eventful narrative force.

Before addressing the question it is necessary to recall, however, as no doubt many of you have already recalled to yourselves, that everything I have said so far in a loose, informal way about the integration of event and context has of course been said before in far more formal and more pressured fashion in the philosophical reflections on history, historiography, and historicism that come out of the experienced aftermath of Hegel's end of history. It is often said these days—I am thinking here, in particular, of Jean-François Lyotard's remarks on the subject—that we live now, especially when it comes to historiography, after the age of the *grand récit,* i.e., in an epoch for which the large story of the exigent unfolding of beginning, through middle, to end, no longer carries any urgency.[16] Hegel's philosophy of history, with its narration of the spirit's gradual arrival at its own final self-realizing self-reflection, is the purest model of such an historical *grand récit,* and, from Dilthey on, the problem posed to history by such an absolutely and inevitably determined integration of historical event and historical context has been, precisely, that, properly speaking, such a history is not historical. Governed by an absolute, inevitable, inexorable teleological unfolding, so that, in principle, nothing can happen by chance, every moment that participates within such Hegelian history, as the Spirit materially unfolds itself into and unto itself, is thereby rendered timeless; such moments, we can say—and here I am influenced by Jean-Luc Nancy's discussion of this issue in a paper on Hegel and "Finite History"[17]—exist, for all intents and purposes, precisely because they are intentional and purposeful, outside of time, or in a timeless present, and this because their momentary durative appearance is already but the guaranteed foreshadow, the already all but realized promise of the concluding end of history towards which tendentiously, as but the passing moments in a story whose conclusion is already written, they tend.[18]

We can say, still speaking at a considerable level of generality, that it has been the project of post-Hegelian philosophy, insofar as it remains Hegelian, and concerned therefore with history, to find some way to introduce into the ahistorical historicality of Hegelian philosophy of history some break or interruption of the fullness and repletion of the Spirit's self-reflection, so as thereby to introduce to history the temporality of time. Thus Husserl, to take the central instance, attempts—I am thinking of *The Origin of Geometry,* but the theme arises elsewhere, notably in *The Crisis of European Science*—at the final limits of his phenomenological deduction of the transcendental ego's relation to its own necessary historicity, to find a way to root the structural a priori of universal historicality in a natural, not a transcendental, origin, so as thereby to return the transcendental subject to an origin in time, and to establish thereby a practical "universal teleology of reason."[19] This is Husserl's late great turn to History—when the transcendental ego reflects alternatively on his place in a specific tradition of philosophical reflection or, instead, on the natural attitude that is necessarily pregiven, as life-world, to his transcendental subjectivity—that marks the novelty of Husserl's late writings, distinguishing them from his earlier—in principle, ahistorical— eidetic, phenomenological reductions of ideas. So too with Heidegger, who attempts in *Being and Time* which is dedicated to Husserl, to establish what he calls "authentic historicality" by developing the broken self-reflection by means of which the subject, through his opening to the finitizing futurality of death, appropriates his tradition, his past, and thereby enters into an existential relation to the temporality of *dasein:*

> Only an entity which, in its Being, is essentially futural so that it is free for its death and can let itself be thrown back upon its factical "there" by shattering itself against death—that is to say, only an entity which, as futural, is equiprimordially in the process of having-been, can, by handing down to itself the possibility it has inherited, take over its own thrownness and be in the moment of vision for "its time." Only authentic temporality which is at the same time finite, makes possible something like fate—that is to say, authentic historicality.[20]

And, for Heidegger, what is true for the subject of history is also true for the methodology of the discipline thereof:

> The question of whether the object of historiology is just to put one-for-all "individual" events into a series, or whether it also has "laws" as its objects, is one that is radically mistaken. The theme of historiology is neither that which has happened just once for all nor something universal that floats above it, but the possibility which has been factically existent. This possibility does not get repeated as such—that is to say, understood in an authentically historiological way—if it becomes perverted into the colourlessness of a supratemporal model . . . Even historiological disclosure temporalizes itself *in terms of the future.* The *"selection"* of what is to become a possible object for historiology *has already been met with* in the factual existential *choice* of Dasein's historicality, in which historiology first of all arises, and in which alone it *is.*[21]

(We should recall in passing that Heidegger's description of the individual's fateful history—*schicksal*—is supposed to become collective with the idea of a communal Destiny—*geschick*—and Being-in-the-world.)[22]

And so too with Jacques Derrida, whose deconstruction of Husserl's natural origin (the origin whose necessity Husserl develops in *The Origin of Geometry*) shows how such a transcendentally required natural origin (as the need for this natural origin is established by Husserl's phenomenological account of the historical a priori), is, *as origin,* necessarily conceived as a deferment, as a structural deferment, and must be so for history to happen:

On the condition that the taking seriously of pure factuality follows after the possibility of phenomenology and assumes its juridical priority, to take factuality seriously as such is no longer to return to empiricism or nonphilosophy. On the contrary, it completes philosophy. But because of that, it must stand in the precarious openness of a question: the question of the origin of Being as History. . . . Here delay is the philosophical absolute, because the beginning of methodic reflection can only consist in the consciousness of the amplification of *another* previous, possible, and absolute origin in general. Since this alterity of the absolute origin structurally appears in *my living Present* and since it can appear and be recognized only in the primordiality of something like my *living Present,* this very fact signifies the authenticity of phenomenological delay and limitation. . . . Could there be an authentic thought of Being *as* History, as well as authentic historicity of thought, if the consciousness of delay could be reduced? But could there be any philosophy, if this consciousness of delay was not primordial and pure? . . . The impossibility of resting in the simple maintenance [nowness] of a Living Present, the sole and absolute origin of the De Facto *and* the De Jure, of Being *and* Sense, but always other in its self-identity: the inability to live enclosed in the innocent undividedness of the primordial Absolute, because the Absolute is *present* only in being *deferred-delayed [différant]* without respite, this impotence and this impossibility are given in a primordial and pure consciousness of Difference. Such a *consciousness,* with its strange style of unity, must be able to be restored to its own light. Without such a consciousness, without its own proper dehiscense, nothing would appear.[23]

(I cite Derrida at such length in part to recall the way he fits into or participates within a relatively familiar historical tradition of reflection on historicity, but also to make the point that people who criticize Derrida for ignoring history—and there are, lately, many such people—simply have not read him carefully enough, in my opinion, since history and the possibility of historicality have been central concerns for Derrida, and also emphatically explicit thematic issues, in almost everything he has written.) In all these cases—Husserl, Heidegger, Derrida, and, let me say, what goes without saying, that I mention these three names only as a way of pointing to a larger continuity of concern—the self-completing self-reflecting of Hegelian historicity is turned over on itself, turned over and turned inside-out, so as to open up in space a space for space to take its place, and to open up the temporality of time so that time can have its moment. (I will parenthetically add, for reasons that will become clearer later, that Jacques Lacan's category of the Real for the subject—different both from the imaginary and the Symbolic—a Real that can be neither specularized nor represented, identifies the same kind of genuinely historical opening).[24]

In this philosophical context, to which, of course, necessarily I here simply gesture, we can see the good historicizing heart and the good historicizing intentions of the New Historicism, of the New Historicism that is properly so-called. The oxymoron, if that is the right word for it, embedded in the rubric—the cheery enthusiasm with which the New Historicism, as a catchy term or phrase, proposes to introduce a novelty or an innovation, something "New," into the closed and closing historiography of successive innovation, "Historicism"—however unreflectingly or naively this oxymoron may initially have been intended, and whatever it was the old and unreformed "Historicism" of the New Historicism may have been supposed to have been before its supplanting renovation—this oxymoron is witness to or earnest of an impulse to discover or to disclose some wrinkling and historicizing interruption, a breaking and a *realizing* interjection, within the encyclopaedically enclosed circle of Hegelian historical self-reflection. This is why the term, "The New Historicism," as a term, is different in kind from the "New Criticism," the term that may have been its model. As a title, the New Historicism strives to perform and thereby to enable the project it effectively entitles, and thus to earn thereby its access to the real through the excess of its name. In this sense, if only in name only, the New Historicism amounts to a gesture which is the very opposite of Fredric Jameson's essentially ahistorical injunction in *The Political Unconscious* to "always historicize."[25]

All this brings us back both to Thucydides and to the anecdote, and, then, eventually, though in the mode of deferment, to Stephen Greenblatt. Given what I have said just now, and using Heidegger's topoi because they are familiar, we can propose the following provisional definition of history: History is what happens, I shall say, provisionally, when you combine Being and Time, the problem with this definition being—what makes it provisional—that it is necessary immediately to recognize that it is not necessarily the case that something happens when you combine Being and Time. To be sure, if it is the case that something necessarily happens when you combine Being and Time, then you do indeed get history, but, specifically, what you get is the history of philosophy, i.e., the story of a philosophically exigent historical *démarche*—in this case, given the topoi with which we began, we get Heidegger's somewhat portentous, melodramatic rehearsal of the inexorable falling off, in Time, from Being, an ontological decline that, according to Heidegger, begins in the West the day after the Pre-Socratics, and from which, according to Heidegger, we still deeply suffer in our Greco-German souls. But, again, such a history of philosophy is, as such, not historical, and again, this is the case because the story it reports is one that leaves no room for chance. It is necessary, therefore, to revise, at the start, our provisional definition of history, by saying that history is what happens when it happens—but as it only sometimes, in particular cases, happens—that something happens when you combine Being and Time.

And I specify the definition in these terms because this is how I propose to understand both the formal literary-referential peculiarity of the anecdote as well as the historical effects of the anecdote on the writing of history—these two features establishing, when they are taken together, what I am calling the history of the anecdote. In formal terms, my thesis is the following: that the anecdote is the literary form that uniquely *lets history happen* by virtue of the way it introduces an opening into the teleological, and therefore timeless, narration of beginning, middle, and end. The anecdote produces the effect of the real, the occurrence of contingency, by establishing an event as an event within and yet without the framing context of historical successivity, i.e., it does so only in so far as its narration both comprises and refracts the narration it reports. Further, I want further to maintain, still speaking formally, that the opening of history that is effected by the anecdote, the hole and rim—using psychoanalytic language, the orifice—traced out by the anecdote within the totalizing whole of history, is something that is characteristically and ahistorically plugged up by a teleological narration that, though larger than the anecdote itself, is still constitutively inspired by the seductive opening of anecdotal form—thereby once again opening up the possibility, but, again, *only* the possibility, that this new narration, now complete within itself, and thereby rendered formally small—capable, therefore, of being anecdotalized—will itself be opened up by a further anecdotal operation, thereby calling forth some yet larger circumcising circumscription, and so, so on and so forth.[26] Understood in this way, we can distinguish the anecdote from a strictly or restrictively literary formation in which what I am calling the anecdotal opening of narrativity either does not occur to begin with or, what turns about to be the same thing, occurs as a prescriptive opening that forever forecloses any finalizing or finitizing closure. Correspondingly, understood in this way, we can distinguish the anecdote from non-literary forms of reference (e.g., direct description, ostention, definition, etc.) that, relatively speaking, do not call up the narration of beginning, middle, and end, in which, therefore, there can be no dilation of narrative successivity, and from which, therefore there exudes no effect of the real.

This double intersection, the formal play of anecdotal hole and whole, an ongoing anecdotal dilation and contraction of the entrance into history through the opening of history that lets history happen, leads me also to what is intended as a large, but nevertheless straightforwardly historical investigation regarding the historical collation of, on the one hand, the anecdote, or, as it is called in French, *la petite histoire,* the little story, and, on the other, the *grand récit,* where the *grand récit* must be understood as a symptomatic system of enveloping, narrativizing encapsulations called forth as response to the historical effect—the opening of history that lets history happen—that is first disclosed by, but that is then closed up by, anecdotal form. On the basis, therefore, of this formal theory of anecdote, I propose, then, to understand the history of historiography as the history of the effect of anecdotal form on the writing of history, a history that would follow out a traceable, genealogical progression from the medical case history of the aphoristic Hippocrates, through Thucydides, through collections, both in late antiquity and in the middle ages (where, in fact, Thucydides is not really powerfully present), of anecdotal historiography—not just things like chronicles or anthologies of narrative exempla, lives of saints and holy men, parables, collected sequences of stories that take place in larger frames, and the like, but also compilations such as dictionaries, riddles, jest-books, etc.— through the Renaissance, up to the present, up to, through, and, therefore, perforce, beyond the New Historicism.[27]

In this large history of historiography, Thucydides, I think, occupies not only an exemplary but also an historically significant place. Exemplary, because it would be possible to show that specific events and figures in Thucydides's historiography illustrate the effect of the operation of the aporetic anecdote on the writing of history—I refer here, in particular, to the way Thucydides discusses the plague, but also to the way Thucydides develops Alcibiades as a trickster figure who is never more Athenian than when he betrays Athens, these being central instances of the way the anecdotal works to introduce historicizing chance into Thucydides's otherwise, would-be Hippocratic history.[28] Exemplary, then, but also historically significant, however, or moreover, because Thucydides in this way, as a writer of the history of the anecdote, thereby stands, despite his totalizing historiographic intentions, for the appearance of contingency, and therefore of History, in the very Athens that at this very moment is inventing and collating, as complicitous alternatives, a programmatically ahistorical Philosophy and Literature of the non-contingent.[29]

So too, in this grand, recognizably comic, universal history of historiography, the Renaissance would also occupy a crucial place, because, as is often said, it is in the Renaissance that there begins to develop a thematic historical consciousness—the subject as a subject *of* history—at the same moment that there begins to develop a correspondingly thematic scientific consciousness as well—Vico, say, on the one hand, Galileo, on the other—though it is important to recall that there also appears in the Renaissance, at least in the English Renaissance, though it only appears very briefly, an intentionally antiquarian historicism that sees itself as a refreshing alternative to large-scale moralizing, narrative historiography.[30] Here I am guided, historiographically, by Husserl, for whom the Renaissance marked the inauguration of what he called "The Crisis of European Science" because this is when the language of science, exemplified by Galileo's mathematical physics, grows so formal that the sedimented meanings embedded within it grow too faint to recall (in contrast to what happens with less formalized language) their origination in the natural life-world—for prime historical example, and from whence derives the significance of Husserl's *Origin of Geometry,* the way the magnitudes of Euclidean geometry are rewritten by Diophantus and Viete in algebraic terms (here I should say that I am very influenced by Jacob Klein's book on the history of mathematics, which is called *Greek Mathematical Thought and the Origin of Algebra,* and also by what Klein elsewhere wrote on Husserl and the history of science).[31] For Husserl, this forgetfulness nestled within formal scientific language marks the beginnings of crisis—a crisis no doubt conceived in medical terms—for the European spirit, for this is what initiates a specifically European tradition of empiricist, technicist scientism that works to divorce knowledge from experience. It is possible, however—indeed, given Husserl—it is *almost* necessary to imagine a corresponding crisis in historical consciousness inaugurated by the emergence in the Renaissance of a correspondingly technicist historicism that carries as its cost its unspoken sense of estranged distance from the anecdotal real. This locates what for me is the primary issue of my research project, at the same time as it suggests why the New Historicism is at once a symptom of and a response to a specifically Renaissance historiographic crisis. It is my suspicion or hypothesis that we can identify in the passage from the early to the late Renaissance, from the first humanist enthusiasm for the revival or rebirth of the past to the subsequent repudiation of the ancients in the name of science—e.g., Francis Bacon—how it happened that historiography gave over to science the *experience* of history, when the force of the anecdote was rewritten as experiment. This is why, if ever it were to happen I give my paper, I want to consider the relation between Bacon's aphoristic essay style, along with the aphorisms of *The New Organon,* and Bacon's formulation in *The New Organon* of the idea of the crucial experiment for science, i.e., the experiment that would allow one to decide, if such an experiment could ever be devised, between competing theories. This is the type of "Prerogative Instance" Bacon calls *Instantiae Crucis*—traditionally translated as "Instances of the Fingerpost," i.e., what happens when one stands upon or at (and, hence, ex-ists) the intersecting "crossroads"—because, as with Oedipus's "crossroads," this marks the point where one decides which road to travel.[32] There is obviously much more to say about this, but I think this explains why the Renaissance is both a period and a period term, like the period and period term of the New Historicism, haunted by its failure to sustain the historical aspirations of its self-pronounced and new historicizing name. In Shakespeare's words—sonnet 59—"If there be nothing new, but that which is/Hath been before, how are our brains beguil'd,/Which laboring for invention bear amiss/The second burthen of a former child."[33]

Finally, in this large history or historiography that I propose to develop in the light of the history of the anecdote, the New Historicism, as such, also occupies an exemplary and historically significant place, if not quite so crucial a place as that of Thucydides at the beginning of the history of historiography, or as that of the Renaissance at a crucial moment of its development. (I should say that, as a period term, "The New Historicism" is less important than the "Renaissance.") For the aporetic operation of anecdotal form not only allows us to understand the characteristic writing practice of the New Historicism—those essays that begin with an introductory anecdote that introduces history, followed by amplification, followed by a moralizing conclusion that serves to put an end to history, this then sometimes followed by another anecdote that strives to keep things open (and here I will just assert that it is the prosaic and considerable achievement of the New Historicism to have reinvented for our time the essay form invented by Francis Bacon in the Renaissance), but also helps us to understand why the initially eager reception of the New Historicism was and is followed almost immediately by yet more eager and profoundly anti-historical impulse to reject it in the name of one or another presumptively more scientific or more ideologically secured and closed, and closing, historiographic approach. To see why this is the case, however, why in both the practice and reception of the New Historicism the opening of history occurs for but a moment, it is necessary to look more carefully at an illustrative and representative example. Turning, therefore, from large things—Thucydides, the Renaissance, the history of historiography—to different—i.e., to Stephen Greenblatt's essay, "Fiction and Friction"—I here conclude my introductory remarks to the talk I will now not finally deliver, "The History of the Anecdote: Fiction and Fiction."[34]

Notes

1.   This paper was originally delivered as a talk at a conference on "The New Historicism: The Boundaries of Social History," at the West Coast Humanities Institute, Stanford University, Oct. 9, 1987; I have retained the marks of oral presentation but have added and amplified some footnotes for the sake of publication in this anthology.

2.   Jacques Lacan, "Television," trans. Denys Hollier and Rosalind Krauss, *October,* 40 (Spring, 1988), 34.

3.   William Shakespeare, *Coriolanus,* 2.1.113–119; all subsequent Shakespeare quotations are from *The Riverside Shakespeare,* ed. G.B. Evans et al. (Boston: Houghton Mifflin, 1974).

4.   For the most part, I will be referring to the essay, "Fiction and Friction," as this originally appeared in *Reconstructing Individualism: Autonomy, Individuality, and the Self in Western Thought,* eds. Thomas C. Heller, Morton Sosna, and David Wellbury (Stanford: Stanford University Press, 1986), 30–63. A somewhat revised version of this essay appears as a chapter in Stephen Greenblatt's *Shakespearean Negotiations: The Circulation of Social Energy in Renaissance England* (Berkeley: University of California Press, 1988), 66–93.

5.   Karl Popper, *The Poverty of Historicism* (New York: Harper and Row , 1977); originally published in *Economica* (1944/5. R. G. Collingwood, *The Idea of History* (Oxford: Clarendon Press, 1946; this book was published posthumously and is based on a lecture delivered at Oxford in 1936); Paul Ricoeur characterizes the way Collingwood conceives history as "reenactment" of the past as a history of the Same, this in contrast to, on the one hand, an exoticizing history of the Other or of individuated Difference, which Ricoeur associates with the work of Michel de Certeau and with post-structuralist historicisms in general, and, on the other, to what Ricoeur calls the history of the Analogous, i.e., tropological history, which he associates with the work of Hayden White; see *Time and Narrative,* Vol. 3, trans. K. Blamey and D. Pellauer (Chicago: University of Chicago Press, 1988), esp. ch. 6, "The Reality of the Past," 142–156. Thomas S. Kuhn, *The Structure of Scientific Revolutions* (Chicago: University of Chicago Press, 1962); for a characteristic conjoining of Kuhn with Foucault see, Hilary Putnam, "Philosophers and Human Understanding," in *Scientific Explanation,* ed. A. F. Heath (Oxford: Clarendon Press, 1981), 106. For what is a traditional pejorative criticism of anecdotal historicism, see Benedetto Croce, *History as the Story of Liberty* (New York: W.W. Norton 1941) chs. 3–4, 118-132.

6.   For responses to the New Historicism, understood as an academic event, see Louis Montrose, "Renaissance Studies and the Subject of History" and Jean Howard, "The New Historicism in Renaissance Studies," both in *ELR*, 16, No. 1 (Winter 1986). In general, it seems right to think of the New Historicism as an academic phenomenon specific to the U.S.A., something that is also true of what is called deconstruction. As with deconstruction, New Historicist criticism is regularly concerned with the "textuality" of its texts, something very foreign to the practical literalism of U.K. "materialism," on the one hand, and, on the other, the theoretical literalism one associates with Derrida. As has often been suggested, this is probably the result of the textualizing legacy left or left over by New Criticism, which opens up a specifically U.S.A. space for "textuality." As with a deconstructive critic such as Paul de Man—who is profoundly influential in the U.S.A., but who has no urgent currency in either England or France—one suspects New Historicism, as a specific critical practice, will remain firmly rooted in the sensibility of the U.S.A. literary academy.

7.   One should note in this contextualizing context "The New History" *(Nea Historia)* of Zosimus, the sixth-century pagan historian of the decline of the Roman empire; see *Zosimus: New History,* trans, and ed. R.T. Ridley (Canberra: Australian Association for Byzantine Studies; Australian National University Press, 1982).

8.   Thucydides, *History of the Peloponnesian War,* C.F. Smith (Boston: Harvard University Press, 1962), 1.22.4; unless otherwise noted, all subsequent reference to Thucydides will be to this four-volume edition of *The Loeb Classical Library.*

9.   The terms are familiar from Jean Hippolyte's *Structure and Genesis in Hegel's Phenomenology,* trans. S. Cherniak and J. Heckman (Evanston: Northwestern University Press, 1974).

10.   Thucydides, Loeb, 1.22.4; an alternate translation, by John H. Finley Jr., makes the point more clearly: "As for the speeches delivered by the several statesmen before and during the war, it proved difficult for me to report the exact substance of what was said, whether I heard the speeches myself or learned of them from others. I have therefore made the speakers express primarily what in my own opinion was called for under the successive circumstances, at the same time keeping as close as possible to the general import of what was actually said," *Thucydides* (Ann Arbor: University of Michigan Press, 1963), 94–95. Thucydides' practice should be contrasted to the way Livy, for example, stylistically and characterologically individuates the voices of particular speakers. In this connection, consider Freud's remarks at the beginning of his report of the case of Dora:

> The wording of these dreams was recorded immediately after the sitting, and they thus afforded a secure point of attachment for the chain of interpretations and

recollections which proceeded from them. The case history itself was only committed to writing from memory, after the treatment was at an end, but while my recollection of the case was still fresh and was heightened by my interest in its publication. Thus the record is not absolutely—phonographically—exact, but it can claim to possess a high degree of trustworthiñess. Nothing of any importance has been altered in it except in several places the order in which the explanations are given; and this has been done for the sake of presenting the case in a more connected form.
Sigmund Freud, *Dora: An Analysis of a Case of Hysteria* (1905), trans. J. Strachey (New York: Collier Books, 1963), 24.

11.   Finley, cited above, discusses *ta deonta*, p. 95. For discussions of Thucydides's style and its relation to the Sophistic tradition, see also John H. Finley Jr., *Three Essays on Thucydides* (Boston: Harvard University Press, 1967), esp. ch. 2; Michael Grant, *The Ancient Historians* (New York: Charles Scribner's Sons, 1970), 88–101. In this context, Francis M. Cornford's objections to the absence of social or cultural history in Thucydides's strictly military history of the war amount to a criticism of Thucydidean style as well as of substance, (*[Thucydides Mythhistoricus]* London: E. Arnold, 1907).

12.   Thucydides, 1.1.1; as does Herodotus, Thucydides begins his history by marking his own proper name, describing himself—though this was not exactly the case—as an Athenian.

13.   On the relation of Thucydides to the Hippocratic corpus, see C.N. Cochrane, *Thucydides and the Science of History* (London: Oxford University Press, 1929); also Grant and Finley cited above; also Roland Barthes, "The Discourse of History," in *The Rustle of Language*, trans. R. Howard (New York: Hill and Wang, 1986), 127–140; see also, though in a somewhat different context, Carlo Ginzberg, "Morelli, Freud and Sherlock Holmes: Clues and Scientific Method," *The History Workshop*, 9 (1980), 5–36.

14.   Hippocrates, the Loeb Classical Library, ed. E. Capps et al., trans. W.H.S. Jones, Vol. 1 (London: William Heinemann; NY: G.P. Putnam's Sons, 1923), 227–9.

15.   Hippocrates, the Loeb, Vol. 2 (London: William Heinemann; Cambridge, MA: Harvard Univ. Press, 1923), 7–9.

16.   "In contemporary society and culture—postindustrial society, postmodern culture—the question of the legitimation of knowledge is formulated in different terms. The grand narrative has lost its credibility, regardless of what mode of unification it uses, regardless of whether it is a speculative narrative or a narrative of emancipation," Jean-François Lyotard, *The Post-Modern Condition: A Report on Knowledge* (Minnesota: University of Minnesota Press, 1984), 37.

17.   Jean-Luc Nancy, Lecture delivered at Berkeley, Spring, 1987.

18.   "While we are thus concerned exclusively with the idea of Spirit, and in the History of the World regard everything as only its manifestation, we have, in traversing the past—however extensive its period—only to do with what is *present;* for philosophy as occupying itself with the True, has to do with the *eternally present.* Nothing in the past is lost for it, for the idea is ever present; Spirit is immortal, with it there is no past, no future, but an essential *now,*" G.W.F. Hegel, *The Philosophy of History*, trans. J. Sibree (New York: Dover Publications, 1956), 78–79. There is an enormous literature that discusses post-Hegelian philosophy of history; I cite here some works I find especially useful for thinking about the topic: Michael Murray, *Modern Philosophy of History: Its Origin and Destination* (The Hague: Martinus Nijhoff, 1970); Rainer Nägele, "The Scene of the Other: Theodor W. Adorno's Negative Dialectic in the Context of Poststructuralism," in *Postmodernism and Politics,* ed. Jonathan Arac (Minnesota: University of Minnesota Press, 1986), 91–111; Rodolphe Gasché, "Of Aesthetic and Historical Determination," in *Post-Structuralism and the Question of History,* eds. Derek Attridge, Geoff Bennington and Robert Young (Cambridge: Cambridge University

Press, 1987), 139–161. Stanley Cavell, criticizing Paul Ricoeur's criticism of the would-be "eventless" history of *Annales* school history, develops what in this context is an extraordinarily suggestive distinction between the "eventless" and the "uneventful;" see "The Ordinary as the Uneventful: A Note on the *Annales* Historians," *Themes out of School; Effects and Causes* (San Francisco: North Point Press, 1984), 184–194. I have also greatly benefited from discussions of the concept of "event" with John Rajchman; see his "The Events of 1968," in the forthcoming *Harvard Encyclopedia of French Literature,* ed. Denys Hollier (Cambridge: Harvard University Press, 1989); also his "Lacan and the Ethics of Modernity," *Representations,* 15.

19. "If the usual factual study of history in general, and in particular the history which in most recent times has achieved true universal extension over all humanity, is to have any meaning at all, such a meaning can only be grounded upon what we can here call internal history, and as such upon the foundations of the universal historical a priori. Such a meaning necessarily leads further to the indicated highest question of a universal teleology of reason." "The Origin of Geometry," trans. David Carr, p. 378, included as appendix to Edmund Husserl, *The Crisis of European Sciences and Transcendental Phenomenology* (Evanston: Northwestern University Press, 1970), 353–378.

20. Martin Heidegger, *Being and Time,* trans. John Macquarrie and Edward Robinson (New York: Harper and Row, 1962), 437.

21. Heidegger, *Being and Time,* p. 447.

22. It can certainly be said, especially if one recalls Heidegger's relation to fascism, that this idea of a communal destiny is too fateful indeed; similar objections can be raised to Gadamer's Heideggerian approach to hermeneutics and literary history; see Hans-Georg Gadamer, *Truth and Method* (New York: The Seabury Press, 1975).

23. Jacques Derrida, *Edmund Husserl's "The Origin of Geometry": An Introduction,* trans. John P. Leavey Jr. (Stony Brook, New York: Nicolas Hays Ltd., 1978), 151–153.

24. I cite Lacan in order to account for a specifically psychologistic subject of history and to explain thereby a corresponding fetishization of time, e.g., the tidal wave of history; Lacan helps us to understand why the phenomenological experience of historicity is eroticized; see footnotes 26 and 34, below. Lacan's formulation of an unimaginable and unspeakable "real" accounts for my use of the word "anecdote," which, at least etymologically, means that which is "unpublished." For an anecdotal history that lives up to the erotics of its name, see Procopius's *Anekdota,* usually referred to as *Secret History.* On the erotics of the contingent real, see also the end of Jean-Paul Sartre's *The Psychology of Imagination* where Sarte explains that the perfectly beautiful woman is not desirable because she does not elicit contingency. (New York: Citadel Press, 1961 [c. 1948]), 282.

25. This is the opening sentence and also, Jameson says, the "moral" of *The Political Unconscious: Narrative as a Socially Symbolic Act* (Ithaca: Cornell University Press, 1981), 9.

26. cf. Jacques Lacan's account of the *objet a* and the mark of the real:
    The very delimitation of the "erogenous zone" that the drive isolates from the metabolism of the function (the act of devouring concerns other organs than the mouth—ask one of Pavlov's dogs) is the result of a cut *(coupure)* expressed in the anatomical mark *(trait)* of a margin or border—lips, "the enclosure of the teeth," the rim of the anus, the tip of the penis, the vagina, the slit formed by the eyelids, even the horn-shaped aperture of the ear. . . . Observe that the mark of the cut is no less obviously present in the object described by analytic theory: the mamilla, faeces, the phallus (imaginary object), the urinary flow. (An unthinkable list, if one adds, as I do, the phoneme, the gaze, the voice—the nothing.) For is it not obvious that this feature, this partial feature, rightly emphasized in objects, is applicable not because these objects are part

of a total object, the body, but because they represent only partially the function that produces them? These objects have one common feature in my elaboration of them—they have no specular image, or, in other words, alterity. It is what enables them to be the "stuff," or rather the lining, though not in any sense of the reverse, of the very subject that one takes to be the subject of consciousness. For this subject, who thinks he can accede to himself by designating himself in the statement, is no more than such an object.

"The Subversion of the Subject and the Dialectic of Desire in the Freudian Unconscious," *Ecrits: A Selection,* trans. A. Sheridan (New York: W.W. Norton, 1977), 314–315.

27.   For example, it is generally agreed that the *The Chronicle (chronikoi kanones)* of Eusebius, the fourth-century historian of the church, is the first attempt to compile a universal history of history, beginning with Abraham and extending up to the relatively recent past. Passed on through St. Jerome's Latin translation, Eusebius's history is enormously influential; it is not too much to say that Eusebius's Chronicle *is* the history of the West *in* the historiography of the West for the next twelve hundred years. What is worth remarking is that, though Eusebius's *Chronicle* is designed to unfold in tabular form the exigencies of providential history, its very format seems to call forth what I above characterize as the aporetic structure of the anecdote. Eusebius's *Chronicle* appears originally to have been organized so as to line up in its left-hand column events from sacred history, Jewish and Christian, and in its right-hand column what are chronologically corresponding events from secular or pagan history. Between the two columns, vertically descending down the page, were columns of numbers marking or dating successions of Olympiads, the reigns of different kings, etc., (for the sake of brevity, my description here somewhat distorts and very much oversimplifies the layout of Eusebius's manuscript). In principle, therefore, one reads the resulting table both vertically and horizontally, reading down the page for the progress of time, and across the page so as to compare and to contrast events in sacred and pagan history. Collating horizontal and vertical axes, one can thus behold the calendaric display of providential Christian history. However, in the light of scholarly reconstructions of Eusebius's original manuscript (the oldest extant version of the manuscript is not reliable), it is possible to see, at least for some crucial dates, the operation of an aporetic chiasmus in the horizontal collation of sacred and pagan events, with the result that the intersection of paradigmatic and syntagmatic axes seems to stand at odds with, rather than to confirm, straightforward Christian teleology. My remarks here are perfunctory (I intend to discuss Eusebius's *Chronicle* in more detail elsewhere, so too its relation to the Aristotelian idea of time as numbered, countable motion); I cite the example, however, for the sake of what I say later about a specifically Renaissance translation of the real of history into the real of science. For, speaking historically, it is significant that Eusebius's history receives its first deeply critical revision when subjected to the pressure of Humanist, scientific philology—Joseph Scaliger's *Thesaurus temporum* (1606), a genuine instance of "New Historicism"—which is something that eventually will altogether undo "canonical" history as such. For a marvelously detailed account of the history of scholarly attempts to reconstruct Eusebius's original manuscript, see Alden A. Mosshammer, *The "Chronicle" of Eusebius and Greek Chronographic Tradition* (Lewisburg: Bucknell University Press, 1979); for Scaliger's revision of Eusebius, see Anthony T. Grafton, "Joseph Scaliger and Historical Chronology: The Rise and Fall of a Discipline," *History and Theory,* 14 (1974), 156–185; also, Anthony T. Grafton, *Joseph Scaliger: A Study in the History of Classical Scholarship* (Oxford: Clarendon Press, 1983).

28.   With regard to the plague what is important to note is that Thucydides both suffers and survives it, as opposed to the doctors who, Thucydides stresses, were especially and mortally susceptible to the disease: "For neither were the physicians able to cope with the disease, since they at first had to treat it without knowing its nature, the mortality among them being greatest because they were the most exposed to it, nor did any other human art avail," 11.47.3. Thucydides's description of the plague is usually taken to be the most Hippocratic moment in

his history: hence, according to my argument, Thucydides's description of the plague is a precise Hippocratic description of what exceeds the Hippocratic, i.e., the doctor's account of what, as doctor, the doctor does not understand. Moreover, Thucydides stresses the surprising and chance appearance of the plague, introducing its report immediately after Pericles's "Funeral Oration," so that the plague appears as the diegetic surprise that determines, by inexorable chance, the history and "The History" of the Peloponnesian war. The inevitability of this accident corresponds to the equivocal prediction and retrospection with which Thucydides codes the plague. Thus, discussing the plague, Thucydides reports the following prophecy: " 'A Dorian war shall come and pestilence with it' "; Thucydides then elaborates: "A dispute arose, however, among the people, some contending that the word used in the verse by the ancients was not *loimos,* "pestilence," but *limos,* "famine," and the view prevailed at the time that "pestilence" was the original word; and quite naturally, for men's recollections conformed to their sufferings. But if ever another Dorian war should visit them after the present war and a famine happen to come with it, they would probaby, I fancy, recite the verse in that way," 2.54. The always available indeterminacy of the determining prophecy establishes what I call the historeme as an equivoceme that generates the aporetic structure of the anecdote. Compare the fungibility of Thucydides's *loimos-limos* with Greenblatt's "the simple change of one letter" in the example of Marie/Marin that I discuss in footnote 34, below.

What I say above about the anecdotal Alcibiades—ie., Alcibiades as Mr. Anecdote—is intended to refer to the traditional question raised by Thucydides's characterization of this famous hero-villain: i.e., is the personality of Alcibiades representative of the personality of Athens? The answer to this question is yes, but this is precisely *because* Alcibiades betrays Athens, his person and his city both being the essence of that which lacks essence; this is related to traditional characterizations of democracy in terms of the lawless and unstable

29.   The question at issue is the historical specificity of the invention in fifth-century Athens of the concatenated interrelationship between Philosophy, Literature, and History, each of these categories calling for or forth what will eventually become fixed forms of formal narration, i.e., the eventual and consequential striation of *logos* (Philosophy), *muthos* (Literature), and *historia* (History). This concatenation in turn establishes a specific psychology, which is why I speak of a psychologistic "subject of history." Thus, for example, anticipating what I say later about Bacon, the *De Augmentis Scientiarum* begins by "dividing" and "deriving" "human learning" "from the three faculties of the rational soul, which is the seat of learning. History has reference to the Memory, poesy to the Imagination, and Philosophy to the Reason," *The Works of Francis Bacon,* ed. James Spedding, Robert Ellis, Vol. 4 (London: Longman's and Co., 1875), 292. Bacon's anatomy here is traditional, but it suggests why invocations of, or appeals to, what is called "History," regularly presuppose, whether this is recognized or not, a particular faculty psychology that predetermines the results of what is called historical investigation; we can call this presupposition the subjective "burden of 'History.' " (Note to deconstructionists: Bacon is careful in his next sentence further to subdefine "poesy" as "nothing else than feigned history or fables," but this does not freeze him in his tracks.) It is often said that the historical invention of "History" in fifth-century Athens is one consequence of the arrival of writing: e.g., "History becomes possible only when the Word turns into words. Only verbatim traditions enable the historian to reconstruct the past. Only where words that were lost can be found again does the historiographer replace the storyteller. The historian's home is on the island of writing. He furnishes its inhabitants with subject matter about the past. The past that can be seized is related to writing." Ivan Illich and Barry Sanders, *The Alphabetization of the Popular Mind* (San Francisco: North Point Press, 1988), ix. It is surely the case that the invention of writing is an instrumental or material cause of the invention of "History," but this is why it is all the more plausible, as I say below, to recognize in the Renaissance, which is when the invention of the typographic printing-press makes its mark, a decisive reinflection of historiographic textuality.

30.   On Renaissance antiquarian historicism, see D.R. Woolf, "Erudition and the Idea of History in Renaissance England," *RQ*, 60, No. 1 (Spring, 1987), 11–48. We should also note that it is in the Renaissance that Thucydides returns to the history of historiography; thus, as M. I. Finley notes, Lorenzo Valla produces the first Latin translation in 1450–52, the first vernacular translation (in French, from Valla's Latin) appears in 1527, and the first English translation appears in 1550 (also, Hobbes's first publication is his translation of Thucydides, 1628); see M. I. Finley's introduction to *Thucydides: The Peloponnesian War* (New York: Penguin Books, 1972), 31. There are other indications of a Thucydidean revival, e.g., Boccaccio's paraphrase in the *Decameron* of Thucydides on the plague, the many references to Thucydidean events in various historiographic projects (e.g., by Raleigh and Bacon). In general, there is a movement or development in Renaissance Humanist historiography away from a markedly rhetorical historicist tradition (Isocrates, Livy, Plutarch) to what would be conceived, instead, as a more "scientific," presumptively Thucydidean, historicism, e.g., Machiavelli. It is in this context that Bacon can establish, as an impetus to scientific discovery, "A Catalogue of Particular Histories by Titles," e.g., "History of the Heavenly Bodies; or Astronomical History," "History of Rainbows," "History of Flame and of things ignited," etc., or, under the subcategory of "Histories of Man," such items as "History of Humours in Man; blood, bile, seed, etc.," "History of Excrements," "History of the Generation of Man," "History of Life and Death," or—thinking of Greenblatt's "Fiction and Friction"—"History of Venus, as a species of Touch," "Catalogue of Particular Histories," *Works*, ed. Spedding and Ellis, Vol. 4, 265–270

31.   Jacob Klein, *Greek Mathematical Thought and the Origin of Algebra*, trans. Eva Brann (Cambridge, MA: M.I.T. Press, 1968). (in the same volume, see also Winfree Smith's introduction to this translation of Viete, printed as appendix); also, Jacob Klein, "Phenomenology and the History of Science," in *Philosophical Essays in Memory of Edmund Husserl*, ed. Marvin Farber (New York: Greenwood Press, 1968), 164–186.

32.

> Among Prerogative Instances I will put in the fourteenth place *Instances of the Fingerpost*, borrowing the term from the fingerposts which are set up where two roads part, to indicate the several directions. These I also call *Decisive and Judicial*, and in some cases, *Oracular* and *Commanding Instances*. I explain them thus. When in the investigation of any nature the understanding is so balanced as to be uncertain to which of two or more natures the causes of the nature in question should be assigned on account of the frequent and ordinary concurrence of many natures, instances of the fingerpost show the union of one of the natures with the nature in question to be sure and indissoluble, of the other to be varied and separable; and thus the question is decided, and the former nature is admitted as the cause, white the latter is dismissed and rejected. Such instances afford very great light and are of high authority, the course of interpretation sometimes ending in them and being completed. Sometimes these instances of fingerpost meet us accidentally among those already noticed, but for the most part they are new, and are expressly and designedly sought for and applied, and discovered only by earnest and active diligence.

Francis Bacon, *The New Organon*, ed. F. H. Anderson (New York: The Liberal Arts Press, 1960), Book 2, sec. 36: 191.

Bacon's method, it will be recalled, is to be applied to "everything":

> It may also be asked (in the way of doubt rather than objection) whether I speak of natural philosophy only, or whether I mean that the other sciences, logic, ethics, and politics, should be carried on by this method. Now I certainly mean what I have said to be understood of them all; and as the common logic which governs by the syllogism, extends not only to natural but to all sciences, so does mine also, which proceeds by induction, embrace everything. For I form a history and table of discovery for anger,

fear, shame, and the like; for matters political, and again for the mental operations of memory, composition and division, judgement and the rest; not less than for heat and cold, or light, or vegetation, or the like. But nevertheless, since my method of interpretation, after the history has been prepared and duly arranged, regards not the working and discourse of the mind only (as the common logic does) but the nature of things also, I supply the mind such rules and guidance that it may in every case apply itself aptly to the nature of things. And therefore I deliver many and diverse precepts in the doctrine of interpretation, which in some measure modify the method of invention according to the quality and condition of the subject of the inquiry.
Organon, Book 1, sec. 127; 155–116.

In such quotations we can glimpse the force of the much remarked movement towards scientific method in the Renaissance—Port Royal, the Royal Society—a methodism or "doctrine of interpretation," that not only encompasses "natural philosophy" but also what will eventually come to be called "the sciences of man:" "logic, ethics, politics," and all "the mental operations of memory, composition and division, judgement and the rest; not less than for heat and cold, or light, or vegetation, or the like." Hence, as Husserl noted, the scientism of seventeenth-century psychologism—Locke or Hume, or any purely "natural history of ideas"— a scientism that, according to Husserl, inexorably grows increasingly dissatisfying, to the point at which it potentiates a "crisis." It is in the context of this, for Husserl, historically momentous event that Bacon's identification of "*instantiae crucis*" is important, for it is precisely the idea or idealization of the so-called "crucial experiment" that will subsequently come to pose the greatest problem in the philosophy of science for establishing the scientificity not only of science but, specifically, of the *history* of science.

The classic essay on the matter is Pierre Duhem's essay of 1906, "Physical Theory and Experiment," in which he argues that "A 'crucial experiment' is impossible in physics" because it is never possible to devise an experiment that will unambiguously falsify a theory; trans. P. Weiner, reprinted in *Can Theories Be Refuted? Essays on the Duhem-Quine Thesis,* ed. Sandra G. Harding (Boston: D. Reidel, 1976), 1–40. For this reason, for Duhem, *"In the course of its development,* a physical theory is free to choose any path it pleases provided that it avoids any logical contradiction; in particular, it is free not to take account of experimental facts."(27) For this reason also, the history of science becomes a matter of ethical rather than experimental judgement, as Duhem says in conclusion: "The sound experimental criticism of a hypothesis is subordinated to certain moral conditions; in order to estimate correctly the agreement of a physical theory with the facts, it is not enough to be a good mathematician and skillful experimenter; one must also be an impartial and faithful judge.(39)

Subsequent to Duhem, and often discussed in relation to the famous Michelson-Morley experiments regarding the properties of light, the very idea of a crucial experiment has grown increasingly problematic. Despite a variety of attempts to support the idea of experimental falsification (e.g., Karl Popper, Adolf Grünbaum), philosophers of science for the most part strive, though in very different ways—e.g., the "(w)holism" of W.V.O. Quine and Carl Hempel, the "research programs" of Imre Lakatos, the "paradigm shifts" of Kuhn, the "Dadaism" of Paul Feyerabrand—to draw the moral for science that follows from the fact that there is no such thing as a "crucial experiment," i.e., that it is not possible to devise an experiment capable of deciding between competing theories (because the interpretations of the results of any such experiment are themselves "theory-laden," and because there is no unambiguous way to resolve the differences between "incommensurable theories"). In general, therefore, philosophy of science translates the logical or epistemological problems associated with the crucial experiment into a discussion of the sociology or the psychology or the politics of knowledge, and it is by no means clear such problems are altogether resolved by thus changing the merely thematic register of the discussion. What *is* clear, however, is that the aporias embedded in the idea of the crucial experiment—which I take to unpack the aporetic, chiastic structure of the anecdote, as I discuss it above—have obliged science to replace the idea of an inexorable *démarche* of scientific history with, instead, an ethics of the real. This was clearly not the case for Bacon, whose simple faith in inductive reasoning led him to see in the crossroads of the crucial experiment a way of establishing the inevitable narration of scientific history. For Bacon, scientific "history" functions as a version of "Sacred History; like divine prophecy, the predictions of the scientist, as "history," report a "memory" of the future: "Prophecy, it is but a kind of history: for divine history has this prerogative over human, that the narration may be before the event, as well as after," *De Augmentis Scientarum,* 426. Contemporary philosophy of science, which possesses the courage of the convictions that give it its intellectual coherence, no longer believes in such "memory of the future"—it certainly distinguishes between prediction and prophecy—and this is a loss of faith that properly responds to the paradoxes embedded in the idea of the crucial experiment. It remains for historicism, which still for the most part believes in the crux of the crucial experiment, to do the same with its equally pious fidelity to the memory of the past.

33.   As I have argued elsewhere, the "second burthen of a former child," defines the "re-" of the late Renaissance as a baby born *as* abortion, i.e., as the issue of the "invention" *of* secondariness, *Shakespeare's Perjured Eye: the Invention of Poetic Subjectivity in the Sonnets* (Berkeley: University of California Press, 1986), 48, 145–146.

34.   Gesturing towards the paper to which the above stands as introduction, I would like here briefly to remark both what I disagree with and what I admire in Stephen Greenblatt's essay, "Fiction and Friction." First, however, it is necessary to rehearse the argumentative movement of Greenblatt's essay, which begins by recounting a striking story—indeed, an anecdote—about a certain Marie le Marcis, a household servant in Rouen, who, in 1601, surprises a fellow woman servant, a woman named Jeane le Febvre, with the revelation that she, Marie, is not the woman she appears to be but, in fact, a man. Following out the story, as its outlines emerge from surviving documentary evidence, Greenblatt goes on to narrate how, subsequent to Marie's revelation, the two servants, Marie and Jeane, engage in sexual relations, including penetrative copulation, fall in love, and propose publicly to marry, an announcement that not only scandalizes the local community but also provokes from the relevant ecclesiastical and juridical authorities an inquisitorial investigation designed to identify the gender of Marie. For all concerned, the consequential question at issue is at once medical and juridical: either Marie is a woman who with her prodigiously enlarged clitoris has committed what would have been understood as sodomy, a serious crime punishable by death, or, instead, Marie is a man, although a peculiar one, and, as such, his proposed marriage to Jeane is neither unnatural nor illegitimate. To resolve the question, one way or the other, a number of doctors are called in, among them Jacques Duvall, a doctor with a special interest in hermaphroditism, who, more conscientiously and carefully than the other doctors, examines Marie's sexual organs—though Marie now calls herself by a man's name, Marin—and is able thereby successfully to establish that he/she is indeed a man, for, as Greenblatt puts it, "the friction of the doctor's touch caused Marin to ejaculate" (p. 32). At least for Duvall, this medically manipulated outcome amounts to a piece of decisive evidence, one that settles the gender question once and for all.

More narrative attaches to the incident but what primarily interests Greenblatt in the story is the way, as he understands it, the example of Marie/Marin serves to illustrate a system of paradoxes and tensions informing what, Greenblatt claims, is a perennial biological or medical imagination of how the two sexes, despite the differences between them, stand to each other, at least with regard to the anatomy of the sexual apparatus, in a relation of introverted homology. Greenblatt cites Galen on the matter—"Turn outward the woman's, turn inward, so to speak, and fold double the man's, and you will find them the same in both in every respect' " (p. 39)—and he also cites some contemporary Renaissance gynecological commentary—e.g., Ambrose Parey (who is translated into English in 1634)—that discusses and conceives the issue in similar terms. What specifically interests Greenblatt in this model of the introverted collation of the anatomical sexuality of the two sexes is the way the model's topographic homology, its depiction of an essential anatomical similarity obtaining between the two sexes, calls forth a developmental principle or dynamic through which to explain the differences—not just the anatomical differences but so too the different social and cultural valuations—also understood to obtain between the sexuality of the two sexes. Hence the "friction" in the title of Greenblatt's essay, for it is the presence of greater or lesser amounts of heat—of specifically bodily heat, as the formation and operation of such heat is imagined by gynecological orthodoxy—that accounts not only for the translation, as the foetus develops, of the inferior sex into the superior (a movement from female to male) but also for the experienced phenomenality, by both men and women, of erotic affect and effect.

In persuasive and suggestive ways, Greenblatt then teases out a series of typological gender consequences packed into this caloric model of anatomic sexual destiny and psycho-physiologized desire, all the outcome as Greenblatt puts it, of the way "the topographical account imagines gender as the result of the selective forcing out by heat of an originally internal organ—like reversing a rubber glove—so that where there was once only one sex, there are now two" (p. 41). And this is of critical interest to Greenblatt not simply for what it suggests about a purely medical imagination but also because, for Greenblatt, the same model of transformative, effective heat also informs Shakespeare's "representation of the emergence of identity in the experience of erotic heat" (p. 48). Accordingly, towards the end of his essay, Greenblatt turns briefly to *Twelfth Night* in order to advance and to argue for the thesis that the gynecologist's heat or erotic "friction" is "figuratively represented" (p. 49) by Shakespeare, "fictionalized" (p. 49), in the "chaffing," "sparring" (49) language through which Shakespeare's lovers both express and come to experience their erotic life. As exemplary evidence, Greenblatt quotes the playful, punning, bickering dialogue that takes place between Viola and the Clown in the third act of *Twelfth Night*, where we find the same metaphor of the inside-outside glove ("chev'ril" now, not "rubber") as was already deployed by Greenblatt in his explication of the gynecological tradition:

> *Clown*, You have said, sir. To see this age! A sentence is but a chev'ril glove to a good wit. How quickly the wrong side may be turn'd outward!
> *Viola*, Nay, that's certain. They that dally nicely with words may quickly make them wanton.
> *Clown*, I would therefore my sister had had no name, sir.
> *Viola*, Why, man?
> *Clown*, Why, sir, her name's a word, and to dally with that word might make my sister wanton. (*TN*. 3.11–20)

Greenblatt's argument here is straightforwardly New Historicist literary criticism in so far as it is concerned to establish a specific relation between a field of medical discourse, on the one hand, and Shakespeare's literary representations of human relations, on the other. Greenblatt is careful to avoid simplistic, naturalizing reductions and associated New Historicist clichés about the so-called social-cultural construction of the body; instead, he wants to identify how a particular medical discourse—a "discursive field," to use Foucault's somewhat incoherent and reifying concept—influences Shakespeare's literary imagination of the erotic, as this appears in characteristically Shakespearean literary language. The influence Greenblatt describes is fluid but pointed. Greenblatt does not say the biological discourse decisively determines Shakespeare's literary or linguistic imagination; neither does he say a traditionary conceptualization of biological erotic friction is responsible for the erotic "friction," to use Greenblatt's metaphor, of Shakespeare's language; nor does he attempt to establish an opposition between two "discursive fields"—the biological and the Shakespearean—by reference to which either can be seen as either cause or consequence of the other. Rather, Greenblatt is concerned to identify what he will later, in his book, call a "negotiation" between the two, a set of reciprocities and exchanges, one set among many others, through which we can understood how it happens each discourse achieves some of its independent force and charge. Thus, Greenblatt says, "at moments the plays seem to imply that erotic friction originates in the wantonness of language, and thus that the body itself is a tissue of metaphors or, conversely, that language is perfectly embodied" (p. 49). This reciprocal negotiation—Greenblatt's "conversely"—is not, on Greenblatt's part, a way of absolutizing or compromising the difference between two altogether comprehensive or preclusive alternatives; rather, the emergence, in this particular case, of this particular reciprocal negotiation amounts to the substance, modestly restricted, of Greenblatt's "New Historicist" claim.

I stress this point because it is with the substance of this claim—Greenblatt's "conversely"—that I disagree, and on historical grounds, for, as I have argued elsewhere (in connection, precisely, with this "love-glove" in *Twelfth Night),* it is Shakespeare's historical achievement, in literature, to have derived desire from the "wantonness" of words, and to have done so in a way that precludes the possibility of putting things the other way around, i.e., as though the erotic charge of language might be derived from the experience of desire (see, *Shakespeare's Perjured Eye*; also my "Shakespeare's *Will:* The Temporality of Rape," *Representations,* 20 [Fall, 1987], 25–76). For Shakespeare, I have argued, language, either as a theme or as a performed practice, does not figure or "embody," to use Greenblatt's metaphor, some biologized erotic impulse (however it happens such impulsion is thematically conceived); rather, for Shakespeare, desire is the very literal consequence of the figurality of language—a figurality or "wantonness" that Shakespeare characteristically imagines in terms of the "duplicity" of language, where "duplicity" not only carries with it the erotic metaphorics of the anatomic double "fold" but is at the same time the motivating mechanism of erotic intentionality. Greenblatt says this too, and says it explicitly, when he relates the Marie/Marin anecdote to the quoted passage from *Twelfth Night:* "It is as if the cause of Marin le Marcis's sexual arousal and transformation were now attributed to the ease—the simple change of one letter—that turns Marie into Marin: Her name's a word, and to dally with that word might make my sister wanton" (p. 49). But Greenblatt also says "conversely," i.e., he says that the gynecologists' erotic heat is figuratively represented by Shakespeare's language, and in doing so Greenblatt loses, as I understand it, the historical particularity of the fact that, and also the novelty of the particular way that, Shakespeare introduces personhood or subjectivity into literature by registering desire as the particular and specifiable effect of the duplicity of speech. My objection to Greenblatt's claim, therefore, is that I want to say only half of the two things Greenblatt says, but I want to say that half univocally rather than to put the two halves together, as does Greenblatt, for the sake of an equivocal "negotiation."

This is not the place to argue in extended detail the point about the relation of desire to language in Shakespeare; nor is it the place to attempt historically to situate this post-idealist, Renaissance recharacterization of the language of desire—though one gets some sense of the historical novelty attaching to the insight in the lines that continue what Greenblatt quotes from *Twelfth Night:*

> *Clown,* Why, sir, her name's a word, and to dally with that word might make my sister wanton. But indeed, words are very rascals since bonds disgrac'd them.
> *Viola,* Thy reason, man?
> *Clown,* Troth, sir, I can yield you none without words, and words are grown so false, I am loath to prove reason with them. *(TN.* 3.1.19–25)

It is important, however, in the context of what I have argued above about the New Historicisms's subjective relation to the anecdotal real to note that Greenblatt's essay gains its own powerful authorial voice from a mechanism very similar to the one through which, as I see it, Shakepeare's literary subjects come to be the desiring agents of their speaking voice. I have already noted that when Greenblatt explicates the gynecological commentaries on the anatomy of the sexual apparatus he introduces, on the basis of what seems to be his own volition, the metaphor of the inside-outside rubber glove, a metaphor that then subsequently appears to be historically significant when it reappears in the quotation from *Twelfth Night*. (We can find the same glove, by the way, folded inside out, in Auguste Dupin's description of the disguised purloined letter: " 'In scrutinizing the edges of the paper, I observed them to be more *chafed* than seemed necesary. They presented the *broken* appearance which is manifested when a stiff paper, having been once folded and pressed with a folder, is refolded in a reversed direction, in the same creases or edges which had formed the original fold. The discovery was sufficient. It was clear to me that the letter had been turned, as a glove, inside out, re-directed and re-sealed' "; italics in the original, "The Purloined Letter," *The Complete Tales and Poems of Edgar Allan Poe* (New York: Vintage Books, 1975), 221. But because the metaphor comes to Greenblatt from Shakespeare, and not from the gynecologists—leaving aside the not insignificant difference between leather and rubber—it seems very clear that it is Shakespeare's literary text that controls Greenblatt's reading of the history of medicine, and that, correlatively, it is not the case that the history of medicine opens up, on this reading, a novel way to read Shakespeare. Hence the subtitle of my paper, "Fiction and Fiction," a way of noting that the medical texts Greenblatt discusses, and so too their "friction," are as "fictive" as is *Twelfth Night*, which is just another way of saying that the medical texts are, for Greenblatt, nothing but Shakespearean. Quite apart from the question of Shakespeare, however, it is important to notice this because, if this is the case, then we can conclude that the literary exigencies that determine the ways in which Shakespeare writes his literary subjects not only write the medical texts that are supposed to have influenced Shakespeare but, in addition, so too, the "Stephen Greenblatt" who in his turn will come to write about those medical texts. (It should also be noted that, given the predeterminative force of these literary exigences—i.e., that they precede Shakespeare, the gynecologists, and Stephen Greenblatt—objections to Greenblatt's essay such as E.A.J. Honigmann's "The New Shakespeare?" in *The New York Review of Books*, Vol. 35, No. 5(March 31, 1988), 32-35, which complain that the gynecological texts Greenblatt cites are posterior to the Shakespeare texts they are supposed to influence, rather completely miss the point).

"A signifier," says Lacan, in his famous definition, "is what represents the subject for another signifier," "The Subversion of the Subject," *Ecrits*, p. 316. For Lacan, this accounts not only for the intrinsic figurality of language (i.e., that language begins with the primal metaphoricity that substitutes, from the beginning, the signifier of one signified for another signifier) but also for the constitution of the subject as a desiring subject in relation to the signifying motion of these fungibly sliding signifiers. Lacan also speaks of this subjectivizing process in terms of the capture of the imaginary by the Symbolic, in the course of which capture, as both condition and consequence, something slips out; that something which is elided by the achievement of representation is what Lacan calls the "real," a "real" that, because left out, can be neither imaginatively specularized nor symbolically represented. For Lacan, this real, neither here nor there but always elsewhere, accounts for the fact that "there is no sexual relation," which in turn accounts both for the arrival and for the endurance of desire. See *Television*, 12. Hence the relevance of the passage from Lacan's *Television* that I take as my first epigraph, for it seems clear that the Marie/Marin anecdote Greenblatt relates—"the simple change of one letter"—is for Greenblatt an instance or insistence of the way a signifier represents the subject— in this case, "Greenblatt"—for another signifier, a substitution that leaves over as remainder only the mark of the real, *"Marin le Marcis"* (49), to which Greenblatt's essay wants to give a meaning. Accordingly, we can conclude, in accord with the Lacanian formula I take as epigraph, that Greenblatt's essay amounts to one of those "fictions"—in this case, the empiricized "friction"—exuded by the sexual impasse in an attempt to rationalize the impossible "real" from which it orginates. On the one hand, the persistent insistence of this "real" accounts for what calls forth the authorial voice of Greenblatt's essay, just as it accounts for the way the essay stands as ongoing invitation to the real that underwrites both it and what, by convention, we can call its author. By the same token, however, but on the other hand, this accounts for what is comic about the "empiricutic" in the lines from Shakespeare's *Coriolanus* that I take as complementary epigraph; this is something Menenius says early in the play, when he looks forward to the return of the conquering Coriolanus, and when he can still eagerly anticipate, because he does not know what is going to happen, the triumphant display of the hero's "wounds."

5

English Romanticism and Cultural Production

Jon Klancher

Renaissance new historicists have been "dancing an attitude," in Kenneth Burke's phrase, as they probe the delicate semiosis of history, culture, and power. The attitude appears in their most influential gestures, like Stephen Greenblatt's echo of Kafka—"There is subversion, no end of subversion, only not for us"—which aligns a Renaissance culture saturated with power with a postmodern culture powerless to resist.[1] This peculiar identification of a Renaissance moment, when politics and literature were still undifferentiated realms, with postmodern culture, when power is felt to saturate discourse of every kind, helps make the Renaissance the paradigmatic field in current English studies. But the allegory of past and present also makes a number of new historical critics uneasy. When the new historicism "discloses power" and the postmodern age "displays and worships power," Don Wayne observes, "we run the risk of seeing the opposition between these two kinds of unmasking collapse into what will be merely two aspects of a fascination with the same imposing spectacle."[2] The risk lies in making historical criticism a transhistorical echo of the politics of the present.

So firm a bond between past and present ideologies is what an emerging historical critique of English Romanticism is attempting to break. Only a few years ago, the rhetorics of English Romantic literature sponsored a criticism that prized imagination, sublimity, and the "politics of vision"— not because Romantic literature and English politics were felt to be identical, but because they seemed to be so separate. The new work in Romantic studies refuses the distancing of culture from politics that Romantic writers often brilliantly proposed. It sets out, as one practitioner puts it, "to oppose our ideological structure to that of the Romantic period" rather than reproduce it.[3] What now makes English Romanticism so complex to read historically is that we can assume neither a new historicist's identification of power and culture, nor their Romantic opposition. This is why, as I'll argue here, the questions posed in English Romantic studies increasingly need to engage issues raised by "cultural materialism." As developed in England, cultural materialism ranges between social history and semiotic or deconstructive reading strategies to ask how literature is produced, read, and reproduced among institutions, cultural formations, and social structures. To some degree, cultural materialism shares these interests with the new historical enterprise in Renaissance and American Renaissance studies. But the cultural materialist strategies inquire into relations of cultural practice and politics that cannot be posed as alternative between "subversion" and "containment." That postmodern version of the older conflict of "self" and "society" is just what the institutional and political history of English Romanticism puts into doubt.

I.

New historical and political critiques of Romantic culture have only recently emerged in an array of "historicist," "deconstructive-materialist," Marxist, social-semiotic, Foucauldian, and feminist critiques in the work of Marilyn Butler, James Chandler, Kurt Heinzelmann, Theresa Kelly, Marjorie Levinson, Alan Liu, Jerome McGann, David Simpson, Clifford Siskin, Gayatri Chakravorty Spivak, and others. Unifying these diverse projects is the shared claim—forcefully projected in Jerome McGann's critique of "the Romantic ideology"—that the Romantic influence on critical thinking has reached its end. McGann's polemic aims against the critical discipline's transhistorical faiths: its "uncritical absorption in romanticism's own self-representations."[4] Such absorption was the hallmark of the Romantic studies revival led by Northrop Frye and Meyer Abrams in the 1950s and 1960s. Their new Romanticism had emerged, with the splintering of New Criticism, in a rather complex way. In Renaissance and American studies, the large historical frameworks permitting formalist idealisms were contructed in the 1940s—in E.M.W. Tillyard's *The Elizabethan World Picture* (1943), F.O. Matthiessen's *American Renaissance* (1941), and Robert Spiller's *A Literary History of the United States* (1948). An "English" Romantic studies, however, had just then begun to be disentangled from a wider European Romanticism whose meanings had been, since 1919, deeply ensnared in the politics of a revolution and two world wars. Hence Walter Jackson Bate's *From Classic to Romantic* (1946) and M.H. Abram's *The Mirror and the Lamp* (1953) began a long, slow process of institutional recuperation fully consolidated only in the early 1960s. It was then that Romantic studies established its period journal, launched definitive editions of major writers, and—at the 1962 English Institute session "Romanticism Reconsidered"—officially signaled the recovery of Romantic discourse from a long night of critical and ideological marginality. By this time Frye had used Blake to rewrite T.S. Eliot into the spiritual democracy of *The Anatomy of Criticism*, while powerful new readings of Wordsworth's *Prelude* were being prepared to focus critics on the modernity of Romantic consciousness.[5] But it may have been M.H. Abrams's English Institute paper "English Romanticism: The Spirit of the Age" that most firmly grounded English Romanticism as an historical moment capable of becoming paradigmatic for a new generation of readers. In one grand historical scheme, Abrams portrayed the Romantic writers as triumphantly internalizing their traumatic encounter with history and politics—the French Revolution—into a greater Romantic imagination and sublimity that was shortly to become the new orthodoxy of English studies.

Here Abrams carefully teased out the meaning of "spirit" from Hazlitt's "spirit of the age" as a means to argue that the English Romantics retextualized their encounter with the French Revolution in a complex, threefold way. They absorbed it historically by rewriting Revolution as a moment in an essentially English Protestant and providential history (the poets' Christianizing sequence of "hope, despair and redemption"). They translated it socially by sublimating demands for political and economic equality into the leveling of styles and genres (Wordsworth's "democratic" esthetic). And thus they also projected a new sense of politics over the ashes of the old: a Blakean, imaginative "politics of vision." Subtle and even inspiring, Abrams's historicizing both surprised his 1962 audience—no one had spoken of the English Romantics as "political and social poets" since the beginning of World War II—and convinced them that Romantic imaginations grasped the power of surpassing all political and social moments in a transhistorical act of imaginative will.[6]

Despite its sense of authority, the Abrams "world picture" was politically and theoretically contested in the decade after it was produced. E.P. Thompson's New Left history of "the making of the English working class" taught a generation of younger students to start reading cultural history "from below," building implicitly on a still compelling account of the French Revolution by the French Marxist historians (Albert Mathiez, Georges Lefebvre, Albert Soboul). Meanwhile, the Abrams account, as fleshed out in *Natural Supernaturalism* (1971), met a more internally devastating challenge in the deconstructive critique made by Jacques Derrida and inflected into Romantic studies by Paul de Man. De Man demonstrated the way literary texts rigorously resist being recuperated by historicism and other institutionalizing stratagems. The result was not simply, as Frank Lentricchia charges, to glimpse the apolitical void. In a fundamental sense, de Man's work both enabled and complicated the effort to forge more materialist and worldly reading strategies insofar as such strategies now tried to locate the uses of texts for culturally hegemonic or resistant ends.[7]

Without a credible secular theology to make the transition from political/historical realms to imaginative or ideal ones, Abrams's mode of historicism collapsed. But those critics who now pick up both ends of the critique also have to engage a methodological and theoretical dialogue between poststructural and materialist stances. So, for example, Gayatri Chakravorty Spivak deploys Derrida and Marx to read "sex and history" in the 1805

Prelude; McGann forms a complex dialogue among Frankfurt School ideology-critique, philology, and the work of de Man; Marjorie Levinson proposes a "deconstructive materialist" reading of Wordsworth's idealizing sublime.

The diversity of method and strategy in the new work suggests that—contrary to the assumption of an absolutist state in Renaissance new historicism—there is no single material or political framework against which to read Romantic texts. English Romantic writings were staged within an unstable ensemble of older institutions in crisis (state and church) and emerging institutional events which pressured any act of cultural production—the marketplace and its industrializing, the new media and their reading audiences, the alternative institutions of radical dissent, shifting modes of social hierarchy. Reading Romantic texts historically will therefore often mean trying to position those texts among institutional pressures and possibilities.

The complexities appear in a strong version of the recent historical critiques. Marjorie Levinson's controversial and vigorously polemical *Wordsworth's Great Period Poems* subjects the short masterpieces of Wordsworth's "great decade"— "Tintern Abbey," "Intimations Ode," "Michael," and "Peele Castle"—to a reading-against-the-grain that means to recover a repressed social and political history obscured in Wordsworth's "sense sublime." Levinson opens the rhetorical enclosure of "Tintern Abbey" to the history of the Dissolution of monasteries by the Protestant reformation. The abbey Wordsworth saw in the Wye valley was not only an emotionally resonant ruin, however, but also something of an industrial wreck. From this palpable evidence of painful historical change, Wordworth's poem turned resolutely and lyrically away. This analysis combines a politics of space— the historicity of local places rent by political and industrial change—with a study of the way Wordsworth's poem both claims and denies its historical contacts. Most odd is the poem's advertising and then masking of its relation to the French Revolution. Wordsworth's "five years" of personal anguish ties Bastille-Day Eve of Year I of the Revolutionary Calendar to the poem's date of composition, July 13, 1798. It is both this political occasion and its personal consequence for a troubled English liberal that the poem then buries in its extravagant lyricizing of the recovered self. Levinson pursues these contradictions in a furious reading that, unlike the dance-style of most Renaissance new historical essays, performs a kind of jujitsu upon the idealisms of Wordsworth scholarship.[8]

Polemically and theoretically, Levinson's reading of Wordsworth leans closer to the strategies of English cultural materialism than do any of the comparable new historical Romantic critiques. Her program of a "deconstructive materialism" forges the combination of poststructural reading methods with reconstructive social history that has also been invoked by Alan Sinfield, Jonathan Dollimore, or Malcolm Evans in British Renaissance studies but has had little impact on American new historicism. Characteristically, the cultural materialist stance produces less a book to watch, like a new historicist performance, than a book to argue with. Readers of Levinson's work may want to argue about how the skeptical reading of Romantic poetic idealism should be reconciled with the dynamic social history she reconstructs. Her method of "deconstrutive materialism" more often uses symptomatic Machereyan strategies, to show where the text represses its historicity, than a deconstructive destabilizing of the poem into textual and historical move and countermove. Thus Levinson restores social history as a wilfully repressed content—what the poem should have shown—rather than using it to situate the text in a field of complex strategies of cultural production. The effort to join a "de-" and "re-construction" of text and social history faces the question of grounding that all versions of ideology-critique must grapple with. Levinson's often brilliant readings do not settle that question so much as raise it forcefully and unavoidably for both historical and textualist modes of criticism alike.

The tensions that Levinson's work reflects—between poststructural and ideological reading, difference and dialectic, textuality and history—have not been resolved either by resorting to an alternative model that conflates language with power, discourse with discipline. In *The Historicity of Romantic Discourse,* Clifford Siskin attempts a critique of Romanticism that equates its cultural production with all its subsequent uses, quarrels, institutionalizations, and critiques. Siskins' "Romantic discourse" is a monumental affair that entails "disciplinary boundaries (literary vs. nonliterary), hierarchical differences (creative vs. critical), aesthetic values (spontaneity and intensity) and natural truths (development and the unconscious)" as well as "the distinction between organic and the ironic/deconstructive that informs contemporary critical debate."[9] In a remarkably undefended way, Siskin mingles categories from the earlier and later works of Michel Foucault to present a kind of epistemic Romanticism that tends to swallow nearly everything in its path, from Romantic poetry to Austen's fiction, Marx's class analysis, Malthusian population theory, ideological criticism, and deconstructive critique. What results is an "historicized" romanticism so all-embracing as to be indistinguishable from the generic understanding of "romantic" as a floating cultural category. By identifying such a Romantic discourse too simply with literary criticism as an institutional discipline, Siskin merges the notions of "institution" and "discourse" as a monolithic mode of "discipline" centered in the "Romantic" idea of "self-development." The postmodern critic can then rather easily solve the problem of his particular relation to the cultural past. The mirror opposite of the Renaissance new historical self whose subversion is always contained, Siskin's postmodern critic transcends an unhappy Romantic self-disciplining regime to become that strangest of phoenixes, the happy consciousness. This is a new, culturalist version of the traditional and still unworkable liberal problematic of "self" against "society." But the most difficult questions of our critical relation to the culture and power of the past remain unresolved.

What the best work in cultural materialism has been able to show—and here the work of Raymond Williams becomes exemplary—is that such historical, theoretical, and political questions call for a more complex mapping of the cultural field than literary study has allowed. Williams pointed to the uneven and contested relationships of "cultural formations," "emergent, dominant, and alternative" tendencies, and particularly the heterogenous institutions within which texts are produced and read.[10] In his later career, Williams skeptically negotiated the claims of both Marxist ideology-critiques and semiotic language-critiques in works from *Keywords* and *Marxism and Literature* to late essays like "The Uses of Cultural Theory."[11] But William's principal and most suggestive strategy was to rearrange the contours of cultural study within which questions of ideology, culture, and history would be pursued.

For English Romanticism that kind of map has special importance because of the intensive cultural and ideological *organizing* to which Romantic texts and English literary studies of the Romantic era have equally been subject. Romantic writers and their interlocutors profoundly reorganized British cultural production and reception—and its textual relation to history and power—in what I have argued elsewhere was a culture-wide struggle over the control of signs and meanings.[12] Seen from the wider view of a "cultural studies," English Romanticism appears as a complex negotiation between that struggle of the years 1790 to 1830 and the institutional and political history of its outcome, English Romantic literature. The cultural production of English Romanticism embraces both its origins and the reproductive energies that have kept Romanticism variously and tendentiously current. In the following notes toward a larger study, I want to suggest what such a view of producing Romanticism may entail.

II

English Romantic studies has always had a double rather than singular focus, no matter how univocal its particular way of defining "Romanticism" might be. The main focus has been the literature and theory produced out of late-eighteenth- and early-nineteenth-century cultural strategy and conflict. But this focus has been doubled and blurred by the category of "English Romanticism" imposed after the fact, mediated through European notions of the "Romantic," and always aligned with one or another institutional mode of cultural appropriation. In the pivotal term "Romanticism," two distinct realms of text-making and reading make contact. One can be situated between 1790 and 1830; and as Marilyn Butler's work shows, much of it was not in our sense Romantic.[13] But the other realm, familiar now as English Romantic literature, was then reconstructed as a way for later nineteenth- and twentieth-century cultures to read, institutionalize, and "use" an earlier one they regarded, in either deeply troubled or in exhilarated ways, as their own modern origins. This is why the heatedly disputed meaning of what constitutes "Romanticism" is inseparable from its institutional history and thus its cultural emplotments.

The cultural stories told about English Romanticism have been constructed among diverse institutional crises and consolidations. But they have also been controversially political stories, since they engage Romanticism in a general rereading of the history of politics and power.

The great reactionary critiques of Romanticism, for instance, viewed it as a fundamentally though perversely political stance. With a startling polemical violence, Irving Babbitt's *Rousseau and Romanticism* (1919) repudiated Matthew Arnold's thesis of great divide between Romantic culture and Enlightenment political ideology. Babbitt's cultural history read all Romantic departures from politics—including the "imagination," "aesthetics," Romantic irony, and the egoist self—as proof of their saturation in power by filtering the culture of 1789 through the German imperialism and Russian revolution of 1917. It was not only Rousseau's will to power that explained modern political catastrophe, but the self-condemning effort of the Romantic subject to mold the world into the shape of his desire. The more that subject struggled to project his desire into history, the more fiercely did his desire double back onto him as the collective violence of politics and power. Babbitt mobilized this radically anti-historicist critique against the nineteenth-century human sciences—including psychology, historicism, and philosophic positivism and pragmatism—to show what he considered the fatal collusion of Romantic culture with post-1789 European political power. All this was complexly laced with Babbitt's local struggle against two contemporary institutional antagonists, the Germanic scholarship of Harvard philology and the progressive pedagogy of Chicago pragmatism, which themselves have ironically become ancestral to the politics and methods of the current new historicist criticism.

At about the same time, the German political theorist Carl Schmitt was implicating Romanticism in a more intricate relation to politics in *Politische Romantik* (1924). The contradictory Romantic allegiances to right-wing authoritarianism or left-wing revolutionism suggested to Schmitt that "Romanticism" cannot be said to have any fixed political tendency, but rather becomes a modern, secularized version of theological "occasionalism." Romantic thinking transforms the idea that God uses the world as the occasion for His omnipotent creativity into the position that the bourgeois subject can use the world "occasionally" as a creative plaything, or fiction, that in turn guarantees the subject's own freedom. Hence "Romantic irony" adopts an "indecisive" stance toward any and all political positions, particularly authoritarian and democratic ones, by entertaining them as aesthetic fictions. Yet it is just this "indecisive" aesthetic fictionalism that makes Romanticism infinitely absorbable by a classical liberal state. "Everything that is romantic is at the disposal of other energies that are unromantic, and the sublime elevation above definition and decision is transformed into a subservient attendance upon alien power and alien decision."[14] Hence the two sides of Romantic power relations—either political commitment to Left or Right, or aesthetic detachment—come full circle in a historically elastic but self-preserving accommodation to all existing forms of power itself.

The full emergence of an "English Romantic" studies after World War II depended partly, it seems, on putting an end to such political questions. Both might well be credited to Jacques Barzun, whose *Romanticism and the Modern Ego* (1943) retained Babbitt's comparatist perspective but now tried to assimilate European Romanticism into the American pragmatist idioms of John Dewey and William James. Barzun's detoxified Romanticism eased the terrors of Rousseauism, Russian collectivism, and Fascism by gently disengaging Romantic writers from the politics of Modernism and the brutalites of modernization. Such a move meant historicizing Romanticism as a pragmatist commitment to individual responsibility, so that the political theory of Rousseau or Hegel could now appear as more benignly liberal theses in which the subject would give up a measure of freedom to accept a measure of coercion. With such readings, Barzun helped weld Romantic culture to Columbia University's humanities program and the "colloquium on certain great books from Bacon to William James" he conducted with his colleague and collaborator, Lionel Trilling.[15] The Trilling connection helps explain the strategic importance of Barzun's work—to find American social virtue embedded in Romantic and particularly English Romantic culture. As Don Wayne argues in an inportant essay on postwar American criticism, Trilling made Arnold's humanism a "means of social and political emancipation" by reducing "cultural diversity to what appeared, from an intellectual standpoint, to be the highest common denominator, the English cultural tradition."[16] Other critics would then rediscover the complexities of a particularly "English" Romanticism and inflect them, by Abrams's moment, as more characteristically American cultural claims. The Arnoldian reading of Romanticism as autonomy from politics would be renewed in the forthcoming work of Richard Fogle, Morse Peckham, Earl Wasserman, Abrams, and others over the next two decades. But this road toward a consensually idealized English Romanticism could only emerge after a long, wayward dialogue with European power and the darker moments of ideological entanglement Americans now needed to forget.

Thus when Abrams reminded his audience of 1962 that English Romantic poets were "social and political" writers, he had a remarkably different historical filter through which to read the politics of Romanticism. Perhaps the most effective of all Abrams's tactics was to mold his propositions in a borrowed poetic language of rising libidinal and spiritual hunger—Blake's "I want! I want!"—that in 1962 happened to echo the discourse of a new American kind of self-representation. As bearers of the "politics of vision," Abrams's English Romantics began to sound ancestral to the great historical moment Arthur Schlesinger, Jr., was proposing for his own generation of American intellectuals:

> One feels that . . . the mood which has dominated the nation for a decade is beginning to seeem thin and irrelevant; that it no longer interprets our desires and needs as a people; that new forces, new energies, new values are straining for expression and for release . . . a widespread yearning for spiritual purpose . . . All this means that our intellectuals are beginning to draw the new portrait of America out of which new political initiatives will in due course come . . . . ("The New Mood in Politics," *Esquire,* January 1960[17])

The Kennedy era could also be visualized—to make the picture somewhat more contradictory—in Robert Frost's extraordinary inauguration poem, as ushering in a new Augustan era of world-historical ambition. The time had come, as Frost exalted the occasion of January 20, 1961, for "A golden age of poety and power / of which this noonday's the beginning hour" ("For John F. Kennedy His Inauguration"). Equally "visionary" was Norman Mailer's countercultural sense of a uniquely American "subterranean river of untapped, ferocious, lonely and romantic desires" bubbling just beneath the surface of a self-repressive middle class. New Hazlitts of various political and philosophic kinds surged forward in these years to bespeak their sense of some emergent and irresistible new "spirit of the age."[18] So it is far from clear whether an early 1960s revival of English Romanticism was, for a generation of intellectuals now emerging from a dark decade of post-political despair, just academic. It seems plausible to think that, at the same time that Abrams's paper brilliantly reconciled French Revolutionary politics with Romantic transcendent imaginations, it also evoked a suggestive bond between liberal intellectual formations of the English 1790s and the American early 1960s. The latter would, however, be slow to comprehend that its own political trauma was not, like Wordsworth's, receding in the mists of re-imagined time, but coming up in Schlesinger's "due course"—even as the policies leading to Southeast Asia were now already underway.

These notes are meant to suggest that the most powerful readings of English Romanticism have entailed complex relations to politics and institutions that belong to the historicizing of Romantic culture. Such a history of institutional readings is not finally separate from the more locally historical British culture that formed after 1789. English Romantic arguments were constructed within a specific field of dispute about reading and institutions, culture and power. That field should be understood as strategically as well as ideologically and culturally productive. Cultural-strategies, often put into play by groups as well as by individuals, are ways that readers and writers make their history, but not always as they please. Historical intentions misfire; the logic of the social and cultural field is often, as Pierre Bourdieu has shown, the logic of "unintended effects." To these effects both the English culture of 1800 and the institutional history of Romanticism have given rich evidence. One unintended effect of Romanticism's modern institutionalizing might thus serve to signal many more.

When the Bollingen Foundation and Princeton University Press announced the vast *Collected Coleridge* edition in 1960, the editors' intent was in large part to memorialize the powerful Romantic theorist whose program for symbolic interpretation and cultural order had underwritten much of the postwar success of a formalist literary study. Yet as those volumes have unfolded since 1969, they have had the unintended effect of exposing the conflicted social and political struggle for meanings and cultural control that Coleridge's massive writings were meant to master. A magisterial product of the modern critical institution, these volumes ironically have helped open up English Romanticism to the historical, political, and epistemological critiques with which Coleridge's cultural authority was supposed to settle accounts. *The Collected Coleridge* displays a decidedly uncollectable Coleridge whose "texts" are enmeshed with those of his radical, mass cultural, middle-class, political, religious, skeptical, and literary interlocutors. As the traces of their languages and cultural strategies contest his, so too does the early-nineteenth-century production of an English Romanticism begin to appear entangled in the questions of power, culture, and institution that will later mark the history of its rereadings. This edition does not memorially enclose a Romantic Coleridge so much as open up the phenomenon of English Romanticism to the strategies of cultural contention that first composed its complex "history."

Notes

1.   Kenneth Burke, *The Philosophy of Literary Form* (New York: Vintage, 1941), 9. I want to thank David Suchoff, Susan Mizruchi, David Wagnenknecht, and Anne Janowitz for their astute critical readings of this essay in manuscript.

2.   Greenblatt's phrase appears in "Invisible Bullets: Renaissance Authority and Its Subversion," in *Political Shakespeare: New Essay in Cultural Materialism,* ed. Jonathan Dollimore and Alan Sinfield (Ithaca: Cornell Univ. Press, 1985), 18–47. See Don Wayne, "Power, Politics, and the Shakespearean Text: Recent Criticism in England and the United States," in *Shakespeare Reproduced,* ed. Jean Howard and Marion O'Connor (London and New York: Methuen, 1987).

3.   Marjorie Levinson, quoted in "Literature's Romantic Era," *Chronicle of Higher Education* (13 April 1988): A7.

4. Jerome McGann, *The Romantic Ideology,* (Chicago: Univ. of Chicago Press, 1983), 1. See also the work of Kurt Heinzelmann, *The Economics of Imagination* (Amherst: Univ. of Massachusetts Press, 1985); Alan Liu, "Wordsworth: The History in 'Imagination,' " *ELH 51* (1984): 505–48; Gayatri Chakravorty Spivak, "Sex and History in *The Prelude* (1805): Books Nine to Thirteen," *Texas Studies in Language and Literature* 23 (1981): 324–60; Marilyn Butler, *Romantics, Rebels and Reactionaries* (New York: Oxford University Press, 1981); Theresa Kelley, "Submitting to Scale: Imperial Images and Romantic Rhetoric," forthcoming; Robert Maniquis, "Lonely Empires: Personal and Public Visions of Thomas de Quincey," in *Literary Monographs 8,* ed. Eric Rothstein (Madison: Univ. of Wisconsin Press, 1976), 47–129.

5. Herbert Lindenberger, *On Wordsworth's Prelude* (Princeton: Princeton Univ. Press, 1963); Geoffrey Hartman, *Wordsworth's Poetry 1787–1807* (New Haven: Yale Univ. Press, 1964).

6. M.H. Abrams, "English Romanticism: The Spirit of the Age" in Northrop Frye, ed., *Romanticism Reconsidered: English Institute Papers,* (New York: Columbia University Press, 1963), together with papers by Frye, Lionel Trilling, and René Wellek. There had been, of course, the rare reminder of politics in such monographs as F.M. Todd, *Politics and the Poet* (London: Methuen, 1957).

7. See in particular "Shelley Disfigured," de Man's most explicit confrontation with historicism, in *Deconstruction and Criticism,* ed. Harold Bloom (New York: Seabury, 1979), 39–70. Lentricchia's critique appears in *After the New Criticism* (Chicago: Univ. Chicago Press, 1980): 282–317; and *Criticism and Social Change* (Chicago: Univ. of Chicago Press. 1983). On the "worldly" turn of deMan's influence, see Barbara Johnson, *A World of Difference* (Baltimore: Johns Hopkins Univ. Press, 1987); and for an important engagement with his assumptions, see Jerome McGann, *Social Values and Poetic Acts,* (Cambridge: Harvard Univ. Press, 1988), "Introduction."

8. See Marjorie Levinson, *Wordsworth's Great Period Poems* (Cambridge: Cambridge Univ. Press, 1986), 14–57.

9. Clifford Siskin, *The Historicity of Romantic Discourse* (New York: Oxford Univ. Press, 1988), 1.

10. His term "cultural materialism" means "a theory of the specificities of material cultural and literary production within historical materialism" —a definition he later made proximate to a deconstructive "radical semiotics." See Raymond Williams, *Marxism and Literature* (New York: Oxford Univ. Press, 1976), 1–7; and "Crisis in English Studies," in *Writing in Society* (London: Verso, 1983), 208–11.

11. In the latter, he embraced the work of V.N. Voloshinov, P.N. Medvedev, and Mikhail Bakhtin as an historical semiotics that advances the materialist study of cultural production. See Raymond Williams, "The Uses of Cultural Theory," *New Left Review* 158 (July/August 1986): 19–31.

12. See my study of *The Making of English Reading Audiences, 1790–1832* (Madison: Univ. of Wisconsin Press, 1987).

13. See Marilyn Butler, *Romantics, Rebels and Reactionaries* (New York: Oxford Univ. Press, 1981)

14. Carl Schmitt, *Political Romanticism,* trans. Guy Oakes (Cambridge: MIT Press, 1986), 162. Schmitt bases this argument on his own commitment to a *Realpolitik* "decisionism" (he notes with satisfaction that Metternich was not a Romantic) with roots in Edmund Burke and Joseph DeMaistre; Schmitt himself was easily adaptable to the needs of the Third Reich. For a troubled debate on the apparent proximity of Schmitt's political and aesthetic analysis to the

work of the Frankfurt School, see contributions by Ellen Kennedy and Martin Jay to the forum in *Telos,* No. 71 (1987): 37–66, 71–80.

15.   The result was a so-called "neo-Romantic school at Columbia." See Jacques Barzun's later account of the cultural and pedagogic context for the 1943 volume, the preface to its second edition: *Classic, Romantic, and Modern* (Chicago: Univ. of Chicago Press, 1961), xii–xiii.

16.   Wayne, "Power, Politics, and the Shakespearean Text," p.54.

17.   Arthur Schlesinger, Jr., "The New Mood in Politics," *Esquire* (January 1960). Reprinted in *The Sixties,* ed. Glenn Howard (New York: Washington Square, 1982), 44–55.

18..   Robert Frost, quoted in Howard, *The Sixties,* p. 28; Mailer, "Superman Comes to the Supermarket" (1960), in Howard, p. 158.

6

The Use and Misuse of Giambattista Vico: Rhetoric, Orality, and Theories of Discourse

John D. Schaeffer

I

The interest literary critics have shown in Giambattista Vico has been limited to his influence on *Finnegans Wake*. During the last decade, however, Vico's thought has been cited by such theoreticians of discourse as Hayden White and Edward Said as containing crucial insights about the dialectic of language and thought.[1] White finds that Vico anticipated the insights of Michel Foucault. In the essay that makes this point, White joined the burgeoning intellectual enterprise of crediting Vico's thought with containing the beginnings of later developments in philosophy.[2] Vico always is presented as the great anticipator, the undisciplined thinker whose insights point to the ideas developed subsequently by more rigorous thinkers. Edward Said has argued that Vico was in fact the beginning of his own study, *Beginnings,* but that the insights of his work had to wait until the present. Even as a beginner Vico was just a beginner.

I hope to show why Vico's thought is critical *to* a theory of discourse and also critical *of* some of the theories which use him. A closer look at Vico's own thought may not only refocus his role in the contemporary discussion, but also revise its agenda.

Vico's importance to any discussion of discourse stems from his being the first to use the nomenclature of the rhetorical tropes of metaphor, metonymy, synecdoche, and irony to describe the interaction of discourse and thought. For Vico each trope represents a specific stage in cultural development and is also the determining characteristic of the discourse at that state. The age of metaphor is the age of the gods; men perceive similarities in a kind of unmediated vision. The age of metonymy is the age of heroes; men perceive difference, especially among themselves, and the social structure becomes feudal, the lords or patricians arrogating to themselves the vision, and control of, the deities. The age of synecdoche is the age of men; men perceive the world in terms of interrelated groups, and social structure achieves the sophistication that comes with conscious interdependency. Finally, irony is the trope of decay; discourse becomes conscious of its powerlessness to reflect accurately the social reality in which it exists and that reality, in turn, is one of greed and strife masked by the discourse of equality and equity. These stages follow each other in dialectical fashion, each succeeding the other as social groups contest the definition and function of social institutions.

This taxonomy of discourse and the ages of civilization is what White claims as Vico's contribution to the current discussion: a dialectical progression which White attributes to Foucault's *The Order of Things*.[3] In making that attribution White claims to have found a way to account for the changes from one discourse, or in Foucault's term, *episteme,* to another. Foucault himself had denied that such an account can exist; he claimed that the various discourses simply emerge out of the silences of the preceding discourse.[4] White criticizes Foucault's position that one discourse is "simply displaced by another one" by finding a Vichian scheme of orderly progression in Foucault's analysis. In so doing White brings Foucault back into historical time, undercutting his claims that an archaeology of knowledge, a study of discursive strategies, gives the lie to history. White, in short, uses Vico to bring Foucault into the camp of the historians of ideas.

Clearly White, as a historian, has a considerable interest in Foucault's challenge to historical methods, but more is going on than a historian defending his discipline. White used Vico previously in analyzing historical writing and has advocated his theory as a way of freeing historiography from the constraints of irony:

> I maintain that the recognition of this ironic perspective provides the grounds for a transcendance of it. . . . Historians and philosophers of history will then be freed to conceptualize history, to perceive its contents, and to construct narrative accounts of its processes in whatever modality of consciousness is most consistent with their own moral and aesthetic aspirations.[5]

The freedom of discursive modes White is calling for would transcend the Vichian account of discourse by creating a fifth period in which all previous modes are possible. While White wishes to transcend periodicity in discourse, Foucault calls for the end of the fiction of discursive continuity behind which the West has hidden its use of power from itself. He calls for the end of historical consciousness itself: "the scattering of the profound stream of time by which he [man] felt himself carried along and whose pressure he suspected in the very being of things."[6] Foucault calls for a return to the Dionysian experience of time, "the explosion of man' s face in laughter, and the return to masks." White describes Foucault's intention as a "will to return to a world which existed before metaphor, before language."[7] Then he adds an interesting comment: "Foucault heralds the rebirth of the gods, when what he means to herald is the rebirth of a pre-religious imagination." This "rebirth of the gods" is what Vico termed the *ricorsi,* but White does not pursue the implications of Vico's religious thought. I would like to do so.

To summarize the terms of the dispute, Foucault sees discourse as discrete, ahistorical strategies of concealment by which the West has hidden its abuse of power from itself. He calls for an end to the fiction of history and a return to a kind of primitive, pre-religious imagination. White maintains that discourse is, in fact, historically conditioned even in Foucault's account of it, and that Vico provides a schema of the historical processes by which discourse and culture interact. Furthermore, though White and Foucault agree that an ironic discourse now holds sway in the human and social sciences, White feels that knowledge of this fact itself allows for the transcendance of the ironic stage to a kind of fifth stage in which all modes can co-exist as writers operate in "whatever modality of consciousness is most consistent with their moral and aesthetic aspirations." In short, White believes that writers can control their discourse and consciously direct its moral implications, while Foucault denies that such transcendance is possible, much less that it would enable the West to take responsibility for power. For White the play can control the power. For Foucault the power controls the play, and the abuse of that power must be abolished by "playing with" the discourse that conceals it, unmasking it and leaving it impotent.

And what of Vico? Has he nothing to add other than to establish the historicity of Foucault's analysis? I believe he offers more. The epistemological ground of Vico's taxonomy transcends the power/play dichotomy with which both Foucault and White are working. That ground antedates the Enlightenment methods which are the subject of both White's and Foucault's attacks and, most important of all, that ground is religious in nature.

This study will fall into three parts: first, a study of the relevant passages of Book II of Vico's *New Science* will allow Vico to speak for himself about the way the tropes relate to language, imagination, and religion; second, an analysis of some of Vico's earlier writings, especially his *De ratione temporis studiorum ratione,* will indicate how Vico's system is controlled by his concept of *sensus communis,* a concept rooted in the oral culture of classical and early humanist rhetoric. Finally, I will indicate the significance of *sensus communis* for the White/Foucault controversy and for the general discussion of theories of discourse.

Vico's discussion of the operation and significance of tropes is not merely abstruse musings, for Vico was not merely a theoretician of rhetoric; he was a teacher of rhetoric and a practicing orator as well. For Vico rhetoric, the art of acquiring eloquence, meant the ability to produce conviction in, or elicit a decision from, an audience by means of an *ex tempore,* or nearly *ex tempore* speech. By rhetoric he meant what George Kennedy has called "primary rhetoric": eloquent performance, as opposed to secondary rhetoric, the packaging of various techniques of eloquence for purposes of teaching.[8] The paradigmatic situation for such eloquence was in the courts of law, and it was for the law that Vico prepared his students at the Universitry of Naples. He taught what we today would call "Developmental Rhetoric" to law students with insufficient rhetorical training. The rhetoric Vico taught was directed specifically to oral performance, and Vico himself was an extremely good extemporaneous speaker.[9] Vico never lost sight of the fact that the various stages of rhetorical training, *inventio, dispositio, elocutio, memoria,* and *pronunciatio* were only stages in training and were not stages to be followed in a temporal succession as in a process of written composition. In oral argument, style and organization had to occur simultaneously. It is within this concrete situation, dramatic oral performance, that Vico conceives the tropes at work.

Vico describes how the tropes function in culture in Book II of the *New Science,* especially in sections one and two. The latter section, the "poetic logic," explains how the tropes generate each other linguistically.[10] The remainder of the book explains how this process operated in the culture of antiquity. Vico multiplies examples of how changes in social structure and in discourse accompanied one another. These examples almost invariably involve the resolution of a religious-legal tension. In one instance Vico describes the way in which the Roman plebs gained access to the auspices and thus also to civil marriage and the right to inheritance (415). This process was a movement from metonymy (difference between plebs and patricians) to synecdoche (each class seeing itself and the other as part of a whole). But the change occurs *pari passu* with changes in the interpretation of law and religion.

The beginning of this process of "poetic logic" can be found in metaphor, the first trope, in which community and value were originally fused. Vico attributes that fusion to the *gigantes,* the *Urmenschen* who Vico says roamed the forests after the great flood. The proximate cause of this metaphor is thunder:

A few giants . . . were frightened and astonished by the great effect whose cause they did not know, and raised their eyes and became aware of the sky. And because in such a case the nature of the human mind leads it to attribute its own nature to the effect, and because in that state their nature was that of men all robust bodily strength, who expressed their very violent passions by shouting and grumbling, they pictured the sky to themselves as a great animated body, which in that aspect they called Jove. . . . And thus they began to exercise that natural curiosity which is the daughter of ignorance and the mother of knowledge, and which, opening the mind of man, gives birth to wonder. . . .
(377)

Having created such a noisy deity, the first men proceeded to interpret what they heard:

> They believed that Jove commanded by signs, that such signs were real words, and that nature was the language of Jove. The science of this language the gentiles universally believed to be divination . . . meaning the science of the language of the gods.(379)

Vico concludes that "Jove was born naturally in poetry as a divine character or imaginative universal to which everything having to do with the auspices was referred . . ."(381). The creation of Jove is a *metaphora*, a "carrying over" to the sky of certain bodily and auditory characteristics of men; these characteristics are then interpreted for direction. Jove's first directive was the prohibition of unrestrained sexuality. The *gigantes* caught copulating in the field by the storm fled to caves, where they eventually founded homes and families (504).

These interpreted meanings persist in social institutions and in the language of the community. That persistent meaning Vico calls "vulgar wisdom": "For the wisdom of the ancients was the vulgar wisdom of the lawgivers who founded the human race . . ." (384). The first men were the first poets and the first lawgivers. These "giants" founded language and religion when they looked into the sky, and their authoritative interpretation of that metaphor constituted the human community. Their interpretation is "vulgar" because it is given to all as the very act by which an "all" is constituted. The poetic and interpretive act of the giants springs from the recognition of the numinous. Hence Vico calls them "theological poets."

These passages illuminate how Vico conceived the relation of the imagination and language to the numinous, and they also illuminate White's critique of Foucault's thesis. White indicates that according to the Vichian system there is no pre-religious imagination. Hence White accuses Foucault of unwittingly wishing a return to the gods while still trying to free men from them. While these passages support White's critique, they also have some consequences for White's own use of Vico which I will discuss in the last part of this essay. For now, however, it is important to note the relation of imagination and divinity in the implosion of meaning in the primal metaphor.

It is significant that Vico ascribes the awareness of divinity to a fear-provoking *sound*. The giants respond to the sound in a metaphoric leap, interpreting it as the sound of a body, the body as the sky, the sky as a god, an angry god. From thence it becomes necessary to respond to the anger; that response creates institutions, laws, and language simultaneously. The central idea that should control our understanding of this stage of Vico's thought is that the metaphors which ground language are formed in perception (hearing) conditioned by emotion (fear), and are used to convey interpretations of divine will. Furthermore, Vico ascribes this primal metaphor to the very structure of primitive thought. That structural principle is Vico's enigmatic "imaginative universal."

The epistemological status of the "imaginative universals" is a thorny problem in Vico scholarship.[11] Vico apparently means by "imaginative universal" the primal metaphors of a language which became categories of perception and value. A valiant man is Achilles, a clever one is Odysseus. Not *like* them, but actually seen to be them. Logic, says Vico, "comes from *logos* whose first and proper meaning was *fabula*, fable . . ." And myth becomes truth: "Similarly, *mythos* came to be defined for us as *vera narratio*, or true speech . . ." (501). Vico then concludes:

> All the first tropes are corollaries of this poetic logic. The most luminous and therefore the most necessary and frequent is metaphor. It is most praised when it gives sense and passion to insensate things, in accordance with the metaphysics above discussed, by which the first poets attributed to bodies the being of animate substances, with capacities measured by their own, namely sense and passion, and in this way made fables of them. Thus every metaphor is a fable in brief. (404)

Metaphor expresses, or rather compresses, the religious, linguistic, and "institutional" *arché* of the human community. The first of these metaphors is Jove, created by the first men, the theological poet and lawgivers. From this first "imaginative universal" come others. They are a "sensory topics" through which the first men interpreted their world, and they form the foundation of the "poetic logic," that dialectical development of discourse which Vico describes and which White ascribes to Foucault. Vico goes on to say: ". . . the first poets had to give names to things from the most particular and the most sensible ideas. Such ideas are the sources, respectively, of synecdoche and metonymy" (406). Vico proceeds to indicate that the tropes developed *pari passu* with social change. The thrust of Vico's analysis is that the poetic logic is an exfoliation of the "vulgar wisdom" compacted in language at its origin in the imagination of the giants when they confronted the numinous.

I have tried here to give a synopsis of Vico's poetic logic and its ground in the imaginative universals. The question now arises as to how Vico conceived the poetic logic occurring, how he thought "vulgar wisdom" really operated. White's criticism of Foucault stops short of analyzing the imaginative procedure by which one discursive period moves to another. It is sufficient for his argument to point out that Foucault's *epistemes* do move in the way Vico described. But how they move is Vico's real contribution to a theory of discourse, and the key to that movement is *sensus communis*, by which I take Vico to mean the vulgar wisdom as it is apprehended, or perhaps "prehended," in the language of a particular human community.

II

The term *sensus communis* occurs in Book I of the *New Science* where Vico cites it as "judgment without reflection" and then as the source for a "common mental dictionary" of all languages which in turn is the locus of the vulgar wisdom (142, 145). To grasp the full significance of this concept one must trace its original in Vico's rhetorical theory and praxis. This will make the radically oral matrix of Vico's thought apparent.

Current Vico scholarship has tried to focus on how Vico relates *sensus communis* to imagination, and to both the language and life of a community. But how the relationship operates is still a matter of dispute. Hans-Georg Gadamer claims that by *sensus communis* Vico means "a moral sense which founds the community."[12] Ernesto Grassi, on the other hand, places *sensus communis*, not in the community, but wholly in "the ingenious structure of work."[13] Finally Michael Mooney assigns a subordinate role to *sensus communis*, saying that Vico intended by that term "what is agreed upon by all or most," the Aristotelian definition.[14] At issue is the relationship between three terms: *sensus communis*, imagination, and language. The terms may be juggled about, but, as is the case with juggling, no matter which two terms one feels he has a grasp of, the other is left hanging in the air. Their relationship, however, is crucial to understanding how Vico conceives the poetic logic working.

Vico developed his ideas of imagination, language and *sensus communis* in his *De nostri temporis studiorum ratione*, an oration he gave to the faculty and students of the University of Naples in 1708 and later published.[15] In this oration Vico defended rhetoric as educational training superior to Cartesian method. I have analyzed how Vico developed his own rhetorical theory in opposition to Descartes in an earlier work.[16] Here I will summarize my conclusions.

Vico contrasted rhetoric with Cartesianism by explicating their different attitudes toward probability. For Descartes a probable truth was, in fact, a falsehood. Methodic doubt would only accept as true those propositions which were demonstrably true. Rhetoric, on the other hand, works with probable truths and tries to argue from them to some sort of conviction which will furnish a motive for action. Vico follows Aristotle in defending rhetoric's use of the enthymeme, syllogisms whose major premise is only probably true. Vico asserts that Cartesian method's exclusive focus on the demonstrably true, to the exclusion of the probable, is harmful to the growth of *sensus communis* which, he says, emerges from perceptions of similitude

(13). These "perceptions of similitude" are recognitions of similarities between the case at hand and previous cases or precedents. *Sensus communis*
is first defined as the ability to perceive concrete events or cases within the
context of "similar" cases.

Vico goes on to say that *sensus communis* is both the "standard of practical
judgment and the guiding standard of eloquence"(13). *Sensus communis* is
the common standard of judgments about both circumstances and discourse
because both involve the imagination. The imagination of the orator finds
the "similarities" in cases and formulates such similarities into arguments.
In other words, *sensus communis* is both the source of the argument and
what the argument appeals to. Here Vico moves into a detailed defense of
rhetoric on the grounds that it trains the imagination and thus provides the
young orator with *sensus communis.*

Vico defends rhetoric by contrasting *inventio* with methodic doubt and
elocutio with geometric logic. In fact he specifically defends the use of the
topoi and the use of metaphor, but in each case he is working with how the
imagination creates arguments from probability.

First Vico claims that the *topoi* insure that a subject is investigated compre-
hensively. The *topoi* constitute a method by which the imagination can
exhaust the probably arguments on a subject. What they work on, however,
is not merely the case or subject but also the orator's *copia. Copia* is the
fund of words and images which the young orator has interiorized by means
of oral and written drills practiced over a period of years.[17] When the orator
scans the *topoi* he notes similarities between the case at hand and all the
formulas, images, quotations, and examples which he has memorized and
recited for years, the common fund of knowledge and precedents which both
the orator and his audience can take for granted. Those relations which
appear relevant to the case he then formulates into arguments. These arguments may not be demonstrably true, but they are persuasive because they
invoke what everyone knows and focus it on the case at hand.

Vico introduces *elocutio* when he moves to the second half of his defense
of rhetoric against Cartesian method; specifically he contrasts the use of
metaphor with geometric logic. In this earlier work, Vico presents metaphor
as the basis of all figurative speech, just as he will later in the *New Science.*
His definition of metaphor is gnomic:

> That which is tenuous, delicately refined, may be represented by a single line;
> "acute" by two. Metaphor, the greatest and brightest ornament of forceful
> and distinguished speech, undoubtedly plays the first role in acute figurative
> expression. (p. 24)

"That which is tenuous" obviously refers to Cartesian logic which prided
itself by proceeding in small simple steps, a "linear" progression. But metaphor is "acute," i.e., it focuses two lines in an acute angle. Metaphor con-

verges two meanings, but is also focused on some "point," the case at hand. In an earlier work, his *Institutiones Oratoriae*, Vico had said that metaphors were drawn from the list of *topoi* in Cicero's *De Oratore*.[18] For Vico, a metaphor is an argument, an argument drawn from perception of similarities, which similarities are then twinned in a metaphor. The orator's discovery of similitude via the *topoi*, and expression of it in a metaphor, are both imaginative acts which occur simultaneously in *ex tempore* performance. The orator must fuse argument and figurality by drawing on the *copia* which he has interiorized, perceiving the "lines" of argument and focusing them on the case in an "acute" expression.

The orator's power of effective persuasion depends not on the logical power of argument alone. The interpenetration, or "play," of meanings generates the possibility of other figures, connotations, and allusions, some shared by the entire language community, some by a part of the community, and some peculiar to each individual and derived from his own experiences. But the orator, ideally at least, understands these shared meanings. They were incorporated during his years of verbal performance, recitation, and declamation. These multiple meanings are what the imagination "incorporates," the somatic nature of language itself. It is at this level that reason meets emotion in Vico's rhetorical theory. The ability to manipulate language at this emotive level presupposes that the orator has interiorized the "feel" of the language, that he is aware of the "common" affective, pre-logical meanings, images, and rhythms which the speakers of the language share. It is these which the orator joins and focuses on the case at hand in a way which fuses argumentation and aesthetic pleasure, power and play.

The ground of these shared, pre-logical meanings is *sensus communis*. The orator invokes the pre-logical affective power which underwrites the ethical consensus of the community. As Gadamer says, *sensus communis* "is the moral sense which founds the community," but that sense has to be available to the orator, and he has access to it in the poetic nature of his language, the "common sensuality" which the audience shares and which embodies the consensus. It is at this level that the perceptions of similitude supply force to the argument. Learning to inhabit this world and to incorporate it into his imagination is the young orator's primary task. It is from this unclear and indistinct substrata that metaphor and the other figures derive their force and that force "reinforces" the civic community when it decides upon an action. The "common" pre-logical, pre-reflective, affective dimensions of meaning and conventional signification constitutes *sensus communis* in the *De nostri*. It is both the ground of the tropes within the orator's imagination and it is also the ground of their intelligibility and effectiveness in directing the audience's choices. This inseparable relationship between imagination and *sensus communis* forms the basis of the operation of Vico's "poetic logic" in the *New Science*.

One way of looking at the *New Science* is that Vico is trying to reveal the *arche* of what the orator works with. How did that rhetorical *sensus communis* get into the language in the first place, and what is its role and function in cultural development? The answer to the first question is the imaginative universal: the answer to the second is the poetic logic. The imaginative universals implode into language the meaning, passion, and values which were fused when the first men responded to the numinous and formed human communities. The poetic logic traces how those meanings are adapted by eloquent speech to new circumstances and new solutions are presented "in terms of" old values, the "similarities" which it is the orator's job to find and express. *Sensus communis* is, indeed, "judgment without reflection with regard to needs and utilities" and also the source of a "common mental dictionary." It is what keeps language wedded to community life and makes eloquence, and perforce rhetoric, possible.

The aspects of *sensus communis* to which I want to call attention are, first, its origin in religious experience, second, its relation to a language community and a civic community, and, finally, its relation to the oral matrix of rhetoric. These aspects of *sensus communis* create some problems for both White and Foucault's use of Vico's thought.

It should be clear from this discussion that the heart of Vico's poetic logic is a religious event. That event establishes the *logos* and the community simultaneously and begins the development of the poetic logic. While White wishes to transcend this process through historical consciousness, Foucault simply wishes to erase it and begin again. Neither is fully cognizant of the central role Vico gives to religion in his poetic logic. For Vico the *logos* originates in the religious and derives its power from it. The *sensus communis* is the *sensus numinous*. Despite their differences over the historicity of discourse, both Foucault and White seem to agree on the desirability and possibility of a secular, pluralistic discourse, but Vico's entire epistemology seems to frustrate such a desire.

The religious origin of *sensus communis* challenges the objectives of both White and Foucault. The price for Vico's theory of periodicity is acceptance of its basis in religion. The "capital" of pre-logical, affective meanings and judgments out of which eloquence and discourse is formed is constituted by religious experience and imaginative response to it. White is quite right to chide Foucault for seeking a return to a pre-religious imagination when, in fact, according to Vico, no such time existed. For Vico human time begins with the *mysterium tremendum et fascinans*. But Vico claims not only that religion initiates human language and culture, but that the meaning which inheres in language and community, the *sensus communis*, remains at base a religious meaning. What prevents Foucault from returning to a pre-religious discourse also prevents White from advancing to a post-religious one. White succumbs to the temptation to extend our notion of religious relativism, inherited from the Enlightenment, to a pluralism or relativism of discourse.

The *sensus communis,* as Vico describes it, makes White's critical objectives suspect. It is *community* which makes discourse possible at every stage of the poetic logic. A choice of discursive modes in which each writer "pursues his own moral and aesthetic aspirations" would, in Vico's view, relegate each writer to his own linguistic, moral, and religious universe. White refers to the writer's "modality of consciousness" as if his discourse were only a matter of individual preference. In effect White reduces Vico's discursive modes to rhetorical strategies. But the whole thrust of Vico's poetic logic is that it limits the available effective rhetorical strategies: these strategies are limited by historical, social, and linguistic prejudices inhabiting the community. Or to put it another way, if White seriously holds to Vico's poetic logic, then to realize his ideal of multiple discursive modes he must posit that each individual has a right to his or her own sense of the community. Perhaps such a thing is not unimaginable for a writer, but if the writing is to be intelligible there needs to be a *sensus communis* for *readers* so they can understand and judge the various discursive modes, and that sense must be communal.

Readers need a *sensus communis* to read, even if it is the sense that the *sensus communis* is absent. I think that is what White's relativism requires. While he wants to use Vico to transcend the historical progression of discursive modes, especially of irony, he in fact only accomplishes what Wayne Booth has called the "destabilization" of irony, releasing it from any overt claims of reflecting a *sensus communis.*[19] Destabilized irony draws upon a *sensus communis* that the reader knows has vanished. The meaning of the ironical text is always elusive, always evaporating, as in the works of Beckett and Kierkegaard. For White, what began as an escape from irony becomes an escape into infinite irony.

What, then, does Vico have to contribute to a theory of discourse? I think he contributes the beginning of a much more radical critique than that offered by either White or Foucault. Vico's poetic logic rests on a rhetorically oriented theory of human thought and human community. That theory was constructed from humanist rhetoric out of its oral praxis in order to meet the challenge of Enlightenment rationalism and its attendant pedagogy. The orality of Vico's paradigm allows it to be holistic in its account of the "power" and the "play" that constitutes the interaction of discourse and history, while the Enlightenment paradigm divorced power from play and concealed it behind a tone of ironic objectivity, a tone available exclusively to writers. The duplicity involve in that divorce fuels Foucault's moral indignation at history as well as White's disenchantment with the ironic mode. Vico's poetic logic derives from a tradition which predates the ironic posture of the Enlightenment, humanistic rhetoric. As such it challenges the Enlightenment's assumptions about the possibility of secularity and relativism as permanent contexts for intelligible discourse.

Vico's poetic logic is not a mere theory of periodicity; it is a rhetorical paradigm for discourse which challenges rationalistic assumptions behind current attempts to construct such a theory. Vico's challenge, originating in a performative, imaginative, communal, and religious account of discourse, makes clear how these attempts still rest on the models of secularity and irony inherited from the Enlightenment.

Notes

1. Hayden White, "The Tropics of History: The Deep Structure of *The New Science,*" *Giambattista Vico's Science of Humanity,* ed. Giorgio Tagliacozzi and Donald P. Verene (Baltimore and London: Johns Hopkins University Press, 1976), pp. 65–86. Edward W. Said, *Beginnings: Intention and Method* (Baltimore and London: Johns Hopkins University Press, 1975).

2. Hayden White, "Foucault Decoded: Notes from Underground," *History and Theory,* vol. 12 (1973), 23–54.

3. White, "Foucault Decoded," p. 48.

4. Michael Foucault, *The Archaeology of Knowledge,* trans. A. M. Sheridan Smith (New York, Hagerstown, San Francisco, London: Harper & Row, 1976), p. 199.

5. Hayden White, *Metahistory: The Historical Imagination in Nineteenth-Century Europe* (Baltimore and London: Johns Hopkins University Press, 1973), p. 434.

6. Michel Foucault, *The Order of Things: An Archaeology of the Human Sciences; A Translation of Les mots et les choses* (New York: Random House Inc., 1973), p. 385.

7. White, "Foucault Decoded, p. 44.

8. George Kennedy, *Classical Rhetoric and Its Christian and Secular Tradition from Ancient to Modern Times* (Chapel Hill: University of North Carolina Press, 1980), pp. 3–5.

9. In his *Autobiography* Vico describes how he gave a long speech on a point of law with only one page of notes as part of the competition for a chair of jurisprudence. *The Autobiography of Giambattista Vico,* trans. Max Harold Fisch and Thomas G. Berbin (Ithaca and London: Cornell University Press, 1944), p. 164.

10. All references are to *The New Science of Giambattista Vico,* trans. Max Frisch and Thomas G. Bergin (Ithaca: Cornell University Press, 1944) and will be indicated by paragraph number.

11. The imaginative universals have become a kind of no-man's land in the battle over a Marxist or idealist interpretation of the New Science. For example, Ernesto Grassi makes the argument for interpreting the imaginative universals as concretizing the emotional domain of work in community life, thus investing work with a value beyond itself, while Donald P. Verene argues that the universals supply a "genetic epistemology" which relates thought to culture, and he concludes that imaginative univerals supply a first stage to the development of myth as it has been described by Ernst Cassirer. See Ernesto Grassi, "The Priority of Common Sense and Imagination: Vico's Philosophical Relevance Today," *Vico and Contemporary Thought,* ed. Donald P. Verene, Michael Mooney, and Giorgio Tagliacozzo (Atlantic Highlands, N.J.:

Humanities Press, 1976), pp. 163–85, and Donald P. Verne, "Vico's Philosophy of Imagination," *Vico and Contemporary Thought*, pp. 20-35. Michael Mooney has argued that language can mediate between these two views of the imaginative universals. See Michael Mooney, "The Primacy of Language in Vico," *Vico and Contemporary Thought*, pp. 191–211. These studies all argue for one concept or another as grounding or controlling Vico's imaginative universals. I am arguing that this concept is grounded in humanist rhetoric which in turn saw these various mental and linguistic phenomena operating holistically and simultaneously in oral performance.

12. Hans-Georg Gadamer, *Truth and Method* (New York: Seabury Press, 1975), p. 29.

13. Grassi, "Priority of Common Sense and Imagination," p. 163.

14. Mooney, "The Primary of Language in View," p. 185.

15. Published in English as *On the study methods of our Time,* trans. Elio Gianturco (Indianapolis: The Library of the Liberal Arts; Bobbs-Merrill Inc., 1965).

16. John D. Schaeffer, "Vico's Rhetorical Model of the Mind: *Sensus Communis* in the *De nostri temporis studiorum ratione,"* *Philosophy and Rhetoric*, Vol. 14, No. 3 (Summer 1981), 152–67.

17. For a good description of the education of young rhetoric students in ancient Rome see Stanley F. Bonner, *Education in Ancient Rome: From the elder Cato to the younger Pliny* (Berkeley and Los Angeles: University of California Press, 1977), pp. 189–277.

18. *Institutiones oratoriae*, Vol. VII of *Opere di Giambattista Vico,* 8 vols. (Naples: Morano), p. 96.

19. Wayne C. Booth, *A Rhetoric of Irony* (Chicago: University of Chicago Press, 1975), pp. 240–77. See also Walter J. Ong, "From Mimesis to Irony: Writing and Print as Integuments of Voice," *Interfaces of the Word: Studies in the Evolution of Consciousness and Culture* (Ithaca and London: Cornell University Press, 1977), pp. 272–304.

7

The Sense of the Past: Image, Text, and Object in the Formation of Historical Consciousness in Nineteenth-Century Britain

Stephen Bann

Until quite recently, there has been a substantial obstacle to the understanding of historical consciousness as it developed in 19th-century Britain and Europe. Quite simply, this has been the historian's own sense of the factors which determined the emergence of their own discipline as a field of scientific study. Every historian knows, or thinks he knows, that in the 19th century the pioneers of the modern study of history emancipated themselves from the cloying embrace of literature, and developed a critical method which would make it possible to elicit the truth of the archives. Every historian knows, or thinks he knows, that the German Leopold von Ranke committed himself to the stern assignment of recounting "what actually happened," and from that point onwards gave historiography a new and noble destiny, teaching his successors—as Lord Acton was later to phrase it, "to be critical, to be colourless, and to be new."

Yet historians and others have started to wonder about what has been omitted from this mythic reading of the 19th century—this seemingly parthogenetic birth of a new historical science. They have started to inquire, for example, into what was swept under the carpet when the new professional historiography emerged. Philippa Levine's recent study, *The Amateur and the Professional,* charts the maze of 19th century research into the past, and shows how its different areas separated out into the distinct pursuits of antiquarian, archaeologist, and historian proper—a process which she does not consider to have begun in any significant degree until the foundation of the Public Record Office in the second half of the century necessitated the training of a new professional caste of archivists. Yet she also makes no bones about the fact that such a view leaves the titanic figures of mid-19th-century historiography high and dry. Neither Carlyle nor Macaulay, she insists, "was ever part of the wider historical community but found their associates and friends rather in literary and political circles of a more general kind." They belonged instead, she suggests, to "an older tradition of essayists and reviewers."

There is however more than a hint of paradox about an interpretation which consigns to an "older tradition" precisely those historical-minded writers who galvanized the imagination of the contemporary public. Surely their work must have been new in some significant sense, even if it was not new in the precise sense that the archival method at the Public Record Office was? Much recent writing on 19th-century historiography, taking its lead from Hayden White's fine study *Metahistory*, has countered this problem by insisting on the sheer creative power of these mid-century writers. John D. Rosenberg, in his book *Carlyle and the Burden of History,* raises the poetic stakes when he describes the effect of the extraordinary section entitled "The Ancient Monk," in *Past and Present:* "But for Jocelin, Carlyle feels and communicates a lived affection. 'The Ancient Monk' radiates a power of pure delight akin to a child's in finding buried treasure or in witnessing magic." But this graphic evocation of Carlyle's success is not the kind of thing which will impress the historians. Indeed it is just the kind of thing which will put them on their guard against the blandishments of the poetic imagination, as grandfather Ranke taught them to be against the seductive siren-song of Sir Walter Scott.

What I am therefore proposing at the start of this paper is the need for a historical view which will include both the amateur and the professional, Carlyle and Ranke, the historical novel and the text edited by the Public Record Office—rather than insisting that they differ like chalk and cheese. I have only come across one historical thinker who has tried to establish the theoretical preconditions for such a view, and this is Michel Foucault, who argued in *Les Mots et les choses* that "the lyrical halo which surrounded [in the 19th century] the awareness of history, the lively curiosity for the documents of traces which time had left behind" was a reaction to an overpowering sense of loss: to "the bare fact that man has found himself to be emptied of history, but that he was already at the task of re-discovering in the depths of himself . . . a historicity which was linked to him essentially." Now I cannot go into the detail of Foucault's argument, which is based on a complex study of the development of ideas about domains such as language and the natural world, and their 18th-century tendency to separate off into specific areas of knowledge rather than mere attributes of humanity which reaffirmed man's central place in the cosmos. But the main point is, I hope, clear. Foucault's dialectical model of loss and retrieval helps to account for the fact that 19th-century man did not simply discover history: he needed to discover history, or, as it were, to remake history on his own terms. It is this overriding cultural need, it seems to me, which can be shown to be common both to Ranke's deeply motivated objectification of the protocols of historical reconstruction, and to Carlyle's passionate evocation of subjective response to the past.

However I am not concerned here primarily with the "why" of 19th-century historical awareness. My concern is with the "how." How did not only historians and writers, but painters, collectors, and architects, articulate their relationship to history in their work? I hope it will not seem unduly arrogant if I suggest that this is a question which has so far hardly begun to be answered. This is not because art historians have neglected the rich materials of 19th-century historicism. Quite the opposite, they have been actively concerned with it for a long while. It is because they have, on the whole, completely neglected to ask the right questions. I have my own explanation for this, which is that art history, in defining itself as a discipline over against connoisseurship, understandably took over the positivist paradigm of 19th-century archival research. But in so doing, it also inevitably (though no doubt unconsciously) took over the prejudice which was so ingrained among archive-based historians against the serious historical value of artistic representations of history. I am not saying that this dominant direction of contemporary art history systematically devalues its objects of study. What I am saying is that by driving a wedge between the status of the work as object—with its own "history," made accessible by studies of patronage and so on—and the status of the work as representation—which is reserved for the purely artistic, and hence cognitively null domain—normative art history tends to occlude the ways in which visual representation itself helped to concretize the awareness of the past.

What I intend to do, therefore, is to sketch the basic outline of what might be called a rhetoric of evocation, in which objects, texts, and images all contribute to the materialization of the past. I shall deliberately be using a series of rhetorical tools which allow me to make conjunctions between these different registers, looking at texts for images, objects in images and so forth. And rather than alienate the reader with a series of Greek or Roman technical terms, I shall simply identify my rhetorical tools by a set of three present participles: *framing, focalizing,* and *filling* are the three operations which I shall try to trace in a very diverse series of historical representations of the period. But I should suggest at the same time that my approach is to a certain extent governed by a wish to be attentive to the particular sensory stimuli which are being employed to stimulate an awareness of the past. The well-established art-historical opposition of the visual and the haptic—appeal to the vision and the sense of touch—will here, I hope, cease to be a merely formal opposition, or one used to establish broad comparisons between the stylistic characteristics of the works of different epochs. Instead, I shall attempt to show how the senses are inveigled into an act of identification with the otherness of the past.

Of course this mode of interpreting the shifts in consciousness of the 19th century, and the way in which they are mirrored in the creations of verbal or visual art, is far from original. Rosenberg's discussion of "The Ancient Monk" details the stages by which Carlyle converts a potent visual metaphor into an even more potent tactile metaphor as he begins to describe the exhumation of the embalmed corpse of King Edmund by the medieval Abbot Sampson. First he promises us, in overtly biblical language, that we shall "look face to face" upon an ancient century. Then he follows the process by which Samson "strips away layer upon layer of outer cerements" until he comes to the body itself, finally touching the eyes, the nose, the breast, the arms, and the toes. As Rosenberg puts it, "the reader senses the presence of the double miracle, the one palpable to Abbot Samson's touch, the other performed by Carlyle, through the medium of Jocelin, of bringing 'that deep-buried Time' back to effulgent life. A 'laying on of hands' takes place on the page, Samson touching the long-buried Edmund, Carlyle touching us through the freshly unearthed words of Jocelin."

I certainly agree that Carlyle's account works in the way that Rosenberg decribes, and in a sense all historical fiction has to demonstrate to a certain degree that implicit contract with the reader which is evoked so vividly by Charles Reade's intradiegetic vignette of clasped hands, in his preeminent late 19th-century historical novel, *The Cloister and the Hearth*. But the escalation of metaphors in Carlyle, from percipient sight to reverent touch, has its own dynamic correlative, so I would argue, in the way in which the antiquarian sensibility had already liberated the historical object from the ahistorical zone of Neo-classical perfection. To take just one comparative example, William Weddell's splendid Sculpture Gallery at Newby Hall, in North Yorkshire, is a manifestation of the neo-classical drive to flawless and timeless perfection; no fragmented limbs or historical abrasions are allowed to remain here, and even the recent placement of a fine contemporary bust of the collector beside the rehabilitated sculptures seems intrusive, precisely because it lends a note of inappropriate subjectivism. By contrast, the Kentish antiquarian Bryan Faussett constructs the now vanished Faussett pavilion on an immeasureably humbler scale. While Weddell is collecting in Rome, Faussett is excavating in Canterbury, and the fruits of his labors are installed, in all their fragmented and abraded state, with inscriptions which denote both the pathos of the truncated figure ("TRUNCAM [PROH DOLOR!] FIGURAM") and the temporary nature of its resting place ("ASYLUM QUALE QUALE"). It is precisely in his investment in the historical fragment both as an object and as a vestige of history that Faussett anticipates the sensibility of 19th century, while Weddell celebrates the triumph of the ideal over the material, and the synchronic over the diachonic.

After that parenthesis, I want to return to the three-stage analysis which I introduced with the terms *framing, focalizing,* and *filling.* Just to give a brief initial definition of these terms, *framing* is concerned with the physical operation of delimiting an area and designating it as authentic; *focalizing* is concerned with identifying objects of special interest within that area, and in that way contributing to the authenticity of the whole; *filling*, which I shall refer to at a later stage, is the final operation of establishing the otherness of history not simply as a visual or verbal system of references but as a perceived or imagined fullness—no less concrete than the everyday world.

To frame, then, is to set apart and designate for attention. In terms of Nicholas Poussin's well-known advice to Chanteloup, "un peu de corniche" will allow the rays of sight to be concentrated in the painting. But as a supplementary move, the frame can be used to signal the special kind of authenticity which is historical authenticity. When David Erskine, then Lord Cardross and later Earl of Buchan, presented a portrait of Queen Elizabeth I to the national collection in 1765, he took care to have inscribed around the frame that this was a "true effigy"—*hanc veram effigiem*—of the great Queen. A few years later, when he chose to erect a few pseudo-medieval monuments at Dryburgh Abbey on the River Tweed, he used this niche-like arrangment to bracket off the improbable impostor who is identified on the upper band of stone as "James Ye First" of Scotland.

Of course the painter, more than the stonemason, has a ready-made opportunity of delimiting a space, which can then be invested with historical values. Yet I would argue that it is well into the 19th century before this can be realized, in the fullest sense, by any British painter. Thomas Stothard's famous composition of the Canterbury Pilgrims, in particular the version dating from 1817, shows the results of the painter's study of medieval dress. Nevertheless, in two respects, it fails to achieve, or refrains from attempting, the type of authenticity which I am describing. The first point is that History is mediated by the literary text: we see not the Middle Ages, but the visual counterpart to the poetic world evoked by Chaucer. The second point relates to composition: the frieze-like sequence of figures, in a format comparable in other versions to the longitudinal form of a *cassone* panel, draws attention to its own formality, rather than establishing a scene for our attention.

By contrast, Bonington's *Henri III and the English Ambassador,* painted just a decade later, frames and represents a historical scene with a skill which is not merely painterly but rhetorical. As Marcia Pointon has suggested, Bonington was an avid reader, first of contemporary historical works like Barante's *Histoire des Ducs de Bourgogne* and secondly of the original chronicles of Jean Froissart and Monstrelet, which were the basis of Barante's account. This delightful work is literally programed by a quotation from the historical memoirs of Don Juan d'Autriche, which reads, in English translation, as follows: "I went to the Louvre in the morning under the auspices of the Gonzagas—the king had just been presiding over the Council, we found him in the dressing room with half a dozen little dogs, his favourite minions, some parrots and a monkey which leapt onto his Majesty's shoulder—they sent out the dogs and the minions. We remained with the parrots." Now when I say that Bonington's skill is not merely painterly but rhetorical, I mean that there is far more to the work than Bonington's fresh and vivid technique, luxuriating with the diversity of velvets and the multi-colored plumage of the remaining parrots. In choosing the moment of the reception of the English Ambassador, Bonington converts the traditional Albertian principle of the witness figure—the figure who mediates between the spectator and the represented scene—into a historical go-between. We are received by the King, just as the Ambassador is received, and the historical moment—taking place, like the original reception of Don Juan, in the margins of more momentous occasions like the sitting of the Royal Council—is entirely taken up with our induction into what is traditionally called the "presence" of the King.

It will, I think, be obvious how different Bonington's strategy is from that of Stothard. Nor is there any obvious connection between his historical costume-dramas and the tradition of Dutch genre painting with which they are sometimes compared. A painter like Gerard Ter Borch, for example, makes inventive use of the very interface between the framed world and the impossible world beyond the frame which Bonington succeeds in negating. Ter Borch's strategy is characteristically to set up a sequence of gazes: the young page is intently scrutinizing the fashionable lady, with Cherubino-like devotion, while her gaze is directed to a zone the secret of whose magnetism remains unknown to us. In Bonington, the rhetorical elements are not outward-straying, but bound in. Reception by the King and reception into the past are inseparably identified. One wonders if there might be a covert as well as an overt meaning to Delacroix's celebrated comment on works by Bonington such as these: "you are king in your domain, and Raphael would not have done what you do." Bonington was not only an original artist, but one concerned precisely with kings being secure in their domain—the domain being a purely represented past. Delacroix's small, turbulent oil painting of the *Assassination of the Bishop of Liège,* also painted in the late 1820s, is certainly no attempt to move in on Bonington's territory. But it does suggest a new sophistication in the ability to manipulate conventions of style and composition to the ends of historical recreation. Bonington counteracts the solemnity of the royal reception by a delightful informality that strays almost to the boundaries of the burlesque. Delacroix precipitously inverts the motif of reception by a potentate directing our eyes to the wide embrace of the endangered prelate.

Of course, in this case Delacroix is evoking an incident which comes straight from the pages of *Quentin Durward.* Sir Walter Scott might serve as the paradigm, in the literary field, for inventive use of the appropriate devices of framing, as in *Quentin Durward* itself, where the narrative is introduced by a lively introduction which tells of the finding of family papers in an old French château. To say that this conventional authenticating device is analogous to the "framing" effects of the painter is perhaps to stretch the term too far. But the common point, at least, is that a certain intervening layer—whether it be a novelist's prologue, or a carpenter's frame–edges us, or eases us, into the action. What I am claiming is that particular new strategies become appropriate, and certain others inappropriate, when it is the historical authenticity of that action that must be foregrounded.

Scott had by the late 1820s given historical painters much more to think about than *Quentin Durward*. He had, for example, provided the type of enthusiastic, indeed excessive cultivation of the objects of the past in his novel, *The Antiquary*. When Bonington paints his own version of *The Antiquary*, he chooses to render it as what Michael Fried would no doubt refer to as an "absorptive" picture. The elderly scholar is entirely bound up in his intense scrutiny of goodness knows what, as the dog begins to realize that it is useless to compete for attention, and the young lady, like Uccello's wife, seems wan from the exertion of trying to get the Antiquary to pay the ordinary dues of nature. Bonington obviously used the same male model for his similar painting of *Old Man and Child*. But there the opposition between the two ages is rendered in terms of a tender complicity. *The Antiquary*, by contrast, suggests the hypnotic attraction of the tiny object at the center of it all, which threatens to draw us into the vortex of receding time.

There were certainly other ways of representing antiquaries in the 1820s, and other ways of dealing with the lure of the historical object than realizing it as a kind of cultural black hole. Renoux painted the French collector Alexandre du Sommerard as "The Antiquary" *(L'Antiquaire)* in 1825, and it is interesting that in his work a more public character has been given to the protagonist's activities. Du Sommerard is engaged in dialogue with a visitor, presumably about the object which he holds in his hand. Our own eyes are free to range over the admittedly disordered state of the room, picking up in one corner a decorative ewer, in another a jumble of armor. I referred at the outset to the different systems of arranging objects in William Weddell's splendid sculpture gallery at Newby and Bryan Faussett's much more humble pavilion near Canterbury, suggesting that Faussett's aim is precisely to lend historicity—what Riegl might have called "age-value"—to the object by stressing its checkered career and its fragmentary state. But the complex development of modes of exhibiting objects over the century which followed Faussett's modest installation seems to show not so much a growing recognition of the historicity of historical objects, as a tendency to accentuate the overall picturesque character of a display by the use of dramatic light effects. This seems to have been the aesthetic program of Alexandre Lenoir's Musée des Petits-Augustins in Paris, if we can trust the surviving images of the various rooms, and particularly Hubert Robert's evocative picture of lateral light flooding into an interior replete with monumental fragments. It was also, in a very different way, the program of Sir John Soane's remarkable museum at Lincoln's Inn Fields: the young French scholar Beatrice Jullien has in my view rightly assimilated Soane's strategies of display with 18th-century concepts of associationism and the picturesque, and Gandy's contemporary water-colors tell us a good deal more than the present-day photograph about how the diverse fragments were intended to merge into each other within the diffused, golden circumambient light.

However I would claim for Renoux's Antiquary, Alexandre du Sommerard, that he personally invented a museum type which differed radically from all these immediately prior examples—one which was distinguished precisely by the fact that it did not dissolve objects in a picturesque luminosity, but reassimilated them to a notion of lived History. Ironically enough, the present-day Musée de Cluny only testifies vestigially to his pioneering work, and the sale of postcard images there points glaringly to a mode of presentation which is the exact opposite of his innovatory procedure. For Du Sommerard's achievement could be summed up simply in two stages. First, he brought together for the first time in a collection the sheer breadth of objects surviving from the later Middle Ages and Renaissance which had had no status at all for former collectors; secondly, he installed his collection in the medieval Hôtel of the Abbots of Cluny in such a way that each room contained a plethora of objects relating to a particular overall theme. Each egregiously odd reliquary would have merged into the overall richness and diversity of the furnishings of the chapel of the Hôtel de Cluny, represented effectively by a contemporary lithograph which even seems to incorporate a cowled monk for greater medieval authenticity.

It will, I hope, be clear by this stage in my argument that the procedures of framing and focalizing which I spoke of previously are complementary rather than totally distinct. Broadly speaking, the strategy of the historically minded pioneer in the 1820s is to delimit an area designated as authentic, and to people it with objects which will collectively attest that authenticity, though never drawing one's attention overridingly to a single object, which would fracture the recreated patina of age. This very loose definition would fit both Bonington and Du Sommerard. And it can be interpreted in another way as an attempt to conciliate the haptic and the visual, leaving enough roughness in the paint-work, or heterogeneity among the objects, to provide a vivid haptic stimulus while never abandoning the overall evenness of tone. This is, I believe, why Bonington was drawn particularly to water-color, and Du Sommerard, in his publication *Les Arts au moyen âge* and earlier, to the relatively new medium of lithography. A plate from Cotman's *Architectural Antiquities of Normandy* may be a finer work of art than the undistinguished lithograph of the Chapel, but it is infinitely less effective as a historical evocation, since it allows the fine linear texture gouged by the engraver's burin to obtrude, and so infiltrates the level of conscious craft.

It will also be clear by now, or so I hope, that I am setting up specific conditions for the success of a historicizing project that are not merely coincident with those of 19th-century art in general. Not every work of the period which takes history as its subject matter, in the broad sense, is a successful exercise in historical evocation. Indeed, there are many instances where, in my view, the artist totally misconceives the strategies which are appropriate to achieving a framing or focalizing effect. And after Bonington, it must be said, the proportion of British artists perpetrating this kind of misconception seems higher than the proportion of French artists. In France, there is Delacroix, but there is also Delaroche, who strays almost as far as it is possible to stray away from the framing and towards the focalizing effect. His famous painting of the *Princes in the Tower,* of which there is a small version held in the Wallace Collection, effectively inverts the strategies of the Boningtons in the same collection. The chink of light in the door, and the alertness of the dog, warn us of the approach of the assassin: we are not received, through our surrogate the ambassador, by a diverted and delightful monarch, but trespass upon the drama of regicide that is about to take place. And Delaroche's much less vigorous technique enables him to single out for particular attention, to focalize, an object which gives a vivid charge of additional authenticity: the open illuminated book of hours held by the doomed brothers.

Once again, there is a literary parallel to this focalizing of objects in the works of Scott, not only in the general use of devices like the "Talisman" in the novel of the same name, which perform integral functions in the plot, but also in the fashion by which the novelist will periodically designate an object as historic. In Scott's late novel, *The Pirate,* set in the Scottish Isles of the early 18th century but taking for granted a society whose roots lie back in the Middle Ages, a young girl rather diffidently approaches a kind of Nordic witch called Norna to work a "curative spell" on her. The episode begins like this: "Minna moved with slow and tremulous step towards the rude seat thus indicated to her. It was composed of stone, formed into some semblance of a chair by the rough and unskilful hand of some ancient Gothic artist." In Scott's novel, this is a telling introductory device, which is reiterated when the chair is again referred to at a later stage of the narrative. But in the engraving of John Houston R.S.A., included in a collection sponsored by the Royal Association for the Promotion of the Fine Arts in Scotland, Minna's chair cannot summon up the same imaginative picture, trapped as it is in the dry and laborious texture of the print. Another episode in Minna's adventure, which was drawn by W.E. Lockhart and engraved like its fellow by John Le Conte, vividly suggests the leakage of historicity that takes place when the artist seems to have considered everything in detail and nothing overall. We might consider his anomalous ladies, half out of fiction, half into art and historically nowhere, as mere wraiths compared with the photographed Newhaven fisherwomen recorded by Hill and Adamson a quarter-century before. As Walter Benjamin wrote in his fine essay of photography, the essence of the historicity of these images is that they "remaining real even now, will never yield [themselves] up entirely into art." Minna has given up the struggle years ago.

This mention of photography as a kind of paradigm for historical concreteness is, of course, not a mere intrusion into the field of representation with which I have been concerned. As an invention, if we choose to look at it as such, photography only breaks surface around 1840. But it is clear that the effects which photography achieved were sought after, through different techniques, in the previous half-century, not only in spectacular manipulations of light such Louis Daguerre's diorama, but also, arguably, in the tonal values of Du Sommerard's cherished medium of lithography. Indeed the notions of *framing* and *focalizing* which I have been pursuing find an obvious, non-metaphorical application in the techniques of photography and subsequently cinematography, which might be seen as the Utopia to which 19th century historical representation is valiantly striving. In his study *And when did you last see your father?*, Roy Strong notes the loss of conviction experienced by the late Victorian painter G.A. Storey, who realized that Velásquez presented him with "a true page of history" and not "a theatrical make-up of a scene dimly realized in the pages of some book written many years after the event." Whether or not he admitted it to himself, Keeley Hallswelle A.R.S.A must have been pursuing the second rather than the first alternative when he contributed to the edition of Scott's *The Pirate* his posturing and preposterous images. By contrast, a modern master of cinematography like Stanley Kubrick can deploy a whole range of techniques in a period film like *Barry Lyndon* (1975): special filters to make the woodland scene reminiscent of Gainsborough, establishing shots rather than tracking shots to accentuate the impression that the milieu is discovered as pre-existent by the camera's innocent eye, and of course movement of the characters within the scene to enact the process of coming into focus. Not all the techniques of cinematography are conducive to historical representation, I would argue. But as we follow the gradual manifestation of the two lovers in the woodland scene, we participate in a non-theatrical event, which is experienced as the coming-into-being of a relationship to the past.

But I would not wish to imply that only cinema can fulfill the urge to historical representation which so concerned the artists and writers of the last century. What I would claim is that, as the century progresses, the outstanding successes in this domain belong more and more to the avant-garde, and not to the honest academicians. The Pre-Raphaelites and younger associates like William Morris revive a vision of the past, in the proper sense of the term, which is at once purer and more cogent than anything seen in British art since Bonington. And if, in this case, the stimulus does not lie in the thrilling rediscovery of authentic medieval texts, it is produced hardly less effectively by a kind of self-stimulated transport of the senses which is often associated with the dream. William Morris, writing as an undergraduate in the *Oxford and Cambridge Magazine* of March 1856, concludes a story of medieval romance entitled precisely "A Dream" with a vision of "the moon shining on the tomb, throwing fair colours on it from the painted glass," and a final brief verse:

> No memory labours longer from the deep
>   Gold mines of thought to lift the hidden ore
> That glimpses, moving up, than I from sleep
>   To gather and tell o'er
> Each little sound and sight.

It is indeed the precision of Pre-Raphaelite imagery—"each little sound and sight"—that makes it distinctive. But that is not, of course, the focalized precision of Delaroche and the academic tradition. Pre-Raphaelite painting in its most historical vein, like the small gouache of "The Blue Closet" by Dante Gabriel Rossetti which Morris bought around 1858, crowds the picture plane with decorative detail, stimulating the tactile sense with what Marshall McLuhan called the "mosaic approach." Such works are an amalgam of effects, which disperse our focalizing gaze and often ease the transition from outer to inner world with the device of a splendidly elaborate frame. But what is perhaps less obvious is that a positive strategy of historical time-traveling is implied in them. Against Rossetti's *Wedding of St. George and Princess Sabra*, from 1857, it is fascinating to put yet another undergraduate extract from William Morris, which captures the bewilderment of travel through time, but also celebrates the intense spectacle that awaits the arriving traveler:

> I have been dreaming then, and am on my road to the lake: but what a young wood! I must have lost my way: I never saw all this before . . .
>   May the Lord help my senses! I am *riding!*—on a mule; a bell tinkles somewhere on him; the wind blows something about with a flapping sound: something? in Heaven's name, what? *My* long black robes.—Why—when I left my house I was clad in serviceable broadcloth of the nineteenth century.
>   I shall go mad—I am mad—I am gone to the Devil—I have lost my identity; who knows in what place, in what age of the world I am living now? Yet I will be calm; I have seen all these things before, in pictures surely, or something like them. I am resigned, since it is no worse than that. I am a priest then, in the dim, far-off thirteenth century, riding, about midnight I should say, to carry the blessed sacrament to some dying man.

Soon I found that I was not alone; a man was riding close to me on a horse; he was fantastically dressed, more so than usual for that time, being striped all over in vertical stripes of yellow and green with quaint birds like exaggerated storks in different attitudes counter-changed on the stripes: all this I saw by the lantern he carried, in the light of which his debauched black eyes quite flashed. On he went, unsteadily rolling, very drunk, though it was the thirteenth century, but being plainly used to that, he sat his horse fairly well.

I have no time to analyze this passage minutely, as it deserves. But I should like to point out that, by the end of the passage, the multi-colored vision so contrasted with the black priest's robe of the intermediary has been hedged in with irony: "very drunk, though it was thirteenth century." Morris recognizes the necessity of not holding the vision too long, and he so to speak empties it out, re-emphasizing the modern viewpoint. "I watched him in my proper nineteenth-century character . . . ," the text continues.

For my final examples, I would like to turn from framing and focalizing to the third notion, mentioned briefly at the outset; that of *filling*. How can we follow, in the world of images and objects, that delicate but crucial process by which historical plenitude is rhetorically conjured up, for the spectator's attention, and then dissipated, since that attention cannot, after all, hold for very long? While I cannot claim to answer that question definitively, I can point to a way in which the issue of historical plenitude was metaphorized, in the 19th century, being linked with the development of the taste for collecting arms and armour.

Picture Sir Walter Scott in his Castle Street study, while behind him, on guard, is a suit of armor. This is Sir J. Watson Gordon's frontispiece to the edition of *The Pirate,* but both of Edwin Landseer's paintings of Scott and Abbotsford, which date from the 1820s, feature arms and armor: in the case of the 1824 portrait, Scott is juxtaposed with the lower half of a suit of armor thought at that time to have been worn by the tallest man at the Battle of Bosworth Field. We know that, in Britain at any rate, the habit of collecting arms and armor was pioneered by Meyrick in the early part of the 19th century. But although part of his collection has survived in the congenial company of the Wallace Collection, it is of course one thing to see a piece like this in a museum, and another to rediscover what was invested in it by Meyrick and his contemporaries. My hypothesis is that the suit of armor serves as a metonymy for the human body, a body representative of the otherness of history, in the most direct way. Even today, we can see figures in armor guarding the Entrance Hall at Abbotsford, but we are not of course likely to enter into the spirit of the thing by imagining, as does Washington Irving in his visit to Newstead Abbey, that the armor is tenanted: "on arriving at angle of the corridor, the eye, glancing along a shadowy gallery, caught a sight of two dark figures in plate armor, with closed visors, bucklers braced, and swords drawn, standing motionless against the wall." Then Irving has to spoil it with a grudging admission: "They seemed two phantoms of the chivalrous era of the Abbey." But Du Sommerard's visitors to the Musée de Cluny, from the early 1830s onwards, must have been faced with a still stranger challenge to their imaginations when, in the plethoric surroundings of the François Premier room, they espied two suits of armor sitting opposite one another in the window embrasure, bathed in the light of a stained-glass window, and possibly enjoying a game of genuine medieval chess.

My suggestion is not that people were taken in by these effects, but that they were willing to play the game whose cycle led from pleasurable illusion to ironic dismissal. As the century developed, the ironic element tends inevitably to predominate, just as the neo-medieval whimsy of Barham's *Ingoldsby Legends* succeeds the full-blooded romance of Scott. When Horace Walpole's Strawberry Hill collections are sold in the 1840s, the whimsical concatenation of historical properties including armor which introduces the sale catalogue would seem to imply that the medieval has reverted to being mere decor, just as it was for Walpole himself. But there is an amusing pendant to this brief sequence in a painting whose irony is certainly not whimsical: Manet's *Le Déjeuner,* from 1867. Contemporary critics confronted with this splendid work agonized about their inability to construct a plausible narrative setting out of the properties included, which comprise not simply lunch things, but a jumbled heap of assorted armor. "Is it a lunch which precedes or follows a duel," asked Théophile Gautier. The answer is, of course, that Manet is expertly playing upon the capacity of pictorial space to seem empty or full, with the non-committal figure of Leon Koella-Leenhoff jutting out into our space, only to be reabsorbed again. It is surely appropriate that armor, the vehicle of a Romantic subterfuge in imagining what was empty to be full, should clutter the place up in an arbitrary, unmotivated fashion. It is also worth pointing out that Napoleon III's director of cultural affairs, the Comte de Nieuwekeerke, was a celebrated collector of arms and armor, who would, perhaps, have been specially put out by this casual treatment of the studio properties.

I have traced quite a variety of themes in the attempt to illuminate what I called the "how" of historical representation in the 19th century. It will be evident that I believe this to be something which can be well done, or badly done, and that the peaks of achievement, for me, are the ambassadorial works of Bonington and the gouaches of Rossetti: indeed I would go so far as to say that it is crucial that Rossetti's works, unlike Bonington's, represent no authentic historical figures (or very rarely so) since by that stage, it has become apparent that the intensity of the vision can only come from within— from the self-induced dream which poetry, as well as painting, is able to support and communicate. The artist is present in Pre-Raphaelite work not like the English Ambassador, or in this case the Spanish Ambassador, being received into the royal presence, but as the dreamer "gather[ing] and tell[ing] o'er each little sound and sight." Yet when Henry James finally comes, in his unfinished novel, *The Sense of the Past,* to the point of propelling his hero back into the past, he does in a sense readopt the ambassadorial model. The American Ambassador, who has shared Ralph Pendrel's passionate ruminations on the possibility of time travel, is present as he fades through the door dividing him from the past, and shrinks away as James escalates his vocabulary through the sensory gamut, and ends up so to speak under the water, but back in time:

> Our young man was after that aware of a position of such eminence on the upper doorstep as made him, his fine tat-tat-tat-ah of the knocker achieved, see the whole world, the waiting, the wondering, the shrunkenly staring representative of his country included, far, far, in fact at last quite abysmally below him. Whether these had been rapid or retarded stages he was really never to make out. Everything had come to him through an increasingly thick *other* medium; the medium to which the opening door of the house gave at once an extension that was like an extraordinarily strong odour inhaled—an inward and inward warm reach that his bewildered judge would literally have seen swallow him up; though perhaps with the supreme pause of the determined diver about to plunge just marked in him before the closing of the door again placed him on the right side and whole world as he had known it on the wrong.

If the Royal Scottish Academy had got hold of that, they would simply have manifested Ralph putting on the clothes of his Regency counterpart. But James, like Carlyle, recognizes that the rhetoric has to be screwed to a point where sensory evocation is almost excessive, in order that the need for the plenitude of the past can be expressed with an adequate power.

8

The Struggle for the Cultural Heritage: Christina Stead Refunctions Charles Dickens and Mark Twain

Jonathan Arac

The received cultural values with which we academic literary intellectuals most closely involve ourselves are the values of the "cultural treasures,"[1] the canonized masterpieces, for which we serve our students as intermediaries. In the years between the first and the second world wars, the established canon and its transmission faced strenuous challenge and probing discussion, not just, as our training leads us to expect, because of modernism, but also through the revolutionary and reactionary political struggles of those years. The debates over Proletarian Culture and Socialist Realism in the Soviet Union counted heavily for the production and mediation of literature through the western world. The French political strategy of the Popular Front first became visible, the year before the Blum government was elected, as a cultural force, when in 1935 the League of Writers for the Defense of Culture sponsored a gigantic international conference.[2] Prominent on the agenda for that conference stood the topic, "The Cultural Heritage," and at the second League conference, held in 1936, André Malraux addressed this topic with remarkable vigor. Amplifying observations from 1935, he defined the "cultural heritage" as created by each civilization "out of everything in the past that helps it to surpass itself." This is no passive reception but an active struggle: "A heritage is not transmitted; it must be conquered."[3] The antithesis of this position emerged a few years later in Walter Benjamin's "Theses on the Philosophy of History," written at a moment when the Popular Front (which Benjamin had never supported) could be judged a dreadful mistake. Benjamin emphasized that "cultural treasures" form part of "the triumphal procession in which the present rulers step over those who are lying prostrate," for "there is no document of civilization which is not at the same time a document of barbarism."[4]

The dialectic between these positions emerges through the case of Christina Stead's novel of 1940, *The Man Who Loved Children*, which takes two cultural treasures of Popular Front leftist humanism, Charles Dickens and

Mark Twain, and shatters them as false idols, even while finding within their works resources that make her own work possible. This critical redeployment of cultural power exemplifies what Brecht and Benjamin called "refunctioning" (*Umfunktionierung*).[5] This exploration will touch on issues that are still relevant to our current cultural and political debates, ranging from the values of "totality" and the strategies of feminism to the methods by which literary studies may be put in touch with the study of mass media and popular culture, a contemporary intellectual refunctioning.[6]

I

Little direct connection can be positively established between Charles Dickens and Mark Twain. If Sam Clemens was seen carrying volumes of Dickens in Keokuk in the 1850s, he was ashamed to admit that he never really read them.[7] If he attended a performance of Dickens's reading tour in America in 1867, he doubtless paid more attention to Olivia Langdon, his future wife, with whom he was on his first date.[8] From such incidents I take the moral that Dickens was for Twain, as Twain himself later became for many Americans, a cultural presence that extended far beyond the merely literary act of really reading.

Typically, Dickens and Twain have been brought together for the purpose of contrast. From the beginning, Twain's originality was set against the Dickensian imitativeness of Bret Harte,[9] and if the project that led to *Tom Sawyer* bore some relations to *David Copperfield,* that relation was burlesque. James Cox has strikingly remarked the disappearance of Dickens's early pseudonym "Boz," while "Mark Twain" wholly displaced Samuel Clemens.[10] In *The Ordeal of Mark Twain,* the study that formed twentieth-century critical debate on Twain, Van Wyck Brooks some half-dozen times set Dickens against Twain: Dickens succeeded in using "experience" as the basis for socially independent satire, in contrast to Twain's socially disarming and disarmed humor.[11]

The most telling connection was made by William Dean Howells, who linked the two as pre-eminent among the world's great comic writers for their "humanity."[12] More recently this has been elaborated by students of popular culture: Dickens and Twain each became a "celebrity" by representing "the common sense and basic goodness of the mass of the people."[13] In the 1930s, however, such insights were only formulated about each of the writers separately. George Orwell singled out in Dickens a "good tempered antinomianism," an opposition to laws and codes that Orwell considered characteristic of "western popular culture."[14] Newton Arvin, in a centennial evaluation of 1935, judged that Twain would survive as a "grand half-legendary personality," loved for his "largeness and sweetness."[15]

Yet it was also in the 1930s that Christina Stead's major novel achieved what I still find the most powerful specific conjunction of Dickens and Twain. Stead was born in 1902 and died in 1983. From her native Australia, she came in 1928 to London, where she met and loved a Marxist journalist and financier named William Blake, with whom she lived until his death in 1968. They were in Paris from 1929 through 1935 and then in the United States from 1937 through 1946.[16] *The Man Who Loved Children* was written here, has an American setting, and offers an intimate yet distanced interpretation of America.

Stead's link to Dickens is already well established by Joan Lidoff in her standard introductory study. Stead herself observed in an interview that "Dickens was in the family" as she grew up.[17] She was pleased to speculate that her grandfather left England for Australia inspired by Magwitch's success as a sheep-farmer in Dickens' *Great Expectations*. In *The Man Who Loved Children*, the man's father puts on a Dickensian family entertainment:

> "Come on, granddaughter! The Old One's about to present 'Mr. Wemmick and the Aged Parent.' Come along, come along, roll up, roll up, come right in, the show's just about to begin! All star performance: manager, Charles Pollit; business manager, Charlie Pollit; stage manager, Chas. Pollit; and the Aged, played by Charles Pollit. You must excuse, not stare at, the redundancy of that beautiful name Pollit, in the cast, ladies and gentlemen, if there be any of that name here, for it's all in the family. And the play written by Charles—Dickens, the greatest Charlie!"[18]

Sam Pollit, the "man" of the title and son of Charles Pollit, shares with his father the manic verbal inventiveness that is here attributed to Dickens as source. In such details as the ringing of changes on the name (Charles, Charlie, Chas.) Stead has caught and transmitted precise Dickensian characteristics, but also more largely in the whole parental mode of Sam Pollit's "love," enchanting in its constant flow of names, games and rhymes.

If Dickens and Stead is a familiar topic, however, Twain's significance for her has not been discussed. Yet we learn on the very first page that the title character, Sam Pollit, has as his full name, "Samuel Clemens Pollit" (as if there were a genealogy from Charles the father to Sam the son, from the English comic genius to the American). Perhaps only an Australian, and a woman at that, could have sufficient distance to allow the images of Dickens and Twain thus to superimpose, and from the perspective of "down under" they will come out topsy-turvy as well.

Stead's constellation of Dickens and Twain may suggest something like what Harold Bloom calls the creation of a "composite precursor," or else the kind of process Sandra Gilbert and Susan Gubar have followed Virginia Woolf in analyzing for women writers, who must conjure away the "Milton's bogey" of male literary authority. As opposed to the theories of unconsciousness and repression that undergird both these positions, however, the debate in the 1930s over the cultural heritage makes it possible to understand Stead's novel in terms of more conscious revisionary polemic, that is, refunctioning. To understand this more precisely will require some immersion in the book's specifics.

The Man Who Loved Children presents the life of a family from 1936 into 1938: Sam Pollit, in his late thirties; his second wife Henrietta ("Henny"); his daughter Louisa ("Louie") whose mother died in Louisa's infancy; and the five, later six, children of Sam and Henny. From the Baltimore fish market to world conferences on fisheries, Sam has risen from poverty to become a federal conservation bureaucrat, self-made with the help of connections from Henny's wealthy family. From the first page, man and wife rarely sleep, or even speak, together, and things get much worse, both financially and emotionally, yet Louie achieves a precocious adolescent independence, which carries the book's positive weight.

Sam and Henny, father and mother, are both terrible and wonderful, and above all *different* from each other: "He called a spade the predecessor of modern agriculture, she called it a muck dig: they had no words between them intelligible" (139). Different languages mean different ways of seeing the world:

> What a dreary stodgy world of adults the children saw when they went out! And what a moral, high minded world their father saw! But for Henny there was a wonderful particular world, and when they went with her they saw it: they saw the fish eyes, the crocodile grins, the hair like a birch broom, the mean men crawling with maggots, and the children restless as an eel that she saw . . . all these wonderful creatures, who swarmed in the streets, stores, and restaurants of Washington, ogling, leering, pulling, pushing, stinking, overscented, screaming and boasting. (9)

The grotesque energy of Henny's language is inseparable from her vision, saying and seeing cohere, and these different ways of seeing the world further ramify into differing ways of being in the world: "There were excitement, fun, joy, and even enchantment with both mother and father, and it was just a question of whether one wanted to sing, gallop about, and put on a performance ('showing off like all Pollitry,' said Henny), or look for mysteries ('Henny's room is a chaos,' said Sam)" (32). The surface clarity of "performance," in Dickens and Twain, Stead has isolated in Sam, while Henny shares their literary, textual "mysteries."

Stead explains these differences less by sheer human idiosyncrasy or by any biological distinctions between the sexes than by a socially produced dynamic of inequalities. Henny is aware of sinking from a higher economic position and of being oppressed because she is a woman, and her dark poetry springs from this consciousness. Despite setbacks, Sam is rising from a lower economic origin, and as a man he is master in the family. Louie will become an artist and thus (in the book's logic) declassed, yet she also belongs to a rising sex.

Henny's angry claims for the "rights of woman" (92), not just the American rights of man always on Sam's lips, her siding with "all women against all men" (36) in the "outlawry of womankind" (258), comes only through painful recognition, across class lines, of women's fellowships as "cheap servants" (61), an equality in degradation: "I hate her but I hate myself" (463). Even the power available to women through marriage can only be grasped in self-torment, as Henny mediates on her wedding band:

> If this plain ugly link meant an eyeless eternity of work and poverty and an early old age, it also meant that to her alone this potent breadwinner owed his money, name, and fidelity, to her, his kitchen-maid and body servant. For a moment, after years of scamping, she felt the dread power of wifehood; they were locked in each other's grasp till the end—the end, a mouthful of sunless muck-worms and grass roots stifling his blare of trumpets and her blasphemies against love. (145)[19]

Sam's position blends classic patriarchy with modern social progressivism. The book powerfully suggests that, while patriarchal family relations persist, there is little good to be hoped from many otherwise promising developments. Here Stead tellingly challenges the limitations of "humanity" as Howells found it in Dickens and Twain, but also as it was found in the Popular Front rhetoric of Roosevelt's second term, a blissfully strange moment when "Marxists were not revolutionaries and liberals were not pessimists."[20]

Sam's paternalism is unembarrassed in his explanation to Louie that "a woman must not leave her father's home until she goes to her husband: that is what I am here for, to look after you" (364). Later he more menacingly insists, "You are coming home to me, and I am going to watch every book you read, every thought you have" (523). Over the whole globe he wishes for the same knowledge he desires to have of his daughter:

> "to know my fellow man to the utmost . . . to penetrate into the hearts of dark, yellow, red, tawny, and tattooed man. For I believe that they are all the same man at heart and that a good one; and they can be brought together sooner or later by their more advanced brothers into a world fellowship, in which all differences of nationality, creed, or education will be respected and gradually smoothed out, and eventually the religion of all men will be one and the same." (49)

The next paragraph displays this fantasy of penetration and homogenization, omniscience and omnipotence, as inseparable from Sam's masculinity and misogyny:

Louisa was propping herself up against the railing. She was staring at her father absently. The morning was hot, and Sam had nothing on beneath his painting overalls. When he waved his golden-white muscular hairless arms, large damp tufts of yellow-red hair appeared. He kept on talking. The pores on his well-stretched skin were very large, his leathery skin was quite unlike the dull silk of the children's cheeks. He was not ashamed of his effluvia, thought it a gift that he sweated so freely; it was "natural." The scent that women used, he often remarked, was to cover lack of washing! (49–50).

As the passage goes on, the political ugliness of Sam's vision becomes manifest:

"My system," Sam continued, "which I invented myself, might be called *Monoman* or *Manuity*!" . . .
Louisa said, "You mean Monomania." . . .
Sam said coolly, "You look like a gutter rat, Looloo, with that expression. Monoman would only be the condition of the world after we had weeded out the misfits and degenerates." There was a threat in the way he said it. (50)

Stead makes us imagine an etymology in which "*wee*ding" means to form by exclusion a purified "*we.*"
After Sam returns from the expedition to Malaya that had in prospect stimulated the fantasy of Monoman, his plans elaborate in a panoptic hope of the sort to which Michel Foucault's *Discipline and Punish* sensitized us:

Sam, a great partisan of the Roosevelt Works plans . . . and seeing with pleasure new works being acquired from several states and placed under the surveillance or control of federal bureaus, saw in President Roosevelt the first great socialist ruler. . . . He favored a bureaucratic state socialism with the widest possible powers and a permanent staff, a bureaucracy intricately engineered, which would gradually engulf all the powers of [government]. . . . In his mind's eye he saw internations within internations; and overnations over nations, all separate functions of Federal Government rising to one crest of supreme judgment, sitting in a room; all glass, no doubt, with windows on the world. (315–16)

This "modern" American imperial administration, spurred by "public necessity's eminent domain," will replace the outmoded British Empire (as "Sam" follows "Charles").
The continuity that extends from the familial to the global in Sam's vision does not overlook, rather it intends to oversee, the local as well: "If I had my way—if I were Stalin or Hitler . . .—I would abolish schools altogether for children . . . and would form them into communities with a leader, something like I am myself, a natural leader, for only man learns in communities, he is a social animal" (352). Here the rhetoric of "community," so

prevalent in the American thirties, is inseparable from a powerfully individualizing desire.[21]

Sam's vision returns to the domestic Sunday when he was "to superintend the housework and show them all how easily it could be managed by 'system' and 'scientific management' "; in other words, the household was to enjoy what Sam called a "new deal." So, "commanding from his honorable position behind the coffee cup," he "made Little Womey [for "Little Woman," the Dickensian sobriquet Sam accords to Henny's daughter] and Looloo scrape and stack the dishes in the washbasin" (372). In America of the 1930s, it was widely understood that the phrase "New Deal" for Roosevelt's programs to combat the depression derived from what Hank Morgan promised to Arthurian England in Twain's *Connecticut Yankee*.[22]

Even after the debacle of his family life and loss of his government career, Sam is eager to rebound with a radio show, in which he will be known as "Uncle Sam" and will teach the lore of America (518). Here it is relevant to recall the great frequency with which in the last decade of his life Mark Twain was identified with the American national icon of Uncle Sam.[23]

II

Let me now try to specify what Stead is doing with Samuel Clemens Pollit, her composite figure of Charles Dickens and Mark Twain as petty-bourgeois paterfamilias and socialist booster of the 1930s. She offers an exploration, at once critical and imaginative, into the cultural meanings that Dickens and Twain have taken on in their historical afterlife. She forces upon us the question, "What are they good for now?" Such revisionary inquiry was provoked, not only for Stead but also for many others, by the social and economic crises of the 1930s, in which a whole way of life across the western world was felt to be changing, and further to *need* changing. The Popular Front relied upon the belief that change could happen without a painful struggle against existing values. Stead came to think otherwise. Her criticism of the Popular Front is inscribed not only in her critique of humanism through Dickens and Twain but also, very precisely, in the family name of Samuel Clemens Pollit. For Harry Pollitt (1890–1960), a founding member of the Communist Party of Great Britain and its Secretary from 1929, became a nationally visible political figure after 1936 when the Popular Front allowed his gifts as a "warm-hearted personality" to flourish (according to the *DNB*).[24]

Revisionary undertakings by some of Stead's contemporaries are better known to history. Our current institutional forms of literary study owe much to F. R. Leavis's journal *Scrutiny* (begun 1932) and to the overall project summarized in the title of his book *Revaluation* (1936). In the United States, F. O. Matthiessen's *American Renaissance* established a canon of great

American authors with such authority that we tend to forget its recent creation. In Europe during these same years, to meditate on the relations between form and life in the classic novel, especially that of the nineteenth century, seemed of crucial moment to George Lukács, the Hungarian Communist activist seeking refuge in Moscow; to Erich Auerbach, the German Jewish civil servant fled to Istanbul; to Mikhail Bakhtin, the Russian Christian polymath exiled to Kazakhstan.[25]

These great European critics of the novel stimulate insight into *The Man Who Loved Children*. Following Auerbach, it is at once more "everyday" than work by Dickens and Twain in its attention to sheer domestic routine, and more "serious" because its existential problematic is not discounted by the *conventions* of comedy, funny as the book often is. Following Bakhtin, its play of voices comes closer to Dostoevsky than to Dickens or Twain, in presenting alternative ways of life, embodied ideologies, among which the choice is not obvious. In contrast, Twain's scrupulous verisimilitude in rendering dialect variations does nothing to challenge the priority of Huck's values. Above all, Stead's work, as Solzhenitsyn's does later, vindicates Lukács's claim, against both naturalism and modernism, that the power of critical realism remained available to a writer who was not afraid to face history. I think there is no doubt that the apparent anachronism of Stead's technique helps account for the neglect of her novel when first published, no less than what seemed the anachronism of feminist concerns.[26]

Yet such textually oriented reading as these great critics point to is somewhat beside the point for Stead's work with Dickens and Twain. She operates on the *images* of Dickens and Twain that the various media of culture had elaborated from their books, and at least equally from their lives. Once worked up and set loose, these images could circulate as signs for cultural value. Stead here approaches certain concerns of postmodern fiction such as E. L. Doctorow's *Ragtime* (1974) and Robert Coover's *The Public Burning* (1977). How could she acquire such a perspective so precociously? In the first place, even more than Pound, Joyce, and Eliot she came from an imperial margin that knew the heart of western culture only at a painfully felt distance of symbolic mediation (see her Australian revision of Hardy's "Tess" in *For Love Alone* [1944]). And then she went on to discover, through Blake's emphasis on economic theory and through her own immersion in international finance and commodity trade, that what drove that heart was itself another circulation of signs (see *House of All Nations*, 1938).

By cultural "images," I mean what Newton Arvin referred to as Twain's "grand, half-legendary personality," his immortality "less as a writer . . . than as a figure" (87). A decade earlier, Edmund Wilson had observed of Twain that "the man is more impressive than his work,"[27] and later he would insist of Dickens that "it is necessary to see him as a man."[28] Orwell concludes his essay on Dickens with the sense that what remains is "the face of a man who is generously angry."²⁹ This strikingly, and independently, echoes Walter Benjamin's "The Storyteller," which ends by defining the storyteller as "the figure [*Gestalt*] in which the righteous man encounters himself."³⁰

Criticism had at this time the half-avowed task of humanist mythmaking, the production through reading of culturally potent images by which to sustain and orient ourselves in a time of historical crisis. Orwell, Wilson, Arvin, Benjamin were all politically on the left, and at least in Wilson and Orwell, writing after the disillusions experienced from the Moscow Trials, the Spanish Civil War, and the Molotov-Ribbentrop pact, the image of human comprehensibility, a face that could be reliably known, compensated for political duplicity. The prestige of the *Gestalt* ("figure," "shape," "totality") appears also in radical social theory. Drawing upon not only his Resistance work but also upon his attendance at Alexandre Kojève's lectures on Hegel during the thirties, Maurice Merleau-Ponty wrote, "To be a Marxist is to believe that economic problems and cultural or human problems are a single problem and that the proletariat as history has shaped it holds the solution to that problem. In modern language, it is to believe that history has a *Gestalt*."³¹ This context renders even more telling the force with which Jacques Lacan analyzed the role in ego-development played by the "imaginary" production of an ideal figure (he uses the German *Gestalt*) of human wholeness. His theory of the "mirror-stage," first proposed in 1936, turns away from such humanism.

Stead for her part draws little cheer from the human face of history. Her figure of Sam Pollit as Dickens and Twain appropriates human images that had been displaced from the relatively autonomous realm of literature into the culture at large, then combines those images, and sets them to work again within a new piece of literature, which allows for a fresh exploration of their possible effects, thus giving them a different force when they again are shifted from her literary work into the larger culture, and her readers' lives. This is refunctioning.

If her view of Dickens and Twain, and their meaning for America, is less positive than Wilson's or Orwell's or Arvin's, it is not because she is reactionary (like T. S. Eliot who opposed "apeneck" Sweeney to Emersonian humanist historical optimism), but because she is writing as a woman. The worst trouble with Sam, her book shows, is patriarchy, his position within a socially established structure of sex and gender domination that even the organized left of the 1930s neglected. Only a few years earlier, Stead had not criticized but had herself enacted such neglect. When in 1935 the first great cultural event of the Popular Front, the Congress of the League of Writers for the Defense of Culture, was held in Paris, Stead reported on it for the English journal *Left Review*. Her language in this report is routinely sexist; writers are always "he" (e.g., "He rises to defend what has come to him from his father").[32] More than that, however, she writes with a normative, positivist biologism that in *The Man Who Loved Children* only Sam approaches: Writers who "enter the political arena" and "take lessons from workmen" will then "use their pen as a scalpel for lifting up the living tissues, cutting through the morbid tissues, of the social anatomy" (454). And as their art is hygienic, so are their bodies: "The hall was not full of half-feminine masculine revolutionaries and half-masculine feminine rebels. They were neat, had no postures and poses" (456). Many years later, interviewed in 1973, Stead denied any identification with the contemporary women's liberation movement: "It's eccentric. It's not a genuine movement. It's totally, purely middle class."[33] Nonetheless, I think any reader now will find *The Man Who Loved Children* a serious feminist critique of domestic patriarchy and its larger ramifications.[34]

The composite figure of Dickens and Twain adds something special. It emphasizes how marvelously, almost irresistibly fascinating and attractive that patriarchal power can be. Michel Foucault made a fundamental observation: "If power was never anything but repressive, if it never did anything but say no, do you really believe that we should manage to obey it? What gives power its hold . . . [is that] it does not simply weigh like a force that says no, but that it runs through and produces things; it induces pleasure."[35] Not only for men, but also for women, escaping patriarchy requires abandoning pleasures that we know as cultural treasures, and as forms of daily life; it requires learning to resist the "love" which "the man" offers and which keeps up "children" by producing and reproducing a system of domination.

All biographies make clear the magnetic personal power that Dickens and Twain enjoyed over those who knew and loved them, but what was their family life like? Already by the thirties, serious questions had begun to arise. Bechofer Roberts's novel *This Side Idolatry* (1928) imagined Dickens's cruelty to his wife (Orwell, 454), and Gladys Storey's *Dickens and Daughter* (1939) offers filial testimony that "nothing could surpass the misery and unhappiness of our home."[36] So Stead's Louie never tells outsiders about home life because "no one would believe me" (356), but she can no longer bear the "daily misery," the "horror of everyday life" (405). More recently, Hamlin Hill in *God's Fool* has exposed the last years of Twain's life, but sensitized by Stead, we may reinterpret even material that Albert Bigelow Paine had considered appropriate for his adulatory biography. At the same early adolescent age as Stead's Louie, Twain's daughter Susy began to keep a diary, above all to capture her father's performances, which he made sure to put on for her: "He told us the other day that he couldn't bear to hear anyone talk but himself, but that he could listen to himself talk for hours without getting tired, of course he said this in joke, but I've no doubt it was founded on truth."[37] As Sam launches one of his enraptured monologues, he notices Louie writing. Flattered by the expectation that she is recording his wisdom, he looks over to see, "Shut up, shut up, shut up, shut up, shut up, I can't stand your gassing, oh, what a windbag . . ." (363).

In *The Ordeal of Mark Twain*, Brooks presented his case for attention to Twain's domestic life: since what writers think and feel is "largely determined by personal circumstances and affections," and since "no one will deny that Mark Twain's influence upon our society has been, either in a positive or in a negative way, profound," we must therefore reckon with such matter. Brooks's debunking has certain affinities with Stead's, but they are separated by a fundamental gap, that of Brooks's virulent misogyny. For he argues that New England was "literally emasculated" and that cultural power consequently passed to "old maids" who worked their will through Twain's wife Olivia, ensuring that his subservience to her dulled any serious critical edge his work might have had.[38] In Stead's book, by contrast, Sam carries on Victorian sentimental petty-bourgeois prudery, while Henny practices nihilistic critique. Stead has reversed the gender values and thus suggests, as against Brooks, that our culture needs but suppresses the criticism women could offer.

Edmund Wilson found in Brooks's Twain a model for repressed duality that gave Wilson the basis for his revaluation of Dickens as a covert rebel. In Wilson's appropriation of Brooks's model there occurs a transvaluation with large consequences for academic literary study. For in Brooks the structure of psychological duality explained the divided forces in Twain's work and thus accounted for his failure to achieve the highest literary greatness. Wilson, however, adopts the structure of Brooks's Twain to analyze Dickens, while carrying on from Brooks the positive judgment that Dickens's laughter was socially subversive (as Twain's had not been). By Wilson's dialectic of "the wound and the bow" (like Yeats's insistence on choice between perfection of life or work), the misery of the life explains the great energies of the work. Even though Wilson has been understood as differing from new critics by his emphasis upon history and biography, the principle of paradox works as crucially for him as for them, the wish to find in division not damaging fracture but strengthening tension. George Orwell judged otherwise the effect of Dickens's duality: "Dickens seems to have succeeded in attacking everybody and antagonizing nobody. Naturally this makes one wonder whether after all there was something unreal in his attack upon society."[39] Compare Paine's description of *Innocents Abroad* as "the most daring book of its day," yet received with overwhelming acclaim.[40] I think too how hard it proves to persuade students that the slavery denounced by *Huckleberry Finn* already had been abolished when Twain wrote. I do not mean that popularity automatically makes it impossible for a work to exert socially critical effects; however, some forms of liberal self-criticism are almost impossible to separate from complacency, and therefore radical refunctioning may be needed to set loose the work's potential power.

Both Dickens and Twain were phenomenal successes, parvenus who married up from declining, marginally respectable families and then skyrocketed far beyond. So in their own lives they were always at once the progressive opposition and the status quo itself. Indeed, Marx and Baudelaire could agree that it was the nature of the bourgeoisie to be progressive.[41] And Foucault's work made us increasingly alert to the support individualists like Dickens and Twain gave to the growth of the repressive state apparatus. So Sam Pollit is a self-made man devoted to the growth of agencies of social control, both one who is already a master (as a male) and one whose day is yet to come (because of his economic deprivation).

III

My argument, then, holds that neither Dickens nor Twain is absolutely, objectively critical, complacent, subversive, or anything else. If we accept Benjamin's claim that "there is no document of civilization which is not at the same time a document of barbarism," then it will depend upon circumstances which aspect we emphasize. There are different ways of using cultural objects. To take this seriously requires that we reconceptualize the books and authors we study. It requires abandoning "literature" as an autonomous sphere of aesthetic contemplation, and it requires instead thinking about "media" as potentialities for mediation between the parties in particular cultural transactions. Dickens and Twain, of course, never distanced themselves from either journalism or the speaker's platform, and Sam Pollit's move onto radio charts the next step.

At the 1936 Congress of Writers for the Defense of Culture, held in London, André Malraux defined the "cultural heritage" as created by each civilization "out of everything in the past that helps it to surpass itself," for, "A heritage is not transmitted, it must be conquered." With less grandiloquence, but to the same effect, Orwell began his essay on Dickens, "Dickens is one of those writers who are well worth stealing." That is, he begins as another's and must be made one's own. This dialectic of alienation and appropriation motivates Orwell's pioneering exploration of mass-culture "Boy's Weeklies" no less than his study of Dickens: he wants to figure out how to write such things with a left-wing slant, to reach an otherwise inaccessible audience. For to Orwell, "All art is propaganda."[42]

This process of redeploying cultural powers I have been describing (after Brecht and Benjamin) as refunctioning. So we could say of Stead that her technique refunctions the modernist use of myth. She does not take hallowed myths like Joyce's *Odyssey* or Eliot's grail quest but cultural images just beginning to acquire the apparently independent power of myth. Her content refunctions the critical *Gestalt* of Dickens and Twain. Refusing to validate them either by showing their continuing relevance (Ulysses in Dublin) or by decrying their contemporary degradation (the waste land in London), instead she criticizes them. Her tone refunctions the very "irreverence" that characterized the masculine comic philistine humanist genius of Dickens and Twain and makes it into a woman's weapon against them. In adapting the novel of adolescent development, so vividly revitalized in English by Charlotte Brontë in *Jane Eyre,* Stead does not return directly to the passionate intensity of her female predecessor; she works with and against the literary history by which men had remade Brontë's form, as in *David Copperfield* and *Huckleberry Finn,* and she obliquely refunctions it.

Finally, her book itself contains a model of such refunctioning; it not only enacts but also represents the process. A remarkable sequence begins with Sam's trying to educate Louie about sex. He gives her three books: "Shelley's *Poems* (to help her poetry, said he), Frazer's *Golden Bough* (for the anthropological side of the question, said he), and James Bryce's book on Belgian atrocities (to explain our entry into war and the need for America's policing the world, said he). . . . From the latter two books Louie was able to fill her daydreams and night thoughts with the mysteries of men's violence" (378–79). Not Frazer and Bryce, but Shelley most captivates her. At one point she declaims some startling verses from *The Cenci,* Shelley's tragedy of rape and murder, the conspiracy of fathers against a daughter, which disturb Sam until he "was reassured by the book in her hand, the very one he had given her" (383). She writes her own "Tragedy of the Snakeman," made up of one terrible scene between father and daughter, clearly derived from her excited response to *The Cenci.* She casts it in a language she has invented, which baffles Sam completely. It begins with the father, "Ia deven fecen sigur de ib. A men ocs ib esse crimened de innomen tach. Sid ia lass ib solen por solno or ib grantach." The daughter replies, "Men grantach es solentum. . . . Men juc aun. . . . Ben es bizar den ibid asoc solno is pathen crimenid" (401). (This soon is translated, for Stead deranges the process of signification only as a moment in something larger).

This fascinating performance bears manifold significance for our concern with refunctioning. First, *The Cenci* itself is a revisionary drama. Just as Shelley's *Prometheus Unbound* reverses gender stereotypes by making the female Asia an active quester and the male Prometheus her still, suffering goal, so *The Cenci* presents a Lucrece-figure who kills her victimizer rather than herself, though she finally is condemned to death. Second, Shelley was under severe attack at the time Stead wrote. After his Victorian prestige as the exemplary lyricist, New-Critical modernism dismissed him as technically unsound, illogical, emotionally adolescent, indeed effeminate, compared to the cool, witty logic of the Metaphysical poets. This attack was partly political: Shelley's personal and social radicalism was unwelcome to Eliot and the Agrarians.[43] Stead, then, polemically renews Shelley's cultural dignity by endorsing the use an amateurish, adolescent girl makes of him. Third, Stead shows how what has been handed down as part of patriarchal oppression ("the very [book] he had given her") may be refunctioned. Through her "Tragedy of the Snakeman," which in itself echoes the deaths of Lucrece and Beatrice Cenci, Louie finds the strength to survive her own life, and Stead lets her live. To see this process of use, revision, and transformation worked through within the book helps us to understand Stead's right not only to attack the humanist images of Dickens and Twain that had been transmitted as cultural treasures but also and in the same work to exploit the literary resources that Dickens and Twain left.

This much clarity about its procedures still does not make *The Man Who Loved Children* wholly lucid. In presenting Louie as the young artist breaking free of bourgeois origins, the novel seems too little aware that this model of free artistic development depends upon the bourgeois society it appears to transcend.[44] Yet a version of this issue remains with us today as a crucial topic for debate within feminism. It might be phrased, "Should women's goal be an 'autonomy' comparable to that which men have individually enjoyed?" Or, put another way, "Must the agenda of feminism include a bourgeois revolution for women?" These questions endure, unfinished matters from the thirties and before.

Notes

1. Walter Benjamin, "Theses on the Philosophy of History" (1940), in *Illuminations,* trans. Harry Zohn (1968; rpt. New York: Schocken, 1969), 256.

2. On details of the conference see Herbert R. Lottmann, *The Left Bank: From the Popular Front to the Cold War* (Boston: Houghton Mifflin, 1982) and Roger Shattuck, "Writers for the Defense of Culture," *Partisan Review* 51 (1984).

3. André Malraux, "The Cultural Heritage," trans. Malcolm Cowley, *New Republic* 88 (21 October 1936): 316–17. For further ramifications of this statement, see my essay on F. O. Matthiessen in *The American Renaissance Reconsidered,* ed. Donald E. Pease and Walter Benn Michaels (Baltimore: Johns Hopkins University Press, 1985).

4. Benjamin, "Theses," 256. On further implications of this position for the study of American literature, see Jonathan Arac, "The Politics of *The Scarlet Letter,*" in *Ideology and Classic American Literature,* ed. Sacvan Bercovitch and Myra Jehlen (Cambridge: Cambridge University Press, 1986).

5. Benjamin, "The Author as Producer" (1934), in *Understanding Brecht,* trans. Anna Bostock (London: NLB, 1977).

6. Cf. Laura Kipnis, "Refunctioning Reconsidered: Toward a Left Popular Culture," in *High Theory; Low Culture,* ed. Colin MacCabe (Manchester: University of Manchester Press, 1986).

7. Albert Bigelow Paine, *Mark Twain* (1912; rpt. New York: Chelsea House, 1980), 1:106; 3:1500.

8. Paine, *Mark Twain,* 1:353.

9. Paine, *Mark Twain,* 1:451. See also Twain on Harte as early as 1864 in *The Works of Mark Twain, Early Tales and Sketches* (Berkeley: University of California Press, 1981), 2:470.

10. James M. Cox, *Mark Twain: The Fate of Humor* (Princeton: Princeton University Press, 1966), 20.

11. Van Wyck Brooks, *The Ordeal of Mark Twain* (1920; rev. 1933; rpt. New York: Meridian, 1955), 61, 99, 121, 161, 204, 213.

12. William Dean Howells, review of Paine in *Harper's* (1913), rpt. in Louis J. Budd, ed., *Critical Essays on Mark Twain, 1910–1980* (Boston: Hall, 1983), 37.

13. Louis J. Budd, *Our Mark Twain: the Making of His Public Personality* (Philadelphia: University of Pennsylvania Press, 1983), 121, quoting a formulation about Dickens from John G. Cawelti, "The Writer as Celebrity," *Studies in American Fiction* 5 (1977).

14. George Orwell, "Charles Dickens" (1940), in *Collected Essays: Journalism and Letters* (1968; rpt. Harmondsworth: Penguin, 1970), 1:503.

15. Newton Arvin, "Mark Twain: 1835–1935," *New Republic* (1935), rpt. in Budd, *Critical Essays,* 87.

16. For biography I rely on Joan Lidoff, *Christina Stead* (New York: Ungar, 1982).

17. Lidoff, 203.

18. Christina Stead, *The Man Who Loved Children* (1940; rpt. New York: Holt, Rinehart & Winston, 1965), 259.

19. Stead is aware of further complications. Sam's sister "was neither a married woman nor an old maid, nor a schoolma'am, she was a landlord" (106), while to Ernie, the oldest boy, it is clear that father and mother alike enjoy the power of adults, against whom "children had no rights" (109).

20. José Yglesias, "Marx as Muse," *Nation* (5 April 1965): 369.

21. On relations between nineteenth-century individualism and agencies of social control, see Michel Foucault, *Discipline and Punish,* trans. Alan Sheridan (New York: Pantheon, 1978).

22. *Saturday Review of Literature* 10 (December 16, 1933), 352, cited from Thomas Asa Tenney, *Mark Twain: A Reference Guide* (Boston: Hall, 1977), 108.

23. Budd, *Our Mark Twain,* 12, 71.

24. Professor Philip Collins, University of Leicester, recalled Harry Pollitt when I presented an earlier version of this paper at a conference on Dickens and Twain sponsored by the University of California Dickens Project, August 1984.

25. See, for example, Georg Lukács, "Narrate or Describe?" (1936), in *Writer and Critic* (1971); Erich Auerbach, *Mimesis* (1946), of which the section on Flaubert dates from 1937; Mikhail Bakhtin, "Discourse in the Novel" (1934–35), in *The Dialogic Imagination* (1981).

26. On the apparent irrelevance of feminism during the period in which Stead's novel was neglected, the following testimony is especially striking because it concludes a valuable account of Twain's dealings with Isabella Beecher Hooker, a neighbor and active feminist, in Kenneth R. Andrews *Nook Farm: Mark Twain's Hartford Circle* (Cambridge: Harvard University Press, 1950), 142–43: "Feminism—now of little more vital interest than mohair furniture—was a crucial issue in Mark Twain's Hartford, absorbing all the reformist energies of the city. The

feminists thought the emancipation of women fully as important as the liberation of the Negro. . . . [M]ore persons were active in this reform than in the extension of economic justice."

27. Edmund Wilson, [Review of Van Wyck Brooks] "The Pilgrimage of Henry James" (1925), in *The Shores of Light* (1952; rpt. New York: Random House, 1964), 227.

28. Edmund Wilson, "Dickens: The Two Scrooges" in *The Wound and the Bow* (1941; rpt. with corrections New York: Oxford University Press, 1965), 9.

29. Orwell, "Charles Dickens," in *Collected Essays,* 1:504.

30. Walter Benjamin, "The Storyteller" (1936), in *Illuminations,* 109; German in *Illuminationen* (Frankfurt a.M.: Suhrkamp, 1964), 486.

31. Maurice Merleau-Ponty, *Humanism and Terror* (1947), trans. John O'Neill (Boston: Beacon, 1969), 130.

32. Christina Stead, "The Writers Take Sides," *Left Review* 1, no. 11 (August 1935), 453.

33. Lidoff, *Christina Stead,* 207.

34. I do not have the opportunity here to pursue the problems of how far Stead moves from a purely critical position to a feminism that emphasizes women's positive values for each other.

35. Michel Foucault, "Truth and Power" (1977), in *Power/Knowledge,* ed. Colin Gordon (New York: Pantheon, 1980), 119.

36. Cited from George H. Ford, *Dickens and His Readers* (Princeton: Princeton University Press, 1955), 166.

37. Paine, *Mark Twain,* 2:823.

38. Van Wyck Brooks, *The Ordeal of Mark Twain,* 111, 75, 77.

39. Orwell, "Charles Dickens," in *Collected Essays,* 1:455.

40. Paine, *Mark Twain,* 1:383.

41. This point is strongly emphasized in Marshall Berman, *All That is Solid Melts into Air* (New York: Simon and Schuster, 1982), esp. chs. 2–3; and strongly qualified by Perry Anderson, "Modernity and Revolution," *New Left Review* 144 (March–April 1984).

42. Orwell, *Collected Essays,* 1:454, 529–31, 492.

43. On Shelley's role in theoretical debate, see my "To Regress from the Rigor of Shelley: Figures of History in American Deconstructive Criticism," *boundary 2* vol. 8, no. 3 (Spring 1980). Shelley is associated specifically with left-wing positions at moments in Stead's *House of All Nations* (1938) and *Letty Fox* (1946).

44. For a fuller, nuanced exploration of Louie's development, see Judith Kegan Gardiner, *The Hero as Her Author's Daughter: Jean Rhys, Christina Stead, Doris Lessing* (Indiana University Press), forthcoming.

9

The Asylums of Antaeus: Women, War, and Madness—Is there a Feminist Fetishism?

Jane Marcus

I. New Historicism as Forgetting

The sign of the suffix in the name of the New Historicism indicates a radical dissociation from history as an autonomous form of intellectual inquiry. The "ism" signifies philosophical cynicism about what can be known about reality, past or present. As a literary critical practice, New Historicism names itself as an operation upon a text with no pretensions toward "truth value." As an enhancement of the text, it is the setting for the jewel, the scenery for the play. The text is the thing, of course.

New Historicism is a gargantuan gloss which almost "disappears" the text (as they say in Latin America), a monumental form of marginalia which makes the critic's antiquarian skills superior to the power of the text over the reader. Helpless before history, the postmodern intellectual invents historicism as a game which helps to deny our fears about the relation between what was written and what really happened in the past. This reversal of the not so distant relegation of texts to the marginalia of History indicates a concern with discourse, an insecurity about human agency over language which displaced the hegemony of history as explanation of culture with literary theory as the newly acclaimed master discipline.

The fear of remembering, putting the pieces of our past together, is nowhere more apparent than in the recent revelations about the anti-Semitic and collaborationist essays written by the late Yale critic, Paul de Man, in Belgium during the Second World War. The anti-historical effort of his work, powerful and brilliant as it was, is instantly historicized by this news. We cannot escape from history. Clio claims yet again that memory makes us moral, that history is a primary structure in the kind of culture critique which might explain why de Man's theories were so attractive to American intellectuals.

Historicism is the return of the repressed desire for history, for knowing what happened. The effort to forget is so fierce that its displacement engages the critic in a tremendous effort not to be forgotten himself, to see to it that he and his work are remembered with the same ferocious force as his forgetting. The drive to erase triggers the drive to make a mark. I do not mean that de Man's work derives from guilt over his political past, but that forcing the forgetting of history and politics in the study of texts, he demands that his students remember *him*. Milan Kundera defines forgetting as "absolute injustice and absolute solace at the same time." He argues that the message of *The Book of Laughter and Forgetting* is not Mirek's claim that "The struggle of man against power is the struggle of memory against forgetting." He points out that the character who struggles to ensure that he will be remembered is also doing his utmost to make people forget someone else. "Before it becomes a political issue, the will to forget is an anthropological one: man has always harbored the desire to rewrite his own biography, to change the past, to wipe out tracks, both his own and others."[1]

When New Historicism plays with history to enhance the text, its enhancement is like the colorizing of old movies for present consumption. The denial and defacement of the black and white originals prevents the possibility of cultural critique. Feminist versions of New Historicism allow the recovery of women's texts with the selective enhancement of only certain historical evidence which colors the reader's response with presentist concerns. To learn political lessons from the past we need to have it in black and white.

II. Helen's Plot

If all history (or at least historiography) is a fiction, as contemporary theorists tell us, an interesting question for literary critics is whether all fiction is history. It is easy for the literary critics to accept the new narrativity of historians and, since Michel Foucault, the study of history as a discourse. Can historians, accustomed to raiding the literature of an age for examples, accept an equal revelatory force in fiction as in events as evidence of lived reality? Does a battle lie the way a poem lies, to get at "the truth"? Certainly Elsa Morante's devastating *History: A Novel*, recording as it does the personal experience of politics, anti-semitism, and fascism, the Nazi occupation of Rome and the aftermath of World War II from the point of view of a frightened widow schoolteacher, her epileptic child, "Useppe," born from her rape by a German soldier, and two extraordinary dogs, is a straightforward answer to the literary question.[2] The historical question is increasingly vexed by the work of the "new historicists." And even radical critics like Gayatri Chakravorty Spivak in *In Other Worlds* would suspend postmodern suspicion of "truth-value" in special cases like the Subaltern Studies Group's work on Indian history, but would not extend this to the history of women.

The writing of history is all a matter of the construction of more or less plausible plots. When women read traditional male history, like Virginia

Woolf in *Three Guineas,* they throw up their hands at its bias and prejudice—she claims that for truth, authenticity, and authority, one is forced to use biography, autobiography, and fiction as the true histories of women's lives and interpreters of political events. As Isa Oliver in *Between the Acts* cries, "Is there another plot? Will the author come out of the bushes?"[3] Foucault, like Woolf, has taught us to read the two rhetorics together, the high drama's discourse against the conversation going on between the lines and between the acts, and to see the author/historians' controlling ego like Miss LaTrobe's blood-filled shoes, trampling on the grapes of wrath so that his or her particular truth may go marching on.

How can feminist criticism construct the *other plot* by reading the fictions of history and history in fictions differently? In the marriage of the two disciplines history has often used literature as a handmaiden to provide comic or tragic relief, human interest as a distraction from an unrelenting procession of facts. And for many literary critics those facts have been used as "masculine" proof or support for literary readings. Can this marriage be saved? Can the two work together as partners?[4] Can the plotters recognize that there are other plots as well?

The purpose of the present essay is to destabilize the standard plot of the literature of World War I and its relation to history through a supposedly feminist history by Sandra Gilbert, to demonstrate that history and literature deserve equal narrative force in a cultural text. I find a "double voice" in her text and a reaffirmation of the traditional male plot. I propose a theory of the *feminist fetish,* collating and adapting recent work of Naomi Schor on female fetishism and Tom Mitchell on iconography and commodity fetishism to discuss the poster art and political dress of British Suffragettes.

Early in Virginia Woolf's anti-war novel *Between the Acts,* Lucy Swithin finds in the story of the giant Antaeus in Lempriere's classical dictionary the origin of the superstition to "knock on wood," to ward off evil (the particular evil here is World War II). The wood is the tree of the earth mother, archetypal nurse. Antaeus is the archetype of the patriarchal ethos of war, heroism, and death, calling itself civilization. Because the mother goddess revives him whenever his body falls to earth or touches wood, he is invincible. Ironically this plot depicts death and destruction as protected and perpetrated by the maternal life force. (Antaeus is eventually killed by being crushed in the air with his body separated from mother earth.) Woolf's novel is about what the state does to women when it makes war. *Between the Acts* argues, like *Three Guineas,* that the militaristic patriarchal state needs the collaboration of women to make war and casts her in two crucial and needed roles of mother and nurse. (Women workers, of course, always work.) The state and its servant soldiers need her physical presence as war-nurse or mother in a fetishization of her force as healer.[5]

Whether she collaborates or not, the patriarchy's poet will still claim that the Trojan War was fought over Helen whatever its real economic or imperialistic motives may have been. The "asylums of Antaeus" may be seen as the real and imagined places where the contradictions of her state-enforced roles drive woman mad (where she fights fetishization and fails). She speaks out of the confusion and fear derived from this condition in a double voice.

Studying the rise of Italian fascism, Maria Macchiocci has brilliantly analyzed the state's projection of the roles of mother and nurse on to women, depriving them of other identities while investing the myths of sacred motherhood and war nurse with mysterious powers symbolized in blood. One sees how "She gives life and heals wounds" becomes "men die for her; she caused the wounds," in a deliberate confusion of signs and signifiers.[6] Like Roberto Rossellini's film, *The White Ship* (1941), the propaganda posters of the British War Office contained this double message and it is repeated in the misogynous poems of D. H. Lawrence and Wilfred Owen and in Ernest Hemingway's *The Sun Also Rises*. Virginia Woolf protested against the state's distorting propaganda about war nurses in the scene in *The Years* where Peggy and Eleanor pass the statue of the martyred war heroine, Nurse Edith Cavell, shot by the Germans in Belgium. Eleanor thinks that the only sensible words uttered in the Great War were Cavell's "Patriotism is not enough." Though these words are inscribed in small letters at the base of the statue, the state has erased its enemy by bannering the opposite sentiment "For King and Country" in large letters at the top, denying Cavell's radical pacifism and imaging her for their own ends.[7] Peggy sees the figure as like "an advertisement for sanitary napkins," linking menstrual blood and soldiers' wounds precisely as the war propagandists wished its observers to do.

The *double voice* of the statue of Nurse Cavell, its feminist pacifism overlaid by the patriarchal state's jingoistic "For King and Country," like Isa's confusion about "what we must remember, what we must forget" in *Between the Acts,* is a text for studying women in war-time. Sandra Gilbert in *The Madwoman in the Attic* (written with Susan Gubar), already a classic in feminist criticism, has taught us to hear another intonation of the double voice in women's texts. Consequently, it is disheartening and confusing for readers to make sense of her "Soldier's Heart: Literary Men, Literary Women and the Great War."[8] My problem with reading the essay suggests that we need to understand the implications of our methodologies and to analyze the plots of our own essays. In replacing the double message of "soldier's heart" with Nurse Cavell's bandage, the image of "No Man's Land" with the image of the "asylums of Antaeus," one is offering another plot, but not *the* plot. Ideologically, the essay reassures man that certain forms of feminism will not foil their ancient plot or attempt to topple the temple. Gilbert speaks a plot as double-voiced as the writers whose subtexts she so brilliantly explored in *The Madwoman in the Attic*. But the voices don't speak together.

The over-voice is critical; the under-voice raids history for real examples of male fantasies about women, neglecting the recent works of feminist historians to replace women in the period, e.g. Martha Vicinus's *Independent Women*. Gilbert's essay also confirms the status of the male canon of war literature from Lawrence to Hemingway to Owen. It argues that their vision of women as bloodthirsty vampires who gloat over men's death and derive pleasure and profit from war is correct.

Had the essay centered itself on women's war writing rather than men's, had it been addressed to women readers instead of confusing and "othering" women readers, "Soldier's Heart" might have critiqued the patriarchy. World War I in fact wiped out women's culture, one might argue instead. At the height of the suffrage movement in 1911 there were twenty-one regular feminist periodicals in England, a women's press, a feminist bookshop, the Fawcett Library, and a bank run by and for women. The war decimated that impressive coalition.

Gilbert's essay is illustrated with several posters from the Imperial War Museum, but it does not examine the ideological propaganda machine which produced these mythic mothers, nurses, and young jingoes who demand that men go and fight. It assumes uncritically that women created these images or approved them: it agrees with male writers that war "suggests female conquest" (424) and that during wartime women become "even more powerful," a contradiction of her previous argument (423) that women were "powerless." Each of these statements is directed to a different audience. Gilbert states that the war dispossessed men of "patriarchal primacy" while it gave women votes and jobs. In actual fact, British women did not get the vote until 1928; in 1918 only women over 30 with the property qualifications got votes.[9] Gilbert's characterization of women's "sexual glee" as well as guilt at surviving the war seems to me utterly wrong. Elizabeth Robins records her rage in *Ancilla's Share* that women workers were dispossessed of their jobs when the men returned and thinks the suffragettes were mistaken in suspending their activities, since they were worse off economically after the war. Over 66,000 enlisted women and 1,200 officers lost their jobs, as well as thousands of W.A.A.C.'s, W.R.A.F.'s, W.R.E.N.'s, V.A.D.'s, and women police, not to mention that wholesale turnout of women in Civil Service and the new rule against marriage for teachers and civil servants.[10]

What does Gilbert mean when she says that women had "no sense of inherited history to lose?" The suffrage movement had produced, just as our own movement today has done, a spate of histories of women; "The Pageant of Great Women" was regularly produced on stage and every reader of the weekly *Votes for Women* knew by heart the fifty-year history of the struggle for the vote, for education, for jobs, and professional training. The state asked women to forget that newly acquired "history" and to sacrifice yet again their own desire for social freedom and political equality.[11] Many of them did not. The women's movement provided its own plot and for the first time women did have a "sense of inherited history."

Gilbert might have compared the figures in the government posters to the figures designed by women themselves. Not nurses or mothers, the suffragettes' icon was Joan of Arc, the militant maiden out for vengeance. Armed and chaste, she symbolized struggle, a *real* battle of the sexes for ownership of women's sexuality, and a conscious feminist fetishization. That she was armed, and neither maternal nor a nurse, was part of her power. The state's posters were a direct response to the suffragettes' images of themselves as virgin warriors.

When Gilbert asks "Does male death turn women nurses on?" (436) and "Was the war a festival of female misrule . . .?" (437) one can only reply that she is asking the wrong questions. In the "war of the images" which Gilbert declares is our heritage from this war, she has declared her partisanship with the images created by the state propaganda machine, with Owen and Lawrence, and male establishment historians. Women workers, writers, and political thinkers deserve more than the lower half of a double discourse. Critical fetishization of these familiar female figures is not inscribed in a feminist plot.

The plot of Gilbert's history is prophetically overturned by a fiction of Antonia White called "Surprise Visit" in which the heroine, a publisher's assistant in London, revisits Bedlam, the madhouse, where she, like so many other women who were not "empowered" by World War I, was incarcerated. The plot of this fiction proposes another history. The women's asylum has become the Imperial War Museum. Among the tanks and guns and uniformed figures, Julia Tye is driven mad again by a statue of a nurse, the figure of the propaganda machine created to keep women in line, as well as men: "Then she saw the figure standing deceptively still . . . a uniformed nurse, staring fixedly at her and coldly smiling. Now she knew for certain where she was and who she was. She sagged down on her knees, whimpering: 'No . . . Not the pads! I'll be good, Nurse Roberts, I'll be good.' "[12]

The pads may be read as the patriarchal straitjacket, and Julia Tye's voice the feminist who is intimidated by a powerful restraining woman's voice insisting that women be read as men see them. In the "surprise visit" to her own past and the horrible connection between men's war and women's madness expressed vividly in the spatial metaphor of institutional enclosure, the hospital for madwomen turned into the museum of war and death, Antonia White treats the unspoken and unwritten history of the suffering of her own generation of war widows. When she sees the church-like dome of the old Wren Building her mind reverts to its sepia image stamped on the asylum's plates—from inside the patients see the outside, the image a reward for having cleaned their plates, suggesting an anorexic subtext to the script of women's madness in which the matriarchs enforce patriarchal prescriptions. The story reaches far beyond its autobiographical subject, the madness treated in *Beyond the Glass*. Written late in White's life, in 1965, this story expresses the *"abjection"* Julia Kristeva defines as that which is excluded from phallocentric discourse, a gesture of the feminist "political unconscious" against the kind of male history which buries women's madness in the war museum. It is an effective antidote to Gilbert's treatment of the "sexual glee" of women in wartime Britain. The horrors of Bedlam are erased, as women's history always is, by airplane propellers and gas masks. The ideology of male valor remains a powerful force so that women are still ashamed to claim their mental suffering as equal to that of crippling or death on the battlefield. White's fiction is women's history.

In her autobiography, *As Once in May,* Antonia White vividly recalled her first clear memory of her father, the classics master, standing at the hearth under "the gilt and marble clock in the shape of the Parthenon," with the black marble fireplace framing her in memory forever in woman's place in a Mausoleum of Classical Patriarchy. Daddy's Girl under the middle-class mantle is like Sylvia Townsend Warner's young Osbert's lost mate in "Cottage Mantleshelf." White's father taught her to recite, at age three, in Greek, the first line of the *Iliad*: "Sing, oh Goddess, the wrath of Achilles . . ." He taught her "to give things their right names" and would not tolerate "baby talk," initiating her into the "symbolic" order of language very early. Women, goddesses or not, have been singing the wrath of Achilles for far too long (228).[13] Yet, Antonia White eventually sang her own wrath, the missing song in men's war memorials, refusing to be "good" for the patriarchal nurse. Bedlam become the Imperial War Museum is the "asylum of Antaeus," the site of convergence of the female with war and madness, the heart of one of the unsung *other* plots.

"Patriotism is not enough" is what Nurse Cavell really said. It is her voice we need to hear, not the voice of the propaganda portraits of the nurse as the patriarchy's policewoman.

A more fruitful inquiry might be to translate Fredric Jameson's "political unconscious" so that gender becomes a workable component of the theory. The effect of Gilbert's essay is to affirm male hegemony in action in World War I, male literary hegemony over writing in this period, and male cultural hegemony over images of women, to insist that Helen's text must record only Achilles's wrath. A "feminist" New Historicism is thus even more limited and dangerous than other varieties of this technique.

The ideological conjunction of women, war, and madness is expressed even more dramatically by Antonia White's 1928 story, "The House of Clouds." Lyrically surreal, it captures the historical reality of the mental instability of war-widows because it breaks down the stable relation of narrative authority and the text floats in hallucination, forcing the reader to experience Helen's visions as Woolf does with Septimus in *Mrs. Dalloway*. Hints of ambiguous sexuality and transvestism unsettle both texts. Septimus's moment of joy comes in Rezia's hat covered with roses. Helen is whisked off to the madhouse in a nightgown and her husband's army overcoat. The dirty trench coat is a recurring figure in women's writing of WWI. "The House of Clouds" details the stages of making a grieving woman into an "Inmate" of an institution, straitjacket, drugs, forcible feeding, cold baths, solitary confinement.

When she is first put in the asylum White's Helen recalls her fear of her father and the doctor: "They were going to take her away to use her as an experiment. Something about the war" (47). This personal "neurosis" seems to me an "accurate" historical account of what happens to women in wartime. " 'Morphia, morphia, put an M on my forehead,' she moaned in a man's voice" (47). Her vocal transvestism makes her a female Orpheus, Orphia/Ophelia speaking women's madness and poetry. She is marked as a prisoner of Man, ventriloquist of his mandate that she must not kill herself, marked as war always marks woman, for Motherhood. She hears voices and she conflates the two oppressive war poster figures of nurse and mother.

White here deconstructs the valorization of valor in the literature of heroism. Those militant mothers who willingly sacrifice their sons in war, pictured in the papers opening bazaars with stiff upper lips, also figure in Woolf's portraits of the matriarchal Lady Bruton and Lady Bradshaw in *Mrs. Dalloway*, and even more powerfully in Helen Zenna Smith's (Evadne Price) *Not So Quiet*... Virginia Woolf, Antonia White, and Sylvia Townsend Warner, unlike Sandra Gilbert, understood the true obscenity of British official war propaganda in its mobilizing of icons of motherhood and nursing for their destructive patriotic ends. Gilbert reads the enormous abstract *pietà* of nurse-mother, holding a small wounded soldier on a stretcher as proof that women were thrilled at their power over invalid men. The poster is titled "The Greatest Mother in the World," and it may have been constructed by a clever propagandist to appeal to the recruits' fears of the maternal, but the abstraction of the figure and her iconographic relation to the virgin mother also signals that war and motherhood are complicit. It is also perfectly obvious that this poster is an insidious simple reversal of the famous forcible-feeding suffrage poster in which the doctor and nurses appear to "rape" a suffragette victim.

Antonia White's "House of Clouds" is another of the asylums of Antaeus, where the forbidding nurse-mother figure is seen for what she is, the policewoman of patriarchy, the woman who enforces in other women the continued complicity of motherhood and war. White sings Helen's song, not the wrath of Achilles, but woman as horse in men's war games. Helen sees herself in the mirror as a fairy horse "ridden almost to death" or a stag with antlers, and "dark, stony eyes and nostrils red as blood. She threw up her head and neighed and made a dash for the door" (53). The nurses drag her along iron tracks to her room:

> She came out of this dream suddenly to find herself being tortured as a human being. She was lying on her back with two nurses holding her down. A young man with a signet ring was bending over her, holding a funnel with a long tube attached. He forced the tube down her nose and began to pour some liquid down her throat. There was a searing pain at the back of her nose: she choked and struggled, but they held her down ruthlessly. At last the man drew out the tube and dropped it coiling in a basin. (55)

This scene of forcible feeding of a woman in a mental hospital after the war recalls with vivid intensity the experiences of the suffragettes who hunger-struck in Holloway Gaol before the war and were forcibly fed on government orders, a particularly violent response to passive resistance as a political strategy by the feminists, and a very ugly chapter in British history depicted in a well-known suffrage poster. Women died and were disabled by forcible feeding. Their lungs often filled with liquid. Constance Lytton never recovered. The madwoman and the suffragette are joined in this scene, as they are joined in *women's history*. (Constance Lytton's 1914 memoirs, *Prisons and Prisoners* has been reprinted with a new introduction by Midge Mackenzie, London: Virago, 1988).

This joining sharply indicates the necessity to free women's history from the yoke of male periodization, as Joan Kelly asked, "Did Women Have a Renaissance?", and as Joan Scott argues in her essay, "Rewriting History," in *Behind the Lines*. If Gilbert's study had been written as women's history rather than "historicism," it would have avoided centering on men's war and seeing women only in subordinate relation to it. In women's history, the pre-war cultural achievements of women in politics and art reached a high point from 1906–1914. The War Office's propaganda posters (and those of British Rail) of nurses, mothers, and wives sending their men to war were a *response* to the overwhelming powerful public iconography of the women's suffrage movement, a challenge to the figures of Amazon Joan of Arc, the virgin warrior and the professional single woman drawn as the protector of mothers and children. The image of the powerful single woman at work or as the champion of her sex, the great posters of female victimization, the woman being forcibly fed and the Cat and Mouse Act poster which drama-tized the Liberal Government's release of hunger-strikers only to pounce and re-arrest them when they spoke in public, had to be wiped out of the public mind by the only images of women allowed by a nation at war, the nurse, the mother, the worker. One could argue that the propagandists had to work particularly hard to erase the powerful new images created by women for women at the height of the movement. Certainly the symbolic purple, white, and green colors of the Women's Social and Political Union, their glorious banners, buttons, parades, processions, pageants, and public displays, as well as the weekly posters produced by the suffrage atelier and distributed all over the country, were a daunting feminist propaganda machine, whose effects had to be countered by an equally powerful official propaganda. The enormous matriarchs and fearfully forbidding phallic mothers and stern young wives pointing equally phallic fingers, urging men to go and fight, cannot in any sense be seen as women's images of themselves, but rather as such effective patriarchal projections that ordinary soldiers and university-educated poets could blame the women at home for the deaths of their comrades. Psychologically sophisticated, the War Office "artists" provided the people with a phallic mother fetish which deflected their sexual anxiety and controlled the (natural) fear of castration and wounding in war-time. If we make a feminist revision of Tom Mitchell's fine study of the history of the rhetoric of iconoclasm, we may begin to understand the process. The idol-smashers historically see the childish pagan and primitive "others" as irrational and obscene, he argues. "The rhetoric of iconoclasm is thus a rhetoric of exclusion and domination, a caricature . . . The images of the idolators are typically phallic . . . and thus they must be emasculated, femi-nized, have their tongues cut off by denying them the power of expression or eloquence" (113). (Of course, Mitchell is concerned here with male high art and politics and aesthetics in Gotthold Lessing and Edmund Burke.) Official government idol-smashing of women's self-images in World War I works on the popular level of taste, and functioned well in Punch cartoons and newspaper drawings, where valorous virgins became hateful spinsters, or comic viragoes. Especially effective were captions in newspaper photos of police beating the suffragettes, which declared that violent revolutionaries were attacking law and order. (The text denied the image.) Well-dressed women in the photos are shown with their hair being pulled by rowdies and the violence is projected onto the victim. Thus the male script of iconoclasm toward women's images may be seen as a masculinizing of the female image, the war posters being a particularly good example of the *exclusion* of figures of happy and successful unmarried women and the substitution of phallic mothers.[14]

Proof of the power of the male iconoclastic script of devaluation of women's self-image is that the suffragettes' extraordinary renaissance of women's political art came to be seen, not only by the public, but by socialist feminist Labour Party leaders, as the suspicious *cause* of fascism. In 1939 in *The New Propaganda* (Left Bookclub), Amber Blanco White, twice a Labour candidate in parliamentary elections, and daughter of Mrs. Pember Reeves, an active Fabian feminist, wrote:

The actual methods now so widely used were first made use of by the Suffragettes. They introduced the practice of advertising a political movement by deliberate "publicity stunts" as an adjunct to the preaching of its doctrines. Such devices as chaining one woman to the railings in Downing Street and posting another as a parcel addressed to the Prime Minister—their processions, their window-smashing, their self-imposed martyrdoms—would all have commended themselves (if used by his own side) to an up-to-date Minister of Propaganda. The Suffragettes also adopted, for use among their own followers as distinct from the public, the same means for whipping up excitement, the same emotional appeals for sacrifices, the same technique for arousing irrational hostility against their opponents as the Fascist dictators are now employing to keep their followers in order. Theirs was in fact, towards the end, an organization run on Fascist lines and characterized by an authentically Fascist violence and emotionalism and exaggerations. (11)

This chilling analysis, comparing fascism to the violence and emotionalism of women, repeats exactly the Tom Mitchell formula for historical iconoclasm. Fascism, this most patriarchal of political movements is feminized by its left-wing enemy in order to be discredited. Amber Blanco White has been dispossessed of her own history as a woman and has internalized a male moral judgment of her sisters, who did in fact, win the vote for her, as monsters.[15]

III.   The Semiotics and Somatics of Woman's Suffrage[16]

The somatics and semiotics of Women's Suffrage in England deserves a much more thorough study than I can outline here. A massive feminist iconology was created from 1906–1914, drawing one imagines on traditional symbolism in the purple (suffering or loyalty), white (purity), and green (hope), of the colors of the W.S.P.U. In the first concerted effort of women to create their own self-images after centuries of imprisonment by male images of women, the suffrage artists—including Clemence and Laurence Housman in the Suffrage Atelier in Kensington, and the Artists' Suffrage League in Chelsea—used every conceivable style from Slade School of Pre-Raphaelitism to the socialist realism of Sylvia Pankhurst's prison sketches. Women also moved into public space in a great body, literally and figuratively. Aware of the dangers, they costumed themselves for each occasion, in their rose-laden hats and best Edwardian ladylike dresses, in academic gowns or clothes and banners symbolizing their work, processions of girls in white dresses flanked by vanguards of Joan of Arcs on horseback. They dressed up as historical heroines in *The Pageant of Great Women*; Annie Kenney was paraded at Christabel Pankhurst's side in the clogs and apron of a mill girl long after she had left Lancashire behind. The leaders were photographed and enshrined on posters in their Holloway Prison uniforms to glamorize their hunger strikes. Photographs of Mrs. Pankhurst and a host of other leaders were as popular as those of actresses, and middle-class married women in the country worked long hours on eloquent silk flags and banners signifying regional, religious, or occupational women's organizations, to be carried in mass demonstrations.

The art of the posters, flyers, and pamphlets ranged as wide as support for suffrage across classes and varied in intensity, class bias, or idealization of women. Some of it draws deliberately on fashion or sentimental ideals, while other posters burst with the cartoon vigor of revolutionary propaganda art. Deliberate fetishism in costume and disguise in the W.S.P.U. loosened rigid ideas about dress. Some young women cropped their hair and wore tailored coats and skirts with Byronic silk shirts and ties, like Cicely Hamilton and Christopher St. John of the Actresses' Franchise League. Ancient Mrs. Wolstenholme-Elmy marched in her beaded black Victorian gown and bonnet. Militant Christabel Pankhurst, who planned the window-smashing demonstration in Bond Street, was photographed for her followers in the most ethereal Paris dresses. Then she would appear on the platform in the academic gown, which symbolized the law degree she had earned but could never use as a woman. The signs changed in the feminist semiotic system. They played every aspect of public attitudes toward women, sliding the signifiers of powerlessness marking the inferiority of classical feminine stereotypes into their opposites, exploiting even the most appalling victimization through forcible feeding when they were on hunger strike, or the Cat and Mouse Act, which allowed the suffragettes to go without food until the point of death, then released them to re-arrest them as soon as they spoke in public.

These two posters—on forcible feeding and Cat and Mouse—strike me as particularly important in the semiotic "discourse" of suffrage. The crude "rhetoric" of these posters allowed them to be read as rape scenes, and invested them with a permissible rage on the part of the viewer at male violence, in the government cat who molested the mouse, the doctors and nurses who held down the victim and forced liquid into her nose. The forcible-feeding/rape poster also recalls the famous picture of the French psychiatrist, Jean Martin Charcot, hypnotizing a hysterical patient, conflating the government treatment of women political prisoners who were struggling for the vote with helpless victimized women in insane asylums. (For forcible feeding of pacifists see John Rodker, *Memoirs of Other Fronts,* [London: Putnam, 1930].) I raise this issue of clear expression of male violence in suffrage semiotics, because it is expressly denied by Paula Hays Harper in a misinformed essay on suffrage posters, drawing on an extremely small sample and unaware, apparently, of the enormous collections in the London Museum and the Fawcett Library, as well as their rich variety of artistic styles.[17] Arguing that the posters "have little aesthetic quality," Harper claims that they are all "conventional" and reflect the collusion of women "with the social status quo," and represented an appeal by middle-class women to men. Their tremendous range, from conservative to radical aesthetically, as well as in terms of content, actually reflects a much more complex situation. The suffrage agitation represented all classes and many special interest groups of women from right to left politically, from anarchists and socialists to Catholics and members of the Primrose League. Iconography was the field on which they fought out their political differences. Decorative art nouveau frames and borders for idealized Pre-Raphaelite figures were early movement appeals to popular images of women, but the art changed as the movement changed.

It seems to me that women's poster art, and its borderline status between commercial art and painting, should be as important to modern women's history as photography is to Modernism in general. Women naturally drew on commercial fashion art which was aimed at them and transformed it for political purposes—one might say they *translated semiotically the signs of commodity fetishism into a deliberate feminist fetishism*. Their first move was to de-eroticize the common images they stole from the Pre-Raphaelites. Their last move, before they were crushed by atavistic matriarchal martial iconoclasm, was to depict rape and male violence against women, including the "bestiality" of the cat and mouse. Their effectiveness is quite obvious in Amber Pember Reeves's iconophobia of the thirties, in which fear of fascist propaganda causes her to remember and blame the suffragettes' posters. She does not remember the pretty Pre-Raphaelites but rather the women chained to the railings. Harper claims that suffrage posters lack audacity and refuse to attack men and are thus weak both artistically and politically. The innocent reader would be convinced that women didn't deserve the vote, as Gilbert's essay argues that women gained a wicked pleasure from the deaths of men in World War I. Neither essay does justice to women's history, though both may eventually be seen as functioning within criticism as certain wings of the suffrage movement did in reassuring men that feminists mean no harm to the establishment.

Stories of the somatics of the suffrage struggle enliven all the memoirs of its participants. They all take particular pleasure in recounting the ways in which exploitation of their femininity foiled the police or the government. When the beatings of police and rowdies at demonstrations grew severe, they carried hat pins and wore cardboard "armour" *under* their dresses to carry off their ladylike image. Elizabeth Robins, the American actress, contributed her experience of the effect of dress to the policy of the board of the W.S.P.U. She wrote of dressing as a poor woman in London at night and the response of men, convincing upper-class women that the same men who were good husbands and fathers were violent and rude to women of other classes. There was obviously a great deal of play-acting and political "travesty" in cross-class dressing within the movement, which brings out the conjunction of the Freudian concept of fetishism with the Marxist in this instance of what I shall call *feminist fetishism.*

Lady Rhondda, the founder of *Time and Tide* and the Six-Point Group, recalls a characteristic experience:

> Aunt Janetta, carrying a small and unobtrusive parcel, which was in fact a hammer done up in brown paper, strolled down Oxford Street. She was a beautiful woman . . . with soft curly hair and a very gentle and spiritual face— the face of a saint—and she dressed well. It would have needed a wily policeman to identify her with the popular view of the Shrieking Sisterhood. Opposite the windows of D. H. Evans she stopped, and, murmuring to herself "Whatsoever thy hand findeth to do, do it with all thy might," upped with the hammer and splintered the window. (162)[18]

After breaking several windows she was arrested. As soon as she was out on bail, Lady Rhondda relates, she went back to D. H. Evans and bought a hat, "for she was a most scrupulous woman." The smashing of the Bond Street windows by women dressed exactly like the mannequins on the other side of the glass is telling example of feminist semiotics in the service of an attack on commodity fetishism. It also doesn't take a Freudian to explain the effect of feminine sexual solidarity in those masses of huge, flower-bedecked Edwardian hats as they marched in the West End, smashing the icons of their oppression while wearing them as emblems of class and gender. One of the funniest moments in Dame Ethel Smyth's *Streaks of Life* is the story of the dignified Mrs. Pankhurst's determination to overcome her inability to throw rocks and the composer's devotion of a day to teaching and practice before one of their "raids." Her self-sufficiency as a pure warrior and her chastity frightened men as much as it excited women, and it epitomized a valorous concept of female chivalry, exploiting all the iconography of lady and knight inside an expanded definition of the female. During the war Christabel was able to translate this figure directly into a phallic and jingoistic Britannia, but at the height of the suffrage movement, she stood for invincibility against male sexuality and a code of honor among women which played on medieval chivalry by role-playing on the field of femininity, rewarding with favors and ribbons and celebratory dinners and breakfasts the heroic women who survived the horrors of forcible feeding in jail and those who were molested and beaten in brutal police attacks, like "Black Friday."

This brilliant political use of pageantry and ritual eroticized real danger and the threat of death, honoring wounded veterans of the "sex war" as heroines for their physical courage. It is one of the few recorded historical moments of concerted public physical bravery on the part of women as a sex, and consequently has received little attention from historians except those wishing to discredit the somatics of suffrage chivalry as collective "hysteria." Joan Kelly has pointed out that cross-dressing, the carrying of weapons and chivalric codes existed before the seventeenth century among European women. Thus Christabel may be seen as the restorer of arms to the women. The suffrage movement was the training ground for disciplined V.A.D. nurses and ambulance drivers who served in WWI the state which had molested and imprisoned them.

For Edwardian women to expose themselves deliberately to the bullying and brutality which accompanied their demonstrations and to suffer the searing pain of hunger striking and forcible feeding was to make explicit the sexual dimensions of state-condoned misogyny, to point out to the public and to themselves that their common experience as women was unmistakably the experience of rape. In the libidinal economy of suffrage a political rape victim was a heroine, not a social outcast, thus they established their solidarity with poor prostitutes and unwed mothers. The suffrage struggle fetishized female suffering so that women of all classes could identify with its production of a specifically female code of honor, a serious threat to male historical dismissal of women as creatures without a sense of honor, or as Freud would put it, without a superego. Women were outraged by heavily circulated suffragette photos of frail Mrs. Pankhurst fainting in the arms of a policeman and the staged photos of Emmeline and Christabel in prison uniform, fusing the lady and the criminal.

Another example comes from the recent memoirs of actress Elsa Lanchester.[19] I quote them because they may serve to dispel the myth that the suffrage movement was totally middle class and also because they indicate the use of asylums in political reprisals against feminists. The memoirs are interesting in themselves. The reader who expects to find only the story of her marriage to Charles Laughton is instead confronted with Lanchester's life-long obsession with her radical mother, Edith, known as "Biddy." As one of the first generation of Cambridge-educated upper-class women, Edith joined the S.D.F., became Eleanor Marx's secretary and set up housekeeping with Elsa's father, an Irish working man named Shamus Sullivan. Edith's father and brothers "kidnapped" Elsa's mother and had her certified as insane. The document committing her listed the "supposed cause" of her madness as "over-education" (2). The incident became an international *cause célèbre* on the left and crowds of demonstrators outside the asylum soon won her release to "live in sin" with Shamus. She remained a staunch communist and feminist until her death. Elsa recalls that she went often as a small child with a contingent of leftists to march in suffrage demonstrations, and her mother went to jail:

> Instead of waving red flags and wearing buttons saying S.D.F., we waved green, white and purple flags and wore clothes of those colors, with buttons saying W.S.P.U. There was one awful rally when, encircled by the police in chain

formation, the vast crowd became a jellified mass moving as one. Biddy shouted to me, below her waist level, "keep your arms down!" "Yes!" screamed Shamus, "Keep your arms down, girlie, don't reach up, they might get broken." Another time when I was with Biddy at a suffragette rally I was pushed into a doorway in Scotland Yard. The police all had truncheons and were banging women on the head. I screamed a lot, I think but the whole thing now is oddly still a *picture with no sound at all*. (17; emphasis added)[20]

Elsa Lanchester's vivid memory, after seventy years, of male violence against woman as a "*picture with no sound at all*" suggests an iconophilia bred by the somatics and semiotics of suffrage, which taught her to see women's bodies as feminist fetish. Their words are erased even in dreams. Exactly the opposite is true of Amber Blanco White's iconophobia, linking feminist fetishization with fascism. Both women were the daughters of active political mothers. Amber Blanco White was actually the mistress of H. G. Wells, and the model for the suffragette in his novel, *Ann Veronica*. What Lanchester and White have in common is an identification of feminism with pictures, not words, with spatial modernism, for the suffrage campaign's visual iconography does indeed anticipate all contemporary political campaigns in its non-verbal rhetoric. In their breaking of the images of male false goddesses and creation of new female forms, the iconoclastic suffragettes were self-subverted by the war posters and the historical accusation of serving fascism. Tom Mitchell quotes Jean Baudrillard on how this rhetoric of fetishism comes back to haunt those who use it (205).

Mitchell argues, however, that Marx's concept of fetishization could be more useful to aesthetic analysis than the concept of ideology. It is clear from the suffragettes' art that commodity fetishism serves more than a bourgeois class function, and equally clear that psychological fetishism rises from the female unconscious as well as the male, and that both are inscribed in cultural texts. They may also be consciously exploited by political artists (see Lillian Robinson's *Sex, Class and Culture*). What I have tried to do in this paper is to use Mitchell's suggestion along with Naomi Schor's work on a revision of Freud's concept of fetishism to extend to the female case. Schor follows Sarah Kofman's argument in *The Enigma of Woman* that fetishism is not a perversion peculiar to men and that female fetishism articulates a paradigm of undecidability, an oscillation between denial and recognition of castration, a strategy which allows a woman to keep her human bisexuality from being anchored to one pole. Schor examines female fetishism in George Sand: "Indeed, I would suggest that ultimately *female travesty,* in the sense of women dressing up as or impersonating other women, constitutes by far the most disruptive form of *bisexuality*: for, whereas there is a long, venerable tradition of naturalized intersexual travesty in fiction, drama and opera, the exchange of *female* identities, the blurring of difference within difference remains a largely marginal and unfamiliar form" (370).[21]

In my extension of Mitchell's Marx to female subversion of commodity fetishism and Schor's Freud from female to feminist fetishism, I am suggesting that the suffrage movement deliberately created multiple new images of women as a political act, unsettling female identity in the process. The fetish was less a maternal phallus (as is clear in the war posters) or an "oscillation between denial and recognition of castration," than an oscillation between denial and recognition of *rape* as the common denominator of female experience. The question for the suffrage propagandists was whether or not to depict (and therefore call down on themselves) representations of their own victimization at the hands of male violence.

Examples of Schor's *bisexuality* may be found, however, in the poster rhetoric of W.W.I and the "trench coat" in women's war fiction, Antonia White's "inmates": the narrative rejection of firm boundaries between characters in Virginia Woolf's *The Waves* and much women's fiction up to and including Grace Paley, and especially Marilynne Robinson's *Housekeeping* (1981). The perfect case of "bisextuality" is in the lesbian costume party in Djuna Barnes's *Nightwood*, as well as the tattoos, writing on the body, and the merging of costume and flesh in the whole novel. Miss Bruce in Jean Rhys's short story, "Illusion," who collects sensuous dresses but dresses in public in tweeds is another example of female fetishism. Female identity is startlingly unsettled in the recently reprinted novels of Molly Keane (M. J. Farrell) where one character's harelip becomes an erotic attraction and women characters wear each other's clothes. The phenomenon of female fetishism was only marginal and unfamiliar until Naomi Schor named it. My naming of *feminist fetishism* and the narration of its failure to survive wartime iconoclasm is clearly complicit in a new iconoclasm and placed in opposition to "feminist" versions of "New Historicism." The reprinting of women's novels about World War I by the Feminist Press and Virago should encourage historians to answer historicists. Standard versions of Modernism may then be interrogated and classic men's war novels will look very different in justaposition to the women's texts. It all depends on the way one reads Woolf's "what we must remember, what we must forget."

Notes

This essay is a short version of a paper which appears in *The Differences Within: Feminism and Critical Theory,* ed. Elizabeth Meese and Alice Parker (Philadelphia: John Benjamins, 1988). My thanks to the editors, Angela Ingram, Tom Foster, Blanche Cook, and Catharine Stimpson for their helpful comments.

1. Milan Kundera, *New York Times Book Review,* March 6, 1988. For a feminist discussion of New Historicism see Lynda Boose, "The Family in Shakespeare Studies or Studies in the Family of Shakespeareans or the Politics of Politics," *Renaissance Quarterly,* vol. XL, no. 4, 1987, 707–42. For a discussion of these issues see Paul Veyne, *Writing History* (Middletown, Conn.: Wesleyan University Press, 1986); Domonick LaCapra, *History and Criticism* (Ithaca:

Cornell University Press, 1986); and Hayden White's review essay, "Between Science and Symbol," *TLS* (Jan. 31, 1986): 109–10.

2. Elsa Morante, *History: A Novel* (New York: Random House, 1984). Focusing on the experience of catastrophic events by domestic animals, children, and women, this novel transgresses the borders between the two disciplines and questions the unspoken division in Western culture between the virility of "history" and the femininity of "art," which clearly privileges the former as truth-bearer.

3. The formalist nature of much post-structural exegesis has dismissed biography, autobiography, historical and textual studies as uninteresting literary practice. However, like Woolf, feminists are searching women's autobiographies, debating—as in the 1986 Stanford Conference on Autobiography and Gender and several forthcoming collections of essays edited by Domna Stanton (*N.Y. Literay Forum*), Shari Benstock (*The Private Self*, University of North Carolina Press), and Celeste Schenck and Bella Brodsky (*Life/Lines*, Cornell)—their value as "truth" in relation to the concept of the fictionality of all texts. Problematic for feminists is the issue of maintaining skepticism about authority in uncanonized and unread texts and the wish to share our reading pleasure with a large audience. We are often unwilling to make that last deconstructive turn of undermining our own readings of these neglected works until they have been recuperated fully into literary history, though critics like Gayatri Chakravorty Spivak, Elizabeth Meese, and Shari Benstock are negotiating a plot which unites deconstruction with feminism.

4. For a provocative discussion of disciplines as couples, see Alice Jardine, "Death Sentences: Writing Couples and Ideology," *The Female Body in Western Culture*, ed. Susan Suleiman (Cambridge: Harvard University Press, 1986), 84–96.

5. In "The Matrix of War: Mothers and Heroes," in *The Female Body in Western Culture*, Nancy Huston argues from "myth and historical archtetypes" that "men make war *because* women have children" (119). For a terrifying example of the post-war militarization of motherhood comparable to Rosemary Manning's novel about the militarization of women's education (*The Chinese Garden* [London: Brilliance Books, 1962]), see Enid Bagnold's *The Squire* (1938; rpt. London: Virago/Penguin, 1987). Her 1917 *A Diary Without Dates* got her dismissed as a V.A.D. nurse, and *The Happy Foreigner* (1920; rpt. London: Virago, 1986) is a documentary novel about her stint with the French First Aid Unit just after the war in devastated France.

6. Maria Macciocchi, "Female Sexuality in Fascist Ideology," *Feminist Review* 1:75, 1979. See my discussion of this point in "Liberty, Sorority, Misogyny," in *The Representation of Women in Fiction*, ed. Carolyn Heilbrun and Margaret Higonnet (Baltimore: The Johns Hopkins University Press, 1982). Celeste Schenk's essays "Feminism and Deconstruction: Reconstructing the Elegy," *Tulsa Studies in Women's Literature* 5 (1986), and "Exiled by Genre: Modernism, Canonicity and the Politics of Exile" in Broe and Ingram's edited volume *Women's Writing in Exile* (Chapel Hill: University of North Carolina Press, 1988), are useful here on the valuing of women poets only on the experimental male model. Alex Zwerdling calls Isa's poems the "geriatric pastoral" in *"Between the Acts* and the Coming of War," *Novel* 10 (1977). Compare the rape narrative of the girl at home raped by one's own soldiers in *Between the Acts* to the black woman's experience in Gayle Jones's *Eva's Man* (rpt. Boston: Beacon Press, 1987).

7. William Kent's *Encyclopedia of London* reports that "Patriotism is not Enough" was added to the statue by the Labour Government in 1924 (524).

8. See my essays on *The Years* in *Virginia Woolf and the Languages of Patriarchy* (Bloomington: Indiana University Press, 1987). The canonical status of Gilbert's essay is evidenced by its reprinting; it first appeared in *Signs* 8 (3): 422–50. See especially Margaret Higonnet et al., eds., *Behind the Lines: Gender and the Two World Wars* (New Haven: Yale

University Press, 1987), where its practice is in direct contradiction to Joan Scott's foreword, "Rewriting History." Judith Newton and Deborah Rosenfelt, *Feminist Criticism and Social Change* (New York and London: Methuen, 1986), cites this essay as a sign of a new commitment to history on the part of Gilbert, an improvement on *Madwoman*.

9.   In "The Indescribable Barrier: English Women and the Effect of the First World War," Laura E. Mayhall (Stanford) argues that Gilbert's thesis is incorrect and proves the case with statistical evidence: "The experience of war itself, however, did not create a barrier between men and women. The division occurred when women who aided the war effort threatened the exclusivity of the male power structure." For new readings of women writers of World War I, see the work of a group using the University of Tulsa archives from this period, Jan Calloway, Claire Culleton, George Otte, Linda Palumbo, Celia Patterson, and Susan Millar Williams. The strongest critique of Gilbert's essay is Claire M. Tyler's "Maleness Run Riot—The Great War and Women's Resistance to Militarism," *Women's Studies International Forum*, vol. 11, no. 3, 199–210 (1988).

10.   Elizabeth Robins joined Lady Rhondda in the founding of *Time and Tide* in May, 1920, along with Rebecca West and Cicely Hamilton. They (all feminists) founded the Six-Point Group, to influence legislation affecting motherhood, health, women's wages, equal pay, pensions, and custody of children.

11.   See Ellen N. LaMotte, *The Backwash of War: The Human Wreckage of the Battlefield as Witnessed by an American Hospital Nurse* (Putnam's, 1916), banned for its pacifism; and Angela Ingram's "Un/Reproductions: Estates of Banishments in Some English Novels after the Great War" in *Women's Writing in Exile*. Sylvia Pankhurst's *The Home Front* (London: Hutchinson, 1930) is also valuable. Ingram's discussion of Rose Allatini's banned novel *Despised and Rejected* is especially good on the links between the mother/hero theme and homosexuality and pacifism. Kristeva's concept of abjection is developed in *Powers of Horror* (New York: Columbia University Press, 1985).

12.   For the treatment of the nurse and women's madness, see a different view in White's friend, Emily Coleman's *The Shutter of Snow* (New York: Viking, 1930; rpt. Virago/Penguin, 1986). In Susan Fromberg Shaeffer's *The Madness of A Seduced Woman* (New York: E. P. Dutton, 1983), the nurse is a savior and friend and the narrative is addressed to her. A horrifying nurse like Antonia White's appears in Virginia Woolf's *The Voyage Out*, frightening Rachel in her dying fever. The transformation of Bedlam to the Imperial War Museum gives one the same uncanny chill as a visit to Les Invalides in Paris, where the ex-hospital now houses Napoleon's Tomb and a vast collection of war memorabilia. Antonia White's *As Once in May* (London: Virago, 1983) ed. Susan Chitty, includes her autobiographical writings. For the recurring trench coat, see Helen Zenna Smith, *Not So Quiet . . .* (rpt. New York: The Feminist Press, 1988), afterword by Jane Marcus.

13.   In "Surprise Visit," Julia recalls being frightened by her two former nurses at a dance. In "Clara IV" (in *As Once in May*), which was to be the fifth novel after the *Frost in May* quartet, Julia (Clara) meets two of the nurses on a channel steamer in 1928. She sees them in the mirror, her recurrent image of female madness. Jones and Smith remain sadistic and kind, still playing their old roles of good cop and bad cop. See W. J. T. Mitchell, *Iconology: Image, Text, Ideology* (Chicago: University of Chicago Press, 1986).

14.   This *textual* denial of what the image of state violence against protesters actually shows (and this is true of television newscasting as well) and the projection of violence onto the victim, continues to operate very effectively and actually makes clear that, socially, words may still dominate pictures as vehicles of rationality, though this is obviously changing.

15.   Gilbert's affirmation of the standard patriarchal interpretation of women's role in the war is a similar case.

16.   I use the word 'somatics' as body-language after the fine essay by Catharine Stimpson, "The Somograms of Gertrude Stein," in *The Female Body in Western Culture.*

17.   Like Gilbert, Paula Hays Harper in "Votes for Woman? A Graphic Episode in the Battle of the Sexes" (in *Art and Architecture in the Service of Politics,* ed. Henry A. Millon and Linda Nochlin [Cambridge: MIT Press] 150–61), accepts the standard valuation of the war posters over the suffrage art, failing to distinguish between the enormous resources of official government propaganda and the art produced by volunteer artists in a movement for social change. She also does not see the war posters as an iconoclastic destruction of the previous self-made images of the women's movement. Harper claims that few suffrage posters survive and that they have been ignored. This is not the case. An enormous selection was mounted on exhibit several times in the 1970s in London. They may be seen in the London Museum or the Fawcett Library, or, far more easily, on the library shelves, illustrating all the histories of women's suffrage. A particularly large selection is reproduced in Midge McKenzie, *Shoulder to Shoulder* (New York: Knopf, 1975, rpt. 1988). For a thorough study of suffrage iconology, see Lisa Tickner's *The Spectacle of Women: Imagery of the Women's Suffrage Campaign 1907–1914* (Chicago: University of Chicago Press, 1988). Tickner argues the suffragettes' use of the phallic mother image works with the hysterization of women's bodies and also describes the battle over possession of the image of the "womanly woman."

18.   Margaret Haig, Viscountess Rhondda, *This Was My World* (London, 1933). For a further discussion of the politics of dress, see my "Translatlantic Sisterhood," *Signs* 3 (1978): 744–55. Elizabeth Robins was fond of pointing out that the French fashion house of Worth invented the "hobble skirt" which was very tight at the bottom, at the height of the suffrage movement when women were striding through the streets.

19.   Elsa Lanchester, *Elsa Lanchester Herself* (New York: St. Martins, 1983). Other memoirs relate cloak and dagger stories of the Pankhursts' escape from the police in the garb of working women, as widows in heavy black mourning, in wigs and shawls, a whole costume party of political cross-dressing.

20.   Lanchester also recalls marching in the great demonstration for Emily Wilding's funeral. A brilliant "new woman" with two university degrees, Emily Wilding was killed by running in front of the king's horse at the Derby. Historians have invariably treated her as a hysteric or a joke, quoting someone who says he felt sorry for the horse. It is perhaps too embarrassing to relate that women actually died for the vote, as British propaganda still denies heroism to hunger-striking martyrs to the Irish cause. Elsa Lanchester's child's eye view of the occasion is a memory, after seventy years, of the colors and the shiny steel nuts, bolts, and screws on the road, fallen from cars and buses.

21.   Lillian Robinson, *Sex, Class and Culture* (Bloomington: Indiana University Press, 1978; rpt. Methuen, 1986), Naomi Schor, "Female Fetishism: The Case of George Sand," in *The Female Body in Western Culture,* ed. Susan Suleiman (Cambridge: Harvard University Press, 1986), 363–72.

10

History as Usual? Feminism and the "New Historicism"

Judith Lowder Newton

Many of the assumptions and practices currently identified with "new historicism" are intensely familiar. Those engaged in "new historicism," we are told, generally assume that there is no transhistorical or universal human essence and that human subjectivity is constructed by cultural codes which position and limit all of us in various and divided ways. They assume that there is no "objectivity," that we experience the "world" in language, and that all our representations of the world, our readings of texts and of the past, are informed by our own historical position, by the values and politics that are rooted in them. They assume, finally, that representation "makes things happen" by "shaping human consciousness" and that as forces acting in history various forms of representation ought to be read in relation to each other and in relation to non-discursive "texts" like "events."[1] All are assumptions which inform and have informed a number of critical practices for many years.[2] The constructions of "history" attributed to "new historicism" are also familiar from other contexts. There is the notion that "history" is best told as a story of power relations and struggle, a story that is contradictory, heterogeneous, fragmented. There is the (more debated) notion that hegemonic power is part but not all of the story, that "history" is a tale of many voices and forms of power, of power exercised by the weak and the marginal as well as by the dominant and strong. Even the technique of "cross cultural montage,"[3] or the juxtaposition of literary, non-literary, and social texts is not unknown. In the afternoon, indeed, when I am no longer writing this essay I sit at my well-laden desk, patiently working through a series of connections between Parliamentary debate, women's manuals, medical writing, novels, and the ascension of Queen Victoria. It's enough to make me think I'm a new historicist too.

But self-definition in this case is contingent upon the larger process of defining what "new historicism" itself is to mean, and in the histories of "new historicism" which I have read so far, whether "new historicism" is defined as a school or more loosely as a set of assumptions and techniques given different articulation depending on the politics of the practitioners,[4] my own entry into these same assumptions and techniques has only partially been mapped. "New historicism," we are variously told, comes out of the new left, out of cultural materialism, the crisis of 1968, post-modernist response to that crisis, out of post-structuralism as part of that response, and most particularly out of the historiography of Michel Foucault.[5] "New historicism" is also to be read as a reaction to the formalism of structuralism and post-structuralism and as a response to the perception that American educational institutions and culture are rapidly forgetting history. "New historicism," finally, has also emerged out of fear on the part of literary critics that they are being further marginalized within their culture. The upshot, in this country at least, has been a nagging sense of "professional, institutional, and political impotence."[6]

Some parts of these "histories," of course, do tell the story of my own trajectory into the assumptions and strategies attributed to "new historicism." The new left and cultural materialism, in particular, are central to my own construction of my heritage, both intellectual and political. But barely alluded to in most of the histories of "new historicism" so far are what were in fact the mother roots—the women's movement and the feminist theory and feminist scholarship which grew from it. Indeed, discussions of "new historicism," as of "post-modernism," deconstruction, and the "new history," are often carried on as if their assumptions and practices had been produced by men (feminist theorists, if they are mentioned at all, are often assumed to be the dependent heirs of male intellectual capital), and yet feminist labor has had much to do with the development of these literary/ historical enterprises.[7] The "post-modernist"[8] assumptions which inform new history and new historicism, for example, were partly generated by the theoretical breaks of the second wave of the women's movement, by feminist criticism of male-centered knowledges for their assumption of "objectivity," by feminist assertion of the political and historically specific nature of knowledge itself, and by feminist analyses of their cultural construction of female identity. Since the late sixties, moreover, feminist work has emphasized the role of "ideas," or symbolic systems in the construction not only of identities but social institutions and social relations as a whole. It has done so, by and large, not in response to post-structuralism but because the subordination of women, who have always been at least half of humankind, has seemed ideological to a large degree.

Sisterhood is Powerful (1970), in fact, in its critique of androcentric discourse, reads like a compendium of the "post-modernist" assumptions currently attributed to "new historicism"—no universal humanity, subjectivity culturally constructed, readings of literature and history biased and political, our readings of history, representation and social relations interacting, representation, in particular, having material effects, producing our very bodies.[9] In its juxtaposition of cultural texts, moreover, in its reading of the cultural codes which inform academic disciplines, advertising, sex manuals, popular culture, diaries, political manifestoes, literature, and political movements and events. *Sisterhood* also sounds like a blueprint for "cross cultural montage," the methodology currently patented as new in "new historicism." (I hardly need to point out to anyone who was doing feminist work in the early 1970s that this blueprint also reads like a syllabus for early versions of Introduction to Women's Studies 101.)

Feminist historians both drew upon and helped to generate feminist "postmodern" assumptions in their development of a "New Women's History." The earliest women's history, for example, sought to challenge traditional, masculinist, "objective" "history" by making women visible, by writing women into "history." Early on, moreover, many historians of women, although they drew heavily upon the work of social historians before them, saw that the study of women would be different from the study of other oppressed groups. Women, as Gerda Lerner put it in an early issue of *Feminist Studies,* are the majority now and always have been at least half of mankind." It is their "culturally determined and psychologically internalized marginality" that has made their "historical experience different from that of men." Writing women into "history" might well mean that traditional definitions of "history" itself would have to change.[10] One way in which this "New Women's History," in conjunction with social history, began to change what "history" was going to mean lay in making representation, role prescription, ideas, values, psychology and the construction of subjectivity, a point of focus. The difference between feminist versions of this emphasis and social historical or cultural materialist versions (which came later) was that subjectivity was gendered and was often female and that women were at the heart of historical study. In feminist history, moreover, sexuality and reproduction, both constructed, both seen as sites of power and struggle, were central to the subjectivity of women and of men both. (These early investigations of sexual knowledge as power, of course, predated Foucault's work on sexuality by several years.)[11] As these once invisible persons, relations, institutions, ideologies, and cultures became visible, became part of "history," their relation to the already visible, the larger economic and political structures usually assigned to men began to be explored. That exploration often involved a species of "cross cultural montage" in which (once) untraditional sources, women's letters and diaries, women's manuals, women's novels, even seances were juxtaposed with more traditional and public texts, Parliamentary debate, sociological writing, medical literature, news reports, and medical journals.[12]

Like social historians, finally, feminist historians operated out of an experience of and a commitment to social change. Thus they were alert to the ways in which hegemonic ideologies and oppressive social relations might operate unevenly across an entire culture. One early focus in the "New Women's History," for example, was on the gap between role prescription and women's actual behavior, which might register "role anxiety" or "role resistance."[13] Another focus was on the tensions between dominant values and the values of woman's culture and on the domestic sphere as a site of female status and power. Feminist history also explored the multiplicity of women's roles and identities and the intersections and contradictions between the roles and identities imposed by race, sex, and class. The tensions and contradictions between these roles and identities implied that hegemonic ideologies were far from being unified or static and suggested that anxiety, resistance, and power struggles in general might have many local sites.

What emerged in the "New Women's History," then, and in feminist literary/historical work with which it intersects, are emphases and practices which overlap with those currently attributed to "new historicism." But the important difference between most "new historicist" and feminist literary/ historical work still lies in the degree to which gender relations, gender struggle, women, and women's activities and power are seen as being within "history," are seen as having significant or causative relation to the political and economic realms traditionally associated with men. This difference, as I will suggest later on in more detail, makes for other differences in what "history" looks like, makes for differences in what is included as "history" in the first place and differences in what constitutes an historical period. It makes for differences, finally, in the degree to which dominant representations and hegemonic ideologies are imagined as monolithic and anonymous or as composed of many voices. It makes for differences in the degree to which hegemonic ideology and power are seen as stable and impervious to change and the degree to which they are imagined to be internally divided, unstable, and in constant need of construction and revision, creating the conditions which make social change and the agency of the weak possible.

II

In an effort to make feminist literary/historical work more visible and to investigate the potentially transformative effect of feminist politics and analysis on some of the points of focus, critical assumptions and techniques currently identified as "new historicist." I want briefly to consider three complex and often brilliant works on nineteenth-century culture which share many of the assumptions and employ many of the practices attributed to "new historicism." Each is particularly marked, for example, by a focus on the cultural force of representation and by an interest in the intersection of literary, non-literary, and social texts. Each also employs the strategy of "cross cultural montage" by which literary texts are read in relation to Parliamentary debates, women's manuals, medical writing, legal codes, and, more occasionally, "events" or "material developments." Despite their shared assumptions and techniques, however, each book produces "history" differently. The differences, I will suggest, have much to do with their different relation to traditions of feminist scholarship and feminist politics. The three texts are Catherine Gallagher's *The Industrial Reformation of English Fiction: Social Discourse and Narrative Form, 1832–1867* (1985), Nancy Armstrong's *Desire and Domestic Fiction: A Political History of the Novel* (1987), and Mary Poovey's forthcoming *Uneven Developments: The Ideological Work of Gender in Mid-Victorian England.*[14]

Uneven Developments is most explicitly identified with feminist politics and theory, although its theory and politics are also cultural materialist to a large degree. *Desire and Domestic Fiction* is identified with feminist and cultural materialist politics and with politically informed criticism generally—Armstrong is less comfortable than Poovey with the strategy of situating herself in one group more than in another. *The Industrial Reformation of English Fiction* does not explicitly situate itself in any politics although its definition of terms and its conception of history suggests its indebtedness to cultural materialist theory and to Foucault.[15] Given the different ways these texts are placed in traditions of theory and politics—and there is always a gap between the political heritage of a text and the politics of an author, site of discourse though she may be—there are predictable differences in the degree to which gender and gender relations play a role in "history." What is not so predictable is the degree to which a focus on both helps produce histories which break with or raise questions about familiar historical paradigms and categories.

In one basic way at least each of these books breaks with the ideological division of the world into "public" and "private," man and woman, class and gender and so works within a central insight of feminist theory, that public and private are not separate but intersecting. Each book, that is, examines the way in which a mode of structuring gender relations informed the ways in which women and men imagined the relations of class. This investigation, of course, is only part of Gallagher's study, the larger focus of which is a series of paradoxes (of which the public/private division is only one) that centrally informed the Condition of England debate. In Armstrong and Poovey the division of the world into public/private, culture/nature, man/woman, mind/body is explored across a wider range of middle-class debates and institutions and is discovered to be a crucial, and in Armstrong, the primary, organizing principle of middle-class ideology and culture as a whole. In this important way, by placing gender along with class at the heart of middle-class culture, Armstrong and Poovey radically break with the Marxist and cultural materialist models of history from which they also draw.

In all three texts, as one might suspect, the centrality or marginality of gender as an organizing category in "history" informs what counts as "history" in the first place, informs the choice of historically significant discourse, social relations, and "event." Gallagher, for example, writes of debates traditionally seen, and seen here, as having to do with class—the Condition of England question and Parliamentary debate over reform. She also focuses on texts which she looks at in their relation to class issues—novels, reports, Parliamentary speeches, women's manuals. Although a way of structuring gender (the division of the world into domestic and social) enters into the way class relations are represented, gender relations, the intersection of class and gender, are not really points of focus in this book.

Armstrong concentrates on texts which are centrally informed by a focus on gender—manuals for and often by women and novels, which Armstrong sees as an essentially feminine genre in the nineteenth century. She then draws on sociological writing and Parliamentary debate over the Condition of England question to suggest how a fully elaborated discourse on gender began to structure debates traditionally seen and seen here as having to do with class. Poovey, finally, focuses on a system of differences in the form of binary oppositions—legal subject/non-subject, property owner/commodity, etc.—which were based on the "natural" differences between women and men. She then examines this system as it informed five controversies in the 1840s and 1850s and suggests the complex and shifting ways in which this system of differences was deployed and the multiple ways in which constructions of gender intersected with constructions of class and also race and national identity.

Both Poovey and Armstrong, then, deal centrally with discourse over gender, but their strategies for placing gender in "history" are different. Armstrong's strategy is to suggest how texts informed by discourse on gender acted upon representations of class, modern institutions, and class relations. Armstrong also suggests how centrally, how dominantly, a way of structuring gender was a feminine affair, feminine in the sense of being authored by women, or by men writing in feminized genres, and feminine in the sense that the way middle-class women's subjectivity and sexuality were constructed became a model for the way in which men's subjectivity and sexuality were constructed later on. Thus the first modern individual, modern because her value lay in personal qualities rather than in rank, was a female—a radical break with traditional histories of the "bourgeois subject." Desire for this ideal female, moreover, unified the middle-class before the middle class officially existed. The moral authority attributed to this figure, the authority of the heart, became the authority of the middle class as a whole while the officially feminine and apolitical power which was attributed to her, the power of moral surveillance, became the mode by which modern institutions were to operate and the mode by which the problem of the working class, newly redefined as domestic and as sexual, was to be resolved.

Although Armstrong does not, and might not wish, to situate herself in the traditions of the "New Women's History," she certainly pursues two of its central projects, the exploration of women's cultural power and the investigation of connections between what have been seen as separate—public and private. Thus Armstrong tries to "defamiliarize the division of discourse that makes it so difficult to see the relationship between the finer nuances of women's feelings and a capitalist economy run mainly by men," and she insists that "those cultural functions which we automatically attribute to and embody for women—those, for example, of mother, nurse, teacher, social worker and general overseer of service institutions—have been just as instrumental in bringing the new middle classes into power and maintaining their dominance as all the economic takeoffs and political breakthroughs we automatically attribute to men" (26).

This is an extremely significant challenge to traditional political history, one which should open up our investigations of the nineteenth-century past, and yet the challenge is uneven. For Armstrong chooses to focus on the way that representations of gender informed representations of class, shaped class relations, and structured an otherwise male dominated public sphere. But she chooses not to explore the way in which representations of gender also shaped gender relations and women's lives. And she chooses not to consider the way in which representations of class structured gender relations as well. One effect of these choices is that the book seems to privilege the traditional, political, class-centered history that it also self-consciously and very powerfully challenges.

Poovey has a different strategy for widening our sense of what social relations are to count as "history." The strategy is to examine controversies in which gender is prominently at work, controversies which, by and large, have been invisible in traditional political history—debate over the use of chloroform in childbirth; the debate over the Divorce and Married women's Property Bills; debate over governesses, the entry of women into the labor market, and women's sexual aggression; debates over the professionalization of literary writing and the development of nursing as a profession for women. Poovey then explores the ways in which systems of difference based on sex were deployed within these controversies to structure both class and gender relations. One effect of this strategy is to place discourse over gender less centrally at the service of class relations, to give gender relations a more autonomous historical significance and in this way to suggest a more thoroughgoing redefinition of what relations count as "history."

The division in these works over the degree to which class and gender relations finally count as "history" is tied to another split over the implied definition of significant "events." In the works that most privilege class, "events" (especially those which stimulate controversy) and what one used to call "material conditions" without quotation marks remain fairly male-centered. This correlation, I would argue, between a focus on class and a focus on male-centered material developments, suggests the persistence of a tendency still familiar in much cultural materialist work, a tendency to define class in terms of men's economic and social relations with each other, a tendency to define class consciousness in terms of men's values and interests, and a tendency to associate the development of class identity with events in which men played the central role or in which women's participation has not been fully explored.

Thus in *The Industrial Reformation of English Fiction* events or social developments are largely male, and/or are those which have been traditionally seen, and are seen here, in terms of men—anti-slavery and proslavery agitation (represented here by men), the Ten Hours Movement, Chartism, factory bills, and Parliamentary reform. The labor of working-class women and children also enters in but is seen largely as a class issue and in this instance, I think, class has not been redefined to reflect women's values, interests, and social relations. In *Desire and Domestic Fiction,* as well, although Armstrong's consciousness about the masculine nature of traditional political history is very high, and although she does redefine middle-class consciousness so as to make feminine values and feminine modes of representing subjectivity and sexuality not only central but dominant, events are still largely masculine or their traditional association with men is not explicitly questioned. Thus Armstrong deals with the introduction of machines, working-class protest, the development of Chartism, factory reform bills, and the development of a national curriculum.

In Poovey, however, there is a more thoroughgoing effort to widen our assumptions about what events or social developments count in "history." Many of the events or material developments in this text have to do with women and women's activities—women's entry into the labor force is a point of focus, as are feminist organization and agitation over property reform, the development of female professions (governessing and nursing) and of female institutions (women's colleges and the Governesses' Benevolent Institution.) The Parliamentary bills which Poovey investigates also have to do with women and more generally with gender. *Uneven Developments,* of course, also makes reference to more traditionally significant, traditionally class-focused and masculine developments such as the realization of England's imperial ambitions, but this too is read in relation to women's activities, in this case the development of nursing as a female profession. The goal, therefore, is not to propose a completely alternative "history" to the class-centered histories of the past, but to suggest the lines along which we will have to rethink what significant "events" in fact are and how historical periods might be newly delimited if gender is to be written into our histories.

The most politically charged differences in the histories produced by these three texts have to do with the ways in which, and the degrees to which, social change is imagined to be possible and the degree to which the conditions for social change are imagined to be a function of contradictions in discourse itself or of human agents struggling for power or liberation. In works so focused on the cultural power of representation, these distinctions are largely expressed in the way that representation itself is represented. Although the differences I shall discuss are undoubtedly overdetermined by complexities I can't hope to account for here, they may also be related I would argue to the following political considerations: the degree to which each author situates herself as author of her text within feminism seen as a vital political movement and the degree to which she thereby expresses a political predisposition to see social change and human agency as possible; the degree to which gender relations are made central to history; and the consistency with which each text takes material conditions into account in its analysis of representation.

The Industrial Reformation of English Fiction, for example, which challenges the usefulness of the term "bourgeois ideology," with its implication of a unified class position, is scrupulous in laying out the many different and overlapping strands of discourse and intellectual tradition that informed the Condition of England Debate. These strands of discourse, moreover, have their origin in groups taking political positions—over slavery, over the plight of the working class. But the book's strategy is to focus on a set of central paradoxes—freedom/determination, public/private—that variously informed each strand and that then had impact upon the form of the English novel. Thus, the initial focus is on a multiplicity of voices and positions, but the voices tend to blend together and to lose political affiliation as the recurring and fairly homologous sets of paradoxes are examined. Ultimately, the emphasis of the book fails, to a large degree, on logical and internal contradiction within representation rather than on, say, even local struggles between interested groups to control representation itself. Although the debate over political representation "impinged" on the "theory and practice of literary representation," change, in the construction of representation and culture, emerges to a large degree from logical contradictions in representation itself and from a generalized need for new principles of cohesion (xiii). Change does not emerge for the most part from human agents acting out of specific historical positions and with historically determined politics.

Gallagher's complex analysis of representation is always impressive, but the book's focus on the formal properties of representation, its lack of continuing attention to the social position of the various speakers, works against a consideration of what might be read as politically charged differences in the way that different speakers articulate what would otherwise seem to be the same set of ideas. Representation, therefore, although it is beset by internal logical paradox, appears more cohesive, more stable, more resistant to change than it otherwise might. This muting of what might be read as politically charged nuance, is also tied to the absence of gender relations as a point of focus in this work. This second connection is, for me, most dramatically evidenced in Gallagher's discussion of two ways of thinking about the division between public and domestic, a way of structuring the world which informed much of the debate over the working class. With her usual impressive thoroughness Gallagher lays out two traditions, that of domestic ideology and that of social paternalism. Domestic ideology, she mentions in a footnote, was an essentially female tradition and was developed in manuals by women for other women. In contrast to the discourse of social paternalism, domestic ideology does not see the family as a metaphor for social relations and therefore does not look for the replication of familial hierarchy in the public sphere. Rather, in domestic ideology family and society are contiguous, are related but different.

What Gallagher outlines here are two ways of seeing the world that might be read as having significant political implications. Upper and middle-class men look for the extension of familial hierarchy into the public sphere and middle-class women do not. One narrative, moreover, that of social paternalism, is briefly imagined to be informed by a gendered position—elite men sought to control women's independence as well as the independence of the working class in imagining the world as a patriarchal family with themselves at the head. But the other narrative, women's narrative, is given no politics to speak of although the political nature of this feminine representation of the relation between public and domestic trembles just below the surface. Gender politics, for example, seem particularly striking in some of the women's factory novels which Gallagher explores, novels which are informed by fantasies of women rescuing factory children and setting up female-headed households in Rhenish castles, novels informed by fantasies in which well-meaning men are largely impotent while men in power are often villains. What Gallagher's text points to but does not investigate, in part because gender relations and the different social positioning of subjects in ideology are not consistent points of focus, are deep-seated and potentially destabilizing tensions within middle-class ways of imagining the world.

In Armstrong change comes very centrally from struggle, largely between classes and over control of representation: "In the model of culture I am proposing, culture appears as a struggle among various political factions to possess its most valued signs and symbols" (23). The middle class, for example, comes to power when it wins "the intellectual war to determine the definition of culture itself" (162). The effects of representation, of course, are not neatly defined by class interests, but are more complex and less predictable than this would suggest: and yet middle-class ideology in this book is a fairly unified and therefore fairly stable affair. There is, for example, little sense of tension between men in subgroups of the middle class and little sense that the different social and economic situations of middle class women and men might have affected their relation to middle-class ideology differently. Here is where greater attention to "material conditions" might once again have altered the representation of representation itself.

Armstrong, of course, has deliberately chosen not to deal with the power relations of gender and with women's oppression, wishing instead to focus on "the contrary political affiliations for which any individual provides the site," in this case the affiliations of class (24). This is an important emphasis and it has not been pursued much in literary critical/historical work. But one effect of this single focus is to reaffirm some traditional equations, the equation of "political resistance," for example, with matters of class (252). Until late in the book, with the introduction of Dora and Woolf, women have class politics but they scarcely have any politics of gender. Cultural struggle and politics itself, therefore, remain inter-class issues. Middle-class ideology is implicitly challenged from without, by upper-class and working-class modes of representing the world, but it is internally fairly stable, beset neither by tensions between middle-class men differently positioned in the social formation nor by tensions between middle-class women or between women and men.

Poovey's conception of middle-class ideology, of its relative stability and vulnerability to change, is significantly different from Armstrong's and from Gallagher's, although she draws on insights from both. Her focus, I have suggested, is upon a system of difference based on the "natural" divisions of sex and articulated as a series of polar oppositions that imply and order one another and that centrally inform Victorian middle-class ideology and institutions. Since the oppositions depend on the subordination of one term, they are internally unstable, and it is in part because of this internal instability that middle-class ideology "was both contested and always under construction; because it was always in the making it was always open to revision, dispute, the emergence of oppositional formulations" (4). But this system of middle-class ideas and institutions was also "developed unevenly," hence the title of the work. It was uneven in the sense that it was "experienced differently by individuals who were positioned differently within the social formation (by sex, class, race, for example), and it was uneven in the sense that it was "articulated differently by the different institutions, discourses, and practices that it both constituted and was constituted by" (4). It is in large part, I would argue, that Poovey more consistently takes "material conditions" into consideration that she imagines women positioned differently inside middle-class ideology than men, that she also imagines some men positioned differently from other men, and some women positioned differently from other women. Thus the conditions for social change, as constructed by this book, are not merely a function of internal ideological contradiction but of social positioning and human agency. That agency, moreover, is informed not just by the concerns of class but by the concerns of gender. Hence, dominant ideologies are multiply fractured by contradictions and tensions, many of them internal to the middle class and many of them experienced within the most intimate and most psychically charged relations of middle-class culture—those of home and family.

In some ways, of course, Poovey's construction of middle-class culture belongs to an earlier historical model than Armstrong's, a model according to which men construct a culture and women inhabit it but do not feel entirely at home. Women protest, of course, as individuals like Caroline Norton, or as organized feminist groups, but women do not construct dominant culture in the way that Armstrong suggests and even their protest is severely limited. Opposition, indeed, is more of a theoretical possibility in *Uneven Developments* than a concretely realized phenomenon. This is especially true when Poovey focuses on debates to which women had no access, the debate over chloroform, childbirth, and women's sexuality, for example, as it was carried on in medical journals. But even in debates to which women did have access, in which women did intervene, such as the debate over the Divorce Bill and the Married Women's Property Act, Poovey's emphasis falls not on the voice of organized feminist protest but on the lonely, individual, and ultimately conservative struggles of Caroline Norton.

In both cases a shift in focus might considerably alter the impression of sometimes unrelenting male domination. Women, for example, wrote very differently from medical men about childbirth and mothering in letters and diaries, as well as in novels, and later in the century women allied with the movement to rescind the Contagious Diseases Acts and with social purity crusades sustained public discourse over sexuality that was overtly critical of discourse identified with men. Still, if women's protest remains more of a theoretical possibility than a concretely realized phenomenon, *Uneven Developments* does keep us in touch with a sense of the material basis for female agency and discontent. It impresses upon us, for example, the extreme inequities of women's social position vis-à-vis men of their own class and women's frequent and necessary deviations from the positions they were assigned (many middle-class women also had to earn a wage). Finally, of course, it also reminds us that women's organized protest did exist. Poovey's is the only work to include feminist discourse and feminist institutions.

III

Many questions, to be sure, remain to be asked and explored. Indeed, the distance between Poovey's construction of women's participation in mid-Victorian culture and Armstrong's construction of the same, the first emphasizing the mainly oppositional role of women, the second emphasizing the dominance of feminine values and power suggests one immediate line of inquiry. How might we proceed to investigate these alternative constructions of the past? One strategy is simply to submit more discourse by women and men, discourse that is of course also already gendered, to analysis and examination, to expand what is in "history" and what is seen as having significant relation. We might follow Poovey's example and the example of several feminist historians by juxtaposing the discourse of men and women on the same social topics or in the same organizations and movements. We might investigate too what men and women appropriated from each other. As an index to how widespread the cultural tension or unity between the genders may have been we might pursue another line of questioning laid out over a decade ago in the agenda of the "New Women's History." That is, we might explore the gap between prescriptive and public representations of gender and the way that gender relations were constructed by individuals in their private lives. Perhaps, since literary/historical work poses such a multiplicity of tasks, we ought to work *with* historians more directly, returning to the kind of collective labor which we have always done in women's studies. Perhaps we might share with each other our different strengths and weaknesses, our different strategies for reading and our different standards for historical research.

Feminists doing literary/historical work might also draw upon the work of historians like Leonore Davidoff and Catherine Hall[16] to do more in the way of constructing some version of "material conditions," since texts like Poovey's, which do construct some vision of men and women's different social and economic situations, tend to read representation differently from and more complexly than those which do less with the "material." Family life, moreover, the dynamics of mother/father/child relations (in the modern nuclear family) should be part of our construction of "material conditions." We have yet to try out feminist object relations theory in culturally specific studies of the nineteenth-century past.[17] To what degree, for example, does the nineteenth-century middle-class family approximate the mother-dominant/father-absent family of modern object relations research, and can we see in middle-class men's defense of hierarchical oppositions something like the process of masculine gender identification described there? Perhaps these hierarchic oppositions were fueled not just by the need to deny capitalist alienation, as Poovey argues, but also by unconscious desire to contain the mother, the mother's body and the mother's power, and so to preserve masculine, unified identity. This is one way at least of accounting for the degree to which women's autonomy is often represented by women's bodies and sexuality going out of control and for the fact that the other side of the respectable middle-class domestic woman so often appears to be a monstrous sexualized female, a working-class prostitute.

If, as object relations theory and some current feminist history maintains, middle-class men and women, in their very different daily lives, in their different relation to gender ideology, did articulate different versions of "history" and social relations, we would need to continue to explore the lines along which gender, class, and race united and divided them and the degree to which feminine constructions of "history" had cultural power. Finally, of course, there is much crucial work to be done in bridging the gap between feminist work on gender and gender struggle, always seen in some relation at least to class, and the complex work done on class by those whose focus has not also been on gender. There is crucial work as well to be done in relation to those traditionally understood "material conditions," which so many of us declare at the moment to be "beyond the scope of this book."[18]

But if feminist literary/historical work poses questions for those whose work is already informed by feminist politics, it poses questions and a challenge to those whose work is only marginally or less than marginally defined by feminist concerns. A literary/historical practice that is consistently feminist and materialist, I have argued, tends to produce definitions of representation and of history that are more complex than those which are less consistently both. It also tends to produce "history" in a way which allows us better to account for social change and human agency. To any persons engaged in progressive politics which they still feel to be vital, such models of history, I would argue, are at once more useful and have greater explanatory power than those which tend to deny or to mute radically the possibility of change and agency both. In its emphasis upon the different ways that gendered subjects enter into ideology, moreover, materialist feminist work suggests an important direction for "new historicist" practice no matter what its politics. For if we wish to be serious about our assertion that representation "makes things happen" we will need to explore the way that discursive meanings circulate throughout a culture. It is here that we all have something to learn from feminist historians. A historian like Judith Walkowitz, for example, who also works in a species of "cross cultural montage," does not simply juxtapose isolated written and social texts in order to suggest the homologous operations of dominant ideology throughout an entire culture. Walkowitz not only attempts to construct the different ways in which groups differently placed in the social formation articulate or reproduce ideologies, she also attempts to construct the complex "cultural grid" through which overlapping and conflicting representations passed. That grid, moreover, has much to do with such non-discursive, material (though still constructed) matters as access to social space, a very different access for men and women of the same class and for persons of different classes.

Culture, as feminist historians like Walkowitz and Davidoff and Hall most concretely remind us, is constructed on many levels and not in public written representation alone. As I have argued in this paper, moreover, taking the "material" seriously, a material always apprehended within representation, changes the way that representation itself is represented. Non-feminist "new historicism," for example, in its non-cultural materialist modes, has been widely criticized for its tendency to insist upon the totalizing power of hegemonic ideologies, ideologies implicitly informed by elite male values and often presented as typical of the way culture itself is constructed as a whole. One wonders how such readings might be altered were the material world of the domestic, women's anxiety-producing power as mothers, household managers, and silent participants in enterprise, taken into account. It is only once those levels of culture are actively explored that women's contribution to culture and that of other oppressed groups can be taken adequately into account. It is only once this taking into account begins that any historicism can produce something more than history as usual.

Notes

1.   Louis Montrose, "Renaissance Literary Studies and the Subject of History," *English Literary Renaissance* 16 (Winter 1986): 8. My summary of "new historicist" assumptions and techniques also draws upon Jean E. Howard, "The New Historicism in Renaissance Studies," *English Literary Renaissance* 16 (Winter 1986): 13–43; and Jonathan Dollimore, "Introduction: Shakespeare, Cultural Materialism and The New Historicism," in *Political Shakespeare: New Essays in Cultural Materialism,* ed. Jonathan Dollimore and Alan Sinfield (Ithaca: Cornell University Press, 1985).

2.   Some obvious cases here are cultural materialism and many strands of feminist and Afro-American criticism.

3.   The term is Dominick LaCapra's as quoted by Ellen Pollak, "Feminism and the New Historicism: A Tale of Difference or the Same Old Story?," *The Eighteenth Century: Theory and Interpretation,* forthcoming.

4.   In "Renaissance Literary Studies," Montrose refers to "new historicism" both as a potential orthodoxy and more broadly as a "new historical *orientation* among critics who are heterogeneous in their practice," 6. For other broad definitions of "new historicism" see Howard and Dollimore and Jonathan Goldberg, "The Politics of Renaissance Literature: A Review Essay," *English Literary History* 49 (1982): 514–42. For critics who see "new historicism" more narrowly as a school or as a potential orthodoxy see Pollak; Edward Pechter, "The New Historicism and Its Discontents: Politicizing Renaissance Drama," *PMLA* 102 (1987): 292–303; Dominick LaCapra, remarks delivered as part of a panel on "The New Historicism: Political Commitment, and the Post-modern Critic," MLA, New York, December 1986; Catherine Gallagher, "Critics of Power: Marxists and The New Historicists," paper delivered at MLA, New York, December 1986. See Gallagher, this volume.

5.   Gallagher, for example, mentions the new left, post-structuralism, and Foucault; Dollimore emphasizes the role of cultural materialism; and Howard stresses the "post-modern" tendencies of new historical work. Many critics also specifically mention the influence of Foucault.

6.   Montrose, 12.

7.   For a more detailed argument of these points see the longer version of this piece in *Cultural Critique* (July, 1988).

8. I am using "post-modernist" in the vague way that it is now often employed—to refer to a set of assumptions about knowledge, language, and subjectivity (listed in my text) which call metanarrative or grand theory into question and which problematize interpretation of both literary and social texts. These assumptions may be articulated very differently by "post-modernists" (a term which usually includes Jean-François Lyotard, Michel Foucault, Richard Rorty), French and American deconstructionists (the most cited of whom is Jacques Derrida), and cultural materialists and feminists of various stripes. These categories, of course, are also used in a fluid way.

9. *Sisterhood is Powerful: An Anthology of Writings from The Women's Liberation Movement,* ed. Robin Morgan (New York: Vintage, 1970), 427–28.

10. Gerda Lerner, "Placing Women in History: Definitions and Challenges," *Feminist Studies* 3, no. 1/2 (Fall 1975): 8, 13. See also Carroll Smith-Rosenberg, "The New Woman and the New History," *Feminist Studies* 3, no. 1/2 (Fall 1975): 185–98.

11. For some early feminist work on the construction of sexuality and reproduction see Carroll Smith-Rosenberg, "The Hysterical Woman: Some Reflections on Sex Roles and Role Conflict in 19th Century America," *Social Research* 39, no. 4 (December 1972): 652–78; Ann Douglas Wood, " 'The Fashionable Diseases': Women's Complaints and Their Treatment in Nineteenth-Century America," in *Clio's Consciousness Raised: New Perspectives on the History of Women,* ed. Mary S. Hartman and Lois Banner (New York: Harper Torchbooks, 1974): 1–22. Michel Foucault's *The History of Sexuality,* Vol. I was first published in the United States in 1978.

12. For some examples of "cross cultural montage" in nineteenth-century work see Judith Walkowitz, "Jack the Ripper: And the Myth of Male Violence," *Feminist Studies* 8, no. 3 (Fall, 1982): 37–59, and "The Maiden Tribute," unpublished. See also Carroll Smith-Rosenberg, "Writing History: Language, Class and Gender," in *Feminist Studies/Critical Studies,* ed. Teresa de Lauretis (Bloomington: Indiana University Press, 1986): 31–54.

13. Smith-Rosenberg, "The New Woman," 187.

14. Catherine Gallagher, *The Industrial Reformation of English Fiction* (Chicago: University of Chicago Press, 1985); Nancy Armstrong, *Desire and Domestic Fiction: A Political History of the Novel* (New York: Oxford University Press, 1987); Mary Poovey, *Uneven Developments: The Ideological Work of Gender in Mid-Victorian England* (Chicago: University of Chicago Press, forthcoming 1988).

15. Gallagher does place herself politically in "Critics of Power." See footnote 4.

16. Leonore Davidoff and Catherine Hall, *Family Fortunes: Men and Women in the English Middle Class 1780–1850* (Chicago: University of Chicago Press, 1987).

17. For object relations theory see Dorothy Dinnerstein, *The Mermaid and the Minotaur: Sexual Arrangements and the Human Malaise* (New York: Harper, 1976); Nancy Chodorow, *The Reproduction of Mothering: Psychoanalysis and the Sociology of Gender* (Berkeley: University of California Press, 1978); Carol Gilligan, *In A Different Voice: Psychological Theory and Women's Development* (Cambridge: Harvard University Press, 1982); and Nancy Hartsock, *Money, Sex, and Power: Toward A Feminist Historical Materialism* (Boston: Northeastern University Press, 1985).

18. The words are Poovey's but the strategy is that of Gallagher, Armstrong, and many others, not excluding myself.

19. Louis Montrose begins to integrate these considerations in " 'Shaping Fantasies': Figurations of Gender and Power in Elizabethan Culture," in *Representing the English Renaissance,* ed. Stephen Greenblatt (Berkeley: University of California Press, 1988).

11

Co-optation

Gerald Graff

I recently delivered a talk to the English Department of a midwestern university in which I proposed what I thought was a fairly radical new curricular model for the study of literature. In the usual question period afterward, a number of members of the audience expressed doubts about whether teachers of literature were yet ready for such a bold departure from their normal practices. After some discussion in this vein, a young instructor cut in and objected that from his point of view the problem was that, far from being too radical, my proposal was clearly not radical enough. After all, he asked, would it not be very easily "co-opted" by the established system?

A nice piece of academic one-upmanship of the sort that normally would have stopped me in my tracks. I had been around this particular block before, however, and was ready with a counterploy: "I certainly hope so," I replied. "To say that my proposal figures to be 'co-opted' would be simply to say that it actually has a chance to work. What's the point of advancing ideas in public anyway if it isn't to get them 'co-opted'? That is, to get others to adopt them, to be successful?"

The appreciative laughs from the audience allowed me to feel I had won this small skirmish, but then had I? In refusing the implied premise of my questioner, namely, that every right-thinking literary critic will naturally regard being co-opted by the established system as a fate worse than death, I had declined the role of Uncompromising Cultural Radical that we have a bit too predictably come to expect literary theorists to play. This perhaps, accounted for the appreciative audience response. But in refusing to play the radical, had I not ended up merely playing the cynic? Didn't my questioner's term "co-optation" raise problems that couldn't really be dismissed by the tactic of pretending to treat the term as a mere synonym for legitimate success? This is the question I want to discuss in this essay.

Such a discussion should be relevant to a consideration of the so-called "new historicism," for one of the most powerful themes of this new historicism has been the idea that societies exert control over their subjects not just by imposing constraints on them but by predetermining the ways they attempt to rebel against those constraints, by co-opting their strategies of dissent. In saying this, I don't mean we should identify the new historicism with a particular *a priori* analysis of social control. But it is notable that much of the work that has acquired this label questions the conventional antithesis between established power and agencies of liberation by looking at the way civilization "co-opts" and thus disarms its discontents.

The antithesis between established power and agencies of liberation comes to us as part of the legacy of postromantic aesthetics, in which the arts are defined as a realm of spiritual autonomy set over against an alien and repressive order of material necessity. New historicism tends to call into question this purportedly "oppositional" relation between the arts and their material circumstances, and in doing so it constitutes a challenge—long overdue in my opinion—to the cultural avant-garde's sentimentalization of the arts.

It is in this respect that the new historicism is particularly indebted to the work of Michel Foucault, especially the later Foucault of works such as *Discipline and Punish* and *The History of Sexuality*. It is this later Foucault who rejected "the repressive hypothesis" of his earlier studies of the workings of power and turned to the investigation of the ways in which power operates not by repressing dissenting forces but by organizing and channeling them.[1] Power, for the later Foucault, is positive and productive. It triumphs over opposition not by negating it, but by producing it according to its peculiar requirements. Thus in Foucault's analyses, what passes conventionally for transgression or rebellion against power, as in the case of the modern discourses of sexuality, turns out to be only another of the faces of power, another means by which power reproduces, distributes, and extends itself.

But in developing this argument about the ubiquitous absorptive capacity of power, Foucault was developing a theme which had already been anticipated by the counterculture of the 1960s. Counterculture spokesmen had frequently worried about the ease with which their slogans, imagery, and music were co-opted by the media and even the government. Perhaps the most blatant example was Lyndon Johnson's cynical appropriation of the civil rights slogan "We shall overcome" in a speech Johnson delivered at a moment when everyone knew he was stepping up the bombing of North Vietnam.

It is in the 1960s that the word "co-opt" in the derogatory sense of neutralize or disarm first entered the language. (Did this change in usage have a counterpart in French and German?) Until the sixties, "to co-opt" had only the neutral meaning, to elect or induct into an organization, following the Latin root, "cooptare," *com* = together + *optare* = choose, elect. As late as 1971, "to choose or elect into a body or group as a fellow member" is the only definition given by *Webster's Third International*. In its 1980 edition, however, *The American Heritage Dictionary* gives: "co-opt . . . . 4. to take over (an independent minority, movement, or the like) through assimilation into an established group or culture." And *The World Book Dictionary* (1984) lists, "to take over; secure for oneself; adopt: *what it means is that rock has been co-opted by high culture, forced to adopt its standards (New Yorker)*."[2]

It was not Foucault who initiated the analysis of co-optation as a theme of radical left critique, but Herbert Marcuse, who coined terms such as "repressive desublimation" and "repressive tolerance" to describe the defusing and domesticating of ostensibly oppositional forms of culture by their tolerant acceptance and commercialization. Repressive desublimation was "repressive," paradoxically, by being permissive: it embraced threatening ideas and channeled them into politically unthreatening forms.

But even Marcuse and the new Left were not the first to make co-optation an object of analysis. In my book *Literature Against Itself*, which argued that the self-styled subversions of countercultural aesthetics had been domesticated by consumer capitalism and the academic publishing market, I quoted the following statement by Baudelaire published in 1846: "there are no more bourgeois, now that the bourgeois himself uses this insulting epithet—a fact that shows his willingness to become art-minded and listen to what the columnists have to say."[3] Such a statement suggests that as early as the 1840s some observers saw that the attitudes of antibourgeois art were in the process of being co-opted by bourgeois culture.

My own awareness of this phenomenon had been shaped less by Marcuse and the new Left than by earlier postwar American culture critics, like the critics of "Masscult" and "Midcult" in the 1950s, who had noticed that a good deal of mass-culture *Kitsch* derived from the heretofore "adversarial" vocabularies of modern art. As early as the late 1950s, the domestication of the "adversary culture" was being widely discussed by the so-called "New York intellectual critics," a group too often ignored or discounted today by socially oriented academic theorists. Lionel Trilling, who coined the term "adversary culture," wrote perceptively in essays of the early sixties (collected in *Beyond Culture* [1968]) about how the anarchistic energies of literary modernism had been trivialized by the entry of modern literature into the college curriculum and its easy acceptance in middlebrow culture.

Trilling called this process the "socialization of the anti-social, or the acculturation of the anti-cultural, or the legitimation of the subversive."[4] Though Harold Rosenberg wrote affirmatively of the revolutionary potential of action painting in his 1959 collection, *The Tradition of the New*, several of the essays in this book anticipated the concern Rosenberg would develop more fully in his subsequent writing with the co-optation of radical styles by mass culture.[5] The satire latent in Rosenberg's title would be actualized and made explicit by Irving Howe in *Decline of the New* (1970).[6] Preoccupation with the issue of co-optation, then, is a theme that enables us to link up the Foucauldian new historicism of the 1980s with the cultural criticism of the 1950s and 1960s.

In inheriting the issue, however, the new historicism inherits the unresolved ambiguities which my opening anecdote was designed to illustrate. What makes "co-optation" a paradoxical concept is the negative value it assigns to something that we usually think of as desirable—being accepted or successful, persuading others to one's point of view. The word "co-optation" makes every form of appropriation sound sinister, even the kinds of appropriation normally presuppposed as ends of social action.

The issue has become a particularly elusive one in academic-intellectual culture, where critical and scholarly work has begun to be rated according to its degree of radicalism or complicity, yet where the criteria for judging what is radical or complicitous have become shifting and debatable. On the one hand, it has become obligatory for accredited academic critics to be "oppositional," to oppose the social status quo. On the other hand, it has become less and less clear (or at least less and less agreed upon) what the nature of the "status quo" is, and therefore what being oppositional entails. Now that it is professionally important for critics to be radical and not complicitous, what counts as radical or complicitous has become more debatable. Even so, it can still be useful to distinguish "Left" and "Right" versions of the co-optation argument, especially if we want to gain some perspective on the new historicism.

Left New Historicism

In the sphere of Left academic cultural critique today, the worst thing that can be said about a school of thought or methodology is that it has allowed itself to be co-opted by established institutions. Pushed to an extreme, such a position leads to the kind of puristic position which Richard Rorty objects to in the work of Jean-François Lyotard. Rorty describes it as "one of the Left's silliest ideas . . . that escaping from institutions is automatically a good thing, because it ensures that one will not be 'used' by the evil forces which have 'co-opted' these institutions."[7]

The logic Rorty here ascribes to Lyotard is certainly familiar, and it leads to a curious double bind for Left cultural politics: if the established society represses the Left, it proves itself evil in the way the Left has been saying it is; but if the established society tolerates the Left and even favors it with privileges and rewards, then that society proves itself to be even *more* evil, because its tactics are more subtle and insidious. Feudalism may have cruelly repressed dissenters, but at least the feudal system was "up front" about its tactics, inscribing its punishments directly on the body of the victim for all to see. Far from representing moral progress over feudalism, Enlightenment and post-Enlightenment societies are presumably more evil, since they control their victims by internalizing the modes of control within the subject. By deluding people into feeling that they are sovereign individuals with "natural rights" and liberties, this "carceral" form of society co-opts its subjects into viewing their own subjugation as part of the march of progress. (A friend of mine once remarked that on reading the opening pages of *Discipline and Punish,* an account of a hideous feudal-style drawing-and-quartering, he almost threw up. "Then I read further," he said, "and realized that for Foucault those had been the *good old days.*")

In one respect, the terms of the co-optation analysis appear to be rigged in such a way that the Left cannot lose: however tolerantly established society behaves, it confirms the Left's hypothesis of its evil character. In fact, the more tolerant established society is, the more hypocritical and therefore the more evil it becomes. But if the terms of the analysis are rigged so that the Left can't lose, they are equally rigged so that the Left can't win: for if acceptance by established society is co-optation, then any success is by definition a form of defeat. The only truly authentic "success" is to fail, or at least remain as marginal as possible. Retaining one's radical credentials means remaining marginal—but then remaining marginal means remaining ineffectual.

To put it another way, the problem with the co-optation argument as often wielded by the Left is that it tends to cast an attitude of disapproval on success without *making clear the conditions under which success might be legitimate.* This is the problem many Marxists and other Leftists have with Foucault, though to find fault with Foucault on this score, as a political philosopher, in no way compromises his value as a historian and analyst of institutions. The problem surfaces in Foucault's rejection of the traditional "universal intellectual," the figure who claims to speak for the conscience of the community.[8] To attempt to speak for the conscience of the community is supposedly to "totalize," to arrogate the right to speak for "the Other," to tell the story of a culture from the subject-position of a panoptic overview that deprives the wretched of the earth of the chance to speak for themselves. Only by refusing to totalize, refusing to speak for the Other, can one prevent one's oppositional intellectual project from being co-opted.

What is unclear, furthermore, is how this refusal to play the role of universal intellectual can prevent itself from becoming yet another normative posture in its turn—the normative posture of a new type of universal intellectual modeled along the lines of Foucault. Foucault's celebrity illustrates the problem: no matter how marginal the Foucauldian intellectual may try to remain, there is always the danger that that marginality will be taken up, imitated, and thus made central.

Nor is this the only problem. Another is the fact that self-imposed marginality, refusal to totalize or speak for the Other, do not necessarily confer political innocence or immunity to the corruptions of power. Bruce Robbins has recently spoken of a hypocritical "inverse populism" underlying the refusal of some recent literary theorists to speak for other people: "The proposition that we should never speak for or to the people, just let them speak for themselves, becomes the claim that 'I speak for the people better than you do'."[9] It may be difficult to escape the point that Sartre made long ago (and that Jacques Derrida restated in his critique of Foucault in *Writing and Difference*) that the act of writing or speaking implies inherent commitments or totalizations that are not negated by flamboyant gestures of renunciation. Jürgen Habermas argues along similar lines in another register when he argues that "validity claims" are unavoidably built into communal speech-behavior.[10]

One could conclude from what I have been saying that there is nothing that cannot be "co-opted," and therefore that the very attempt to use co-optation as a critical concept, as the Left attempts to do, is futile. This, in effect, tends to be the fatalistic conclusion of right-wing new historicism, as we shall see in a moment. But it is only a highly abstract way of posing the issues that makes the critical use of the concept of co-optation seem inherently contradictory. Clearly, what makes social success seem compromising is the specific context in which it is achieved, which is to say, within a non-egalitarian and coercively hierarchical social order. Success tends to seem compromising when it is success within a social order that is felt to be illegitimate. Thus it could be argued (and would be argued by any Marxist, but even by some reformist liberals) that if the concept of co-optation seems to lead to a double bind, this is a result of the deformed situation of an intellectual subculture which senses that its society is illegitimate but has lost the vision of an alternative.

Some such description seems applicable to a cultural situation in which being "Left" and "radical" no longer necessarily means being socialist or anti-capitalist. With the decline of socialism as a realistic social alternative, the Left no longer possesses a shared criterion for evaluating cultural phenomena as historically progressive or regressive. With the eclipse of socialism as the privileged standpoint for measuring progress and regress, we get so many disparate and competing criteria that terms like "subversive" and "complicitous" begin to lose their precise meaning and come to seem a form of cant. A point is reached at which almost anything can be praised for its subversiveness or damned for its vulnerability to co-optation, for there is always some frame of reference that will support either description. As a colleague of mine recently put it, when we call something "subversive" nowadays we mean little more than that we *like* it. "Subversive" has become little more than a plus-mark, a gold star awarded to whatever a critic happens to approve of, rather the way an earlier generation of critics used words like "beautiful" and "noble."

Today, certain theories or textual practices are predefined as *inherently subversive*—e.g., any "rupture" of conventional realism or narrative closure, any decentering of the subject, any refusal to read for authorial intentions or determinate meaning. Did not Roland Barthes declare it in "The Death of the Author" when he said that "refusing to assign a 'secret', an ultimate meaning, to the text (and to the world as a text) liberates what may be called an anti-theological activity, an activity that is truly revolutionary since to refuse to fix meaning is, in the end, to refuse God and his hypostases— reason, science, law"?[11]

The assertion that there is something "truly revolutionary" about refusing to assign meaning to a text is perhaps the ultimate descent into the politics of silliness. Given so lax a criterion for being revolutionary, it is not surprising that we have had no scarcity of alleged revolution and subversion in recent criticism. To quote Bruce Robbins once more, "with so much of this subversive quantity about, one would think the revolution was scheduled for next week at the latest."[12]

Though "essentialism" is one of its favorite targets, this line of critique is itself essentialist, a kind of anti-essentialist essentialism. It assumes, in effect that essentialism (as well as any appeal to the natural, the objective, etc.) always and everywhere has the same (sinister) political consequences, irrespective of the contexts in which it functions. What is essentialist, in other words, is to imagine that an idea has its political coloration *in itself,* instead of acquiring that coloration from the way it is used, or the effect it has, in a specific context or situation. To be sure, essentialism (like any other *ism*) always has some political effect, but *what that effect is* cannot be deduced from the idea itself, but only from an examination of how the idea operates in a particular social conjuncture. Appealing to essences (or to the natural, the objective, etc.) is often a way of rationalizing coercive social practices, but not necessarily always. In the recent American and South African racial struggles, to take just one example, the idea that there is an essential human nature that racist regimes violate has had an important "oppositional" effect.[13]

The inflation of the currency of political evaluation is seen in the recent disputes of literary theorists about the politics of deconstruction. Is deconstruction really radical, or has it been co-opted? (The revelation of Paul de Man's early collaborationist journalism has sent this debate into a new phase.) But deconstruction is not alone in this respect—every recent critical movement has been no sooner celebrated for its revolutionary character than it has been damned for its susceptibility to co-optation. The rate seems to accelerate, however, at which a critical methodology goes from being celebrated as a revolutionary to being condemned as complicitous. Whereas it took several years before one heard that deconstruction was really an extension of the establishment, it took only a few months for this charge to be made about the new historicism. Yet again, the criteria on which such judgments are made are often questionable.

So it is not surprising that an attitude of agnosticism has begun to set in toward the current political buzzwords—"oppositional," "masculinist," "logocentric," "panoptic," "hegemonic," "transgressive," "counter-hegemonic," etc. With this, however, has come an attitude of agnosticism toward the validity of *any* political evaluation of culture—which brings me to "Right New Historicism."

Right New Historicism

Right new historicism argues, in effect, that since every form of culture is destined to be co-opted, the very notion of an oppositional position is nonsense. Since there is no "outside" to power, the very question of alternatives to an established regime is foolish. "Theory" is rejected on the ground that it illicitly claims to govern or criticize practice from the outside. I refer not to Foucault, who never acceded to the implicit fatalism of his own logic, but to neopragmatists such as Stanley Fish, Walter Benn Michaels, and Steven Knapp—Foucauldians, in effect, without Foucault's politics. (Rorty, on the other hand, has differentiated his version of pragmatism from conservative politics.)

Whatever their specific politics, these neopragmatists offer a useful corrective to current Leftist criticism when they insist that there is no *logical* connection between a theory and its political consequences, or between any set of ideas and how they may be *used* in particular social contexts. As I have just observed in connection with "anti-essentialist essentialism," the political valence of a theory, idea, or textual practice is *conjunctural*—it does not inhere in the theory or practice *in itself,* but is a function of how the theory or practice is used or appropriated in specific contexts. Such an argument is pertinent in a climate where terms like "oppositional" and "complicitous" are affixed to this or that form of culture as if the contextual analysis that might justify the terms had actually been done. On the other hand, in the hands of Fish, Michaels-Knapp, and Rorty, the valid argument that no theory implies a particular politics in itself seems to be used in such a way as to suggest that any attempt to make political judgments about forms of culture is necessarily pointless.

In his challenging study of American naturalist fiction, *The Gold Standard and the Logic of Naturalism,* Walter Benn Michaels chastizes critics who have debated the question of what attitude Theodore Dreiser's novels take toward capitalism. Michaels argues that it is foolish to ask whether Dreiser "liked" or "disliked" capitalism, because in Dreiser's novels (and presumably in the real world) there is no "outside" to capitalism, nothing outside the marketplace. It is the omnipresence of the market that for Michaels throughout *The Gold Standard* the "logic of naturalism" demonstrates.

Michaels puts the point as follows:

> What exactly did it mean to think of Dreiser as approving (or disapproving) consumer culture? Although transcending your origins in order to evaluate them has been the opening move in cultural criticism at least since Jeremiah, it is surely a mistake to take this move at face value: not so much because you can't really transcend your culture but because, if you did, you wouldn't have any terms of evaluation left—except, perhaps, theological ones. It thus seems wrong to think of the culture you live in as the object of your affections: you don't like it or dislike it, you exist in it, and the things you like and dislike exist in it too. Even Bartleby-like refusals of the world remain inextricably linked to it—what could count as a more powerful exercise of the right to freedom of contract than Bartleby's successful refusal to enter into any contracts? . . .[14]

Michaels adds that he is trying to "transform an argument about the affective relation of certain literary texts to American capitalism into an investigation of the position of those texts within a system of representation that, producing objects of approval and disapproval both, is more important than any attitude one might imagine oneself to have toward it" (Michaels, 19).

Michaels wants to get away from "endless theorizing about the nature and very possibility of realistic representation: do texts refer to social reality? If they do, do they merely reflect it, or do they criticize it? And if they do not, do they try to escape it, or do they imagine utopian alternatives to it?" Like the question of whether Dreiser liked or disliked capitalism, Michaels says, "these questions seem to me to posit a space outside the culture in order then to interrogate the relations between that space (here defined as literary) and the culture. But the spaces I have tried to explore are all very much within the culture, and so the project of interrogation makes no sense; the only relation literature as such has to culture as such is that it is part of it . . . ." (Michaels, 27).

Michaels's argument cuts very effectively against the current way of doing literary-political criticism by hunting down textual practices which have been predefined as liberatory or repressive and awarding ideological pluses and minuses accordingly. The argument also cuts effectively against a more traditional type of critical sentimentality which locates the defining characteristic of literature—or in this instance of the naturalistic novel—in its supposed independence of the realm of material circumstances, commodification, and practical utility. Since Kant, "literature" (or "art") has been defined by the tactic of inverting an essentially negative characterization of the bourgeois market society, namely, functional rationality, predatory objectification, dissociation of sensibility, etc. The definition of "literature," then, comes to be determined by a logic of agoraphobia: literature is anything and everything that the marketplace is *not*—disinterested, autonomous, a communicative mode that does not "mean" but simply "is," and so forth in an endless series of such characterizations.[15]

New historicism joins Marxism and feminism (and bourgeois anti-formalism) in arguing that this anti-market characterization of literature is not essential but historical and contingent. The idea of literature as a special form of discourse, allegedly impervious to standard illocutionary conventions such as reference and assertion, points not to the essential nature of literature at all, but to the way literature has tended to be thought of under certain historical conditions, specifically, in a society where practical, instrumental forms of speaking and writing seem complicitous with the vulgarity of the marketplace. To regard literature as the antithesis of "practical discourse" is to offer a set of ideological preferences masquerading as a definition, preferences generated by a historical situation in which disinterested behavior has come to be valued as an antidote to the market.

Michaels overturns this opposition between literature and the market, not by making theoretical arguments against it but by showing in a series of readings how deeply naturalistic novels are implicated in the "system of representation" peculiar to the capitalist market. These readings demonstrate that naturalist novels not only reveal an obsession with the instabilities of the market, but that their typical characters are constituted and decentered by those instabilities. Tying Marx's analysis of the fetishism of commodities to certain themes of deconstruction, Michaels suggests that commodification is a radically deconstructive force that produces a form of character systematically divided from itself and doomed perpetually to fail in its search for self-identity.

So far so good. But why should the fact that in naturalist fiction the market is all-powerful invalidate questions about the ethical and political implications of that state of affairs, as Michaels maintains it does? One of Michaels's reviewers, William E. Cain, has asked why, after all, is it so foolish to wonder if Dreiser *liked* or *disliked* capitalism: "Why [Cain writes] must Michaels rule out the question whether Dreiser 'likes' capitalism? Such a question may seem to lack sophistication, yet it has just the kind of starkness and crude honesty which Dreiser himself would have found compelling." As Cain observes, there is something arbitrary in Michaels's habit of treating critical questions about a culture as if they were "outside" the culture: " 'Liking or disliking' capitalism, and 'criticizing or endorsing' it, are formulations that are not at all separate from the contexts of capitalism."[16] After all, we often criticize or "dislike" our culture for failing to live up to its own officially professed values.

There is a difficulty here, however, as to what counts as "the culture," a difficulty that arises because of Michaels's overly monolithic use of this word (and terms like "system" or "logic" of representation). Michaels's point, as we have seen, is not that "you can't really transcend your culture," but that the "terms of evaluation" in which you try to do the transcending have to be those of the culture you are trying to transcend. This, however, assumes that a "culture" (or a cultural "discourse") is a monolithic entity whose "terms of evaluation" are specific to that culture and that culture alone and can be identified as such. But if "culture" is being used in the anthropological sense, then it seems fair to say that terms of evaluation cut across different cultures. "Capitalist culture" is not a seamless, monolithic fabric, but carries over some of the "terms of evaluation" from feudal culture and some tribal cultures. It does not follow that because all evaluative vocabularies are culturally *constructed* they are culture-*specific*. It is because Michaels blurs this distinction that he arrives at the odd conclusion that there is something anomalous about asking whether one likes or dislikes one's culture.

Much the same problem arises with the concept of "system of representation" that is so central to Michaels's and other new historicist analyses. Is representation a "system" at all in the monolithic sense which Michaels must give the term in order to classify certain conventions of representation as specifically capitalist? One might argue that though capitalism generates certain characteristic forms of representation, those forms are too heterogeneous for us always to be able to tell whether a particular representational convention is specifically capitalist or not. Michaels cites Bartleby's "I prefer not to" as an example of how an attempt to refuse capitalist logic cannot help exemplifying the capitalist logic of "freedom of contract." Bartleby's "I prefer not to" is presumably constituted by the capitalist system of representation that it attempts to contest. But, how can we know this for sure? For all one can tell, Bartleby's gesture could be in part a residue of feudal culture, or of a quasi-artistocratic aspect of Melville's background. (Bakhtin would argue that such statements are always "internally dialogized.") Such a refusal of capitalism is not necessarily specific to the "culture of capitalism" or its system of representation.

Brook Thomas makes this point in another critique of Michaels's book when he says that "Michaels operates as if, at some moment he does not designate, the country as a whole suddenly became transformed into a unified system of consumer capitalism." In fact, however, the post-Civil War transformation of the United States was marked by uneven development, producing "a culture in which different stages of capitalism overlapped and even came into contact with residual elements of non-capitalist modes of production. Because there was not one uniform 'logic of capitalism' but many different competing logics, it might be safer to speak of cultures rather than a single culture." Paradoxically, then, according to Thomas, Michaels's emphasis on "a structure of internal difference results in a tendency to produce eternal sameness. . . . By conducting his analysis within an overriding logic of capitalism, the very critic who distrusts transcendental categories ends by adopting the Market as a transcendental category, much in the way that mechanical deconstructionists treat Writing, Play, or Differance."[17]

This difficulty with Michaels's use of the concepts of "culture" and "system of representation" can be found more pervasively in the new historicist use of concepts like "discursive practice," "discourse community," and "interpretive community," as if these were unified systems whose characteristics were specific to them and them alone. In fact there is a strong family resemblance between Michaels's monolithic use of terms such as "culture" and "system of representation" and Fish's use of the term "interpretive community." In Fish's case, too, the terminology is used to suggest that there is something philosophically anomalous about radical political critique, as when, in the essay, "Anti-Professionalism," Fish chides Richard Ohmann's critique of certain forms of English department specialization for invoking "a non-institutional standard." Again, it is only on the assumption that "institutions" (or "interpretive communities") are monolithic and distinctly bounded that we would know when a particular discursive move is internal or external to the institution.[18]

In making this argument I have borrowed the Fish-Michaels pragmatic argument and turned it against Fish and Michaels. For what we seem to have in their work is a conflict between the new historicist tendency to overspecify the characteristics of discursive systems, in order to produce analyses of interpretive communities and literary works, and the pragmatist tendency already referred to to dissociate those systems from specific practical uses. That is, if pragmatism is right that there is no logical link between a textual practice and its political consequences, then we cannot identify textual practices with any specific "logic" or "system" of representation.

To put it another way, Michaels's attack on the Left for taking seriously the question of whether Dreiser "liked" capitalism (and Fish's similar line of attack) is an attempt to make an essentially political quarrel look as if it were a philosophical one. Michaels wants us to think that to ask such a question is somehow to be guilty of a philosophical error, the mistaken belief that a theory could govern practice from the outside. But whether there can be something outside the capitalist market is not a problem of philosophy but of practical politics, a distinction which the "against theory" argument effaces.

But then, to revert to my earlier point, asking whether someone likes or dislikes capitalism can seem like a gesture of futility in a society where the possibility of socialism has so receded that for most of us no alternative to capitalism seems conceivable. As Cain suggests, though, in regarding such an "outside" perspective as a philosophical impossibility, Michaels's form of new historicism becomes ahistorical. As Lukács might have argued, the state of life under capitalism has become confused with the nature of reality as it is and always must be.

We come back to the ambiguities entailed by the concept of co-optation and the way they point up the uncertain position of radical cultural politics at a time when the Left is no longer presumptively socialist. Just as the transition from royalism to corporate capitalism has blurred the identity of the Right (today's free market conservative is yesterday's nineteenth-century liberal), the debacle of Soviet and other Communisms and the global expansion of trade has problematized the idea of the Left. It is possible that terms like "radical" and "Left" may be on their way out, both in the larger politics of American culture (where Democrat and Republican are often hard to distinguish) and in academic cultural politics, where the designation "Left" now tends to be replaced by terms like "oppositional" among feminists, gay liberationists, and the more political post-structuralists.

But as I suggested earlier, such substitute terms only disguise the absence of agreement on how oppositionality is to be measured, with respect to what larger vision of society. And in the overheated polemical atmosphere of cultural discussion, it becomes difficult for anyone to admit confusion and ask for clarification. So we go on putting labels like "transgressive," "reactionary," and "complicitous" on texts, theories, and cultural practices, as if we actually knew what we were talking about.

Does the rise of what I have called (perhaps too reductively) right new historicism mean that this name-calling stage of political-cultural discussion is exhausting itself? It is interesting to note that the jacket blurb of *The Gold Standard* (by Philip Fisher) declares that Michaels's book represents a break with an "exhausted oppositional criticism." When I saw this statement I made a mental note to remember it—would this be the moment I would look back on years later, the moment when oppositional criticism officially died? If so, the fact that I first got the news from a publisher's advertisement would be peculiarly apt, a vindication of sorts of the argument that co-optation by the market is unopposable.

If such predictions prove true, will this be a good thing? It will be hard to mourn the passing of the current oppositional phase of criticism. I too dislike it—or much of it—with its conceptual confusion, bullying, and smugness, and I have attacked it often. But the alternatives are never what one would like. If what is to take the place of "exhausted oppositional criticism" is a new, sophisticated complacency, I for one will be sorry to see it go.

Notes

1.   Michel Foucault, *The History of Sexuality: Volume I: An Introduction*, trans. Richard Hurley (New York: Random House, 1978), pp. 17–49.

2.   *Webster's New Third International Dictionary of the English Language* (Springfield, Mass.: G. & C. Merriam Co., 1971), p. 501; *The American Heritage Dictionary of the English*

Language (Boston: Houghton Mifflin Co., 1980), p. 293; *The World Book Dictionary* (Chicago: World Book, Inc., 1984), p. 485.

3.   Charles Baudelaire, *Selected Writings on Art and Artists*, trans. P. E. Charvet (London: Penguin Books, 1972), pp. 33–34; quoted in Graff, *Literature Against Itself: Literary Ideas in Modern Society* (Chicago: University of Chicago Press, 1979), p. 110.

4.   Lionel Trilling, *Beyond Culture: Essays on Literature and Learning* (New York: Viking Press, 1968), p. 26.

5.   Harold Rosenberg, *The Tradition of the New* (New York: Horizon Press, 1959); see especially the essays, "Everyman a Professional" and "Pop Culture: Kitsch Criticism"; later books by Rosenberg include *The De-Definition of Art* (New York: Macmillan Co., 1972) and *Rediscovering the Present: Three Decades in Art, Culture, & Politics* (Chicago: University of Chicago Press, 1973).

6.   Irving Howe, *Decline of the New* (New York: Harcourt, Brace and World, 1970).

7.   Richard Rorty, "Habermas and Lyotard on Postmodernity," in *Habermas and Modernity*, Richard J. Bernstein, ed. (Cambridge, Mass.: MIT Press, 1985), p. 174.

8.   Michel Foucault, *Power/Knowledge: Selected Interviews and Other Writings, 1972–1977* (New York: Pantheon Books, 1980), p. 126.

9.   Bruce Robbins, "Oppositional Professionals," talk (unpublished) delivered at the English Institute, August, 1987.

10.   Jürgen Habermas, *Communication and the Evolution of Society*, trans. Thomas McCarthy (Boston: Beacon Press, 1979), pp. 51–68; Derrida's point on Foucault is in *Writing and Difference*, trans. Alan Bass (Chicago: University of Chicago Press, 1978), pp. 34–36.

11.   Roland Barthes, *Image Music Text*, trans. Stephen Heath (New York: Hill and Wang, 1977), p. 147.

12.   Bruce Robbins, Review (untitled), *Literature and History*, 7, no. 2 (1981), p. 240.

13.   The most incisive critique I have seen of this current anti-essentialist essentialism is Terry Eagleton's essay, "Ideology and Scholarship," in *Historical Studies and Literary Criticism*, Jerome J. McGann, ed. (Madison: University of Wisconsin Press, 1985), pp. 114–25.

14.   Walter Benn Michaels, *The Gold Standard and the Logic of Naturalism: American Literature at the Turn of the Century* (Berkeley: University of California Press, 1987), pp. 18–19.

15.   Agoraphobia is one of the pet themes of New Historicism. See the suggestive essay by Michaels's former student, Gillian Brown, "The Empire of Agoraphobia," *Representations*, XX (Fall, 1987), pp. 134–57. On negatively derived definitions of literature, see my "Literary Criticism as Social Diagnosis," in *At the Boundaries*, Herbert L. Sussman, ed., Proceedings of the Northeastern Center for Literary Studies, I, no. 1, 1983 (Boston: Northeastern University Press, 1984), pp. 1–16.

16.   Realism, Naturalism, and the New American Literary History," *Review*, X, p. 112.

12.   Brook Thomas, "Walter Benn Michaels and Cultural History," forthcoming in *boundary 2*.

18.   For a fuller elaboration of these arguments on Fish, see my "Interpretation in Tlön: A Response to Stanley Fish," in *New Literary History*, XVII, no. 1 (Autumn, 1985), pp. 110–17; Fish replies to my critique in "Resistance and Independence: A Reply to Gerald Graff," in the same issue of the journal, pp. 120–27.

12

The New Historicism and other Old-fashioned Topics

Brook Thomas

I

In the past few years in North America the word "history" has frequently been inserted into our *discours* about the *histoire* of literature. A common label for literary critics' renewed interest in history is the new historicism. The label causes confusion because it has both specific and general referents. Specifically it refers to work associated with the journal *Representations,* especially that of Stephen Greenblatt. Generally it refers to work on the relationship between literature and history that directly or indirectly has been influenced by post-structuralist theory. I will stick to the more general description. Even so, I share the uncomfortableness others have with both words in the label.

"Historicism" causes a problem because it is often used with little awareness of its complicated history in English, a lack of awareness that is damning for any movement claiming to take history seriously. "Historicism" can refer generally to any sort of historical method. But it can also refer to a specific brand of historiography that flourished in the nineteenth century, especially in Germany, where it was known as *Historismus.* Trying to guarantee precision, some translators evoke "historism" to refer to *Historismus.* Nonetheless, "historism" never took. The resulting confusion has caused Herbert Lindenberger to avoid the term historicism altogether.[1] But not all are as restrained as Lindenberger, and it remains a historical fact that in North America the label "New Historicism" has caught on. Rather than quibble over definitions by repeating important, if too often ignored, work done on the term's history, I will accept Fredric Jameson's description that historicism refers to "our relationship to the past, and of our possibility of understanding the latter's monuments, artifacts, and traces."[2] A new historicism in literary studies, therefore, promises a new relationship to our literary past.

One result of defining the new historicism in this more general way is to complicate a comparison Louis Montrose has made between the new historicism in the United States and cultural materialism in Great Britain.

The new historicism and cultural materialism have imporant similarities, but because the British school owes so much to the work of Raymond Williams there is a temptation to argue that it is more concerned with cultural politics than its American counterpart. For instance, Montrose distinguishes between the two by noting that, whereas both British and American scholars of the Renaissance offer new histories, in the United States "the emphasis has been almost exclusively upon a refiguring of the sociocultural field in which Renaissance texts were *originally* produced—although not without an awareness of the role of the present in (re)making the past. In Britain . . . there has been a relatively greater emphasis upon the uses to which the *present* has put its versions of the past."[3]

I don't want to deny a difference between the new historicism and cultural materalism. Indeed, to evoke Greenblatt's alternative description for his work—cultural poetics—is to emphasize an important difference between material and textual emphases. Nonetheless, I do not agree with Montrose that the difference has to do with the degree to which the present makes use of the past. As far as the *English* Renaissance goes, Montrose may be right, but if we look at studies of the *American* Renaissance, we get a different story. It is no accident that American critics are more concerned with the uses the present puts to versions of their own Renaissance rather than England's. As the debate over the canon, the numerous efforts to reconstruct American literature, and the completed and proposed Columbia and Cambridge literary histories demonstrate, there is a concerted effort to make American representations of its literary past more usable to its present population.

I am sympathetic with those who feel the need to redefine our relationship to the cultural past, but to recognize a need is not to minimize problems inherent in the project. Thus, while accepting the term "historicism," I want to raise the question of what is new about present returns to historical analysis. That question is too broad to answer in one essay, so I will focus on one aspect: the narratives that structure these new histories. In fact, my focus will be even more narrow, as I concentrate on a trend within the new historicism that tries to give representation to groups excluded by previous histories. Inevitably my analysis of narrative structures will touch on other aspects, such as subject matter and representational models, that could be topics for other essays. Nonetheless, by concentrating on the narratives commonly used to include the previously excluded I have two goals: (1) to explore the complicated relationship between the new historicism and poststructuralism. (2) to situate the new historicism within the history of historicism.

II

As I have already suggested, the most widespread explanation of how the new historicism distinguishes itself from the old is that it has engaged poststructuralist theory. Thus, its label, which signals a displacement of the

New Criticism, also announces its difference from the old historicism that was displaced (if not completely replaced) by the New Criticism, a difference accounted for by its new theoretical sophistication. Whereas the "discourse" employed by new historicists clearly reveals its debt to poststructuralism, many new historicists make a further claim by arguing that even the poststructuralism to which it is indebted, especially deconstruction, can be as ahistorical as New Critical formalism. Sensing that in and of itself poststructuralism did not take us as far beyond formalism as was first hoped, these new historicists follow Jameson's call, "always historicize."[4]

From this simplistic, but widely held, account of the newness of the new historicism one thing is clear: the relationship between the new historicism and poststructuralism is not at all clear. In examining their complicated relationship I will, unfortunately, use the label "poststructuralism" as generally as I use that of the "new historicism," which will too often cause me to neglect important differences within each. Nonetheless, I risk such overgeneralization because, as I have indicated, I am interested in the historical power of the labels themselves. What, for instance, does their popularity have to tell us about our historical situation?

I'll start my investigation with the work of one of the most outspoken critics of the existing canon, someone who acknowledges her debt to poststructuralist thought and who identifies herself as a new historicist: Jane Tompkins. I do not single out Tompkins in order to make a personal attack on her. Quite the contrary, I have learned from her work. Instead, I use her because she economically illustrates a tension between poststructuralism and the new historicism.

In the Preface to *Sensational Designs* Tompkins promises a "new kind of historical criticsm" that will challenge the canon of the American Renaissance as established by members of a "cultural elite," like F. O. Matthiessen.[5] In order to do so she relies on poststructuralist assumptions similar to those of Stanley Fish, which deny that aesthetic value resides within texts, and argues that texts are constituted by interpretive communities. Drawing on Fish's work she quite effectively demonstrates that the criteria for aesthetic value change as the assumptions uniting interpretive communities change. If this is true, any argument for the intrinsic value of the canon seems seriously flawed.

Now clearly not all new historical challenges to the canon draw on the work of Fish. Nonetheless, most are indebted to some version of poststructuralism in order to deconstruct the canon. Most important is the poststructuralist critique of representation. Emphasizing the gap in any effort to re-present, poststructuralists remind us that the desire for full representation is linked to an impossible to achieve dream of presence. Constituted by both a temporal and spatial gap, representation is structurally dependent on misrepresentation. Since by definition representation can never be full, all acts of representation produce an "other" that is marginalized or excluded.

It is easy to see why such logic serves as a powerful weapon for those attacking existing histories and canons. The supposedly objective criteria used to establish a canon representing the interests of all humanity can be shown to be weighted in favor of a certain segment of the population. Indeed, the notion of objectivity itself is claimed to be a false one, since the inevitability of partial representation makes critical impartiality impossible. Deprived of a position outside society that allows a detached reflection upon it, all literature and criticism—like other social practices—are condemned to remain in the field of the power relations that produce them. In short, literature and criticism do not occupy a detached space free from political pressures, but are inevitably subject to political constraints. All constructions of literary histories are political, and many new historicists consider it their responsibility to redress past political inequities by giving representation to those previously excluded.

As important and valuable as these efforts are to make literary histories more representative, one difficulty with them is obvious. If all acts of representation are structurally dependent on misrepresentation, these new histories inevitably create their own canons and exclusions. This difficulty is concisely illustrated by Tompkins's attempt to offer her version of "The Other American Renaissance," a version that emphasizes the importance of popular works of fiction, like *Uncle Tom's Cabin*, that in making designs on a wide audience produced important cultural work by effecting social change. In order to make a case for the importance of this popular tradition, Tompkins has to discard her theory that interpretive communities constitute texts, for now she is forced to describe a tradition with definable characteristics. Indeed, it is particular characteristics of popular fiction that have caused a "cultural elite" to exclude them. Tompkins's Fishlike assumptions serve her well so long as she asks questions such as, "Is there a text in this classroom?" or "How do readers produce texts?" But they fail her when her attempt to reconstruct the canon forces her to ask "What text should we have in the classroom?" or "How did particular texts influence readers?" Thus when she comes to write her own history, Tompkins abandons her up-to-date poststructuralist pose and returns to old-fashioned assumptions about literature and historical analysis. In terms of literature she adheres to the traditional notion that a text provides "men and women with a means of ordering the world they inhabit" (xiii). In terms of historical analysis she focuses on the cultural work done by texts at their moment of past production not present reception and adheres to the traditional historicists' desire to "recreate, as sympathetically as possible, the context from which [these works] sprang and the specific problems to which they were addressed" (xiii). Reserving criticism of the social and political attitudes that motivated her writers, she "tried instead to inhabit and make available to a modern audience the viewpoint from which their politics made sense" (xiii).

That Tompkins identifies this traditional method of historical analysis with the new historicism confirms how difficult it is to establish a truly "new" historicism. Indeed, she gets caught in a number of contradictions. For instance, her attempt to understand writers on their own historical terms directly contradicts her poststructuralist claim that her book is a product of her own interpretive assumptions, assumptions shaped by her place in history. Furthermore, even the radical thrust of her attack on the canon is compromised. Tompkins's last paragraph is a revolutionary jeremiad announcing that her "study and Matthiessen's are competing attempts to constitute American literature." It ends with the stirring call that, "The literary canon, as codified by a cultural elite, has power to influence the way the country thinks across a broad range of issues. The struggle now being waged in the professoriate over which writers deserve canonical status is not just a struggle over the relative merits of literary geniuses; it is a struggle among contending factions for the right to be represented in the picture America draws of itself" (201).

Since Tompkins spends an entire chapter arguing that Hawthorne owes his literary reputation to "the influence of his friends and associates, and then on the influence of their successors" (4) and since Hawthorne is a writer canonized by Matthiessen, we might suspect that she is attacking the way reputations are made. But this is not the case. "The argument that follows is not critical of the way literary reputations come into being, or of Hawthorne's reputation in particular. Its object, rather, is to suggest that a literary reputation could never be anything but a political matter" (4). A book that announces itself as a radical attack on the canon turns out not to criticize the way literary reputations are made. Rather than demand systemic change, it merely challenges those who have used the system's logic to get ahead. Furthermore, it implies that the only hope for those previously excluded is to use that very logic to their advantage.

Indeed, to persist in maintaining poststructuralist assumptions would seem to guarantee marginality, for whereas they offer a lucid explanation of why exclusions always take place, they seem of little help in reconstructing our literary histories. Thus, the very poststructuralist assumptions that help to attack past histories seem necessarily forgotten in efforts to create new ones. That forgetfulness is apparent in the narrative that Tompkins uses to structure her history of popular writers. Rather than challenge the old historicism's narrative that charts an emerging tradition, a narrative that poststructuralists have discredited, Tompkins adopts it to structure the history of "The Other American Renaissance." Similarly, in a recent talk— "Susan Rowsan, The Father of the American Novel"—her title, however self-ironic, signals that she has merely replaced a male with a female as the originator of our literary tradition. And Tompkins is not an isolated case. Within the field of American literature alone, we have histories of emergent female, black, Hispanic traditions, and so on. Narratives that are politically unacceptable for some are encouraged for others.

In drawing attention to this contradiction, I may seem to be merely indulging in the latest academic sport: pointing out that the new historicism isn't as new as it claims to be. This sport is especially popular with old fashioned historicists because it allows them to dismiss the new historicism as the latest fad—history without footnotes, as some say—and to go on with their work undisturbed. Unfortunately, some new historicist polemics have made this sport all too easy, confirming complaints that the adjective in the label merely appeals to our commodifying cult of the new. (At least it is not advertised as tasting great or being less filling.) Indeed, as Walter Benjamin notes, in capitalist culture the desire for novelty becomes recurrent in both senses of the word. "Fashion," Benjamin muses, "is the eternal return of the new."[6] Without a doubt, much of the recent fuss over the new historicism (including this volume) has occurred because the new historicism has become the latest fashion.

But to dismiss the new historicism because it is fashionable is to deny the possibility that it responds to a felt historical need or that amidst the polemics and posturing something legitimately new might be taking place. It is for this last reason that a poststructuralist critique of the pattern of forgetfulness is more devastating than charges of faddishness, for poststructuralists can interpret the new historicism's forgetfulness as an inevitable lapse from theoretical rigor in any attempt to create the new. Whereas the new historicism's very label implies that the new will be brought about through an understanding of the past, poststructuralists, following Nietzsche, can argue that bringing about the new requires an active forgetting, not remembering.[7] Creation of the new, like representation, inevitably involves an act of repression.

This poststructuralist critique forces those new historicists honest enough to face it into the contradiction that we found in Tompkins. On the one hand, they claim authority for their reconstructions of literary history by appealing to historical evidence. On the other, they have to admit that their evidence is itself an inevitably partial construction of the past from a present perspective. Thus it is no wonder that some new historicists have gravitated to the "Against Theory" position, which claims that theoretical debates ultimately have no consequences for the practice of criticism, that, to use Tompkins's words, "arguments about 'what happened' have to proceed much as they did before poststructuralism broke in with its talk about language-based reality and culturally produced knowledge."[8] Such a position might be subtitled, "How I learned to stop worrying about theory by forgetting it," and it certainly provides an excuse to proceed full-speed ahead with a what-me-worry attitude. At the same time, however, it confirms both the traditional historicists' and the poststructuralists' critiques of the new historicism. Traditional historicists can be reassured that there's nothing new happening anyway, since all of that theoretical jargon doesn't really make a difference when it comes to the practice of history. Poststructuralists can watch with knowing eyes as their theoretical assumptions are actively forgotten in order to produce new histories.

A logical consequence of the "Against Theory" position is to eliminate the tension between the new historicism and poststructuralism by compartmentalizing the two. Poststructuralism becomes the practice of theory; the new historicism that of history. These separate practices can exist at the same historical moment but have no consequences for one another.[9] Our task, however, should be to understand present tensions, not to eliminate them prematurely by fiat. A start toward that understanding is to situate them historically. If that statement seems to align me with the practice of history rather than that of theory, let me add that in order to understand the tension between the new historicism and post-structuralism historically we need to stop thinking of poststructuralism, and even deconstruction, as ahistorical. Indeed, whereas it is commonplace to see the new historicism as a response to poststructuralism, we need to extend our historical horizon to see poststructuralism as a historical response to historicism, especially *Historismus.* To do that requires a very brief history of historicism.

III

The history of historicism reveals one obvious reason why it is so easy to dispute the new historicism's claims to newness: the coupling of "new" with "historicism" is redundant. This is because the historical imagination that gave rise to historicism is unthinkable without a change in the concept of reality that marks the beginning of the modern age. According to Hans Blumenberg, the ancient and medieval world assumed a closed cosmos in which nothing new or unfamiliar was allowed to become real. In contrast, the modern view "removes the dubiousness from what is new and so *terra incognita* or the *munda novas,* becomes possible and effective as a *stimulus* to human activity; if one might phrase the process as a paradox, surprise is something to be expected." The modern concept of reality, in which the *mundas novas* becomes possible, is related to the rise of historicism because it depends upon a changed notion of temporality. Opposed to belief in a closed cosmos, the modern view assumes an open context that "always looks forward to a future that might contain elements which could shatter previous consistency and so render previous 'realities' unreal."[10] Events, therefore, take place not only in history but through history, and temporality has become a component part of reality.

So long as temporality is a component part of reality, reality undergoes continual transformations that necessitate continual rewritings of history. As Goethe confidently announced, "That world history has to be rewritten from time to time is no longer doubted by anyone these days."[11] Put another way, historicism, a product of the modern imagination, assumes that history will always be made new. As a result, the history of historicism is marked by perpetual claims to newness.

For instance, if Goethe recognized the need to rewrite history, his enlightenment belief that universal laws governed world history linked history to moral philosophy, since events were often used to illustrate natural law and the natural rights of man. But Goethe's notion of universal history was challenged by Johann Gottfried von Herder's emphasis on the organic development of peoples and nations, developments that became the object of study for the new science of history. Determined finally to break history's subordination to moral philosophy, the great spokesman for scientific history, Leopold von Ranke, argued that the historian's task was not to judge the past or to instruct the present for the profit of future ages, but "to show only what actually happened (*wie es eigentlich gewesen*)."[12] To accomplish this goal. Ranke emphasized the difference between primary and secondary sources and stressed the need for historians to rely on the former. Reconstructing an era from the materials it produced, the historian could sympathetically reinhabit the past.

Although Ranke's *Historismus* claimed to break with moral philosophy, it smuggled in its own moral vision through the narratives that it used to structure its stories of the past. These narratives yoked together the modern sense of linear temporality with the celebrated logocentrism of Western thought to produce teleological narratives of progressive emergence. According to Ranke, each age was equal in the eyes of God and therefore needed to be understood on its own terms. Combined with a notion of progressive temporality, however, this democratic vision of the various ages implied that the present was an expression of God's will. As Walter Benjamin observes in one of the most severe criticisms of *Historismus,* the result is a history of the victors.[13] Indeed nineteenth-century developmental histories served to justify Europe's imperialist domination of the world as well as the victories of individual nations. World history confirmed God's will to have a higher state of civilization progressively emerge in Europe.

Paradoxically, however, the very success of Western imperialism invited a questioning of the assumptions of *Historismus,* since as the West dominated other cultures it was forced to adjust its narratives about the unfolding of world history to include them. To be sure, these non-European cultures were absorbed into a Eurocentric narrative that denied them proper representation. Nonetheless, the presence of these repressed "others" allowed the possibility of a decentering of the Eurocentric version of history. Registered most forcefully in the thought of Nietzsche, the questioning of *Historismus* led to a general crisis in historicism, a crisis intensified by the destruction wrought by World War I, a crisis that found many thinkers sharing Yeats's anxiety that the center would not hold. If the unfolding of history led, not to a unified European culture, but a shattered and chaotic Europe; not to a higher rationality, but an unleashing of irrational barbarism within European culture; not to an emergent truth, but "the bottomless pit of relativism" feared by German historian Friedrich Meinecke,[14] then the assumptions of *Historismus* needed to be questioned.

Granted, the fragments that intellectuals shored up against Europe's ruin more often than not were a defensive maneuver, an attempt to preserve the order of a culture that perhaps never existed other than in the promise. Few knew better than Paul de Man the dangers of clinging to this reactionary nostalgia for the lost presence of a center that never ever was. De Man, as we now know, with reprehensible consequences faced the crisis in Western thought and politics by embracing the cause of a European culture unified through its literature. Experiencing in an intensely personal way the blindness of Western logocentrism—as well as the need actively to forget—de Man subsequently developed an insight that made him highly skeptical of any revolutionary promise to make history new, especially those depending on teleological narratives of emergence.

To evoke de Man in the present situation may appear sensationalistic but my point is to draw attention to strengths and weaknesses in poststructuralism. First of all, his life and work show to what extent poststructuralism, and especially deconstruction, is a historical response to a crisis in historicism from which Western thought has not yet recovered. Indeed, whereas it is fashionable today, as the subtitle of one essay puts it, to see "Historicism in a Deconstructed World,"[15] it would be more accurate to see deconstruction as a response to a historicized world. To emphasize why there is justification in deconstructive and poststructuralist skepticism toward historicism, especially its narratives of progressive emergence, let me quote, not a poststructuralist theorist, but an American empirical historian, David Hackett Fischer.

> Historicism was many things to many people, but in a general way its epistemology was idealist, its politics were antidemocratic, its aesthetics were romantic, and its ethics were organized around the nasty idea that whatever is becoming, is right.
>
> The classical expression of ethical historicism is Schiller's epigram *"die Weltgeschichte ist das Weltgericht."* This doctrine reduced ethics (and much else) to a province of historiography. And it was radically destructive, not merely of other ethical systems but of itself as well. Ethical historicism commonly took one of two untenable forms. Some historicists—Ranke is an eminent example—unwittingly smuggled an ethical system into history, and then discovered it as the objective teaching of history itself. Others later converted ethical historicism into an ethical relativism. Meinecke, for instance, asserted that "nothing can be

immoral which comes from the innermost individual character of a being." This
doctrine must necessarily become an ethical nihilism. It would prevent any
moral judgment against the filth which flowed from "the innermost individual
character" of many Nazi beings. Historicism, relativism, nihilism. There is *no*
stopping place in this downward descent to nothingness.[16]

Fischer's description places in perspective the charge that poststructuralism
is a nihilistic escape from history. Quite the opposite, at its best it is an
unflinching historical reaction against the nihilism to which at least one
version of historicism led. An important effort to rethink our relation to the
cultural past without succumbing to what William Spanos calls "the West's
Re-collective mania to recuperate the One,"[17] it provides a powerful warning
to those adopting narratives of progressive emergence.

But as powerful as that warning is, poststructuralism does not seem to
speak to the historical needs of important segments of our population. To
understand why is to recognize a limitation that is also highlighted by evoking
de Man's life and work. Clearly de Man cannot stand for all poststructuralists, and many have opposed aspects of his work. Nonetheless, he does show
how the poststructuralist insistence on an inevitable structure of blindness
and insight can be used to excuse the very repressions that it exposes, for if
errors are inevitable how are we to blame those who make them? Put
another way, if the poststructuralist project draws attention to the political
implications of all actions, its own political valence must always be determined situationally. At the same time that poststructuralism can be used
critically to expose repressions, it can be used apologetically to excuse them.
As such, poststructuralism is of limited use for those excluded by previous
histories, who are in a situation in which they need not only to deconstruct
discredited histories of the past, but to construct and legitimate new histories
in which they are finally represented.

The promise of bringing about the new is, as we have seen, indebted to
the modern world view. Indeed, despite the new historicism's acknowledged
debt to poststructuralism, its very label reveals a deeper, if less acknowledged
debt, to the tradition of the modern, that poststructuralism places in doubt.
The tension that we have been exploring between the new historicism and
poststructuralism has to do with the former's alignment with an impulse
contained within the modern and the latter's with what has come to be know
as the postmodern. If, as Spanos puts it, the postmodern is "a destructive
projective impulse" that cannot promise something "new" or a "truly new
epoch" (22), it will remain at odds with the project of new historicism, whose
reconstructive needs cannot be fulfilled solely by the destructive impulse of
poststructuralism and postmodernism. For instance, it may be more than an
irony of history that precisely at the moment when women and ethnics in
this country sense the possibility of emergence and the establishment of a

somewhat autonomous self, a theory is imported from the still predominantly white, male European academy declaring that notions of emergence and a centered self are bourgeois and reactionary. Perhaps those segments in our society that have previously been denied representation feel a need for narratives of emergence that continue to prove so effective in drawing people into a united movement.

But to recognize the legitimate historical need to which present narratives of emergence respond is not to meet the poststructuralist challenge, which at its best is not an abstract theoretical challenge but one based on an acute sense of history. For the new historicism to ignore that challenge or to dismiss it as a theoretical attempt to control practice from without is to make the new historicism, not poststructuralism, prone to charges of escaping history.

So far my brief history of historicism has emphasized the new historicism's unacknowledged debt to the tradition of the modern, a debt that puts it in tension with poststructuralism, which is a serious historical response to the failures of that tradition. Now I want to extend my history to reveal another unacknowledged debt of the new historicism: the tradition of progressive historiography in America.

IV

To suggest that the new historicism belongs to a native tradition is, no doubt, to spark resistance, since, as we have already seen, new historicists generally acknowledge their debt to poststructuralism precisely to announce their break with Anglo-American predecessors. Nonetheless, the most obvious evidence that the new historicism needs to be seen within an American tradition is that it developed on American soil. Perhaps its debt to an American tradition better explains its differences from British cultural materialism than Montrose's argument that the difference has to do with the uses each puts to the past. For instance, the need of Americans to stress "historicism" in their label might result from America's notorious escape from history. After all, the polemical call "always historicize" is most needed when there is a general tendency to do something else. But this explanation serves only to invite another question. If America has a tradition of escaping history, why in the late seventies and early eighties did the call to historicize suddenly reach such a responsive audience among literary scholars? To answer that question we need to add an American supplement to my brief history of historicism.

We can start by noting that America's notorious escape from history is not, paradoxically, an escape from historicism. American exceptionalism, the belief that America broke from Europe's repetition of hereditary wrongs, depends upon the metaphoric distinction between the "old" and "new" worlds. As we have seen, a precondition for that distinction is the modern notion of temporality that is also a precondition for the rise of historicism. Rather than a break with European historicism, American exceptionalism is a product of the belief that history can be made new. Put more simply, the doctrine of American exceptionalism is not, after all, so exceptional. In fact, the belief that America has broken with the European past is similar to the belief ushering in the modern era that the moderns had broken with the ancients. Americans merely claimed that this break with the old did not really occur until the founding of the new world. Thus, what is often seen as America's *escape* from history is better seen as a belief that it *culminates* history. It is only in America that history can truly be made new.

But if there is nothing exceptional about the mode of temporality that produces the doctrine of American exceptionalism, that mode of temporality did enable a spatial metaphor of the "new world" that makes a difference.[18] That difference manifests itself in a contradiction that inhabits both American exceptionalism and the modern self-definition of itself.

As we have seen, an important way in which the modern established its break with what went before was through a different notion of temporality, a belief that the linear progression of time brings about the new. Paradoxically, however, the very notion of progressive linear time rules out radical breaks in the future, since history unfolds in what Benjamin called "homogeneous, empty time."[19] Similarly, American exceptionalism depends upon a belief that in the "new" world the "old" world's repetitive cycle of hereditary sin will be replaced by a better world that gradually unfolds through time. Thus, once the original break with the European past has occurred no more "revolution" is necessary to fulfill the promise of the new.

If these patterns are similar, their difference lies in the historical specificity of the moment and place in which they took shape. Absorbing the ideology of republican virtue and economic liberalism that constituted the foundation of the United States as an independent entity, American exceptionalism linked the progressive unfolding of time with political progressivism. In Europe, the situation was different. As in American exceptionalism, a belief in progressive temporal emergence structured narratives of nationalism and, on a larger scale, of Europe's superiority over non-European cultures. Yet European narratives of temporal emergence were not necessarily linked to republican political progressivism, a difference that was extremely important when historicism started to experience its crisis. We can get a sense of how important that difference was by briefly comparing Nietzsche's late nineteenth-century attitude toward history and that of American pragmatists.

Nietzsche both responded to and contributed to a crisis in historicism by arguing that the new can only be brought about through an active forgetting that releases the burden of history. Abandoning a faith in the progressive emergence of history, he challenges the modern sense of temporality, thus becoming one of the most important "fathers" of poststructuralism. In contrast, the pragmatists, who like Nietzsche are considered antifoundationalist thinkers, retained the modern sense of temporality. Adhering to the historicist's belief that the passage of time necessitates the writing of new histories, John Dewey confirms that "changes going on in the present, giving a new turn to social problems, throw the significance of what happened in the past into a new perspective." The turn that pragmatists gave to the study of the past was influenced by both the American tradition of practicality and Darwinian evolution. In what George Santayana termed "that strange pragmatic reduction of yesterday to tomorrow," the pragmatists saw the study of the past as a tool to help those in the present adapt to their environment in order to bring about a new future. To quote Dewey again, a proper understanding of the past can be "a lever for moving the present into a certain kind of future."[20]

Not professional historians themselves, the pragmatists had a strong influence on James Harvey Robinson, who started a movement known as the New History. Robinson, who studied in Germany under the author of a famous book on American constitutional history, criticized most nineteenth-century histories for being too narrowly political, for telling the story of great leaders and wars while neglecting other areas of human life. In *The New History* (1912) he demanded that historians draw on the newly developed professional social sciences to give a fuller account of the past, an account that covered economic, psychological, and social life as well as political life. He wanted more inclusive histories that took into account the lives of more than an elite few. In addition, he stressed the "new" in his title by calling for histories that served the present. Fearful, as Nietzsche was, that the study of history would lapse into antiquarianism, Robinson joined pragmatism in reaction against the dominant formalism in American thought at the time and denied that the past contained truths applicable to all ages. Instead he believed that the most important truth to be learned from the past was that of change. Emphasizing historical process over product, he urged that Ranke's study of *wie es eigentlich gewesen* be transformed into a study of *wie es eigentlich geworden*. The study of the past was necessary because without it, we had no understanding of our present situation that evolved out of the past.

Robinson's New History exerted a powerful influence on America's progressive historians. The extent to which their democratic reformism was pervaded by historicism's belief that the progression of time brings about the new is indicated by Robinson's description of the French Revolution as "one of the grandest and, in its essential reforms, most peaceful of changes which ever overtook France or Europe."[21] In America, of course, even the "peaceful" reforms as important as the French Revolution were not necessary, since its unique history isolated it from the corruption of the European past.

Nonetheless, not even American exceptionalism made American historians immune to the European crisis in historicism. We can see its effect on Charles A. Beard. Beard, who with Robinson had edited a two-volume textbook on *The Development of Modern Europe,* became the most famous progressive historian when his *An Economic Interpretation of the Constitution* (1913) made a conscious intervention into current political debates. A devoted exceptionalist, Beard worried that America's entry into World War I risked contamination of its special status. Those worries increased when the worldwide depression threatened the belief that America was exempt from the problems affecting Europe. Furthermore, European ideas exerted their influence on American historians. For instance, soon after a careful reading of Benedetto Croce and a book by Karl Heussi entitled *Die Krisis des Historismus,* Beard delivered his famous "Written History as an Act of Faith." Beard's talk and Carl Becker's "Every Man His Own Historian" marked the ascendancy of the school of historical relativism in the United States.[22] Going beyond the New History's argument that histories should serve the present, the relativists questioned the belief that reliance on the methods of the social sciences could produce objective accounts of even *wie es eigentlich geworden.* The recovery of the past was based on an act of faith, not scientific objectivity.

My brief account of the New History and its relativistic aftermath shows that many "poststructuralist" assumptions of the new historicism are in fact part of the tradition of progressive historiography. Most obviously, the acknowledgment that historians do not objectively and scientifically recover the past but construct it from a present perspective is one made by Beard and Becker. Indeed, the influence that relativists had within history departments in the thirties and forties was no doubt one reason why the New Critics felt compelled to attack historically based criticism as relativistic; and insofar as the new historicism hopes to displace the New Criticism, it can be seen as an unacknowledged revenge of the relativists.

Granted, my last point reminds us that progressives did not dominate English departments, that the institutional histories of the two disciplines are different. But if new historicists are to take history seriously, they need to pay much more attention to what was going on in history departments, especially because their own call for interdisciplinarity was anticipated by Robinson's New History. In fact, the fascination of many new historicists with the marketplace recalls Beard's brand of economic determinism, an attempt at finding an American alternative to marxism. Nonetheless, Beard's determinism forces me to pause for a moment to complicate my brief account of the progressive tradition and its relation to the new historicism.

So far I may have implied that progressives were naive optimists, celebrating the past, present, and future state of America. Clearly, this was not the case. Beard, for instance, was highly critical of injustices within American society. The narrative he adopted to expose those injustices presented an almost Manichaean struggle between America's truly democratic progressive spirit and a conservative, monied elite. Thus, his progressive narrative of America's exceptionalism was joined with a narrative that was its mirror image, a version of what Sacvan Bercovitch has called the negative jeremiad.[23] This pessimistic narrative often brought Beard close to a conspiracy theory of American history. After all, something was needed to explain why America's true spirit did not always triumph. Not surprisingly, the new historicism occasionally tends toward a conspiracy theory.

For instance Tompkins's "Other American Renaissance" constructs the story of a "cultural elite" who created a canon by conspiring to exclude popular writers, who for her represent the true democratic spirit. The problem with this narrative becomes clear when we compare it to Beard's narrative of a monied elite, for the values of a cultural elite who play a role in establishing literary canons are not necessarily the same as those of a culture's elite. It was, after all, not just white elites, but also blacks like James Baldwin who were among the strongest denigrators of *Uncle Tom's Cabin*. Especially in the United States, custodians of culture should not be identified with custodians of economic and political life. One of the ironies of attacks on the canon of the American Renaissance is that the present canon was established by cultural critics (many of whom, like Matthiessen, were socialists) who celebrated the way in which it represented America's democratic tradition in opposition to its commercialism. This is not to imply that we should uncritically accept the canon, but it is to remind us that the process of canon formation is extremely complicated. A work within the canon is not necessarily representative of the culture's elite and one excluded is not necessarily representative of the culture's unrepresented. But I don't want this obvious point about the canon to distract from my main point. Tompkins and Beard offer different narratives about elites blocking the triumph of America's truly democratic spirit, but both verge on adopting conspiracy theories.

Canon-busters, especially, tend toward narratives of conspiracy, but a negative jeremiad lacking the taint of conspiracy informs even some of the most subtle new historical analysis. Greenblatt's work is usually synchronic rather than diachronic. At times, however, he reveals that his synchronic analysis works within a diachronic structure of digressive emergence. For instance, in an attempt to historicize Mikhail Bakhtin's analysis of the carnivalesque in Rabelais he asserts, "some of Rabelais's power derives *from* the evanescence of the festive tradition, or more accurately, from the sense of a literary, social, and religious world hardening in its commitment to order, discipline, and decorum," or "Rabelais's fantasy of perfect aristocratic liberty, like his fantasy of unending popular carnival, is generated in response to a culture increasingly intolerant of disorder in society, in the individual, and in art."[24] Other members of the editorial board of *Representations* offer

American narratives of increasing social and cultural control. In his excellent study of Melville, Michael Rogin posits the rise of a secular state that after the Civil War controls more and more aspects of life; and Walter Benn Michaels constructs the rise of an omnipotent capitalist market in the late nineteenth century that dictates the logic of all cultural production.[25]

To mention Michaels is to highlight a final similarity between the new historicism and the progressive tradition. The move of critics as different as Michaels, Cornel West, Ihab Hassan, and Frank Lentricchia from poststructuralism or postmodernism to pragmatism is one reason why it is important to stress the new historicism's unacknowledged debt to what Cushing Strout has called *The Pragmatic Revolt in American History*. That debt should caution us that rather than offer a new way of relating to the cultural past the turn to pragmatism reaffirms the liberal tradition of American progressivism and its sense of temporality, a tradition from which the new historicism has never really broken.

It is in the light of the new historicism's unacknowledged link to American progressivism that I stress the need to maintain its tension with poststructuralism, for that tension makes possible a break with the progressive tradition. Once again there are historical reasons why.

Affected by the crisis in historicism, Beard's relativism focused, not on nihilism, but like William James's pragmatism, on faith,—a faith for Beard in American exceptionalism. In the late thirties, especially with the signing of the Hitler-Stalin pact, there were good reasons for maintaining that faith. For instance, René Wellek, a recent immigrant, chided Van Wyck Brooks for attacking modern writers and for uncritically celebrating America's literary past. Nonethless, Wellek notes, "We may and should deplore Mr. Brooks's bludgeoning attacks on modern writers and his far too crude distinctions between primary and secondary literature, but in his emotional, quite untheoretical way, Mr. Brooks gives voice to a genuine need of our time: a return to the sources of the American national tradition which fortunately is also the hope of all humanity."[26]

Unlike Europe's, America's real confrontation with a crisis in historicism was yet to come, and the period after World War II saw the celebration of American progressive reform by the consensus historians. Thus, in 1970 Fischer could continue his description of historicism with:

> German historicism is dead, or dying, but the same ethical version of the genetic fallacy still appears in other forms . . . . American historians such as Daniel Boorstin came close to arguing in the 1950s that *Die Amerikanischegeschichte ist das Weltgericht,* and they were not alone in that assumption. Something of the fallacy of ethical historicism appears in the absurd and dangerous idea that America's rise to power and prosperity is a measure of its moral excellence—that the history of the Republic can be seen, in short, as a system of morality. How many of us have not, at some time, silently slipped into this error?[27]

The generation of scholars occupying literature departments in 1988 may admit to having slipped into that error, but having experienced the civil rights' movement, the women's liberation movement, Watergate, Vietnam, and the Reagan era, it does so only with a bad conscience. If the belief in American exceptionalism helped to delay America's confrontation with a crisis in historicism, the recent experience of what David Noble has cleverly called *The End of American History* has forced this generation to face it more squarely.[28] That confrontation was a precondition for the "theoretical" revolt that rocked the study of literature in the United States in the seventies and eighties, for (if I am correct) the force of poststructuralist thought comes precisely from its response to the dead-end of historicism.

V

Poststructuralism *has* made a difference in how academic Americans at least relate to their cultural past, as has the continental tradition that poststructuralism has belatedly introduced into literary debates. The most obvious difference is that poststructuralist decentering has rendered notions of an "American character" or "the New England mind" obsolete. If Van Wyck Brooks chided "our American decentralizers" for failing to produce a national culture that was "a living homogeneous entity, with its own faith and consciousness of self," today we celebrate our "decentralized literature."[29]

Even so, the purpose of this essay has been to show that as different as present celebrations are from those in the past, they retain characteristics of that from which they claim to break. Not quite as obsolete as it first appears, the "American character" can be redefined to emphasize heterogeneity rather than homogeneity. Consensus may have yielded to dissensus, but it remains dependent on a pluralistic vision of American society. If we demand that new historical evidence necessitates a revision of the canon, we echo the not-so-naive New Critic Cleanth Brooks, who declared that "a new history is desirable and necessary . . . that new 'facts' emerge that have to be taken into acount, that whole series of problems which have been scanted in the past show themselves to be important, that certain poets deserve a higher place than they have been accorded in the past, and some a lower."[30] And if we condemn established histories as unusable, we follow in the tradition of that old-fashioned historicist Van Wyck Brooks, who urged us to make and find a usable past for the present.

Most important, even the effort to put the past to present use by constructing undiscovered traditions can betray a debt to a repressive tradition when we are not careful about the narratives that we use. This is not to argue that we should stop the effort to discover those traditions, but as poststructuralists remind us, merely to alter the subject matter of traditional narratives of emergence inherited from a discredited historicism is not to escape that tradition. As I have already indicated, the use of such narratives by those previously excluded is extremely complicated. Just as there is no inherent political valence to the poststructuralist project, so there is none to narratives of emergence. Both need to be evaluated situationally. In the current situation a strong case can be made that such narratives respond to felt historical needs, that the establishment of identifiable traditions for excluded groups is politically necessary. Nonetheless, the current situation also indicates why it is politically suspect merely to reoccupy old-fashioned narrative structures. Surveying the field of ethnic scholarship in America, Werner Sollors helps to explain why.

The numerous ethnic histories produced today that are based on a writer's descent, Sollers argues, "all but annihilate polyethnic art movements, movements of individual and cultural interaction, and the pervasiveness of cultural syncretism in America." Rather than increase our understanding of "the cultural interplay and contacts among writers of different backgrounds," individual narratives of emergence too often create new traditions of "insiders" and "outsiders." Furthermore, such histories legitimize a "static notion of eternal groups," much as nineteenth-century historicism's nationalistic narratives of emergence legitimized national and racial identities.[31] Put another way, these histories breed their own version of exceptionalism. If the modern world claimed to break from the closed cosmos of the ancients and America claimed to be exempt from the corruption of the old world, the very narrative that shapes these new histories implies that somehow the traditions that they describe occupy a space of their own.

Sollers's work among others indicates that the tendency within the new historicism to lapse into old-fashioned narratives of emergence is only a tendency, not an inevitability. Refusing to privilege any one tradition or to offer a static pluralism that merely places separate traditions side by side, he interweaves and cross-examines various traditions to produce a dynamic play that decenters all. In my own way I have tried to produce such play between the traditions that I have labeled the new historicism and poststructuralism. There may be nothing new about the new historicism's claim to make history new, but its difference from past historicisms is its effort to take shape in a postmodern age in which poststructuralism has called into question the assumptions of the modern upon which historicism depends. Indeed, the contradictory nature of our present situation can be highlighted by playing against one another the labels "new historicism" and "postmodernism." One promises to make the past new, whereas the other announces that we are past the new. At a time when the contemporary is described as postmodern and that which is considered behind us is referred to as the modern age, the new historicism and postmodernism could be considered complementary descriptions of the same condition. But similarities should not disguise important differences. "Post" implies a belatedness, an age in which everything has always already occurred. Appropriately, postmodernism questions the assumptions of self-consciously modern ages, especially the enlightenment and its belief in progress and rationality. "New," in contrast, implies an impulse toward the very modern that postmodernism calls into question.

It is tempting to find a way to resolve the tension produced by juxtaposing the "new historicism" with "postmodernism." My point has been, however, that the *construction* of legitimately new, decentered narratives depends upon maintaining it. I am well aware that some poststructuralists and new historicists would claim that their projects maintain such play in and of themselves. But since I have frequently used the destructive impule of poststructuralism to draw out a tendency (not inevitabilty) within the new historicism to deny that play. I will end by using the constructive impulse of the new historicism to do the same for poststructuralism.

If there is a tendency for new historicists to reoccupy the narratives produced by the historicism from which they would break, there is also a tendency for poststructuralists to fall prey to the very totalization which they claim to abhor. The totalizing tendency of the non-totalizers is nowhere more apparent than in the uncritical link between domination and Western logocentrism and humanism, as if logocentrism or humanism is the root of all evil. To say this is not to champion logocentrism or humanism, especially insofar as connections between them and Western domination can be established. But the history of domination is clearly different from, if overlapping with, that of logocentrism or humanism. For instance, to take the new trinity of class, race, and gender, my limited knowledge of non-Western culture does not convince me that cultures free from Western thought are superior. Asian women are very familiar with patriarchal domination. Some societies have such firmly entrenched class hierarchies that the introduction of Western thought is welcomed as liberating. And racism is not confined to the West. As much as philosophically-inclined academics might want to believe that what they study is important, domination cannot be explained by simple reference to a philosophical system.

Unfortunately, even the poststructuralist most attuned to historical difference, Michel Foucault, sometimes betrays a slip into such totalization. In "Nietzsche, Genealogy, History" he summarizes Nietzsche on the will to knowledge. "The historical analysis of this rancorous will to knowledge reveals that all knowledge rests upon injustice (that there is no right, not even in the act of knowing, to truth or a foundation for truth) and that the instinct for knowledge is malicious (something murderous, opposed to the happiness of mankind.)" But when he quotes Nietzsche directly we read, "The desire for knowledge has been transformed among us into a passion which fears no sacrifice, which fears nothing but its own extinction."[32] The difference between the blanket statement that "*all* knowledge rests upon injustice" and the historical one that "the desire for knowledge *has been transformed . . .* " is essential. The former implies a deterministic inevitability; the latter a chance for further transformation. Such pronouncements about what allegedly always already has been the case signals the need to keep open the impulse of the modern. For if, with Blumenberg, we define the modern as "always looking forward to a future that might contain elements which could shatter previous consistency and so render previous 'realities' unreal," it is the modern, not postmodern, that works as a continually decentering force.

To bring Blumenberg into tension with Foucault is a useful way to end this essay because Blumenberg's complicated defense of the modern impulse toward the new as a stimulus to increase knowledge places in perspective Foucault's totalizing claim that all knowledge rests on injustice.[33] As we have seen, new historicists have been strongly influenced by Foucault's argument that constructions of the past are inevitably implicated in present networks of power and domination and thus never disinterested. That insight, however, catches new historicists in a seemingly unresolvable contradiction. The authority of a new historicism rests on the faith that knowledge of the past matters for the present. To admit that a history is not an account of how it really was but a present construction intervening into current political debates seems to undermine that authority. The problem has to do with an ahistorical notion of disinterestedness.

To be sure, complete disinterestedness is impossible. As Bacon knew, knowledge is power. Furthermore, the power gained from knowledge can be used to dominate, as the West did in studies of other cultures. But if knowledge inevitably led to domination, exclusion from the canon should be a cause for celebration not protest, since those not studied would be exempt from domination whereas the study of the white, patriarchal tradition of the West would lead to its subordination. Clearly, however, this is not the case, for knowledge can lead to empowerment as well as domination. Granted, empowerment is a political act. But so long as we believe that we are empowered by knowledge of our situation in the world and so long as we believe that that situation has in part been determined by the past, the most empowering study of the past will be the one that comes as close as possible to telling how it really was. To state my point as a paradox: the present has an interest in maintaining a belief in disinterested inquiry into our past. My own inquiry into the history of the new historicism has been a political intervention trying to empower it to recognize the need to serve that interest.

Notes

1. On the term historicism see Georg G. Iggers, *The German Conception of History: The National Tradition of Historical Thought from Herder to the Present* (Middletown: Wesleyan UP, 1968), pp. 287–90; Wesley Morris, *Toward a New Historicism* (Princeton: Princeton UP, 1979), pp. 3–13; and Herbert Lindenberger, "Toward a New History in Literary Study," *Profession 84,* 22, n. 4 (1984).

2. Fredric Jameson, "Marxism and Historicism," *New Literary History* 11 (1979), 43.

3. Louis Montrose, "Renaissance Literary Studies and the Subject of History," *English Literary Renaissance* 16 (1986), 7.

4. Fredric Jameson, *The Political Unconscious: Narrative as a Socially Symbolic Act* (Ithaca: Cornell UP, 1981).

5. Jane Tompkins, *Sensational Designs: The Cultural Work of American Fiction* (New York: Oxford UP, 1985), p. xiii.

6. Walter Benjamin, *Gesammelte Schriften,* 5 vols., ed. Rolf Tiedemann and Herman Schweppenhäuser (Frankfurt a.M.: Suhrkamp, 1972), I, 2, 677.

7. See especially Paul de Man, "Literary History and Literary Modernity," in *Blindness and Insight,* 2nd ed., revised (Minneapolis: U of Minnesota P. 1983).

8. Jane Tompkins, " 'Indians': Textualism, Morality, and the Problem of History," *Critical Inquiry* 13 (1986), 118. See also Steven Knapp and Walter Benn Michaels, "Against Theory," *Critical Inquiry* 8 (1982), 723–42.

9. See Stanley Fish, "Dennis Martinez and the Uses of Theory," *Yale Law Review* 96 (1987), 1773–1800.

10. Hans Blumenberg, "The Concept of Reality and the Possibility of the Novel," *New Perspectives in German Literary Criticism,* ed. Richard E. Amacher and Victor Lange (Princeton: Princeton UP, 1979), p. 33.

11. Quoted in Reinhart Koselleck, *Futures Past,* trans. Keith Tribe (Cambridge: MIT P, 1985), p. 250.

12. Leopold von Ranke, *Geschichten der romanischen und germanischen Volker von 1494 bis 1514,* 2nd ed. (Leipzig 1874), p. vii.

13. Walter Benjamin, "Theses on the Philosophy of History" in *Illuminations,* trans. Harry Zohn (New York: Schocken, 1969).

14. Quoted in Iggers, *German Conception of History,* p. 175.

15. Wendy Steiner, "Collage or Miracle: Historicism in a Deconstructed World,": in *Reconstructing American Literary History,* ed. Sacvan Berovitch (Cambridge: Harvard UP, 1985).

16. David Hackett Fischer, *Historians' Fallacies* (New York: Harper and Row, 1970), p. 156.

17. William Spanos, "Interview," *Critical Texts* 3 (1985), 22.

18. See Myra Jehlen, *American Incarnation: The Individual, the Nation and the Continent* (Cambridge: Harvard UP, 1986).

19. Benjamin, "Theses," p. 261.

20. John Dewey, *Logic: The Theory of Inquiry* (New York: Holt, 1938), pp. 238–39. George Santayana quoted in *Classical American Philosophers,* ed. Max H. Fisch (Englewood Cliffs: Prentice-Hall, 1951), p. 26.

21. James Harvey Robinson, *The New History: Essays Illustrating the Modern Historical Outlook* (New York: Macmillan, 1912), p. 63. For a criticism of Robinson see David Gross, " 'The New History': A Note of Reappraisal," *History and Theory* 13 (1974), 53–58.

22. Charles A. Beard. "Written History as an Act of Faith," *American Historical Review* 39 (1934), 219–29; and Carl Becker, "Every Man His Own Historian" in *Everyman His Own Historian: Essays on History and Politics* (New York: F. S. Crofts, 1935), pp. 233–55.

23. Sacvan Bercovitch, *The American Jeremiad* (Madison: U of Wisconsin P, 1979).

24. Stephen Greenblatt, "Filthy Rites," *Daedalus* 111 (1982), 8, 9.

25. Michael Paul Rogin, *Subversive Genealogy* (New York: Knopf, 1983). Walter Benn Michaels, *The Gold Standard and the Logic of Naturalism* (Berkeley: U of California P, 1987).

26. René Wellek, "Van Wyck Brooks and a National Literature," *American Prefaces* 7 (1942), 306.

27. Fischer, *Historians' Fallacies*, p. 156.

28. A comparable historical situation in Great Britain was the loss of the Commonwealth and entrance into the Common Market.

29. Van Wyck Brooks, "Our Awakeners," *Seven Arts* 2 (1917), 237; and Jules Chametzky, *Our Decentralized Literature* (Amherst: U of Massachusetts P, 1986).

30. Cleanth Brooks, "Criticism, History, and Critical Relativism," in *The Well Wrought Urn* (New York: Harcourt, Brace & World, 1947), p. 237.

31. Werner Sollors, "A Critique of Pure Pluralism," in *Reconstructing American Literary History,* pp. 3, 19.

32. Michel Foucault, "Nietzsche, Genealogy, History," in *Language, Counter-Memory, Practice,* trans. Donald F. Bouchard and Sherry Simon (Ithaca: Cornell UP, 1977), p. 163.

33. See Hans Blumenberg, *The Legitimacy of the Modern Age,* trans. Robert Wallace (Cambridge: MIT Press, 1983).

13

The Nation as Imagined Community

Jean Franco

On the eve of Mexican Independence, the Mexican writer, José Joaquín Fernández de Lizardi, published a letter purportedly from a brother who had been shipwrecked and washed ashore on an island whose multi-racial population resembled that of Mexico. The brother who had unexpectedly become the ruler of the island appeals to Lizardi to "imagine a kingdom in your head and give it laws and a constitution."[1] Lizardi responded not in a letter but with a novel, *El Periquillo Sarniento* (1816), in which he included an episode depicting just such an imaginary kingdom. The link between national formation and the novel was not fortuitous. For well into the twentieth century, the intelligentsia would appropriate the novel and there work out imaginary solutions to the intractable problems of racial heterogeneity, social inequality, urban versus rural society. It was in the novel that different and often conflicting programs for the nation were debated either by "typical" characters in the Lukácsian sense (for instance, the peasants of Mariano Azuela's *Los de abajo* [1816]) or by more properly allegorical figures like the wandering hero of Eugenio María de Hostos, *Pelerinaje de Bayoán* (1863).

Yet it is one thing to recognize that not only the novel but also the essay and the "great poem" have been deeply implicated in the process of national formation and its attendant problems of national and cultural identity and quite another to claim, as Fredric Jameson has recently done, that the "national allegory" characterizes Third World literature at the present time, that is, in "the era of multinational capitalism"[2]—for not only is "the nation" a complex and much contested term but in recent Latin American criticism, it is no longer the inevitable framework for either political or cultural projects.[3] Further, the privileging of a particular genre—national allegory—is a risky enterprise in a continent where literary genres and styles are inevitably hybridized and where the novel, in particular, has often "bled" into other genres such as the essay or the chronicle.

Jameson is, of course, particularly interested in the "era of multinational capitalism" and in the Third World response to Americanization in certain "embattled" societies such as China and Cuba.[4] He is surprised that in such countries, the questions should be formulated in national terms, and that intellectuals should have a major investment in political life. He believes that the novel-as-national-allegory is a response to the "embattled" situation of these countries which are then taken as representative of the "Third World." What I propose in this article is not to refute Jameson's generalization, which like all generalizations provokes us to think of exceptions, but rather to consider whether the term "national allegory" can be any longer usefully applied to a literature in which nation is either a contested term or something like the Cheshire cat's grin—a mere reminder of a vanished body.[5]

The new social movements which have sprung up on the margins of the nation state no longer couch cultural or political projects in national terms. This disaffection is not only a response to military or other authoritarian regimes which have appropriated national discourse but also the end result of a long historical process. It has to be understood in relation to the fact that nation states were in Latin America vehicles for (often enforced) capitalist modernization. The stabilization of the nation state (often built on old colonial bureaucratic infrastructures) occurred for the most part without grass-roots participation or any form of democratic debate and was often vehiculated by autocratic or populist/authoritarian regimes. Most recently, military regimes furthered modernization while banning political parties, censoring the press, crushing unions and any form of opposition.

This cyclical conjunction of modernity and repression in the name of national autonomy or development has been vigorously contested in literature but in terms that are far too complex to be labeled "national allegory." Going back to the forties and fifties, the novel which, in the nineteenth century, had offered blueprints of national formation more and more became a sceptical reconstruction of past errors. The novel made visible that absence of any signified that could correspond to the nation. Individual and collective identity, social and family life were like shells from which life had disappeared. Consider novels such as Carlos Fuentes's *La muerte de Artemio Cruz* (*The Death of Artemio Cruz*, 1962) and Juan Rulfo's *Pedro Páramo* (1955) in which the names of the protagonists "Cruz" (Cross) and "Páramo" (Wasteland) suggest an allegorical reading, or novels such as Mario Vargas Llosa's *La casa verde* (*The Green House*, 1966) and Alejo Carpentier's *Los pasos perdidos* (*The Lost Steps*, 1953) which use generic names such as The Sergeant or the Goldseeker. It quickly becomes evident that the names are signifiers prized loose from any signified and intended more as indicators of loss or absence than as clues to an allegorical reading. In place of an identifiable microcosm of the nation, such novels offer a motley space in which different historical developments and different cultures overlap. What they enact is the unfinished and impossible project of the modernizing state.

This is strikingly born out by the recurrence of one particular motif in several novels written between the forties and early sixties—the motif of the dying community or the wake around the body. This motif occurs in José Revueltas's *El luto humano* (*Human Mourning*, 1943) Juan Carlos Onetti's *El astillero* (*The Shipyard*, 1961) Ernesto Sábato's *Sobre héroes y tumbas* (*Of Heroes and Tombs*, 1961) Gabriel García Márquez's *La hojarasca* (*Leafstorm*, 1955). In José Revueltas's *El luto humano,* a group of peasants slowly and violently sinks to death during a flood which halts the linear time of progress and thrusts the protagonists back into the ritual time of death and vengeance. In Mario Vargas Llosa's *La casa verde*, a series of individual stories are recounted within the framework of a river journey that transports the dying entrepreneur Fushía to his last resting place in a leper colony, thus suggesting the death and corruption of a class that but for dependency might have revitalized the nation. In Carlos Fuentes's *La muerte de Artemio Cruz,* the dying of the protagonist marks the end of some libidinal force which had become displaced from productive national goals and had spent itself in personal satisfaction. Many such novels center on the life and death of an "imagined" community—García Márquez's Macondo, Onetti's Santa María, Fushía's island (in *La casa verde*), the communities in *El luto humano,* and *El astillero*—all of which represent in their different ways doomed enterprises. In fact, the novels describe alternative nations dreamed up by writers whose kingdoms in the head founder on the hard rock of realpolitik. In Onetti's novel, the tragedy of the entrepreneurial protagonist is played out in a shipyard and a city where the nation has been reduced to a few nostalgic signs—the statue of a founding father and a hitching post which is the last remnant of the long vanished rural culture on which the nation had been founded.

No Latin American writer has so persistently parodied and pilloried the nation as García Márquez. Indeed, he has even written the allegory of the transition from colony to nation to nation state in a short story, "Blacaman the Good, Salesman of Miracles" (1968). The story is a Nietzchean account of legitimation which is told by the victor, the self-styled Blacaman the Good once apprentice to Blacaman the Bad, a magician who had invented a snake bite cure that could bring him back from the dead after being bitten. But modern magic proves more potent than these old superstitions. Blacaman the Good, with the help of the American marines, seizes control of the state and becomes a tropical dictator in the manner of Batista or Trujillo. When Blacaman the Bad dies, he has him resuscitated so that the population can hear his wailing in the mausoleum where he is entombed. This modern magic controls the past which is useful as long as it reminds people of how much better off they are in the present. In this brief tale, the modern state is a kind of illusionist which needs the past only as a lament and whose miracle is the economic miracle of dependency.

García Márquez returned to the problem of legitimation and the identification of the dictator with the nation state in *El otoño del patriarca* (*The

Autumn of the Patriarch, 1975), in which the dictator/protagonist epitomizes a grotesque modernization that has been achieved through murder and oppression. Yet the nation and the dictator are clearly shown to be producers of and produced by a particular discursive formation. In one episode, for example, the Dictator tries to legitimate his rule by claiming that he was born miraculously of a virgin birth. The papal nuncio sent to investigate the improbable claim is shot as he rides over the mountains on his mule and falls headlong—not through a landscape—but through pastiche.

> The nuncio fell into a bottomless vertigo, from the mountains covered with *perpetual snow,* through different and simultaneous climates, through the engravings of natural history books, down the precipices and over the tiny springs from which *the great navigable waters flow,* over the escarpments over which European scientists climb on the backs of Indians in search of secret herbal remedies, down the mesetas of wild magnolias on which sheep grazed *whose warm wool gives us generous protection* as well as *setting us a good example* and past the coffee plantation mansions with their solitary balconies and their interminable invalids, past the perpetual roar of turbulent rivers and past *the beginnings of the torrid zone* (my translation and emphasis).

The underlined passages expose the way the nation state is legitimized through pedagogical discourse—for example, the geography text book. The Papal nuncio falls through this secular landscape constituted by a positivist discourse that identifies nation with natural regions (and exploitable resources), and with a literary canon (the invalids in houses probably refers to Columbia's classic nineteenth-century sentimental novel, *María* by Jorge Isaacs). But as soon as the nation is described as discourse, it simply becomes a provisional framework, a fiction that will disappear once the dictator is shown to be mortal. García Márquez underscores the role of nationalism in homogenizing disparate texts which together come to make up our idea of the "nation"; at the same time he shows how national allegory itself is complicitous in a legitimizing ideology. This leads to the realization that the problems which national discourse engendered—problems of patriarchy, of power and its attendant techniques of exclusion and discrimination—could not be resolved by a genre which was implicated in these very procedures. His most recent novel, *El amor en los tiempos del cólera* (*Love in the Time of Cholera*, 1985), can no longer be read in Jamesonian terms at all. It is the private that has become central, a private that cannot be allegorized or transposed into an exemplary national story because there is disjunction between the public and the private. The apocalytic landscape of decay and cadavers bears the scars of modernization and progress, of old national battles and ancient conquests, but the protagonists enacting their anachronistic love story can no longer represent anything beyond their own mortal passion. *Love in the Time of Cholera* thus marks the dissolution of a once totalizing myth which is now replaced by private fantasies lived out amid public disaster. And the novel, rather than an allegory, has become the terrain of conflicting discourses.

In such novels, it is precisely the disappearance of the nation, its failure to provide systems of meaning and belief that undermines referential reading. It is true that they capture referential the continued resonance of certain historical events such as the conquest and the impact of succeeding waves of modernization, visible in the fragmented life forms they have left in their wake. For this untimeliness is the condition of Latin American modernity giving one a sense of reliving the past. Or it is as if the past can speak in the present tense. In Augusto Roa Bastos's *Yo el supremo* (1978), which the author describes as a compilation of "twenty thousand unpublished documents as well as journals, tape-recorded interviews and letters," the compiler (who declines to be author) observes that "unlike the usual text, this one has been read first and written afterwards." The protagonist of the novel is the nineteenth-century dictator, Dr. Gaspar Rodríguez de Francia founder of the Paraguayan nation who can only be known through historical documents. Roa Bastos, however, is not interested in historical reconstruction but in reading the past in terms of the present, since the past has never been transcended and the problems with which Francia struggled—problems of national autonomy, racial diversity, the unrepresented masses—are those of contemporary Paraguay. He therefore transforms third-person historical writing, translating the documents into a first-person narrative in which the "I" is both the nation embodied in Dr. Francia and a personal, mortal "I." As representative of the nation the supreme I is immortal, disembodied, continuous—yet this transcendent I is continually undermined by the I of the mortal Dr. Francia which is always a relationship with a reader or listener and whose language is always inflected by the presence of the other. But the personal is represented as voice and voice can only be recorded in writing which like fatherhood is putative. Thus while the novel itself is motivated by a document apparently written in the dictator's "own" handwriting and bearing his signature, this "authentic" document is also a reproduction and not an original since it is reproduced in the published text we read. The document reads as follows:

> I, the Supreme Dictator of the Republic, order that upon my death, my body shall be decapitated, the head placed upon a lance for three days in the main square of the Republic to which the people will be summoned by the sound of tolling bells.
>
> All my civil and military servants will be hanged. Their bodies will be buried outside the city walls without a cross or mark to commemorate their names. At the end of the said period, I command that my remains be burned and the ashes thrown into the river. (my translation)

The lampoon poses a problem of attribution, for the author is not a person but discourse. In addition, by using the first person in a document in which the first person is inappropriate, it underlines the difference between the impersonal discourse of the state and the "I" of the living "dictator" who cannot control meaning after his own death (nor even during his lifetime). For even what appears to be "living" speech in the novel is constantly revealed to be writing. The dictator's "speech" often breaks off in midsentence and the accompanying gloss exposes the fact that it is not said but written—"Manuscript burned," "torn," "the next folios are missing." The Supreme I speaks both as a person and as a nation, as the Supreme I of an immortal, ungendered abstract state and as a speaking human being who can however not be present in the written word. Further, the illocutionary force of the decree is lodged not in the living Dr. Francia but only in the imaginary body of the nation. The nation as the locus of secular immortality is here shown to be incompatible with the person who momentarily embodies statehood. Once this living person attempts to speak as the impersonal and public "I," the disparity is foregrounded.

Dr. Francia represents the impossible conjunction of the person and writing, a conjunction that is made plausible by the grammatical category of the subject. Roa Bastos transforms the impersonality of historical writing into a speaking subject who is argumentative, plaintive, and resentful because excluded from the discourse of the state. The mortal Francia wants to be a Cartesian cogito, a cogito that can abstract itself from the material world and endure as idea. Yet the "I" is forced to take into account the decomposition of the material body that supports it and the invasion of flies that will devour the corpse. As the body decomposes, the "I" is still hungering for food, for a cooked egg—the egg that like Francia's nation will never generate new life.

Roa Bastos is able to represent Latin American nationalist discourse as an enactment of contradictions—the struggle to tell historical truth when that "truth" is always written from a partisan point of view, the struggle to maintain purity of boundaries when that purity means the exclusion of the heterogeneous. Although *Yo el supremo* is often described as a novel of dictatorship, it goes far beyond the representation of authoritarianism, to show the complicity of language in the constitution of the nation. In other words, Roa Bastos attacks the very basis on which national identity is constructed, making visible the gap—that discourse conceals—between person and institution.

A reverse strategy is exemplified by the Puerto Rican author, Edgardo Rodríguez Juliá in his novel, *La noche oscura del Niño Avilés* (1984). Whereas Roa Bastos tries to invent the living speaker of existing texts, Rodríguez Juliá restores the documents which would correspond to the oral myths, legends, dreams, and pornographic nightmares which have never been part of official history.

The novel uses a Borgian device of describing a city which is mentioned only in apochryphal documents. The city is founded by the Blessed Avilés who, as a child, had been found floating like Moses on the waves. The bulk of the novel consists of rival documents and chronicles describing a campaign led by the Bishop Trespalacios against a heretical sect, the Avilés sect. One of the chronicles is written by Gracián who is on the side of the Bishop and the other by a renegade Spaniard, one of the captains of black leader, Obatal. Yet these chronicles are also digressions. They constantly stray from the campaign in order to pause over a particular succulent feast and the farts that follow it, over drug trips (the bishop is a drug "aficionado") and, in the case of the Renegade, there is a prolonged incursion into the realm of the senses and his love affair with an African Queen. Inserted in the chronicles, there is also the story of Obatal's obsession with the construction of a glass city, a city of forgetting whose entrance is in the form of a vagina.

The period to which the documents supposedly refer date from the end of the eighteenth century, that is, the period of the great slave rebellions which liberated Haiti from the French. Puerto Rican history records no such uprising and its black culture was largely "hidden from history" by a ruling class that was mainly concerned with "whitening" the island. Rodríguez Juliá's novel restores the body to history, rather as Roa Bastos restored the living person to the abstract dictatorship. The two Spanish chroniclers who interpret Puerto Rican history either regard it as a perpetual feast or as a perpetual orgy reading into it the history of their own repressions. That is why their classical language is again and again rudely interrupted by the fart.[6]

The juxtaposition of disparate discourses, the use of pastiche perhaps helps explain why U.S. critics so eagerly embrace Latin American novels as postmodern.[7] But incorporation into postmodernism is no more satisfactory than Jameson's Third World national allegory. Indeed, the two recuperative gestures seem to be motivated by the same operation of extrapolation. Extrapolation reduces the complexity of intertextual allusions and deprives texts of their own historical relations to prior texts. It implies a view of Latin American literature either in opposition to the metropolis or as part of the metropolis's postmodern repertoire. Yet novels such as Augusto Roa Bastos's *Yo el Supremo* and Edgardo Rodríguez Juliá's *La noche oscura del Nino Avilés* which defy facile recuperation as national allegory or as the postmodern demand readings informed by cultural and political history.

Hybrid genres have always abounded in Latin America. Thus, both "national allegory" and postmodern imply an impoverishment for they overlook an entire culture history in which essay, chronicle, and historical document have been grafted onto novels, a history of rereadings and rewritings which give rise to voluminous compendia—such as Jose Donoso's *El obsceno pájaro de la noche* (*The Obscene Bird of Night*, 1970), Lezama Lima's *Paradiso* (*Paradise*, 1966) and Carlos Fuentes's *Terra Nostra* (1972)—that defy categorization, as well as to texts such as *Yo el Supremo* in which the rancorous voice of posthumous knowledge mingles with the murmur of the fictional characters. Such texts may seem "postmodern" because of a sum of characteristics—pastiche, nostalgia, and the like—and because they reflect the dissolution of any universal system of meaning or master discourse, a dissolution which, clearly affects Latin America's relation to metropolitan discourse.

Yet just as national allegory fails to describe adequately the simultaneous dissolution of the idea of the nation and the continuous persistence of national concerns, so postmodernism cannot adequately describe those texts that use pastiche and citation not simply as style but as correlatives of the continent's uneasy and unfinished relationship to modernity. Indeed, it is significant that the last few years have witnessed a proliferation of testimonial fiction and chronicle as well as novelized histories and historical novels that seem to suggest that generic boundaries cannot easily contain the bizarre overlappings of cultures and temporalities. I shall cite one recent outstanding example—Edgardo Rodríguez Juliá's *El entierro de Cortijo* (1983), which is a "chronicle" of the author's attendance at the wake and funeral of a "plena" musician, Cortijo. The writer is one of a mass of people who crowd into the funeral home in a popular quarter of San Juan for the last glimpse of the singer who lies in an open coffin with a guard of honor. The writing moves backwards and forwards between reminiscence, observation, snatches of conversation and song. What we have is a kaleidoscope of minute gestures; of myriads of individuals each one different, unclassifiable; of transient contact; of an event that is clearly an event but defies classification, for it is neither properly speaking a Catholic ritual nor a patriotic demonstration. As the Church, the state, and opposition politicians in turn try to take over the funeral, pluralism always reasserts itself. One man pays homage by straightening the crucifix in the hand of the dead man, another embraces the body. Styles clash—fifties, sixties, eighties. Does anything unite this crowd apart from the corpse? The kaleidoscope constantly shifts to form different and unreconcilable patterns. The author concludes, "We live in a period of ghostly intentions, and unburied gestures, tradition breaks up into a thousand conflicting fragments. How can so much volatility be reconciled with such depth of feeling?"

What is at stake here is precisely the impossibility of the typical, the representative, the Puerto Rican (except as the sum of idiosyncracies). The only unity is mortality, the only way to resist death is to play Cortijo's music. There is no way of converting this into national allegory but neither will it do simply to sweep it under the carpet of postmodernism. *El entierro de Cortijo* presents in the form of a simultaneous kaleidoscope all the unfinished problems of modernity in Puerto Rico, projects which cannot be totalized nor simply celebrated. It is also thick with historical, cultural, and political allusions and therefore forces those of us not familiar with Puerto Rico to do some homework.

Each piece of clothing, the name of a street, a manner of walking represent traces not only of the past but of the past's relationship to modernity. It is the refusal to totalize, however, rather than heterogeneity that distinguishes Rodríguez Juliá from his Modernist and nineteenth-century predecessors. What used to be a source of embarrassment to the intelligentsia—the imitation of the metropolis, the recourse to pastiche—has now come to be seen as an irrepressible process of appropriation and defiance.

In this light, the proliferation of "historical" novels, testimonials and chronicles, the emergence of women writers in Latin America highlight not only a celebration of heterogeneity but also the efforts to contain it by state violence and repression. Because pluralism of style is not equivalent to democratic participation, those texts which open up to the multiple and often antagonistic discourses of the continent represent a political as well as an aesthetic choice, a Utopia glimpsed beyond the nightmare of an as yet unfinished modernity.

Notes

1.   The letters are included in José Joaquín Fernández de Lizardi, *El Pensador Mexicano,* 2, 3, and 4 (January–February 1814) in *Obras* III (Mexico City: UNAM, 1968), pp. 386–99

2.   Fredric Jameson, "Third-World Literature in the Era of Multinational Capitalism," *Social Text,* 15 (Fall 1986), pp. 65–88. There is a response to this article by Aijaz Ahmad, "Jameson's Rhetoric of Otherness and the 'National Allegory' " *Social Text,* 17 (Fall 1987), pp. 3–25.

3.   See for instance Carlos Monsivais, *Entrada libre, crónicas de la sociedad que se organiza* (Mexico: Era 1988) in which new social movements spring up on the margins of the hegemonic national project.

4.   Jameson, "Third-World Literature," p. 69 defines the Third World text thus: "the story of the private individual destiny is always an allegory of the embattled situation of the public third-world culture and society.

5.   Benedict Anderson, *Imagined Communities: Reflections on the Origin and Spread of Nationalism* (London: Verso, 1983).

6.   On the fart as response, see Peter Sloterdijk, *Critique of Cynical Reason* (Minneapolis: University of Minnesota Press, 1987), especially pp. 150–1.

7.   For Jameson, postmodernism is part of the logic of late capitalism in the First World and especially the United States, see "Postmodernism, or the Cultural Logic of Late Capitalism," *New Left Review* 146 (July–August, 1984), pp. 53–92. For the inclusion of Latin American literature in the postmodern, see Brian McHale, *Postmodernist Fiction* (London: Methuen, 1987).

14

Literary Criticism and the Politics of the New Historicism

Elizabeth Fox-Genovese

In recent years, literary critics, surfeited with the increasingly recognized excesses of post-structuralist criticism in its various guises, have discovered history. Or rather, lest one suspect them of a regression to simplicity, they have discovered "historicism." In this enterprise they have, it should in fairness be noted, been wonderfully aided and abetted by a growing number of historians who, for their part, are reveling in this new attention to their own crisis-ridden discipline. A bastard child of a history that resembles anthropological "thick description" and of a literary theory in search of its own possible significance, this "new historicism" consists in a plethora of converging, but also conflicting, tendencies within cultural studies broadly construed.[1]

This move offers an unexpected opening to call contemporary literary theory to the bar of that history on which it had (albeit building on a long formalist precedent) previously declared war. The critics' war on history had its own logic, for the history they had received did not admit of happy endings. Heirs to the whimpering collapse of bourgeois individualism, they sought to wrest victory from apparent defeat by themselves proclaiming the primacy of sign and texts and the attendant deaths of author, subject, and all extra-textual selves. Their project captured the mood of our own and all other post-heroic, times. Like innumerable predecessors, they sought to claim for the epigones the mantles of the giants. In so doing they raised technique over substance, analysis over narrative, and critic over author. Indeed, pressing the limits of credibility for all but the votaries of fashion, they announced that technique had subsumed substance, analysis narrative, and, most important, critic author. There they were standing not, as Newton would have had it, on the shoulders of giants, but sitting, as the second Napoleon pretended—recall Marx's epigram about the second time—on the imperial throne. Yet, as those of us who recognize history as the most demanding of mistresses could have told them, history herself would sooner or later confront them with the naked recognition: The Emperor has no clothes.

History will not down easily: She never does. But her returns are protean, disguised, and no more salutary than we make them. Today's "new historicism" is clearly viewed by its proponents as a good thing. Not one to gainsay this heartening rush of enthusiasm, I cannot withal let it go unchallenged. For the proponents of the new historicism have yet fully to clarify either the "good" or the "thing" of their devotion. History, like criticism, must sooner or later answer to judgment, to discrimination, and, however unfashionable the term, to meaning.[2]

Tellingly, the diverse practioners of the new historicism have yet to issue a manifesto or even a clear statement of their respective purposes. If the new historicism has an official organ, it would appear to be the journal *Representations,* which brings together historians and literary critics in a colorful carnival of cultural readings and thick descriptions.[3] Yet *Representations* does not begin to account for the diversity of new historicist work or even its multiple tendencies. Presumably, we should have to include under the general label of new historicism the growing interest in reader response criticism, notably the work of such feminist critics as Jane Tompkins and Cathy Davidson.[4] Assuredly, we should have to include the work of such historical and theoretical critics as Fredric Jameson, Michael McKeon, Dominick LaCapra, Richard Terdiman, and Timothy Reiss.[5] And what of the growing numbers of literary historians who also have their own journal that explicitly addresses problems of theory and interpretation?[6] The attention to rethinking literary history reminds us, if need be, of the uncertain and contested boundaries between the literati's new historicism and intellectual history. One would look in vain in new historicist pages for references to the great cultural critic, Lewis P. Simpson, or to such younger intellectual historians of the South as Michael O'Brien or Drew Faust, much less to the conservative literary scholar M. E. Brandford.[7] One can only assume that from the new historicist perspective such literary and intellectual historians do not qualify as "new."

The newness of the new historicism derives in no small measure from its continuing affair with post-structuralist criticism—notably deconstruction with which it is much less at war than one might think—and anthropological thick description.[8] It remains, in other words, enthusiastically embroiled in that web of contemporary intellectual fashion which none of us can hope to escape completely. Withal the emphasis on newness bespeaks the central paradox that informs the new historicism as a project: Notwithstanding some notable exceptions, it is not very historical. It is especially not self-critically or self-reflexively historical. For part of the project of any contemporary historicism must inescapably be a fresh consideration of history herself—that is, a hard look at the history of modern historicism and its conflicted relations with other critical strategies.

Today's historicism has developed in response to a series of debates within cultural studies and the human sciences broadly construed, not least to those that contest the validity of disciplinary boundaries themselves. In this climate, the new historicism understandably signifies different things to its various practitioners: to some, mere attention to the past; to others, context, which includes social relations; and to at least some few others, even change over time. Historicism has also been taken to provide an opening wedge for overdue attention to the claims of gender, class, and race—to the claims of the multiple subject and the uncanonized author. If so, it is, if not necessarily a good thing, at least a good intention. But we all know about good intentions and the road they pave.

In general, the devotees of the new historicism have proved less than self-aware about the relation between their concerns and the continuing debates among historians with which they intersect. From one perspective, the new historicism bears a strong family resemblance to the venerable model of history and literature, which, it might be noted, is under serious attack in its most developed form, namely American Studies.[9] Those debates have their own history, which defies neat summary here. But the central conflicts are instructive. They especially concern the relation between the canonized texts of high culture and the culture at large and the appropriate strategies for reading any texts. Or, to put it differently, previous generations have bequeathed to us the interlocking problems of which texts to read and of how to read them. These debates in turn intersect with those about the nature of history, notably the rise of social history in opposition to discredited elite history (especially intellectual and political history), and the related skepticism about the nature of historical "events" and "facts." The main tendency in new historicism has bravely swept over most of these debates without explicitly addressing the nature of the historicism—preeminently thick description—that it is seeking to restore to the reading of texts. But it seems safe to say that the new historicists do view their project as revitalizing the increasingly formalist project of deconstruction. They thus apparently take historicism to imply something about the social life to which texts testify and by which they are informed.

Not long ago, historicism had different meanings or, better, connotations. It signified reductionism, present-mindedness, and teleology. Historicism, in short, stood in direct opposition to history, which itself was not as clearly defined as one might have hoped. The reversals—history's own deceptions—are worth savoring. The bad historicism of the recent past was normally attributed by bien-pensant bourgeois to uncouth, deterministic Marxists. Things, as things are wont, got a little confusing during the great bourgeois declension, for during a brief period the once sanctified "whig interpretation" of history—the view that history consisted in the steady progress of the human race from barbarism towards its present enlightened state—disconcertingly began to resemble historicism. No matter. We know what happens when undesirables move into a neighborhood: property values collapse. So too with intellectual values. Bourgeois individualism a-dying relegated the whig interpretation to the old neighborhood in which it was trying to confine Marxism, never pausing for that self-analysis which would have indeed revealed Marx to have been steeped in the very Scottish Historical School that engendered the whig interpretation. Today the neighborhood is being gentrified, and historicism with it. But it remains unclear whether we are witnessing a reinvigorated attention to historical understanding or a nostalgic retro window-dressing. For, as Fredric Jameson has argued, the related questions of causation and extra-textual "reality" cannot be brushed aside.[10]

History consists in something more than "just one damn thing after another," in something more than random antiquarianism, even in something more than what happened in the past. Some of those who are turning to History to redress the excesses of contemporary literary theory are calling it a "discourse"—a label that at least has the virtue of acknowledging its claims to intellectual status, and more, of acknowledging its possible internal cohesion and rules, of beginning to recognize it as a distinct mode of understanding. But their strategy runs the risk of confusing history as accounts, narratives, or interpretations of the past, with history as the sum or interplay of human actions, notably politics. School children who first learn of history as what happened in the past may lack the intellectual sophistication to grasp that what we know of the past depends upon the records—implicit interpretations of who and what matters—and upon the ways in which subsequent human beings have written about and interpreted those records. Only later do they learn to recognize history as a genre, as one particular kind of text. We still use history to refer, however imprecisely, to what we like to think really happened in the past and to the ways in which specific authors have written about it. Contemporary critics tend to insist disproportionately on history as the ways in which authors have written about the past at the expense of what might actually have happened, insist that history consists primarily of a body of texts and a strategy of reading or interpreting them.[11] Yet history also consists, in a very old-fashioned sense, in a body of knowledge—in the sum of reliable information about the past that historians have discovered and assembled. And beyond that knowledge, history must also be recognized as what did happen in the past—of the social relations and, yes, "events," of which our records offer only imperfect clues.

History cannot simply be reduced—or elevated—to a collection, theory, and practice of reading texts. The simple objection to the subsumption of history to textual criticism lies in the varieties of evidence upon which historians draw. It is possible to classify price series or coin deposits or hog weights or railroad lines as texts—possible, but ultimately useful only as an abstraction that flattens historically and theoretically significant distinctions. If, notwithstanding occasional fantasies, the nature of history differentiates historians from "hard" social scientists, it also differentiates them from "pure" literary critics. For historians, the text exists as a function, or articulation, of context. In this sense historians work at the juncture of the symbiosis between text and context, with context understood to mean the very conditions of textual production and dissemination.

In fairness, many literary critics or theorists seem also to be working at this juncture, and their best work is opening promising new avenues. I am hardly alone among historians in being heavily indebted to the work of Antonio Gramsci and Mikhail Bakhtin in particular, although admittedly both rank more as cultural philosophers than as literary critics.[12] Thus, in important instances, the center of attention can be seen to be shifting from text to context, with a healthy emphasis on the concept of hegemony and the notion of struggle within and between discourses. But only in rare instances have new historicists embraced the full implicatons of this project. In most cases they have implicitly preferred to absorb history into the text or discourse without (re)considering the specific characteristics of history herself.

Such a blanket charge may appear churlish, especially since so much of the work in the new historicism has attempted to restore women, working people, and other marginal groups (although rarely, so far, black people) to the discussion of literary texts. Nor can a blanket charge pretend to do justice to the diversity of works that can be lumped under the general category of new historicism. Understandably, as with any fledgling enterprise, the new historicists, in all their diversity, have worked piecemeal, borrowing from the materials that lie to hand. And, in the vast majority of instances, they have drawn their materials from the new social history and have followed it in substituting experience for politics, consciousness for the dynamics and consequences of power. Feminist critics, to be sure, have attended to the consequences of power—from which they singlemindedly argue women to have suffered—but have tended to homogenize its dynamics under the mindlessly simplistic category of "patriarchy." The end result, despite the uncontestable value of discrete efforts, has been to take as given precisely the most pressing questions, namely the (changing) relations of power and their (multiple) consequences.[13]

History, at least good history, in contrast to antiquarianism, is inescapably structural. Not reductionist, not present-minded, not teleological: structural. Here, I am using structural in a special—or, better, a general—sense, not in the sense developed by Saussure, Lévi-Strauss, or even Roland Barthes or Lucien Goldmann. By structural, I mean that history must disclose and reconstruct the conditions of consciousness and action, with conditions understood as systems of social relations, including relations between women and men, between rich and poor, between the powerful and the powerless; among those of different faiths, different races, and different classes. I further mean that, at any given moment, systems of relations operate in relation to a dominant tendency—for example, what Marxists call a mode of production—that endows them with a structure. Both in the past and in the interpretation of the past history follows a pattern or structure, according to which some systems of relations and some events possess greater significance than others. Structure, in this sense, governs the writing and reading of texts.[14]

This use of structure requires a word of justification. Structure has lapsed in fashion in large measure because of our recognition of the multiple ties that link all forms of human activity, including thought and textual production. In other words, the preoccupation with structure has given way to the preoccupation with system. The very notion of textuality in the large sense embodies the insistence on system, interconnection, and seamlessness, and therefore leads inescapably to what Jameson calls totalization.[15] That recognition is compelling, but it rests upon a denial of boundaries. The concept of structure, not unlike that of discourse, represents a commitment to drawing at least provisional boundaries. In this respect, structure, like discourse, attempts to take account of present and past politics. For politics consists in nothing if not the drawing of boundaries. If indeed, we live in and represent ourselves through a seamless web of textuality, ultimately the spoils of our living and representing accrue to those who draw the boundaries: boundaries of the law, of the literary canon, of superordination in all its manifestations. In this perspective, politics as the will to define and the ability to impose boundaries constitutes the irreducible core of experience, textuality, and history. Politics draws the lines that govern the production, survival, and reading of texts and textuality—of text and Text.

Here again, we have an irony of sorts. Contemporary criticism implicitly, when not explicitly, grants the text a status *sui generis,* as if it somehow defied the laws of time, mortality, history, and politics. But beneath that surface lies an implacable hostility to history as structure and to politics as the struggle to dominate others and thus to shape the structure of social relations. Thus the evocation of history reduces to history as accident (in the Aristotelian sense) of the text rather than its essence, and thus, implicitly, reduces politics to its textual embodiment.

At the core of the contemporary critical project lies the conviction that we think, exist, know, only through texts—that extratextual considerations defy proof and, accordingly, relevance. And how wonderful it is that these critics make precisely the same claims for their theory that the more reductionist, not to say vulgar, cliometricians and psychohistorians make for theirs. In this respect, contemporary criticism as a philosophical project returns through the thickets of modern philosophy to the eighteenth-century Berkeleyan dilemma: Does the falling tree make a sound if none is there to hear it? Or, to take the modern variant, does the thought exist if none is there to write it? The radical attempt to transcend this dilemma, which does command attention, proposes the text as society, culture, history, consciousness, on the grounds that it is all of them or all that we can know. And it further proposes that in addition to being all of them that we can know, it is the only form in which we can know them.

Life would be easier if we could dismiss this challenge to our commonsensical, intuitive apprehension of the solidity of things out of hand. We cannot. In the post-Einsteinian and post-Wittgensteinian universe of intellectual relativism in all spheres, in the post-capitalist world of modern technology and of a restively interdependent globe, our culture's received wisdom about order, about cause and effect, about subject and object no longer suffices. Most of us know all too well that complexity, uncertainty, and indeterminacy govern our world and have effectively shattered our abiding longing to grasp the scheme of things entire. And those who refuse to accept the evidence— notably religious fundamentalists of varying persuasions—engage in a massive effort of denial and self-deception. Bourgeois culture had bravely assumed that the scheme of things obeyed a logic that the individual mind could grasp—had rested on a commitment to what modern critics are now dismissing as "logocentrism." Bourgeois attitudes towards history, notably the whig interpretation, rested upon this commitment. We now know that what we called reality is but appearance, no more than the interplay of self-serving opinions. Historians told the stories that legitmated and served the perpetuation of the powerful's control of the weak. For some, the collapse of this illusion is taken to have opened the way to intellectual anarchism: to each his or her own history. For others, it may be opening the way to a new intellectual totalitarianism, or at least to an elitist thrust that divorces history from the perceptions of the general educated public.

The literary critics cannot absorb history piecemeal, as curiosity, landscape, or illustration. Nor, can the historians restore history in all its innocence. The epistemological crisis of our times itself reflects the crisis of bourgeois society—a crisis of consciousness, certainty, hierarchy, and materially grounded social relations. I am not suggesting that we should return, if indeed we could, to an untransformed Marxism any more than to a sanctimonious whig interpretation. Not least, recent developments in history and literary studies have exposed the bankruptcy of the authoritative white male subject and pressed the claims of women, working people, and peoples of non-white races and non-Western cultures.[16] I am suggesting that a structurally informed history offers our best alternative to the prevailing literary models. For serious attention to the claims of history forces the recognition of the text as a manifestation of previous human societies. The problems of "knowing" history persist. We remain hostage not merely to the imperfection but to the impossibility of precisely recapturing the past and, in this sense, remain bound on one flank by the hermeneutic conundrum. But those constraints neither justify our abandoning the struggle nor our blindly adhering to the denial of history.

The acknowledgment of history's claims, however, confronts us with an especially delicious irony. With the collapse of the whig interpretation, Marxism has inherited the royal historical mantle.[17] This outcome would have delighted, if not entirely surprised, Marx who studiously grounded his own political, philosophical, and historical project in the bourgeois society and ideology he was so resolutely opposing.[18] Today Marxism has, if anything, been tarred with the brush of cultural and philosophical conservatism, although the efforts of some neo-Marxists have succeeded in moving Marxism itself down the road of radical individualism and cultural pluralism. The moral is that, bourgeois pieties to the contrary notwithstanding, Marxism offers no more static a doctrine than any other vital political and intellectual current, and that Marxism is no more immune to the winds of political and intellectual change. At one extreme, neo-Marxists have succeeded in divorcing their work from its political moorings and legacy; at the other they have tied it too firmly to the vicissitudes of specific political regimes and parties.[19] But between these extremes, Marxism continues to develop as an explicitly historical and political theory, even if, as John Frow has reminded us, the "political and theoretical radicalism of Marxism can no longer be taken for granted."[20]

Marxism has, in effect, benefited from the attribute that its harshest bourgeois critics have always reproached in it: a sense—however diluted—of social, which is to say political accountability. In the old days, the same would have been true of its bourgeois opponents. Today, however, bourgeois critics have largely abandoned the political field, or rather, they have abandoned the notion of accountability. Conservatives, how ever much they may be recognized as members of the bourgeois camp, have not made the same mistake. But they, even more than Marxists, have been marginalized and silenced by the academic establishment. To be sure, the popular success of Allan Bloom's *The Closing of the American Mind* should make people thoughtful. But by and large the liberal academy has responded with outraged dismissal rather than serious debate.[21] Thus, by the grace of bourgeois culture in decline, Marxism has emerged as the last bastion of historical thinking.

The philosophical problems persist, not least because of our culture's reluctance to confront the conflicted relation between what Jameson calls "freedom and necessity," and what I should prefer to call "freedom and order." But most of the practitioners of the new historicism are not addressing them at all. To the extent that they implicitly accept the view of society as text and equate history with thick description, they, if anything, implicitly perpetuate the dubious politics of what many are calling our society of information. Their considerable skills are devoted to the decoding of inter-twining messages with little attention to sources or consequences.

Texts do not exist in a vacuum. They remain hostage to available language, available practice, available imagination. Language, practice, and imagina-tion all emerge from history understood as structure, as sets or systems of relations of superordination and subordination. To write in the name of the collectivity, which is what—however narrowly and self-centeredly—all fabricators of text do, is to write as in some sense as the privileged delegate of those who constitute society and culture. Here, the concern with the links that bind different texts to each other genuinely approaches attention to history. It should prompt us to read such antebellum northerners as Nathan-iel Hawthorne and Harriet Beecher Stowe, such escaped slaves as Harriet Jacobs and Frederick Douglass, and such proslavery southerners as William Gilmore Simms, Louisa Susanna McCord, James Henley Thornwell, and John C. Calhoun, as members of an interlocking universe. For texts, as manifestations or expressions of social and gender relations, themselves constitute sets of relations: not relations innocent of history, but essentially historical relations of time, place, and domination. And without a vital sense of the structure of those relations, the reading of texts collapses into arcane, if learned and brilliant, trivia.

With a sense of structure other possibilities open. The best recent example can be found in Michael McKeon's ambitious and compelling discussion of the origins of the English novel.[22] One need not agree with all of McKeon's formulations in order to appreciate his sensitivity to the historical location of discourses and the dynamism of their historical unfolding. For the novel did emerge in tandem with the emergence of the bourgeoisie, even if its early history also embodies a struggle between that bourgeoisie and its recalcitrant aristocratic opposition. Moreover, to take the story beyond the point at which McKeon leaves it, the ensuing history of the novel—as privileged form of bourgeois discourse—continued to enact struggles between new political positions. Bourgeois discourses, in Richard Terdiman's formulation, engen-dered counter-discourses.[23] And what was true for Britain and France was all the more true for the United States with its persisting division among classes, races, and world views. Antebellum southerners, like their northern counterparts, turned to the novel—among other genres—as a powerful weapon in defending their distinct, proslavery culture[24]

Undeniably, an insistence on history as structure is political, although not in any narrow way. It is at once more modestly and more inclusively political than the defense of a specific political position. For texts themselves are products of and interventions in the inescapably political nature of human existence. The point is not that texts defend specific political positions, although they may , but that they derive from political relations from which they cannot be entirely abstracted.

In general, the new historicism, in failing to address these questions, has aligned itself with the post-structuralist criticism the excesses of which it is seeking to redress, and has thus positioned itself in radical opposition to history. For the new historicism is tending to restore context without exploring the boundaries between text and context. In this respect, it is modifying, but not seriously questioning, the premises that have informed post-structuralist textual analysis. And, in so doing, it is obscuring yet more thoroughly the specific character of history and historical understanding.

The defense of history as structure rests on a conviction that texts have the power to crystallize the pervasive discourses of any society and thus to shape their development. This view endows texts with considerable, although not autonomous, power. For texts enjoy a privileged position in the continuing process of fashioning and refashioning consciousness, of defining possibilities of action, of shaping identities, and of shaping visions of justice and order. But that power derives precisely from their inscription in a history reread as structured relations of superordination and subordination.

No more than the author can the text escape history, although history herself assures some texts the power to speak compellingly to more than one historical moment. No more than the author can the text claim political innocence, although a sophisticated politics invariably presents itself as comprehensive world view. The history that informs even the most abstract text is ultimately political in privileging a particular distillation of common experience. Craft and talent play their roles, as does audience response, in permitting the production and dissemination of texts and thereby in establishing their influence. But craft, talent, and audience response themselves result from history and politics. Ultimately, to insist that texts are products of and participants in history as structured social and gender relations is to reclaim them for society as a whole, reclaim them for the political scrutiny of those whom they have excluded, as much as those whom they have celebrated, for all of those in whose names they have spoken or have claimed to speak. And it is to reclaim them for our intentional political action, and ourselves for political accountability.

Notes

1. The preeminent figure associated with thick description is Clifford Geertz. See, in particular, his *Interpretation of Cultures: Selected Essays* (New York, 1973).

2. On the need to reclaim meaning, see Fredric Jameson, *The Political Unconscious: Narrative at a Socially Symbolic Act* (Ithaca, 1981).

3. *Representations* is published by the University of California Press at Berkeley and co-edited by Svetlana Alpers and Stephen Greenblatt. In fact, *Representations*, does not so much stand for a philosophical movement as for a methodological one. Thus, not surprisingly, it encompasses authors of different—or undifferentiated—philosophical positions, or without philosophical concerns. Since method, however important and whatever its most devoted

exponents claim, cannot stand in for philosophy, the privileging of method over philosophy understandably results in the appearance of philosophical eclecticism.

4.   See especially, Jane Tompkins, *Sensational Designs: The Cultural Work of American Fiction* (New York, 1985), Cathy Davidson, *Revolution and the Word: The Rise of the Novel in American* (New York, 1987), and Janice Radway, *Reading the Romance: Women, Patriarchy, and Popular Literature* (Chapel Hill, 1984). These feminist critics are obviously building on the work of other reader-response critics, notably Wolfgang Iser. See, esp., Wolfgang Iser, *The Act of Reading: A Theory of Aesthetic Response* (Baltimore, 1978): but also for a general introduction to the work in the field, Jane Tompkins, ed., *Reader-Response Criticism: From Formalism to Post-Structuralism* (Baltimore, 1980); and Susan R. Suleiman and Inge Crosman, eds., *The Reader in the Text: Essays on Interpretation and Audience* (Princeton, 1980).

5.   Jameson, *Political Unconscious;* Michael McKeon, *The Origins of the English Novel 1600–1740* (Baltimore, 1987); Dominick LaCapra, *Madame Bovary on Trial* (Ithaca, 1982); Richard Terdiman, *Discourse/Counter-Discourse: The Theory and Practice of Symbolic Resistance in Nineteenth-Century France* (Ithaca, 1985); Timothy J. Reiss, *The Discourse of Modernism* (Ithaca, 1982).

6.   *New Literary History: A Journal of Theory and Interpretation* is published by the Johns Hopkins University Press and edited by Ralph Cohen. For the new developments in literary History, see Ralph Cohen, ed., *New Directions in Literary History* (Baltimore, 1974). In truth, *New Literary History* represents a catholicity and diversity that far exceed the bounds of the new historicism, however loosely drawn.

7.   Among Lewis P. Simpson's extensive oeuvre, see esp., *The Dispossessed Garden* (Athens, Ga., 1975), *The Man of Letters in New England and the South* (Baton Rouge, 1973), and *The Brazen Face of History* (Baton Rouge, 1980). See also, Elizabeth Fox-Genovese and Eugene D. Genovese, "The Cultural History of the Old South: Reflections on the Work of Lewis P. Simpson," in J. Gerald Kennedy and Daniel Fogel, eds., *American Letters and the Historical Consciousness: Essays in Honor of Lewis P. Simpson* (Baton Rouge, 1987), pp. 15–41. For Michael O'Brien, see *A Character of Hugh Legare* (Knoxville, Tenn., 1985), his edited collection, *All Clever Men Who Make Their Way* (Columbia, Mo., 1985), and his "Preface" and "Politics, Romanticism, and Hugh Legare: The Fondness of Disappointed Love,' " in Michael O'Brien and David Moltke-Hansen, eds., *Intellectual Life in Antebellum Charleston* (Knoxville, Tenn., 1986). See also, Drew Gilpin Faust, *A Sacred Circle: The Dilemma of the Intellectual in the Old South, 1840-1860* (Baltimore, 1977). For M. E. Bradford, see, for example, *A Better Guide Than Reason: Studies in the American Revolution* (La Salle, Il., 1979).

8.   For a clear formulation of the relation between deconstruction and the new historicism, see Walter L. Reed, "Deconstruction versus the New Historicism: Recent Theories and Histories of the Novel," paper presented at the annual meeting of SAMLA, Atlanta, 1987. I am much indebted to Professor Reed for letting me read his thoughtful paper.

9.   For an introduction to the debates about the nature of American Studies, see Gene Wise, guest editor, "The American Studies Movement: A Thirty Year Retrospective," *American Quarterly* XXXI, no. 3 (1979): 286–409, which includes essays by Wise and Wilcomb Washburn. For recent developments in American Studies, see, for example, Sacvan Bercovitch and Myra Jehlen, eds., *Ideology and Classic American Literature* (Cambridge and New York, 1986), and Walter Benn Michaels and Donald E. Pease, eds., *The American Renaissance Reconsidered: Selected Papers from the English Institute, 1982–83* (Baltimore, 1985).

10.   Jameson, *Political Unconscious*. It should be clear from my discussion that I do not think that Jameson's work can be completely subsumed under the rubric of new historicism, if only because of his proclaimed and serious philosophical concerns.

11.   See in particular, Hayden White, *Metahistory: The Historical Imagination in Nineteenth-Century Europe* (Baltimore, 1973).

12.   See e.g., Antonio Gramsci, *Selections from the Prison Notesbooks*, ed. and trans. Quintin Hoare and Geoffrey Nowell Smith (New York, 1971), his *Gli Intellettuali e l'organizzazione della cultura* (Torino, 1949), and his *Ouaderni del Carcere*, 4 vols., ed. Valentino Gerratana (Torino, 1975); Mikhail Bakhtin, *Rabelais and His World*, trans. Helene Iswolsky (Cambridge, Mass., 1968), and Michael Holquist, ed., *The Dialogic Imagination: Four Essays by M. M. Bakhtin*, trans. Caryl Emerson and Michael Holquist (Austin, 1981).

13.   See, for example, Margaret W. Ferguson, Maureen Quilligan, and Nancy J. Vickers, eds., *Rewriting the Renaissancce: The Discourses of Sexual Difference in Early Modern Europe* (Chicago, 1986); Catharine Gallagher, *The Industrial Reformation of English Fiction* (Chicago, 1985), and her "Embracing the Absolute: The Politics of the Female Subject in Seventeenth Century England," *Genders* 1 (March 1988): 24–39.

14.   For a position similar to my own, see Robert Weimann, *Structure and Society: Studies in the History and Theory of Historical Criticism* (London, 1977), esp. pp. 146–87, in which he criticizes various practices of literary structuralism. In fact, the work of Roland Barthes and Lucien Goldmann, in particular, offer promising directions, even if both ultimately remain unsatisfactory on the nature of historical structures and the relations between social and literary structure. For Barthes, see, for example, Roland Barthes, *Sur Racine* (Paris, 1963); and, for Goldmann, *Le dieu caché: Etude sur la vision tragique dans les "Pensées" de Pascal et dans le théâtre de Racine* (Paris, 1955).

15.   Jameson, *Political Unconscious*, p. 26.

16.   For preliminary statements of my views of these matters, see my "The Great Tradition and Its Orphans: Or Why the Defense of the Traditional Curriculum Requires the Restoration of Those It Has Excluded," in Taylor Littleton, ed, *The Rights of Memory: Essays on History, Science, and American Culture* (University, AL, 1986), and "The Claims of Common Culture," *Salmagundi*, no. 72 (Fall 1986).

17.   Jameson, *Political Unconscious*, p. 19, makes a similar point: "My position here is that only Marxism offers a philosophically coherent and ideologically compelling resolution to the dilemma of historicism evoked above."

18.   For a premier example of Marx's dialogue with his bourgeois predecessors, see Karl Marx, *Theories of Surplus Value*, trans. Emile Burns, ed., S. Ryzanskaya, 2 vols. (Moscow, 1969).

19.   Apolitical Marxism is best represented in the work of Edward P. Thompson and his followers. See, in particular, E. P. Thompson, *The Poverty of Theory & Other Essays* (London, 1978). Political Marxism is best represented in dominant Soviet historiography, but for Western variants, see, for example, Claude Mazauric, *Sur la revolution française: contributions a l'histoire de la révolution bourgeoise* (Paris, 1970). For a more satisfying, yet nonetheless politically engaged Marxist history, which eschews both fashion and dogmatism, see the work of Eric Hobsbawm.

20.   John Frow, *Marxism and Literary History* (Cambridge, Mass., 1986), p. 5.

21.   Allen Bloom, *The Closing of the American Mind* (New York, 1987).

22.   McKeon, *Origins of the English Novel.*

23.   Terdiman, *Discourse/Counter-Discourse.*

24.   See, for a striking example, Carolyn Lee Hentz, *The Planter's Northern Bride* (Philadelphia, 1854).

15

Is there Class in this Class?

Richard Terdiman

This essay is going to implicate the notion of classes, of categories in the most general sense. But no more than the larger society, it cannot do away with them. So let me begin (in the form of some questions I want to keep in mind) by insisting on categories, on distinctions—indeed, just the ones evoked by the occasion for which this paper was originally written. First, what is the difference between Poststructuralism on the one hand, and what we call New Historicism on the other? Secondly, what are their differences from their Others? Finally, what difference do these differences make?

It is crucial to remember that differences are not the same thing as unrelated diversities or disparities. Difference implies a very intimate form of connection. Between Poststructuralism and New Historicism, the underlying relaton invokes language. Let me try on this distinction: in their discourse, poststructuralists are moved by a concern with the constitutive, irreducible *play* of signifiers. And new historicists by a concern with their constitutive, irreducible *power*. Together, both tendencies counterpose themselves against strains of formalism which conceive language as *stable* and as *absolute*. For these formalisms, semiotic effects like play and *différance*, social effects like power and symbolic violence, are simply not pertinent. So beyond their differences and in a very broad sense, there is significant commonality between the axiomatics underlying Poststructuralism and New Historicism.

But what happens when we take a concept which appears to belong to one of these discursive universes and interrogate it, *play* with it, in the spirit of the other's protocols? Specifically, the concept of *class*. At first glance such a notion might seem more comfortably housed within the New Historicist paradigm. As Don Wayne put it in a recent essay, New Historicists have substituted relationships of power for "ideas" as fundamental units of historical analysis.[1] As a perspective attentive to issues of power and ideology, and to the way these regulate and reproduce culture, the New Historicism ought easily to be able to assimilate the idea of "class."

But a question will have occurred to you: which kind of "class" do I mean? For in our context here, clearly there are two. Do I intend the notion of "class" as political economy classifies it? Or rather the academic, the pedagogical "class" in which most of us pass a goodly portion of our lives? By rights I ought to make my categories clear. But my point here is willfully to mean both of these, and to play with *their* coincidence. What happens, then, when I insist upon a paralogism, and refuse to recognize the proper distinction between these very different entities, the social and the academic class?

Such a perverse conflation of the world of scholarship and the world of politics seems to depend upon nothing more than the random polysemy of a single signifier, the common word "class." Purists of numerous stripes— the traditional defenders of academic virtue first among them—will no doubt react in horror at my illicit homogenization of distinct semantic fields. I've mixed my classes. And by means of word play I've engineered an invasion of politics both into the crystalline neutrality of taxonomy and (this may be worse) into the sanctified refuge of the academy.

What I want to argue is that the two modes of criticism which come together in the project of this volume unite across their considerable differences to suggest there may be sense in my verbal hodgepodge—political sense particularly. A poststructuralist take on language gives me some confidence that the play of difference and identity between my two "classes" may be more than adventitious, indeed may turn out deeply consequential. The New Historicism (and, I might add, a whole tradition of historically-sensitive reflection on language, ideology, and power of which New Historicism forms only a recent part) helps me argue for the strongly *conjunctural* meaning of what appears at first glance to be no more than an accidental identity of signifiers.

Let me dip into history at two points which may help to illuminate the terminological convergence that interests me here. In their *The Politics and Poetics of Transgression,* Peter Stallybrass and Allon White recall where words like "class" and "classic" come from.[2] They stem from Latin *classis,* which at the origin had nothing to do with the academic or the esthetic at all. The word designated a category in Roman property and taxation law. In Rome, the *classici* were the most prosperous citizens, and paid the most taxes. In the second century, Aulus Gellius built a metaphor on their pecuniary preeminence, and used their name to designate the best writers. This subterranean valorization of *economic power masquerading as quality* has stuck to "class" ever since. In other words, in the most concrete ways, the reassuringly neutral, analytic resonances of the word "class" are achieved through a purposeful erasure of history.[3]

Now let me consider the thinking of one of the important ideologists of civil society since the twin revolutions of the nineteenth century, François Guizot—historian, and prime minister to the first French bourgeois monarch. Guizot's recommendation to "Get rich" ("Enrichissez-vous"), made in a celebrated speech (1 March 1843) to the French *Parlement,* is rightly believed to have founded the Yuppies. But I want to credit him here with another crucial insight. The great problem of modern societies, Guizot wrote in justification of the Education Law of 1833 which he had proposed to the legislature, is the governance of minds. Consequently he recommended considerable effort to make education in the new secular, liberal French State "a guarantee of order and social stability."[4] Here is where the mixing of our classes began to be carefully programmed.

The academic study of the classic, *prosperous,* writers now begins to make clear conjunctural sense. And the classic values to be taught in class turn out to be less glorious, and less innocent, than Matthew Arnold had told us.[5] But as between the social and the educational senses, a third sense of "class"—as the fundamental register of hierarchy—clearly emerges as the root notion or image which embeds and informs the other two. "Class," in other words, is the basic dialectical operator. In Pierre Bourdieu's terms, class is "a mode of vision and of division."[6] What it asserts is achieved through an implicit but powerful negation: it forcefully excludes what it does not embrace. Social reproduction in liberal societies since the nineteenth-century revolutions has depended upon *realizing* this notion of class in a critical sectioning of social (and indeed personal) reality. To do so has required a considerable dose of what Bourdieu provocatively terms "symbolic violence."[7] We need to ask how and where such violence is perpetrated.

"Symbolic violence" implies the forcible imposition of such principles of division, and more generally of any symbolic representations (languages, conceptualizations, portrayals). The speakers of a language have little choice about whether to accept or reject these: they are embedded in the medium itself. In Bourdieu's and Jean-Claude Passeron's *Reproduction,* the education function of the State is conceived as a quintessential form of symbolic violence. This is because students are obliged—by the law of compulsory education and by the force of pedagogical authority—to conceive their own social situation, like the material they study, in terms of the interpretations of these which are inculcated by their schooling. So following the lead of curricula which have been administered to that end since Guizot's time, *classes* have been made dominant realities within culture. As everyone reading this knows, classes decide lives. It is not only that the class you take determines what class you get into. It is that *in classes we learn to class.*

But so long as we conceive it as simple division, as the fundamental operator in a kind of detached set theory, the notion of class and of classifying remains curiously neutralized. It suggests that the world could be in some sense innocently Boolean. On the other hand, restoring the signifier to history, restoring its history to the signifier, irretrievably complicates its existence as a logical or formal absolute. However much they might be criticized on other grounds, the practices of the New Historicism reinstate a form of relation—to history, to culture, to politics—which it is the function of historicism's or deconstruction's Other to bracket and efface. To class may seem an act in the neutral operation of a logic. But *classes*—both kinds— are irreducibly social. And they sustain each others' realities as if by the most intricately instrumental mechanism. The order into which these concepts and practices are inscribed is itself instrumental, linked with the representation and exercise of power which the formal classification of "class" would simply bleach out.

To put this in terminology I've already suggested, in real social formations, classification always entails symbolic violence. And symbolic violence is always *situated;* violence is always exercised *against* someone. So there is no innocent categorization. In social life, if not in logic, differences are necessarily *hierarchies.* As we learned in *Brown v. Board of Education,* the notion of "separate but equal" is an oxymoron. And as Postructuralism argues, even "separate" is an abyss.

The word "class" is thus in essence a word for distributing power. Even if difference could be neutral, the act of classing itself presupposes power in the form of a superior instance authorized to decide the membership of the categories specified. A system of classes (of whatever kind) always implies evaluation, and hence its inevitable if guilty accompanist, subordination.

But to return to our own class: the university, of course, exists to classify, and thereby necessarily to subordinate. It is the university which decides membership. And as Jacques Derrida points out in "The Principle of Reason: The University in the Eyes of its Pupils," today the academy can do its job of segregation of the classes without employing overt censorship at all.[8] The university simply takes evaluative action—it gives a grade, declines to certify a research project or a course offering. It does not fire personnel, it simply disapproves rehiring them.

These are the forms of the university's internal struggles. But even such a classification as internal vs. external conceals a hierarchy and an apparatus of power. We are all familiar with the theory of the university's fundamental inner-directedness, of its disinclination to implicate itself in the sordid struggles of what it sometimes still naively terms the "world outside." Despite such pretensions, the mediation through which our two senses of "class" converge within the academic realm is the university's preoccupation with "occupations," its self-proclaimed mission of producing professional qualification.[9] This is the determination by which the outside world turns up at the center of that protected academic space which it was thought to surround and even to shelter. Within modern technocratic societies, those professional qualifications are the effective form of social class, as Bourdieu argued in "The Force of Law." Thus there is *always* class in our classes.

The exercise of technopolitical power has been inherent in the university, certainly since the nineteenth-century revolutions, as Guizot's reflection suggested. Such dominant discourses inhabiting our consciousness, our practices, our habitus, can hardly be evaded. There is no verbal or institutional magic (surely not the supposed neutrality of the academy) which would abolish these necessities or undo this domination. In that sense we are subjected. We cannot imagine that the university might make a revolution on its own. Our classes are outclassed by the power of power.

What then? We are left with our counter-discourses, with the subtle and elusive achievements of subversion and of symbolic resistance.[10] Power, however dominating, is always porous. The university's function ought to be, and perhaps in an honorific sense has always been, to find the holes and exploit them when possible. Poststructuralism and New Historicism join in this exploration: both upset received evaluations of fundamental social operators. And they upset the guardians of the university too. One need only read the essays by Education Secretary William Bennett or Harvard English Professor Walter Jackson Bate to which Derrida has recently referred [11] to see the passion which has been elicited among these classics by the iconoclasts, some of whose work I've been referring to here. We thus encounter a live and intense contemporary struggle over the conduct of education and the inculcation of values. Its very intensity suggests the degree to which, while dominated by it, our classes still implicate power. Of course how much and how quietly we accept our own implication in and by such power classes *us* to a significant degree.

Notes

1. Don Wayne, "Power, Politics, and the Shakespearean Text: Recent Criticism in England and the United States," *Shakespeare Reproduced: The Text in History and Ideology*, ed. Jean E. Howard and Marion F. O'Connor (New York and London: Methuen, 1987), p. 48.

2. Peter Stallybrass and Allon White, *The Politics and Poetics of Transgression* (Ithaca, N.Y.: Cornell University Press, 1986), pp. 1–2. As White and Stallybrass tell us, the *locus classicus* of this historical discussion of "*class*" is Ernst Robert Curtius's *European Literature and the Latin Middle Ages* (New York: Harper & Row, 1979), pp. 249–250.

3. As Curtius reminds us, in discussing "What is a classic?" in 1850, Charles Augustin Sainte-Beuve glossed Gellius's metaphor without any apparent false consciousness. He defined the classic writer as "a writer of value and of note, one who counts, who has comfortable possessions, who is not to be confused with the crowd of proletarians." See Curtius, *European Literature*, p. 250. It went without saying, of course, that these classics were the writers to be studied in class.

4. See Eugen Weber, *Peasants into Frenchmen: The Modernization of Rural France, 1870–1914* (Stanford, Cal: Stanford University Press, 1976), p. 331. As quoted by Weber, Guizot's opinion is found in his *Mémoires pour servir á l'histoire de mon temps*, (Paris: R. Laffont-Club français du livre, 1971), p. 200.

5. Etymology and filiation of historical meanings will take us only so far. Still, one more glance at this area. In *Keywords*, Raymond Williams sought to sort out the intertwined meanings of "class." Already upon its passage into English in the seventeenth century it carried above all the familiar special association with education: "A Form or Lecture restrained to a certain company of Scholars." *Keywords: A Vocabulary of Culture and Society* (New York: Oxford University Press, 1976), p. 51. The use of the term in its modern political and economic sense dates from considerably later, between 1770 and 1840 according to Williams.

6. See for example Pierre Bourdieu, "The Force of Law: Toward a Sociology of the Juridical Field," trans. Richard Terdiman, *Hastings Law Journal* 38:5 (July 1987), 829, and my introduction to the essay, p. 812.

7. See Bourdieu, "The Force of Law," p. 812; and Pierre Bourdieu and Jean-Claude Passeron, *Reproduction in Education, Society, and Culture,* trans. Richard Nice (London: Sage, 1977), pp. 13–14 and passim.

8. Jacques Derrida, "The Principle of Reason: The University in the Eyes of its Pupils," trans. Catherine Porter and Edward P. Morris, in *Diacritics* 13:3 (Fall 1983), 13.

9. Derrida, "The Principle of Reason," p. 17.

10. See my *Discourse/Counter-Discourse: The Theory and Practice of Symbolic Resistance in Nineteenth-Century France* (Ithaca, N.Y.: Cornell University Press, 1985), Introduction.

11. See Jacques Derrida, *Mémoires: For Paul de Man,* trans. Cecile Lindsay, Jonathan Culler, and Eduardo Cadava (New York: Columbia University Press, 1986), p. 41, n. 5.

16

Foucault's Legacy—A New Historicism?

Frank Lentricchia

Literature is "not a mere play of imagination," nor is it "a solitary caprice of a heated brain."[1] With those polemical bullets fired off in the opening sentences of his *History of English Literature* [1863], Hippolyte Taine published one of the inaugural works of old literary historicism in the atmosphere of science's positivistic heyday. "Play" "imagination" "solitary" "caprice"— the syntactical proximity of these and related terms in Taine's discourse refashions them into elements of a rhetorical equation in which they operate as figures of a free, autonomous, isolated, single text and as polemical deflations of a perspective (call it idealist, romantic, formalist, humanist) which irresponsibly portrays the author of the literary text as an originary agent—the exemplary instance of the self that is supposed to be prior to society, precisely the sort of self that might create autonomous literature. Historicism, old and new, is always reactive against a prior idealism—an ever-recurring "German Ideology" which produces the historicist's need to slay by satirically sending up ever-recurring young Hegelians. And one enduring achievement of Taine's introduction to his literary history is precisely the creation of a satirical historicist rhetoric, a debunker's style shared by old and new historicists alike.

Historicism, old and new, would replace the originary self of idealism with its prime antihumanist assumption that all cultural and social phenomena, especially selves, like all natural phenomena, are to be understood as effects produced by imperious agents of causality (cultural traditions, institutions, race, ethnicity, relations of gender, economic and physical environments, dispositions of power). In its earlier scientific phase, historicism tends to be deterministic in the hard sense—it casts determining forces as abstract, monolithic, and oppressively exterior to human activity and it suffers no guilt that I can discern for doing so. In its newer phases, historicism rejects the metaphysics of determinism while cunningly retaining (not without discomfort) a complicated commitment to the principle of causality, for without causal explanation there is no historicism, old or new. Raymond Williams has written that "A Marxism without some concept of determination is in effect worthless. A Marxism with many of the concepts of determination it now has is quite radically disabled."[2] Substitute historicism for Marxism and perhaps Stephen Greenblatt for Raymond Williams, and you have a description of the theoretical quandary within which some recent historically minded literary cirtics, with strong and problematical relations to Michel Foucault, and who tend to specialize in the English Renaissance, now find themselves.

In addition to the basic principle of causality, Taine's old historicism includes the following points. Taken all together they constitute the generative incoherence of his legacy: (1) A rejection of Enlightenment philosophy and historiography which marks the origins of modern historicism: in other words, there is no human nature and therefore no subject which can be its free expression. (2) The assumption (following from the first point) that history is no "flow" of continuity (like a stream) but a series of discontinuous spaces (like geological strata) contiguous with each other; the space within which the historical interpreter stands is one of those relative spaces. And from this point epistemological mayhem would appear to follow. Accordingly, the question, In what sense, if any, can a historian know his or her object of study? Marks the self-consciousness of the newest of new historians, it is their badge of hermeneutical sophistication, what they accuse old historicists of lacking. But Taine has more awareness of this limitation placed upon his work by his key assumptions than he is ever credited for,[3] while new historicists tend to be allowed, mainly by themselves, more credit than is necessary for a presumed insight of contemporary critical theory which in practice produces (by intention, I think) an often disarming, if ritualisitc, gesture about the problematic (that is the jargon term) nature of historical study and the need to be "self-conscious" lest we delude ourselves and others into believing that objective historical understanding is possible. (3) A commitment to continuity. Though the relation of different historical spaces appears to be a disrelation of discontinuity, within any given historical space all cultural phenomena bear a relation to one another of strong resemblance because they are thought to be the "expression" of a "cause" or "center," an "essence" never itself visible but which nevertheless makes all else visible. And the degree to which a historicist commits to this theory that a social formation can be interpreted by a principle of "expressive causality," to a theory that any given cultural phenomenon is a synedoche which makes it possible to produce an "essential section" of the formation (a miniature, a quintessence), and that differences in expressive forms are accidental and decorative—so not to be pursued—then to that degree will a historicist be committing to determinism in its boldest sense.[4] In Taine this full commitment to determinism reveals strange bedfellows by overruling differences between the mechanical (physical) causality of positivism and the expressive (spiritual) causality of Hegelian character, both of which he freely draws upon.

Point 4, the last point, and a subversion of all the others: a humanist impulse. The antihumanist drift of historicism from Marx and Taine to Foucault and his American followers turns—virtually without warning— wholly humanistic and individualistic when the historicist in question is a literary one (as in, say, the cases of Taine and Greenblatt), or when, as global theorist, the historicist in question turns his attention to literary and aesthetic matters in the course of his global theorizing (as in, say, the case of Marx and Foucault). The literary historicist (old and new) grants literature precisely what historicist theory (especially new-historicist theory, with its emphasis on the constitutive presence of the historical reader) is not supposed to grant to any distinct cultural form: the very power which formalist theory claims for literature, the unique privilege of putting us into authentic contact with the real thing through the medium of the "great writer" and his canonical texts. Thus Taine:

> a great poem, a fine novel, the confessions of a superior man, are more instructive than a heap of historians with their histories. I would give fifty volumes of charters and hundred volumes of state papers for the memoirs of Cellini, the epistles of St Paul, the table-talk of Luther, or the comedies of Aristophanes. In this consists the importance of literary works: they are instructive because they are beautiful . . . . a grand literature . . . resembles that admirable apparatus of extraordinary sensibility, by which physicians disentangle and measure the most recondite and delicate changes of body.[5] Now Greenblatt: The literary text remains the central object of my attention in this study . . . because . . . great art is an extraordinarily sensitive register of the complex struggles and harmonies of culture . . . So from the thousands [of writers available] we seize upon a handful of arresting figures who seem to contain within themselves much of what we need, who both reward intense, individual attention and promise access to larger cultural patterns.[6]

So in the end, science is most compelling to Taine not in its systematic and impersonal guise but as the activity of a great man, an individual of "extraordinary sensibility"—and this exemplary scientist is his metaphor of the literary penetration of history, a metaphor which survives intact in Greenblatt's "handful of arresting figures," compelling concrete universals who write those "extraordinarily sensitive" registers of cultural conflict and harmony.

In a useful summary of old and new, and the differences between them (he notes no continuity), Greenblatt, now perhaps the leading voice of American new literary historicists, argues that mainstream literary history "tends to be monological"—he means (in Bakhtinian allusion) to say that it is "concerned with discovering a single political vision, usually identical to that said to be held by the entire literate class or indeed the entire population." This single vision is represented by mainstream historicists as what was really and solely there, as historical fact—not the product in the period under scrutiny of "a particular social group in conflict with other groups," not, surely, the product of the historian's own ideological formation. Against this (Taine-like) view of the expressive unity of culture, and against this serene notion of representation (historical interpretation may confidently represent the past at two removes because what it represents, literature, in turn perfectly represents its society, but only at a hair's breadth of barely one remove)—against this, Greenblatt asserts the new self-questioning historicist who views literary works "as fields of force, places of dissension and shifting interests, occasions for the jostling of orthodox and subversive impulses." So for a new historicist literature is no cool reflection on a "background" of stable and unified historical fact. It is at once part of the "fact" itself and what gives shape to what we know as the fact. The mainstream historicist must therefore practice a triple repression: first, of his own active participation in the creation of the history he thinks he objectively mirrors; second, of the interest-ridden complicity of the literature that he studies in the shaping of what we are given as history; third, of the political conflict of dominant and subaltern social groups which presumably constitutes literature's true shape and content. In short, he covers up struggle with monologue.[7]

A strong feature of new-historicist rhetoric and substance is on display in the typical beginnings of Greenblatt's essays, where he would violate the traditional literary sensibility with lengthy citations of bizarre, apparently off-center materials: an account, roughly contemporary with Shakespeare—thickly, arcanely detailed—of a social practice (say, exorcism) far removed from the high literary practice of the Renaissance. With that gambit Greenblatt would shock his traditional reader into the awareness that here, at last, is no literary business as usual. Greenblatt's beginnings seem to promise what, in theory, new historicism, so hermeneutically savvy, isn't supposed to promise—direct access to history's gritty ground-level texture. In that very moment, while doing that sort of rhetorical work in the arena of contemporary critical maneuvering, Greenblatt initiates his reader to a central new-historicist perspective on culture that recalls the debt of new historicism not only to Foucault but also to the *Annales* school and Clifford Geertz's functional anthropology—a strange mix of voices ultimately dominated by Foucauldian tone: the feeling, usually just evoked, almost never argued through, that all social life is organized and controlled down to its oddest and smallest details.

Old historicists are politically innocent—issues of ideology and class conflict rarely touch their literary work. Greenblatt more or less tells us that they needed to open their Marx. New historicists not only have reopened their Marx; they have embraced Michael Foucault (the deeper theoretical influence on their work), and the effect of this (I think, uncritical) acceptance is traced everywhere in new historicism in the coded term "power." The odd theoretical identity of new historicism is constituted by its unlikely marriage of Marx and Foucault, with Foucault as dominant partner.[8] Greenblatt describes his intention as an attempt to

> achieve a concrete apprehension of the consequences for human expression—for the "I"—of a specific form of power, power at once localized in particular institutions—the court, the church, the colonial administration, the patriarchal family—and diffused in ideological structures of meaning, characteristic modes of expression, recurrent narrative patterns.[9]

In the context of the specific analyses he produces in his landmark book, *Renaissance Self-Fashioning* (1980), Greenblatt's statement on power in his introduction rings with all the paranoid resonances sounded in Foucault's account of the death of the "I" in *Discipline and Punish*. The liberal disposition (Greenblatt's and ours) to read "self-fashioning" as free, expressive self-making is repeatedly and wickedly subverted in *Renaissance Self-Fashioning*. Greenblatt's title announces to liberal optimists (we see this with hindsight) Foucault's depressing message, and his description of power endorses Foucault's theory of power, preserving not only the master's repeated insistence on the concrete institutional character of power, its palpability, as it were, but also his glide into a conception of a power that is elusively and literally undefinable—not finitely anchored but diffused from nowhere to everywhere, and saturating all social relations to the point that all conflicts and "jostlings" among social groups become a mere show of political dissension, a prearranged theater of struggle set upon the substratum of a monolithic agency which produces "opposition" as one of its delusive political effects. Greenblatt's account of the "I," like Foucault's, will dramatize its entrapment in a totalitarian narrative coincidental with the emergence of the modern world as dystopian fruition.

To summon the specter of totalitarianism is to summon determinism once again, not in Taine's positivistic manner but in the political style of *1984*.[10] New historicists are officially on record as critics both of determinism and its sentimental alternative (Greenblatt says the "Renaissance English theater in general functioned neither as a simple extension of constituted religious or political authority nor as a counterchurch or subversive assault upon that authority").[11] Moreover, new historicists typically strike more than pro forma attitudes on the issue; Greenblatt is capable of spectacular acrobatic efforts in the analysis of the relationship of literary texts and history in order to avoid determinist schemas of understanding. But the new historicism nevertheless does have a concept of determination; and far from making it worthless, this concept—which just might be the typically anxious expression of post-Watergate American humanist intellectuals—makes new historicism what it is.

Toward the end of a highly detailed and fascinating essay on the relations among theater, the practice of exorcism, and religious and political authority in the Renaissance in France and England—his most recent study of the relations of literature to its contexts—Greenblatt pulls back from his empirical work for a pause of theoretical reflection that may not refresh. He persuades us that English theater is not a reflex of constituted political authority, but in the process of making that point against old-historicist determinism, he may have instituted a profounder version of it. Consider these remarks:

> 1.   It is no accident, I think, that one of Harsnett's tasks as Bishop [of London] Bancroft's assistant was to license plays for publication: this licensing is an element in the fashioning of social categories—the process of demarcation— that confers upon the public theater the cultural meaning that Harsnett wishes to exploit. The official church dismantles and cedes to the players the powerful mechanisms of an unwanted and dangerous charisma: in return, the players confirm the charge that those mechanisms are theater and hence illusory . . . . They therefore do the state some service.
> 2.   Elizabethan theater does not simply reflect the official policy toward the demoniac, it is in part constituted by it and it contributes in its turn to the concrete shaping of the spiritual and political discourse upon which it draws.[12]

With those statements that sit at the heart of his theoretical reflections Greenblatt affirms both ends of the spectrum of Marxist literary criticism, from the legendary vulgarity of reflectionist modes (and the artist as pawn and lackey) to the sophistication of the culturally sensitive Western (modernist-bent) Marxism (which grants literature formative power). Elizabethan theater shapes political discourse and at the same time is constituted by an official policy, which is executed by villainous agents whom Greenblatt can name (Bancroft, Harsnett), who exploit the theater by granting it a little freedom in return for which the players "do the state some service." But there is always something else in Greenblatt—the Foucauldian transposition of an apparent Marxist perspective. He tells us that in order to grasp the pattern of the relations of artistic and other social practices "we must be particularly sensitive to similitudes for in the Renaissance similitudes are the most well-travelled pathways of exchange, the great trade route along which cultural power is circulated." There are various social practices, like those of theater and exorcism (whose similitude is said to be "coercive"); there are—to cite *Renaissance Self-Fashioning* again—institutions, like those of the patriarchal family, church, and colonial administration; and there are characteristic modes of expression, from everyday communication to high literary narrative. The ground of grounds for understanding these practices and institutions is either "similitude" itself—the great Renaissance idea—or cultural power which is indistinguishable from political power and which "circulates" (Greenblatt's master trope for the action of power). In the first instance Greenblatt retrieves Taine and Lovejoy: similitude is the invisible expressive center, a "world view" which functions as the principle of making sense of all things, causing (in this particular instance) all things to be visible and coherent in a relation of similarity. In the second instance he summons up Foucault by suggesting that the ground of all practice—cultural and political power—is not itself either an "idea" or a practice: "circulating" power—the master agency located in, and motivated by, no specific agent—fashions and demarcates all social categories, causes all relations of similitude and enhances and flows through all practices and human agents, is not itself a subject but sweeps up all subjects, even Bishop Bancroft and his personal operative, his intellectual, Harsnett.[13]

Bancroft and Harsnett are triggering or channeling agents only, nothing more. Not free agents. The anonymous power for which they are the medium has the obvious advantage that conspiratorial versions of history in the name of Marx do not have. The "circulating" activity of this power in all social and cultural spaces gives new and shocking meaning to the notion that nothing is outside politics. But the curious (or is it the predictable?) thing about this concept of a power that coerces all practices is that it gives rise in Foucault and (as we'll see) in Greenblatt to the desire to get outside politics—strange new-historicist desire!—and it has no way of explaining (with its but casual interests in class and economics) why some distinctively not marginal types enjoy staying inside, not only feel powerful but act accordingly.

Greenblatt's recuperation, under the mask of power, of Hegelian expressive unity of culture (a monological vision), is one but not the most interesting theoretical anomaly of new historicism. The most interesting anomaly is generated by Foucault's insistence that historians cannot objectively represent the past because they cannot know and therefore put distance between themselves and the circumstances which produced and disciplined them as social beings enmeshed in the practice of a historical *discipline*. At one level a lurking Hegelianism subverts the Foucauldian new-historicist desire to move beyond mainstream historicist practice and guarantees, in advance, the unity of the culture under historical question. At another, deeper level, mainstream historicist desire, under the very mask of its new-historicist negation, resurfaces in Greenblatt's modest statement of limitation. Greenblatt gives voice to Foucault's project of introducing the forbidden concepts of rupture and discontinuity as antidotes to traditional reliance on the grand humanist assumptions of the narrative unity of history, then (in the same breath) he puts Foucault's theoretical program at bay when he speaks of the "impossibility of fully reconstructing and reentering the culture of the sixteenth century, of leaving behind one's own situation: it is everywhere evident in this book that the questions I ask of my material and indeed the very nature of this material are shaped by the questions I ask of myself. I do not shrink from these impurities—they are the price and perhaps the virtue of this approach—but I have tried to compensate for the indeterminacy and incompleteness they generate by constantly returning to particular lives and particular situations." This apology for his limitation as a historian (it is an unwanted echo of an earlier one made by Taine) remarks ruefully on the price of new historicism—we can't help but note the implication in Greenblatt's tone that objectivity, determinacy, and completeness in historical interpretation are values reluctantly being bid elegiac farewell—yet oddly this apology shifts into a subtle claim to virtue. What is called an "impurity" is embraced as the enabling weapon of a new historicism. Forbidden traditional desires for objectivity and a unified narrative of past and present are replaced by open deployment of self-concerns; the supposed discontinuity of present and past (a Foucauldian axiom) is mapped as a continuous narrative whose source and end is "myself."[14]

The question then is, when Greenblatt says "myself," who exactly is he talking about? When he says that he seizes upon a "handful of arresting figures who seem to contain within themselves much of what we need," just who is the "we" in "need" and what is the nature of this need? Greenblatt's "myself" is representative, it finds its home in "we," and "we" is nothing other than the community of disappointed liberal middle-class literary intellectuals—and how many of us really stand outside this class?—whose basic need is to believe in the autonomy of self-fashioning and who find this need dramatized in certain standard writers of the sixteenth century, who find, therefore, the Renaissance to be peculiarly modern, a theme of traditional Renaissance theory with this twist: this need for autonomy is thought to be set up and stimulated in the emerging bourgeois world and then wholly and cruelly denied. New historicism is another expression of the bitter and well-grounded first-world suspicion that modern history is the betrayal of liberalism. The Renaissance turns out to be "modern" not only in a sense not intended by Jacob Burckhardt but in one which would have horrified his liberal confidence: the Renaissance is *our* culture because it is the origin of our disciplinary society. That, I take it, is the final, if unintended, significance of Greenblatt's remark that we study the Renaissance "by analogy to ourselves." The personal story that he tells in the epilogue of his book functions as a cautionary tale of the archetypal political awakening of liberal man to the realities of power. His advice is to imaginatively interiorize the dream of self-fashioning because only by so doing will we keep ourselves from being swept away in history's narrative of repression, in the inevitable movement to the carceral nightmare as the daylight world of everyday life. Greenblatt tells us at the end that the human subject which he (and we) wanted to be autonomous and believed to be so "begins to seem remarkably unfree, the ideological product of the relations of power in a particular society."[15]

The truly revealing (ideological) pages of *Renaissance Self-Fashioning* are those on Marlowe, the creator of "heroes who fashion themselves not in loving submission to an absolute authority but in self-conscious opposition." And yet (a typical new-historicist "yet") each of these rebel heroes is "not the exception to but"—like the Jew of Malta—"the true representation of his society." ("What wind drives you thus into *Malta* road?" "The wind that bloweth all the world besides,/Desire of gold.") Greenblatt at this point brings his Marx to bear with two quotations from *On the Jewish Question:* (1) "Judaism is a universal *anti-social* element of the *present time";* (2) in the world of capital the marketplace is everywhere, and all things—including all human beings—are turned "into *alienable,* saleable objects, in thrall to egoistic need and huckstering." Barabas, Greenblatt argues winningly, is "simply *brought into being* by the Christian society around him," and he expresses this society in a literal sense, since he gives voice to the dominant culture by constructing his speech out of its materials, speech "virtually composed of hard little aphorisms, cynical adages, worldly maxims, all the neatly packaged nastiness of his society," its "compressed ideological wealth," "the money of the mind." Greenblatt follows out his logic: "As the essence of proverbs is their anonymity, the effect of their recurrent use by Barabas is to render him more and more typical, to *de-individualize* him."[16]

The rebellious, oppositional subject, where has he gone? He has disappared, his identity effaced by the society structured (in Greenblatt's Foucauldian code) by "disciplinary paradigms" which produce what we desire and fear, including the modes of social opposition that in the end merely confirm the original paradigms from which the rebel never departs. Greenblatt closes this portion of his analysis with further support from Marx, this time the most famous passage in *The Eighteenth Brumaire of Louis Bonaparte:*

> Men make their own history, but they do not make it just ast they please, they do not make it under circumstances chosen by themselves, but under circumstances directly found, given and transmitted from the past. The tradition of the dead generations weighs like a nightmare on the minds of the living. And just when they seem engaged in revolutionizing themselves and things, in creating something entirely new, precisely in such epochs of revolutionary crisis they anxiously conjure up the spirits of the past.

Greenblatt moves on to other plays, *Tamburlaine* most importantly, but only in order to enhance the basic point—that radicalism is a representation of orthodoxy in its most politically cunning form and that all struggle against a dominant ideology is in vain.[17]

Marx, theorist of social change and revolution, now reread on Foucauldian ground and converted into a forerunner of Foucault, becomes a servant of the councils of cynicism, a theorist of repetition. But even it you've read no Marx at all you see, in the very passages that Greenblatt deploys to make his political point, that Marx is saying something else. The Jew is not a "universal phenomenon," to cite Greenblatt's curtailment of Marx, but a "universal *anti-social* element." And he is a "universal *anti-social* element" not for all time but the *"present time,"* the time of capital and Christianity which he represents. What is historically specific in Marx is metaphysically general and eternally oppressive in Greenblatt and Foucault. What is always clear in Marx—the antisocial is the undesirable condition of society, Marx imagines alternatives—is rarely clear in Greenblatt and Foucault. Likewise, in *The Eighteenth Brumaire,* in that famous passage, Marx was in effect writing a preface to his reading of a specific (failed) effort of class struggle in France to make revolutionary change. He was not saying (as Greenblatt implies) something general about revolutionary praxis—that it is impossible, that acts of social change are really repetitions in disguise of the past—he was saying that we are marked indelibly by the past and that in revolutionary crises (this, I suppose, is his general point) the desire for rupture, what Marx carefully phrases as the "entirely new," is a guarantee that the past will be conjured up. The past survives as residual culture in the present, but survival is not synonymous with repetition. In *The Eighteenth Brumaire* Marx was not writing a preface to Faulkner. Yet it is precisely the "entirely new," the negation of history (strange new-historicist negation!), that Greenblatt and Foucault set up as the proof of authentic opposition, and failing to find *that* feel licensed to say that oppositional activity is a rebel's delusion cagily incited by the powers that be.

Where does this leave Greenblatt? In a political and psychological posture which he, like Foucault, can't really stomach. His alternative, strongly implied by the title of his chapter on Marlowe, "Marlowe and the Will to Absolute Play," is rigorously aesthetic (strange new-historicist alternative!) and a strong echo of Foucault's preference for so-called marginal figures of anarchy. "Marlowe's heroes," Greenblatt concludes.

> nevertheless manifest a theatrical energy that distinguishes their words as well as their actions from the surrounding society. If the audience's perception of radical difference gives way to a perception of subversive identity, that too in its turn gives way: in the *excessive* quality of Marlowe's heroes, in their histrionic extremism, lies that which distinguishes their self-fashioning acts from the society around them.

The inevitable question—so what?—is answered by Greenblatt with a directness usually absent from Foucault's prose: "The will to play," he says, "flaunts society's cherished orthodoxies, embraces what the culture finds loathsome or frightening, transforms the serious into the joke and then unsettles the category of the joke by taking it seriously, courts self-destruction in the interest of the anarchic discharge of its energy. This is play on the brink of an abyss, *absolute* play." Surely what Greenblatt is describing as the aesthetic moment of absolute theatricality is a moment of freedom from dominant, determining ideology and power which presumably can't be escaped except in such moments of aesthetic extremity. This is a literary politics of freedom whose echoes of Nietzsche and his joyful deconstructionist progeny do not disguise its affiliation with the mainline tradition of aesthetic humanism, a politics much favored by many of our colleagues in literary study, who take not a little pleasure from describing themselves as powerless. This is a literary politics that does not and never has answered the question: So what?[18]

The central commitment of historicists, old and new, is to the self as product of forces over which we exercise no control—the self as effect, not origin: that commitment makes historicists what they are. The central, unacknowledged, and perhaps unacknowledgeable desire of historicism—it is not part of their officially stated position on the self—is to avoid the consequences of that central commitment, to find a space of freedom and so free us from a world in which we are forced to become what we do not wish to become. There is a self-subversive tug in historicist discourse—a need to ensure that there is always something left over, a need to say what historicists are prohibited from saying and which they do not ever quite say: that there is a secret recess of consciousness as yet unmanipulated, some hiding place where we do not feel ourselves to be utterly just entities who have been enabled by vast, impersonal systems. There, in that special place, we know we are because we feel ourselves to be discontented, in that reflective space we make the judgment that no system enables—that we are unhappy. And we locate our unhappiness precisely in those systems that have produced and enabled us as selves. So the Foucauldian new-historicist account in its entirety—both what it believes to be the truth and what speaks through and undoes that belief—is the best if unwitting account of new historicism and its political quandary that I know. Hating a world that we never made, wanting to transform it, we settle for a holiday from reality, a safely sealed space reserved for the expression of aesthetic anarchy, a long weekend that defuses the radical implications of our unhappiness.

The lesson Greenblatt seems eager to impart in the personal anecdote he relates at the end of his book is that we must not abandon self-fashioning even if selfhood is to be conceived as a theatrical fiction—for to give up "is to die." He admits to an "overwhelming need to sustain the illusion that I am the principal maker of my own identity." So we sustain the dream of free selfhood in our disappointed liberal collective imagination, we sustain it there and cherish it there, because we know, or think we know, that we cannot touch the structure of power that denies us such freedom everyplace else. That such knowledge, if that is what it is (I prefer calling it a paranoid fantasy, one especially characteristic of the recent literary mind), is necessary to the sustaining of a totalitarian culture (or, as I prefer to say, to the sustaining of totalitarian culture (or, as I prefer to say, to the sustaining, in ostensibly democratic contexts, of the illusion of totalitarianism): none of this seems ever to give Greenblatt, Foucault, or other new historicists pause. New historicism in its strong Foucauldian vein is an important because representative story of the American academic intellectual in the contemporary moment of literary theory, a moment which we had presumed to be a definitive break with the business as usual of literary study.

Notes

1.   Hippolyte Taine, Introduction to *History of English Literature,* in Hazard Adams, ed., *Critical Theory since Plato* (New York: Harcourt, Brace Jovanovich, 1971), p. 602.

2.   Raymond Williams, *Marxism and Literature* (Oxford: Oxford University Press, 1977), p. 83.

3.   Taine, Introduction to *History of English Literature,* p. 603.

4.   Ibid., p. 604.

5.   Ibid., pp. 613–614.

6.   Stephen Greenblatt, *Renaissance Self-Fashioning* (Chicago: University of Chicago Press, 1980), p. 6. For important accounts of the issues and players of new historicism see the essays by Louis Montrose and Jean E. Howard in *English Literary Renaissance* 16 (Winter 1986).

7.   Stephen Greenblatt, Introduction to *The Forms of Power and the Power of Forms in the Renaissance, Genre* 15 (1982), 3–6 passim.

8.   Though Foucault inhabits *Renaissance Self-Fashioning* mainly in Greenblatt's notes, my point is that Foucault's key obsessions and terms shape Greenblatt's argument, particularly in its "Marxist" moments, more than does the work of Clifford Geertz which appears to be more central to Greenblatt than it is. In any event, Geertz's descriptive and apolitical account of culture enhances Greenblatt's Foucauldian legacy of "political grid-lock" (a phrase I steal from a conversation with Lee Patterson, who invented it).

9.   Greenblatt, *Renaissance Self-Fashioning,* p. 6.

10.   Greenblatt's dissertation was partly on Orwell.

11.   Stephen Greenblatt, "Loudun and London," *Critical Inquiry* 12 (Winter 1986), 343.

12.   Ibid., pp. 341, 342.

13.   Ibid., pp. 341, 343.

14.   Greenblatt, *Renaissance Self-Fashioning,* pp. 5, 6.

15.   Ibid., p. 256.

16.   Ibid., pp. 203, 204, 205, 206, 207, 208.

17.   Ibid., pp. 209–210.

18.   Ibid., pp. 214, 220.

17

The Limits of Local Knowledge

Vincent P. Pecora

Men make their own history, but they do not make it just as they please; they do not make it under circumstances chosen by themselves, but under circumstances directly encountered, given and transmitted from the past.

(Karl Marx, *The Eighteenth Brumaire of Louis Bonaparte*)

. . . the goal, still far enough away to sustain ambition, is an understanding of how it is that every people gets the politics it imagines.

(Clifford Geertz, *The Interpretation of Cultures*)

The assumption with which I begin this essay is that what has come to be called the "New Historicism" in contemporary American literary and cultural criticism is an attempt to find a methodology that could avoid the reductiveness both of formalist (or more traditional literary historical) hypostatizations of the aesthetic object as a mirror or expression of a timeless human nature, and of the Marxian treatment of the aesthetic object as primarily an ideological mediation of changing, but historically determined, social conflicts. For reasons that I will touch upon at the end of this essay, both these positions are deemed to be inadequate—though it is less their inadequacy as such than the "reasons" that will be of greatest interest to me. In order to effect a revision, the new historicism characteristically makes two moves. First, it tries to diminish, or in certain cases to eradicate, distinctions between the "aesthetic object" per se and something called a "historical background," between one kind of "text" and another, and within a hierarchy of genres and audiences—high art versus popular entertainment, literary work versus royal procession, for example. Second, it tries to replace what it sees as a simpler "reflection" model inherent, though in different ways, both in older formalist and in Marxian criticism, with a method which emphasizes the degree to which representation—or a "cultural poetics," in Stephen Greenblatt's term—itself plays a formative, determining social role. Neither of these theoretical moves is unique to new historicist writings; but, as I will attempt to show, their particular conjunction and elaboration does constitute an exemplary strain in contemporary critical writings that is worth careful analysis.

The question of "representation" is thus crucial to the argument, but even a brief glance at new historicist writings will reveal a wide divergence in the uses to which this term is put. In the "cultural materialism" of certain English critics like Jonathan Dollimore, "representation" is construed theoretically to be something that can supersede the older Marxian notion of "mediation": cultural representation works primarily, even simultaneously, as ideological "consolidation, subversion and containment," and thus would seem to expand upon Raymond Williams's well-known triad of residual, dominant, and emergent social forces.[1] Yet in much American new historicism, such as that of Walter Benn Michaels, "representation" has become a code word for the denial that any distinction whatsoever exists between a non-signifying "real" and some realm of cultural production that "reflects," or reflects upon, it. For Michaels and a number of younger Americanists, since everything is always already "representation," representation is where all the "real" action has been all along. What, for many historians, would be more "basic" categories such as material want and material struggle thus lose their privileged position, as these too are merely culturally constructed sign systems.[2] For the supposedly "left" or progressive group of cultural materialists, a key ingredient determining how representations work is an almost mannerist version of Michel Foucault's "power-knowledge relations"; for the supposedly "pragmatic" and apolitical Americanists, representation is primarily a performative function of cultural semiosis, a simplified, ahistorical version of Jean Baudrillard's "political economy of the sign." And in between this polarity is a wide range of other styles of new historicist criticism: Romanticist, reader-response, psychoanalytic, feminist, and what for lack of a better term I will call simply "corporalist."

But, in the face of the wide diversity signified by the new historicist label—which, like all such tags, is clearly itself as performative as it is constative—I would like to address here an issue that runs throughout not only this particular mode of historical criticism, but throughout much of Western intellectual life today: the question of a semiotic interpretation of culture. In order to do that, I would like to concentrate on the work of a figure who, as is often the case in modern, cross-fertilized academic fields, comes to literary criticism from the outside: the anthropologist Clifford Geertz. Geertz is himself exemplary in more ways than one. Indeed, one could find in a 1966 essay the paradigmatic articulation of the search for a method that I have attributed above to the new historicism:

A great deal of recent social scientific theorizing has turned upon an attempt to distinguish and specify two major analytical concepts: culture and social structure. The impetus for this effort has sprung from a desire to take account of ideational factors in social processes without succumbing to either the Hegelian or the Marxist forms of reductionism. In order to avoid having to regard ideas, concepts, values, and expressive forms either as shadows cast by the organization of society upon the hard surfaces of history or as the soul of history whose progress is but a working out of their internal dialectic, it has proved necessary to regard them as independent but not self-sufficient forces—as acting and having their impact only within specific social contexts to which they have, to a greater or lesser degree, a determining influence.[3]

Moreover, not only has Geertz been one of the most popular and influential exponents of cultural semiotics, but his status as an anthropologist has given his writings an authority that is peculiar to Western culture. Like Mead's or Malinowski's or Lévi-Strauss's before him, Geertz's first-hand experience with much that seems to lie outside the "West" automatically endows his work with a privileged vantage on activities—such as "theory" or "interpretation"—whose obvious culture-boundedness haunts every modern critic. In this sense, anthropology is the quintessential post-Hegelian enterprise: it seems to promise, through the ability to understand the other, a clearer definition of self, and at the same moment a vision of the beginnings and ends of that which is human. Even in this regard, Geertz is exemplary, for he has already made the attempt to bring a critical questioning of such promises to bear on anthropology itself, providing his work with an appealing self-consciousness.

And yet, as I will try to show, behind the authority of a storyteller who brings back wisdom from afar, behind the appeal of an intellect which has crossed the invisible thresholds separating one culture from another, all is not quite right. I would thus like the following analysis to raise certain questions—frankly political questions—about the function of our contemporary infatuation with cultural semiotics, whether the avowed purpose of such criticism is "radical" or "pragmatic" or simply speculative. If there is one thing contemporary critics ought to have learned about representation, it is that the signs they use are rarely their own.

I

Clifford Geertz provides an "interpretive" theory of culture that evolves from Weberian typologies of modernization and Parsonian functionalism, and that appropriates the notion of symbolic "structures of signification" and the use of "thick description" from Gilbert Ryle. Further, Geertz introduces into cultural anthropology ideas borrowed, ironically from the present vantage, from literary studies—rhetorical analysis, Kenneth Burke's "representative anecdotes," the interpretation of cultural events as "texts" which represent stories a society tells about itself to make sense of its life-world, the continual tacking between part and whole of the hermeneutic circle elaborated by Wilhelm Dilthey and by critics like Leo Spitzer. Even Geertz's fondness for the shorter, more flexible, and less totalizing essay form has had its influence. But circumscribing all of these, I would like to claim, is Geertz's commitment to "local knowledge," a commitment that has several distinct components. Historically, it is a revisionary elucidation of a more classical (Malinowskian) anthropological desire to assume the "native's point of view," and simultaneously a rejection of the structuralist approach; for Geertz, this yields fundamentally a hermeneutic problem, on the one hand a question of *verstehen* rather than *einfühlen,* and on the other a belief that anthropology is the work of interpreting other "subjects" and their subjective creations, rather than decoding objective, impersonal structures. "The trick is to figure out what the devil they think they are up to."[4] Theoretically, however, "local knowledge" allows Geertz, with the aid of the *Zirkelschluss,* to emphasize the importance of empirical perception, and of theoretical constructions supposedly derived from such perceptions, which can then be reapplied to a wider range of data, and consequently to devalue any theoretical models which appear to be imported from "outside" the local sphere of events. Geertz is of course perfectly willing to admit that all interpretation is a subjective, conceptually laden process, and that "theoretical ideas are not created wholly anew in each study" but are borrowed from previous anthropological work (*IC,* 27). But the approach he suggests nevertheless depends on the practical efficacy of an inside/outside metaphor: "Our double task is to uncover the conceptual structures that inform our subjects' acts, the 'said' of social discourse, and to construct a system of analysis in whose terms what is generic to those structures, what belongs to them because they are what they are, will stand out against the other determinants of human behavior" (*IC,* 27). For Geertz, it might be said, knowledge of anthropological import is knowledge only when it is local.

There are two major problems that emerge here immediately. First, Geertz's emphasis on a "semiotic" concept of culture, "believing, with Max Weber, that man is an animal suspended in webs of signification he himself has spun," is of course hardly unique to his writings, or to "new historicist" criticism. Indeed, given such a broad formula, it is absurd to isolate such ideas as if they constituted a particular mode or theory of criticism, for in the past thirty years they have permeated the humanities and social sciences in France, England, and America (as Geertz himself notes in the "Introduction" to *Local Knowledge*). It would be hard to find a contemporary mode of criticism that had not been influenced to some extent by such thought; we are all (this writer included) in this sense cultural semioticians and "new" historicists under the skin, and the present essay cannot help being in reality a discussion of contemporary critical discourse generally rather than just one "school" within it. But if Geertz's ideas, when expressed on a sufficiently broad level of generality, seem to be simply one version of a larger, modern, Western theoretical perspective, they do not thereby renounce all claims to, and all the burdens of, specificity. In fact, it is precisely the specific workings of Geertz's methods that theoretical debate should be most interested in, for it is only through such scrutiny that the often hidden assumptions carried by new critical languages can be made explicit.

Second, Geertz's work is only one of several theoretical sources for "new historicist" criticism. Without doubt, the other central figure is Foucault, especially the later theorist of power-knowledge relations, the Foucault of *Surveiller et punir*. But no matter how important Foucault's work has been for "new historicist" writing (an issue I will be unable to treat in the present essay), its appropriation has been highly selective, and often the rather profound difference between Foucault's later genealogies of power—which grant a far more "reflective" quality to representation than did his earlier writings—and Geertz's cultural anthropology has been ignored. This difference in fact goes to the heart of the "historical" dimension of much contemporary criticism. One example will have to suffice to illustrate my point. In an essay on "The Politics of Meaning" (1972), Geertz writes:

> The political institutions of all nations are wider and deeper than the formal institutions designed to regulate them; some of the most critical decisions concerning the direction of public life are not made in parliaments and presidiums; they are made in the unformalized realms of what Durkheim called "the collective conscience" (or "consciousness" . . .). But in Indonesia the pattern of official life and the framework of popular sentiment within which it sits have become so disjoined that the activities of government, though centrally important, seem nevertheless almost beside the point, mere routinisms convulsed again and again by sudden irruptions from the screened-off (one almost wants to say, repressed) political course along which the country is in fact moving. (*IC*, 316)

The passage is important both for Geertz's characteristic distinction between external patterns (official "routinisms") and internal forces (in this instance, more real or essential drives, repressed like those of the unconscious), and for the language in which he describes Indonesian social change—"sudden irruptions" from the "screened-off" political life-world of the country. I will return to such matters later. My more immediate concern is with Geertz's invocation of Durkheimian realms of "collective consciousness," even with all its contradictions and conflicts, and with Foucault's explicit rejection of such notions.

In the first chapter of *Discipline and Punish,* Foucault asks the question his book will attempt to answer:

But from what point can such a history of the modern soul on trial be written? If one confined oneself to the evolution of legislation or of penal procedures, one would run the risk of allowing a change in the collective sensibility, an increase in humanization or the development of the human sciences to emerge as a massive, external, inert and primary fact. By studying only the general social forms, as Durkheim did, one runs the risk of positing as the principle of greater leniency in punishment processes of individualization that are rather one of the effects of the new tactics of power, among which are to be included the new penal mechanisms.[5]

That is, what appears to be an unformalized, internal flow of collective consciousness in Geertz could only represent for Foucault an external and inert theoretical hypostasis. More important, Foucault proposes to elucidate discursive practices, but not through an interpretation of symbolic structures that provide, as in Geertz, "control mechanisms—plans, recipes, rules, instructions—for the governing of behavior" (*IC,* 44). Rather, Foucault intends us to see the cultural patterns in processes like "individualization" (a topic Geertz also covers in his work on Bali) as effects of "tactics of power," as discourses intricately caught up in the material patterns of punishment itself. One need only look to John Bender's recent and impressive study, *Imagining the Penitentiary,* to see the important distinction involved here: Bender has taken Foucault's topic, and approached it with Geertz's tools. The result is a study of the rise of the modern penitentiary as it takes shape in an "architecture of mind," in "the symbolic practices through which we manifest our social presence, or subjectivity."[6] The novel, as one medium of such practices, can then be elaborated by Bender as a Geertzian "symbolic structure"—"acting and having . . . impact" on specific social contexts— rather than as an effect of new strategies of power-knowledge.

   To be fair, Geertz often acknowledges the difficulty of his position. Like Weber, he emphasizes that ideas "must . . . be carried by powerful social groups to have powerful social effects" (*IC,* 314); that there is an "ever-present" danger that his style of analysis, in its search for "all-too-deeply-lying" semiotic territory, will "lose touch with the hard surfaces of life— with the political, economic, stratificatory realities within which men are everywhere contained" (*IC,* 30). And, clearly, Foucault's project entails its own dangers, primary among which is the tendency to dissolve the agents who "carry" powerful ideas, in Geertz's sense, and hence those who oppose them, into discursive "regularities" of power and knowledge alike. Having said this, however, I would like to maintain that Geertz's contribution to contemporary literary criticism has certain methodological consequences that have yet to be examined carefully, or critically, by that criticism—a fact of intellectual life that has not been particularly true, it should be added, of anthropology itself. That is, literary studies have appropriated Geertz's insights about as readily as Geertz himself borrowed literary tools, but rarely has anyone stopped to question what social or political "recipes" were being written and followed along the way.

In order to raise that question, I would like to examine briefly not so much what Geertz has had to say about what he is doing as an anthropologist, but rather what he does as an anthropologist, to examine the nature of the insights his interpretive model yields. One of the primary sources of data for Geertz, and hence one of the main locales within which his theoretical knowledge is applied, is Indonesia, primarily the islands of Java and Bali. Geertz's most influential book among literary critics has been *The Interpretation of Cultures,* published in 1973, a collection of essays ranging from 1957 to 1972. (His later collection of essays, *Local Knowledge,* expanded upon the earlier themes, and added discussions of pageantry and law which have also stirred much interest.) Of the fifteen essays *The Interpretation of Cultures* contains, those on an interpretive theory of culture and the now famous "Deep Play: Notes on the Balinese Cockfight" have had the greatest impact. But nearly a third of the book is devoted to what Geertz calls the "New States"—"countries that have gained independence since World War II"— and he counts sixty-six of them. In practice, he focuses in depth only on Indonesia and Morocco, those places where he has done some field work; but he does not hesitate to provide two-to-four page "summaries . . . based on the literature" [Geertz calls them "snapshot pictures"] of "primordial sentiments" and "civil politics" in five other new nations: Malaysia, Burma, India, Lebanon, and Nigeria. It is of course obvious that much of what is called "anthropology" in the West has been done in colonized, or neo-colonial, settings, and Geertz does attempt to confront some of the problems thus raised. But what, exactly, is Geertz saying about topics like ideology, nationalism, modernization, and social change in the "new states"? What does it mean, for example, when Geertz compares the new states to "naive or apprentice painters or poets or composers, seeking their own proper style . . ." or to "immature artists" (*IC,* 278)? What relation, if any, is there between Geertz's approach to such issues and his theoretical observations? And, perhaps most important, what might any of this reveal about the assimilation of Geertzian methods by literary criticism?

I propose then first to look at Indonesia, and at Geertz's "interpretation" of that nation's tortuous struggle for peaceful self-determination. In particular, I would like to focus on what by any account must be a central event in that nation's modern history: the end of Sukarno's rule, and the massacres which followed. How are we to "interpret" Geertz's sense that the Indonesians had failed to "organize a cultural hodgepodge into a workable polity" and had instead produced a "state manqué" (*IC,* 315)? What is the significance, in the context of theories of symbolic interpretation, of passages like the following?

Much of the symbol-mongering that went on under the Sukarno regime, and which has been moderated rather than ended under its successor, was a half-deliberate attempt to close the cultural gulf between the state and society that, if not altogether created by colonial rule, had been enormously widened by it. The great crescendo of slogans, movements, monuments, and demonstrations which reached a pitch of almost hysterical intensity in the early sixties was, in part anyway, designed to make the nation-state seem indigenous. As it was not indigenous, disbelief and disorder spiraled upward together, and Sukarno was destroyed, along with his regime, in the collapse which ensued. (*IC,* 318)

Geertz would read Indonesian history in the 1960s like a grand, tragic *agon*: again invoking that inside/outside metaphor, he blames the Indonesian catastrophe on the fact that Sukarno's regime and the authority it invoked were "not indigenous"; that before 1965, the representation of external ideologies (that is, hysterical "symbol-mongering" rather than authentic symbolic significance) produced an institutional structure which the majority of Indonesian citizens never found "sufficiently congenial to allow it to function" (*IC,* 315); and that Sukarno was in turn destroyed as a result of the chaos, the "disbelief and disorder," which followed. Even more important, Geertz notes that the "eruption of great domestic violence" in Indonesia—for him, in 1972, a repetition of similar events in India, the Congo, Biafra, and Jordan—is more than normally "difficult to evaluate" (*IC,* 323). "Since the terrible last months of 1965, all scholars of Indonesia, and especially those trying to penetrate the country's character, are in the uncomfortable situation of knowing that a vast internal trauma has shaken their subject but not knowing, more than vaguely, what its effects have been" (*IC,* 323). Was the Indonesian trauma of 1965 really such an "internal" affair? Why might "local knowledge"—those systems of self-representation which for Geertz make up the "country's character"—suddenly provide such small explanatory comfort? And finally, were the "effects" of such a trauma, even in 1972, really as vague and confusing as Geertz implies? I will return to Geertz and the "New Historicism." But before that can be done, I would like to address these questions by providing an account of the Indonesian "trauma" that is anything but "local knowledge"—and that provides a sharp, polemical contrast to the discussions of Indonesian politics and culture to be found throughout Geertz's work.

II

In the fall of 1965, the government of President Sukarno of Indonesia collapsed in what has been variously described as a communist takeover that "backfired," an aborted palace coup, a military purge, and a power struggle over nationalist aims. Six top generals were assassinated, "leftist" officers were implicated, and perhaps a half-million communists and suspected sympathizers were murdered. But there is little serious disagreement today, nor was there in the mid-1960s, over the larger geo-political "effects" of this transformation: Indonesia, truly independent from Dutch colonial rule only since 1949, went almost overnight from (a) a militantly anti-colonial nation with an increasingly 'popular communist party (PKI, some 3 million strong by Indonesian estimates) enjoying the overt sanction of the country's charismatic, paternalistic leader and the possibility of close ties to the People's Republic of China; to (b) a military dictatorship under a strident anticommunist general, Suharto, who directed the eradication of the PKI, and who led a regime that was open to American arms and economic assistance, and to new Western investment, and that could become a credible bulwark (especially given the growing difficulties for the West in Vietnam) against the supposed "domino"-like advance of Chinese and communist interests in Southeast Asia.

However complex and difficult to "interpret" it may have become for many in the scholarly community, the "coup" (a misleading but commonly used term) left few in the Johnson White House with an ambivalent reaction. By March of 1966, Max Frankel could report in *The New York Times* that "The Johnson Administration found it difficult today to hide its delight with the news from Indonesia. ... After a long period of patient diplomacy designed to help the army triumph over the Communists, officials were elated to find their expectations being realized."[7] But of course the "news from Indonesia" at this time, especially for administration insiders, contained much that could have occasioned "delight" only from the most cynical and inhuman of observers. The C.I.A., in their own published report on the "coup" (a secret C.I.A. account has never been made public), found space enough in a footnote to mention the salient details:

> Estimates of the number of people killed in Indonesia in the anti-PKI bloodbath after the coup range from 87,000, the official Indonesian government estimate, to 500,000. The figure of 87,000 ... is probably too low. The U.S. Embassy estimated the figure to be closer to 250,000. It would be a mistake to put too much faith in any of the various estimates. ... Undoubtedly, vast numbers were killed. The killings in Java alone put the Mau Mau massacres and the killings in the Congo in the shadow, although the latter got much more publicity. In terms of the numbers killed, the anti-PKI massacres in Indonesia rank as one of the worst mass murders of the 20th century. ...[8]

Nor is there serious dispute over who was in the main responsible for initiating and guiding the massacres, or who stood to gain most from them: the Indonesian military, which had lost six of its generals in the "coup," and retaliated brutally under Suharto's leadership.

With the help of conservative political factions like the Indonesian National Party (PNI) and the Muslim Teacher's Party (NU), which had yielded political ground to the PKI during the previous year, the military was in a position to destroy its primary rival for power.

> The army leadership's goal in encouraging the massacre of PKI supporters was to eliminate the PKI as a political force. The army leaders viewed operations against the PKI as tactically necessary to achieve a strategic objective. Moreover, field officers in Java were drawn largely from the *priyayi* [upper-stratum, only nominally Muslim] section of society, which tended to look on the PKI's activities in mobilizing the lower classes as "non-Javanese" and a threat to the established hierarchy that placed them near the top.[9]

While many have seen "Muslim fanaticism" as a driving force behind the prolongation of the killing, it is also clear that Catholic youths in North Sumatra and Bali Hindus within the PNI played major roles. In any case, as Harold Crouch points out, however factionalized Indonesian society had become as the rising influence of the PKI threatened more traditional and often rural values, army "encouragement" was essential in producing the massacre. "It was only after army officers gave approval of the killing" that "isolated incidents" became systematic bloodshed. "Moreover, the participation of the army gave the supporters of the PKI, unarmed or armed only with bamboo spears and knives, no chance of defending themselves."[10] If there was delight in the White House, and throughout most of the U.S. government, immediately after three of the most gruesome months of modern history, it was not simply due to the identity of the victims—it also depended on the character of the victors, who would henceforth be in a position (though with the slight burden of anywhere between 200,000 and 750,000 political prisoners[11]) to usher Indonesia into "the Free World, where it continues to serve as a loyal outpost of liberty and democracy in the approved style."[12] (The Indonesian invasion of East Timor in 1975, which may have cost another 200,000 lives between 1977 and 1979, made heavy use of the military assistance the United States was providing.[13] Here again, populist elements [Fretilin] which had come to prominence after independence [from Portugal in 1974] were eradicated. And though there were no expressions of delight this time from the Carter White House, the administration did work to block U.N. action against Indonesia at the time.[14])

In hindsight, especially given the expanding U.S. presence in Vietnam during the early 1960s, little besides the sheer size of the slaughter should have been unexpected. Throughout the 1950s, Indonesia was seen by the United States as one of the strategic prizes to be protected by aiding the French effort in Vietnam, and by picking up after them. There is substantial evidence that the C.I.A. helped finance an "outer islands" rebellion against

Sukarno in Sumatra and Sulawesi in 1958.[15] By 1966, such outside interference had become so well known that *The New York Times* could refer to it in passing in the course of a larger discussion of U.S. intelligence operations. Men were trained on Taiwan for action throughout southeast Asia, including Indonesia, and an agent gathering intelligence was often "in reality an activist attempting to create or resolve a situation":

> It is said, for instance, to have been so successful at infiltrating the top of the Indonesian government and army that the United States was reluctant to disrupt C.I.A. covering operations by withdrawing aid and information programs in 1964 and 1965. What was presented officially in Washington as toleration of President Sukarno's insults and provocations was in much larger measure a desire to keep the C.I.A. fronts in business as long as possible.
>
> Though it is not thought to have been involved in any of the maneuvering that has curbed President Sukarno's power in recent months, the agency was well poised to follow events and to predict the emergence of anti-Communist forces.[16]

The article concluded: "Few Americans realize how such operations as these may affect innocent domestic situations. . . ." While it may boggle the ordinary mind to refer to the murder of hundreds of thousands of people as "maneuvering," such euphemistic rhetoric was (and is) in fact standard fare. James Reston, in a column in *The New York Times* later that year entitled "A Gleam of Light in Asia," used similar language; but his point about U.S. involvement parallels the earlier article: "Washington is careful not to claim any credit for the coup and massacres, but this does not mean that Washington had nothing to do with it. There was a great deal more contact between the anti-communist forces in that country and at least one very high official in Washington before and during the Indonesian massacre than is generally realized."[17] Yet the important aspects of the relationship between internal Indonesian struggles and cold-war politics do not rest simply on hints of covert operations against leftist, anti-American foreign leaders—though the earlier Bay of Pigs incident in Cuba and the case of Chile's Allende only a few years later, and subsequent revelations by former C.I.A. employee Ralph McGehee, would tend to lend credence to such reports.[18]

Rather, the crux of the relationship is to be found in the openly expressed expectation that American interests in "disorganized transitional societies" will in the end be served by the growing power of the military itself.[19] Indeed, as Crouch notes, the decade before the "coup" produced a number of studies by Western political scientists which "regarded the army as a likely agent of progress and modernization."[20] In general, such language was simply a code for conditions favorable to Western-dominated economic expansion and political orientation. The army was seen to provide a "more emotionally

secure" kind of leader who would be "sensitive to the needs of modernization" and "a more responsible nationalism," and who naturally found himself "spiritually in tune with the intellectuals, students, and those other
elements in society most anxious to become a part of the modern world."[21]
Indeed, it is in this context that the distinction, so often invoked by Jeane
Kirkpatrick and others in the Reagan Administration, between "authoritarian" (also called "tutelary democracy" in the late 1950s) and "totalitarian"
regimes is developed. As Guy Pauker, arguing for the "leadership potential"
of the officer corps of Southeast Asian nations, wrote in 1958:

> . . . the hope for genuinely representative government is premature. The choice
> is between some form of tutelage that would leave the future open for develop-
> ment in a democratic direction, or political disintegration, economic stagnation,
> and social confusion that would lead the peoples of Southeast Asia toward
> communism. Contemporary history gives strong evidence that totalitarianism
> can be destroyed only by warfare, whereas military regimes do not preclude
> developments in the direction of constitutional democracy. . . .[22]

The position taken by overtly anti-communist political scientists like Pauker
(on whom Geertz says he "relied rather heavily," [*IC*, 279, n33]) and Pye is
especially important, for in emphasizing the "modernization" versus "traditionalism" rift in the societies they study, they leave no way to explain the
peculiar alliance between the army and traditionalist groups like the NU
and its youth organizations in killing even suspected communists after the
"coup."

In 1961, General Nasution negotiated the purchase of arms for an expanded Indonesian military with the Soviet Union.[23] But it is also clear that
many Western observers, including U.S. government figures, agreed with the
thesis that the military could be the West's best friend in developing countries,
and hence a receptive organ of capitalist encouragement. The degree to
which the Indonesian military became central to the economic management
of the country is matched only by the degree to which PKI-led peasants and
unions were instrumental in fostering anti-American sentiment.[24] At the same
time, the conflict between the PKI and the army became one of the central
arenas of class struggle in Indonesia, a struggle exacerbated by Sukarno's
failure to resolve agrarian tensions for a peasantry left impoverished after
the retreat of the Dutch. Especially in the context of *Maphilindo* (a political
alignment of Malaysia, the Philippines, and Indonesia, widely supported at
first, but eventually denounced by Sukarno and the PKI as a neo-colonial
trap to provide a pro-Western "stability" to the region), the military could
hardly ignore the position they were expected to hold in any political environment after Sukarno. "The remarks of Dean Rusk and several other Pentagon
spokesmen about the Indonesian military as the future leader of Indonesia

could not pass unnoticed in the Indonesian military establishment."[25] By 1964, massive U.S. military aid to the Indonesian armed forces had become a condition of implementing the *Maphilindo* plan. Indeed, even during this most strained period of U.S.-Indonesian relations, U.S. military aid was covertly maintained. As Paul Warnke explained to Congress in 1968: "The purpose for which it was maintained was not to support an existing [Sukarno] regime. In fact we were opposed, eventually and increasingly to the then existing regime. It was to preserve a liaison of sorts with the military of the country which in effect turned out to be one of the conclusive elements in the overthrow of that regime."[26] (Recent events concerning the transfer of arms to "moderate" elements in Iran—that is, primarily pro-Western military leaders who would be capable of taking over after, or even overthrowing, Khomeini—appear to be a continuation of this strategy.) Representative Silvio Conte (evidently having forgotten for a moment the reign of terror) claimed in 1976 that, although Sukarno had "told us to get out . . . it was as a result of continuing aid and continuing that small military program that Sukarno was thrown out and a democratic form of government was put in, without firing one shot. . . ."[27] And in March of 1976, Representative William Broomfield pointed out: "Through our training program we trained many of the military people who were able to take over Indonesia and they have become friends of the United States."[28] During the years preceding the "coup," the United States had trained some 500 Indonesian police officials, 1200 military officers, and had helped train over half of the 110,000-member national police.[29]

But the steady erosion of the U.S. position in Vietnam (President Diem's assassination on Nov. 1, 1963 signaled a new phase in the conflict), the repeated failure of the U.S. policy of cultivating "local friends," and its growing military involvement in the region, made any political turning of Sukarno toward American interests practically impossible. Congress in 1964 gave President Johnson nearly unanimous authorization to take "all necessary measures" against communist aggression in Southeast Asia; in March of 1965 "Operation Rolling Thunder" (the full-scale bombing of North Vietnam) began while the first U.S. combat troops landed at Da Nang; and the U.S. Seventh Fleet was in Javanese waters at the time of the Indonesian "coup." The PKI grew in strength, Sukarno embraced their leaders publicly, and the U.S. Congress became disenchanted with any further schemes of military or economic assistance. But this development did not spell the end of American influence: some twenty-six military officers were being trained in the United States prior to 1965, at which time most were sent home. In March of 1965, William P. Bundy told Congress: "We do not support the political, economic or military policies of the Indonesian government, but we do maintain our contact with the people themselves, particularly with those among them who could comprise the leaders of the next generation."[30]

And as Representative William Dorn said after the "coup" (how accurately is unclear): "Some of these good military leaders who were trained at Fort Benning in the United States, and who love freedom, have taken over. . . . They have . . . reentered the good circle of freedom-loving nations in the world, and have rejected communism."[31] The rather bloody taint of that "good circle" was of course not mentioned. Perhaps for good reasons: between 1967 and 1974, Washington spent $1.5 billion in economic aid and at least $94 million in military aid on the "New Order" in Indonesia.[32] Much of it went directly into the pockets of the military elite.[33]

There is of course much of relevance that cannot be addressed in this hurried account: the discontent spawned by the imposition of martial law in 1957 (and the subsequent military acquisition of formerly Dutch-controlled properties), and the postponement of elections at which the PKI was expected to win a major victory;[34] the proposal by Sukarno and PKI-leader Aidat early in 1965 of a "fifth force" of armed workers and peasants to offset the power of the army, navy, air force, and police; the mounting rumors, both within and outside the PKI and around Sukarno himself, that a "Council of Generals" (consisting of the six who were killed plus General Nasution, who narrowly escaped, but minus Suharto, who emerged as the "hero" of the day) was planning a military takeover with the help of the C.I.A.;[35] the links between the PKI and the younger military officers who arrested and murdered the six generals; the mounting dissatisfaction between the younger officers who assassinated the generals and the central military command; the rumors of Sukarno's deteriorating health, which may have stimulated concern over his successor. Moreover, I have only scratched the surface of the long history of sectarian rivalry—so well elaborated by Geertz—that was set free once the Dutch pulled out after World War II: the struggle for dominance between Java and the "outer islands"; the tension between nationalist, religious, and communist sentiment, which Sukarno tried to alleviate through the unifying political doctrine of *Nasakom;* religious factionalism, between Hindu and Moslem, and within each group.

But no matter how such additional information is "interpreted," the events of Oct. 1, 1965 and the months of horror that followed could only reasonably be approached by placing the complex and polymorphous internecine struggles of the Indonesian people for self-determination in the larger context of cold-war, East-West geo-political conflict, by seeing that the *Nekolim* (neocolonialism, colonialism, imperialism) that Sukarno constantly tried to repel was as ubiquitous as the surrounding waters in which the Seventh Fleet sailed. Any interpretation that relies on the notion that the Indonesians could not manage their own locally generated sectarian interests rationally, or that the massacres were simply the result of "popular" discontent that finally erupted into uncontrollable violence, is myopic at best—indeed, such an argument would reproduce precisely the explanation given to *The New York*

Times by the Indonesian chief of security, Admiral Sudomo, in 1978, at a time when he was presiding over the imprisonment of 20,000 political prisoners detained since the aborted "coup." (Amnesty International placed the figures for 1977 at anywhere from 55,000 to 100,000 detained since the coup; according to *The New York Times,* of the hundreds of thousands arrested, only 904 ever went to trial.) In Admiral Sudomo's view, 500,000 died as a result of "unhealthy competition between the parties" which caused "chaos."[36]

Sudomo's interview is also useful in clarifying how those who came to power after the "coup" saw the real source of the conflict. Noting that all prisoners eligible for release would be given a "psychological test" his organization had developed, "to check them for the state of their communist ideology," Sudomo added: "We asked the C.I.A. 'maybe you have some equipment to detect if he is a Communist.' They don't have it." But the language of "unhealthy competition" and "chaos" of course dominated Western perception after the "coup"—only given the supposedly extraordinary socio-political climate of these islands could this "irrationality" have occurred, albeit in the service of rejecting communist tyranny.[37] As Noam Chomsky and Edward S. Herman point out, such rationalization "is useful in suggesting (falsely) that this was a purely spontaneous popular upheaval, a peculiarly Asian form of 'madness,' not a mass murder coordinated by the military forces of the state, which acted with Nazi-like 'ruthlessness,' demonstrating qualities that U.S. specialists had feared they might lack."[38] Geographically, Indonesia may be a collection of islands, but these have not been isolated socio-politically since the Dutch moved in some time ago. Any interpretive method that relies on the assumption that "every people gets the politics it imagines," however much it recognizes that a people may not always desire the results such politics produce, raises important questions that informed critical thinking ought to pursue before it adapts such a method to its own uses.

III

Geertz's reaction to such events—many of the details of which were publicly disseminated before the publication of *The Interpretation of Cultures*—was fairly consistent with the larger trajectory of his project. While noting the horrifying extent of the "savage aftermath" to the "coup," Geertz maintains that the "obsessive concern" about the roles of Sukarno and the PKI may help to understand "the moment," but neither "the country" nor the significance of such events "for the development of Indonesian political consciousness" (*IC,* 322, n10). While admitting that the primary results of the killings have been the destruction of the PKI, and the imposition of military rule, Geertz is far more interested in the "potential for violence in Indonesia society" than in any external ramifications; indeed, neither American involvement, nor Indonesia's wholesale swing to a pro-Western orientation, is ever mentioned in *The Interpretation of Cultures*. Instead, Geertz adds a postscript to his 1963 "snapshot" picture of Indonesia (in which he had reported "a growing conviction of impending political catastrophe"), a postscript worth citing in some detail:

> President Sukarno's frenzied ideologism continued to rise until the night of September 30, 1965. . . . There followed several months of extraordinary popular savagery . . . directed against individuals considered to be followers of the Indonesian Communist Party, which was generally considered to be behind the coup. Several hundred thousand people were massacred, largely villagers by other villagers (though there were some army executions as well), and, in Java at least, mainly along the primordial lines—pious Moslems killing Indic syncretists—described above. . . . Since then the country has been run by the army with the assistance of various civilian technical experts and administrators. A second general election, held in the summer of 1971, resulted in the victory of a government-sponsored and -controlled party and the severe weakening of the older political parties. (*IC*, 282–83)

In "The Politics of Meaning," Geertz goes a bit further along this line of thought: "the economic situation has markedly improved" since 1965, and "domestic security, at the cost of large-scale political detentions, has come to virtually the entire country for the first time since Independence" (*IC*, 324). Moreover, Geertz implies that the mass murders, if understood properly, may be precisely what will help the country emerge from the shadow of the false or hysterical "ideologism" of Sukarno's reign into the clearer light of authentic social integration. "Accepted for what they were, as terrible as they were, the events of 1965 could free the country from many of the illusions which permitted them to happen, and most especially the illusion that the Indonesian population is embarked as a body on a straight-line march to modernity, or that, even guided by the Koran, the Dialectic, the Voice in the Quiet, or Practical Reason, such a march is possible" (*IC*, 324). For Geertz, it is a veil of illusions that has "permitted" the massacres—the one force curiously left out of the catalogue of "symbolic" guidance systems is the Indonesian military itself. Even more curiously, it is Sukarno's admittedly left-leaning attempt to bind the country together ideologically which is seen as "non-indigenous," while the massacres themselves are presented as an "irruption" of primordial, internecine semiotic conflict within the culture that had been dangerously "repressed" by immature symbol-mongering. In this sense, Geertz's conclusions, though arrived at through far more scholarly means, offer nothing substantially different from those presented by *Life* magazine, the Johnson White House, and the new Indonesian regime's chief of security.

My point here is not at all to throw out distinctions between the inside and outside of social events, or political boundaries; we could hardly reason about these matters at all without such distinctions. Rather, I would simply like to confound them somewhat, especially as they are used by Geertz's interpretive anthropology: I would like to recall that where one draws the line between the "indigenous" and external "ideologism" is itself an act of the greatest political significance. What is inside and what is outside in El Salvador? in Nicaragua? in Afghanistan? in South Africa? in Ireland? What would "indigenous" processes of cultural signification mean in Israel, itself a kind of "new state"? The way one answers such questions is not simply an act of semiotic analysis—it is a political choice. Geertz's professed belief in a "civil, temperate, unheroic politics" (*IC*, 200) would be unexceptionable, were it not prone at the same time to narrativize such qualities through the maturing of "naive" nations-in-transition into Western-style parliamentary democracies; because of his desire to penetrate, like Max Weber, what the social actors "thought they were up to," the fact that pro-Western "civil" and "temperate" politics could be imposed from "outside" is never really considered to be a possibility. If "outside factors" like geo-political force are slighted in the kind of anthropology Geertz favors, it is only because "in order to have local effects they must first have local expressions . . ." (*IC*, 325, n12). For Geertz, that is, the local realm of somehow indigenous cultural semiosis is the crux of the matter, since external factors could only come into play on the basis of that already created recipe; and it is only from such a realm that valid anthropological knowledge could be derived and applied to the interpretation of culture at large.

What then is the nature of the knowledge Geertz locally derives? He masterfully elucidates the various *alirans* or semiotic streams of Indonesian life—in terms of language, kinship terminology, religious belief, and political ideology—and persuasively demonstrates how they simultaneously produce and are reinforced by rituals and related cultural "texts," like the cockfight.[39] But however complex such streams turn out to be, Geertz adopts a far more straightforward taxonomy when he confronts the question of nationalism in the "new states." In the main, Geertz reduces the question to two cultural streams, which he calls "essentialism" and "epochalism," and which are meant to supersede the more familiar terms "traditionalism" and "modernization": on the one hand, the desire for a recognizable, public identity, "a social assertion of the self as 'being somebody in the world' "; on the other, a practical "demand for progress," for better living standards, more social justice, and further, for a place on the international scene and for "influence" among other nations (*IC*, 243–49 and 258). Contrary to expectations, Geertz points out, such streams do not necessarily reinforce one another. In fact, it is the conflict between them that creates the fundamental social tensions in the new states, as such conflict traverses what might seem to be coherent ideological elements, like the Communist Party or Islam or a ruling elite. In a sense, this dyad—derived largely from Max Weber and Talcott Parsons—represents the fundamental mechanism of historical change in Geertz's interpretation of post-colonial nationalism. "The interplay of essentialism and epochalism is not, therefore, a kind of cultural dialectic, a logistic of abstract ideas, but a historical process as concrete as industrialization and as tangible as war" (*IC*, 243). Indeed, given Geertz's reading of the Indonesian "blood bath" a few pages later, such interplay is, for an anthropologist, even more "tangible" than war. While the mass slaughter would have to be seen as "the result of a vast complex of causes" which could not be "reduced" to mere "ideological explosion," Geertz is primarily interested in its semiotic results: "the theory [Sukarno's, one is to assume] that the native eclecticism of Indonesian culture would yield easily to a generalized modernism clamped onto one or another element of it was definitely disproved" (*IC*, 246). If Sukarno's regime "drowned" in the blood of its own supporters, it is for Geertz primarily because Sukarno ignored, or did not understand, the depth of the semiotic "interplay" which constituted the fundamental historical process of his people.

This approach to post-colonial nationalism remains largely the same for Geertz between 1963 and 1972, the period during which his most influential theoretical concepts take shape; and it proves adaptable, under the umbrella category of "the integrative revolution" to the diverse range of his "new states"—Indonesia, Morocco, Burma, India, Lebanon, and Nigeria (*IC*, 280–306). Despite his commitment to local knowledge, Geertz's facility in extending his interpretive models sometimes betrays itself in the rhetorical sweep of his language, especially concerning those areas where, having done no field work, he is relying on the "literature": about Lebanon in 1963, Geertz wants to show us that "out of all this low cunning has come not only the most democratic state in the Arab world, but the most prosperous" (295). Presumably, of course, there is no larger semiotic strain of "low cunning" in Lebanese politics than there is in any other. But relatively minor discrepancies like this become crucial questions in the context of Geertz's larger interpretive categories. What really is the epistemological status of the "historical process" that Geertz discovers in the interplay of essentialism and epochalism? Is it true only for the "new states," or for all nascent nationalist movements? Is it central to the idea of a modern nation-state itself, so that one could find such forces at work in the development of Italian, or German, or American political life? The existential quality of the terms indeed lends itself to wide sociological application—where among modern nations is the desire for self-recognition and influence in the world not to be found? But the relation between their "interplay" and the indigenous realm of local knowledge seems more tenuous with each application. And the sense that in the conflict between these deep-lying semiotic strains one has really found the key to the social tensions running through post-colonial Indonesian society soon dissipates.

Hard questions like these have been asked now for the last ten years about Geertz's early and widely praised work on Javanese agriculture.[40] For a number of Marxian anthropologists, Geertz's concern to elucidate a "motivational pattern" at the heart of Java's agrarian malaise led him to mistake an ethic of "shared poverty" for "the actual relations of distribution between classes," an ethic that in Benjamin White's view is a reflection of a folk model of distribution held more by an administrative elite than by villagers themselves.[41] "Shared Poverty," the deep semiotic system which Geertz wishes to use as a template or recipe to explain the resistance to change of the Javanese peasant, may itself already be an ideological expression which a dominant social group—among whom are the most important allies of the military in 1965—uses to explain, and to justify, the present state of things to the society at large.

But I would like to conclude this section with a comment on what has perhaps come to be the best-known example of Geertz's work: his essay "Deep Play: Notes on the Balinese Cockfight." The theoretical framework of the essay is by now quite well known. The function of the cockfight, if it can be said to have one, "is interpretive: it is a Balinese reading of Balinese experience, a story they tell themselves about themselves" (*IC*, 448). And the story told is about the forms of violence peculiar to the Balinese, about "its look, its uses, its force, its fascination" (*IC*, 449). In the artform of the cockfight, the Balinese discovers something about his, and his society's, temperament, discovers "what a man, usually composed, aloof, almost obsessively self-absorbed, a kind of moral autocosm, feels like when, attacked, tormented, challenged, insulted, and driven in result to the extremes of fury, he has totally triumphed or been brought totally low" (*IC*, 450). Simultaneously "only a game," and "more than a game," the cockfight helps the Balinese individual, the way *Macbeth* helps us, "to see a dimension of his own subjectivity" (*IC*, 450).

Geertz must in fact equivocate on the ontological status of the symbolic system at play here:[42] on the one hand, "The cockfight is 'really real' only to the cocks. . . ." (*IC*, 443); yet, at the same time, ". . . it is only apparently cocks that are fighting there. Actually it is men" (*IC*, 417). The overt purpose of this last line is to unpack the obvious pun on "cock," even more obvious to the Balinese than to the American reader. But I would suggest that something more is going on: that, as in other places in his work, Geertz is willing to allow a process of cultural semiosis to be understood, not as a projection, or game, through which human social experience sees itself both reflected and shaped, but as a convenient methodological substitute for social interaction itself. That is, Geertz's thick description of a cockfight, like his earlier "snapshot" analyses of the "new states," becomes a most *immediate* kind of representation; while the careful "tacking" of a hermeneutic circle is invoked, it is barely visible in the analyses themselves. Instead, there is a conflation of orders of experience that in fact makes Geertz's extensive elaboration of "symbolic systems of signification" a rather empty gesture, because by the end of "Deep Play," it is almost impossible to decide what sort of experience would *not* constitute cultural semiosis. Finally, one is driven to ask, what is it that these recipes and blueprints are really shaping other than repeated versions of themselves? But there are other, more questionable results of this equivocation. Despite all his care to define the relation between the internal workings (such as wagering) of the cockfight and kinship structures, to examine the various kinds of fight, and to relate this unique event to what he later calls the Balinese theatrical sense of maintaining an "assigned place in . . . the never-changing pageant that is Balinese life,"[43] Geertz cannot help but read the event's "deep play" in terms of a semiotic system quite familiar to the Western mind. In fact, like the primordial struggle between essentialist and epochalist strains that emerges in Indonesian nationalism, the underlying narrative Geertz reads reduces itself to a well-known Western myth: the struggle between Dionysus and Apollo. What is being expressed is a repressed and deeply rooted psychic, rather than socio-cultural, economy—the deep structure of a Balinese soul that now looks familiar, but all the more fabulous in the bargain.

The equivocation is crucial to the method, not merely accidental, and it raises interesting problems. Near the end of the essay, Geertz provides one more summation of what the cockfight means: it is a paradigm of Balinese experience, he writes, "one that tells us less what happens than the kind of thing that would happen if, as is not the case, life were art and could be as freely shaped by styles of feeling as *Macbeth* and *David Copperfield*" (*IC*, 450). But what is really being said here? Geertz seems to say that the cockfight is really not simply a semiotic template, created by the Balinese out of their shared social life, and upon which in turn behavior can be modeled. Rather, Geertz implies something of a more far-reaching nature: that deep within the Balinese soul are "styles of feeling" that would "freely" express themselves if. . . . If what? If allowed? If not adequately contained by appropriate, authentic rituals and forms of play—that is, if life had as immediate a relation to feeling as, in Geertz's view, art does? What is more, Geertz's readers already know that these Balinese "styles of feeling" are not about deposed kings and rising orphans—they are about violence, about a Dionysian animality that is more or less repressed in everyday Balinese life. Geertz's cultural semiosis turns out to be frankly Freudian, a tale of Balinese civilization and its discontents. From this vantage, it is almost as if Geertz had published the essay in 1972, not so much to illustrate an anthropological method, but to help a confused western world come to terms with just what had gone wrong in Indonesia seven years earlier.

This is anything but an idle hypothesis, for the essay's final footnote lends an eerie credence to such suspicion. The footnote is worth citing at length:

> That what the cockfight has to say about Bali is not altogether without perception and the disquiet it expresses about the general pattern of Balinese life is not wholly without reason is attested by the fact that in two weeks of December 1965, during upheavals following the unsuccessful coup in Djakarta, between forty and eighty thousand Balinese (in a population of about two million) were killed, largely by one another—the worst outburst in the country. . . . This is not to say, of course, that the killings were caused by the cockfight, could have been predicted on the basis of it, or were some sort of enlarged version of it with real people in the place of cocks—all of which is nonsense. It is merely to say that if one looks at Bali not just through the medium of its dances, its shadow-plays, its sculpture, and its girls, but—as the Balinese themselves do— also through the medium of its cockfight, the fact that the massacre occurred seems, if no less appalling, less like a contradiction to the laws of nature. As more than one real Gloucester has discovered, sometimes people actually get life precisely as they most deeply do not want it. (*IC*, 452)

Or rather, as they most deeply *do* want it? What is Geertz really trying to say here in a paragraph whose first sentence syntactically reflects the tortured conception shaping it? If it would be simply nonsense to replace the cocks of the fight with "real people," why does Geertz deliberately make the substitution for us? If the massacres, seen in the light of what anthropologists can tell us about cockfights, seem "less like a contradiction of the laws of nature," how should the West perceive the true nature of the "general pattern of Balinese life"? As a repressed, screened-off realm of violence waiting to irrupt?

To be fair to Geertz's sense of an excessive Balinese zeal during the massacres, it is true that Colonel Sarwo Edhie, the commander of the ruthless RPKAD (Paracommando Regiment) and one of the leaders of the anti-PKI reaction, said in a press interview: "In Central Java the people had to be aroused to oppose Gestapu [the supposedly PKI-led Thirtieth of September Movement] whereas in Bali the spirit of the people was overflowing so that we had to control them."[44] But should we not also question the strong similarity between Geertz's view of the situation and that of an admitted mass-murderer? To what extent does the anthropologist in this situation help to validate views like Colonel Edhie's, ones repeated throughout the Western press, views that justified American support for the new military regime and excused any external complicity in the killings which the new leaders deliberately provoked and directed? In any case, the Balinese killing was hardly a unique event in the Indonesian catastrophe, no matter how "enthusiastic" it may have become after two months of exhortation, the army's dissemination of propagandistic photographs of the mutilated generals, and the army-elite's claim that the atheistic, Java-based PKI had been the main instigator of the growing peasant and anti-American unrest in the months preceding the coup. What are the real political implications of referring to any of this, no matter how equivocally, as the result of "styles of feeling"? In the opening essay of *The Interpretation of Cultures,* Geertz pokes gentle fun at the anthropologist who, "too long in the bush," perhaps, takes an illusory ethical comfort from reducing complex ethnological data to formulas like "the exploitation of the masses" (*IC,* 22). Geertz has a good point; but by the last footnote of this book, it is hard to see how his cultural interpretation has provided any less reductive a vision of human experience. "Local knowledge" has begun to provide existential commonplaces of a far homelier nature than "class struggle," and with decidedly more suspect uses in contemporary Western thought.

IV

What I am trying to do here, then, is to ask a basic new historicist question about the kinds of symbolic significance Geertzian anthroplogy creates, about the kinds of recipes this style of cultural interpretation writes for itself, and by extension for the new historicism. James Clifford points out that "while ethnographic writing cannot entirely escape the reductionist use of dichotomies and essences, it can at least struggle self-consciously to avoid portraying abstract, ahistorical 'others.' "[45] Clifford notes that "textualist" methods like those of Geertz are an attempt to meet this dilemma with a more sophisticated hermeneutics that, while not specifically adopting the "dialogical" model Clifford espouses, nevertheless "has contributed significantly to the defamiliarization of ethnographic authority."[46] But have Geertz's semiotic methods really displaced such authority, or have they simply reconstituted it along more rationalized lines? What I am especially interested in is the degree to which the entire rubric of "local knowledge"— with its promise of greater specificity, its denunciation of totalizing perspectives, and its claim to have found a less reductive way of relating the innately human to the vicissitudes of particular behavior—actually produces a kind of "understanding" whose cultivated abstraction effectively conceals the "essences and dichotomies" with which it juggles under the cloak of thickly described symbolic systems. Geertz solves the ethnocentric dilemma Clifford mentions by showing us that if he, the anthropologist, is the one who actually *writes down* the story of the other, an epistemological link exists precisely because this is what the other has been doing all along for him or herself— we merely need to record and interpret an always-already written text. As I have tried to show, however, the theoretical persuasiveness of this solution is belied by its practical dangers: the illusory elision of the distinction between the ethnographic "text" and the "text" created by the other; the inevitable inclination to mistake the text written by others for the others themselves and to privilege that text above any number of "external" factors—from material want to geo-political coercion—with which they struggle; and finally, the transformation of others into deeply embedded "styles of feeling" which reveal themselves as increasingly reified existential concepts.

The ramifications of this "solution" in new historicist criticism are numerous, but I will try to elucidate the most important resulting tendencies and provide brief examples. I would emphasize the word "tendency" here, for I do not wish to imply that what follows is somehow true of all new historicist writing, or that much of what I will have to say would not apply to a wide range of contemporary criticism influenced by cultural semiotics—my own included. There is of course a great deal of new and interesting scholarship that has been done at the encouragement of new historicist theory. I am nevertheless concerned with the ways in which that scholarly information has been shaped and represented—with the recipes it tends to follow—and with what this might have to say about the larger purposes such criticism serves.

First, there is the tendency, defended precisely in the name of greater concreteness, attention to local detail, and avoidance of "essentialist" totalization, toward rather abstract, general, and ahistorical sorts of conclusions. In spite of Jonathan Goldberg's bold assertion that the new historicism produces the only "genuinely historical criticism," ironically because it is willing to adopt a textualist position where Marxians like Fredric Jameson are not, the evidence he cites is often not convincing. Citing the "radical" conclusion of Louis Montrose that "poetic power helps to create and sustain the political power to which it is subservient" as a more complex and "dialectical" approach than the metaphysics to which Jameson and Christopher Hill are bound, Goldberg shows how this method reveals supposedly more genuinely historical truth: official discourse, for example, reveals "restless energies, disorderly desires, aspiration."[47] But such forces would only be historically interesting if they were differentiated in some way from other desires and other aspirations at other times. For Goldberg, that kind of specificity is relatively unimportant. Thus, a critic like Montrose produces a more "sophisticated marxist analysis": "The crucial dialectic for Montrose is that between generations, the struggle between the aspiring young and the conservative old," a struggle most readers of *King Lear* would call not particularly "dialectical," and hardly "marxist." And in what must be the *pièce de résistance* of new historicist "radical" thought, Goldberg would have us see "grasping peers," with their "bottled frustrations," as members of a now rather attenuated "oppressed" class: ". . . for Montrose, it is in the interests of the oppressed to attempt to speak within culturally sanctioned voices—and there is room in those codes of theatre and court to do so."[48]

My point is not at all that Montrose's scholarship in general reduces itself to such conceptual emptiness—his work on the "Pastoral of Power," for example, seems to me a model of what new historicist criticism can be at its best.[49] Rather, I would like to emphasize the degree to which, even in the hands of its defenders, what seems valuable or significant about cultural semiotics tends to reduce itself to anthropological abstraction in spite of its claim to greater specificity.[50]

Or perhaps, one should say, because of such a claim. Much of what I have called "corporalist" criticism, for example, draws the inspiration for its focus on the body from Foucault's elaboration of power-knowledge relationships. But it is often frankly ethnographic in its methods, and in its theoretical assumptions. Writing of Fanny Burney's mastectomy and Burney's own narrativization of her operation, Julia Epstein provides a thick description of a narrative semiotic system—Burney's letter to her family and friends— which is itself a thick description of a medical semiotic system, the highly ritualized surgical operation. In a sense, the essay is a marvelous example of "local knowledge" as an elaborate, self-reflexive *mise en discours,* a Geertzian conflation of the text produced by the other with the text produced by the ethnographer. But, almost because of this immersion in the wealth of textualized detail, Epstein's analytical assertions must remain as broad and as "deep" as the Nieztschean conflict in Geertz's cockfight: "The formal, stylized operation retold in Burney's letter and her intimately encoded response constitute two approaches to the same timeless human need—the need to avoid pain and suffering—and demonstrate the complex ways in which the act of writing, like the act of surgery, can be simultaneously wounding and therapeutic."[51] Epstein's historical data, which painfully reconstructs a point in time at which the "written" body and the "medical" body could be said to merge, almost always transcends such generalities; yet I would maintain that it is precisely her method that forces such reductions, for in the process all available structures of mediation between Burney and her society have been reduced and compressed into those points of contact between the surgical knife (pictured in the essay) and Burney's body, and between Burney's pen and the sheet of paper. We are told that Burney's letter "questions the nature of representation"—which is perhaps the paradigmatic invocation for *Representations* itself—but all too often what this means is that Burney tells her painful story (thus reliving the pain) in order to relieve that pain, and that this process parallels the surgery itself. One would hardly take exception to such reflections, were it not that, given the long history of mastectomy Epstein recounts, such a psychological relationship between reliving and relieving would itself appear to be timelessly human, in spite of the semiotic inscription of Burney's body that Epstein recalls.

Second, there is the tendency to conflate methodological self-definition with the historical subject's self-definition—a procedure that, as I have tried to show, in Geertz means building a method on the assumption that both the anthropologist and his or her other are engaged in authoring the story of the other. For some new historicists, however, this has created awkward situations. Thus, for example, an analysis of how particular subjects, for reasons lying outside representation, began at a point in history to define (or "fashion") themselves' semiotically, appears simultaneously to be an analysis whose ethno-critical method presumes the universal fact of such semiotic self-definition. For Stephen Greenblatt, who is one of the first to introduce Geertz to literary criticism, "Self-fashioning is in effect the Renaissance version of these [Geertz's] control mechanisms, the cultural system of meanings that creates specific individuals by governing the passage from abstract potential to concrete historical embodiment."[52] What is of course peculiar here is that "self-fashioning" cannot be a specific, historically determined, Renaissance *version* of Geertz's "mechanisms"; "self-fashioning," in other words, is precisely what Geertz means when he speaks of the way systems of signification work, it is the definition of the method itself. The Balinese participating in the cockfight is doing nothing other than "fashioning" himself through cultural self-representation. Geertz wants us to see that the Balinese do this in certain ways (in the ritualized violence of the cockfight, for example), the Javanese in other ways, the Moroccans in still others. Greenblatt wants us to see that Renaissance "middle-class and aristocratic males" fashion themselves through a *version* of this "self-fashioning" that he calls "self-fashioning."

Like other new historicists, Greenblatt's thick and detailed descriptions immerse the reader in the textualized life-world of his literary figures; but inevitably, what they reveal about the Geertzian "systems of meanings"—albeit in neat "dialectical" triads—is an anthropological truism that is indeed already assumed methodologically: that human subjectivity is after all never "pure and unfettered" (though Greenbatt, displacing a methodological contradiction in time, appears disappointed at the end to discover this) and that it proves over and over to be a "cultural artifact," which by definition means that every attempt at "subversion" invariably serves *to some extent* the ends of authority, and may in fact be no more than an effect of that authority. It is of course Foucault who insisted that power not only repressed and controlled, but enabled as well; knowledge could not avoid its complicity with structures of power in whose language it would have no choice but to speak.[53] Yet I would claim that Greenblatt's failed search for genuinely "subversive" moments is primarily a result of the contradiction between anthropological methods and the promise of historical specificity. Greenblatt's rich detail still seems to ask, "historically," why it was that Renaissance writing produced both newly self-fashioned men, and such a diminished sense of "relative" personal autonomy—for "relative" is all there ever could be, by definition, and never the "pure and unfettered" kind that Greenblatt somehow thought actually existed. But in defining his Renaissance subjects' literary purposes as "self-fashioning," by means of a method that assumes that this is the process by which culture in fact always works, Greenblatt has of course answered the question in advance.

In a similar way, Goldberg clarifies one of Shakespeare's best-know tropes by recalling its most obvious sense: "Shakespeare was fond of the metaphor that made all the world a stage not because it reflects back upon him in some self-satisfying manner, but because the metaphor expresses the nature of reality."[54] Thus, as in Montrose's view, Shakespeare's theater "articulates . . . the ideologically anomolous realities of change" for the "social actors" in its audience.[55] But in what sense do such comments reveal the "historical" nature of Shakepeare's theater? Aren't they instead simply the semiotic assumptions of the "nature of reality" defined by Geertzian methods, as Montrose himself announces by referring to a "Shakepearean anthropology" as the object of his study? Indeed, would not a Shakespearean anthropology implicitly call into question a historical Shakespeare, just as Geertz's view of Indonesian cultures cannot help but ignore the specific historical situation in which the Indonesian people, as a people, were caught in 1965?

Third, there is the tendency, already noted in Geertz, to conflate "systems of signification" with the reality that is assumed to be separate from, yet both creative of and determined by, such systems—to substitute men for their fowl-ic symbols, and thus to read an ideological formation at times as unmediated social organization itself, at others as an unconscious "real" that cannot be made present in the life-world. Such reading is largely a resurrection of left-Hegelian techniques: Jonathan Dollimore interestingly discovers a great deal of repressed atheism, ideological self-awareness, and widespread puncturing of the "idols of the tribe"—Renaissance humanism and Elizabethan tragedy already understand ideology (without the term) as no more than a culturally reinforcing semiotic system. This is of course a position that threatens to pull the rug out from under "cultural materialism" altogether, since if Renaissance tragedy is already "radical," how are cultural materialist assumptions any different from Renaissance humanism? Indeed, this is precisely the direction Dollimore's argument must take. That is, as a correlate to the birth of a suspicious, self-centered, and ambitious new bourgeois class, Dollimore's evidence is historically relevant. But for Dollimore, Louis Althusser and Montaigne suddenly appear so alike that the Althusserian "decentering" of man—aimed precisely at undoing the ideological "centering" achieved by humanists like Montaigne—is in fact a repetition of Montaigne's own supposed "decentering" of man.[56] What is of course going on here, in spite of Dollimore's emphasis on "consolidation, subversion, and containment,"[57] is good old-fashioned deconstruction: Dollimore is primarily interested in the way essential categories—whatever their import—are questioned by the period's leading literary figures. Thus, the more traditionally conceived (especially for Vico, Marx, and Weber) transferral of religious or juridical or social authority from a heaven-centered to a human-centered legitimacy in this period is reconceived by Dollimore to imply the simultaneous deconstruction of the "human" itself. Where Foucault would see the invention of the category "man," Dollimore sees its dissolution. I would suggest, however, that, unlike the interests of a new class, such conceptual decentering is itself a function of the cultural semiotics interpreting it, that, like the Derridean deconstruction it begins to imitate, it is theoretically and anthropologically given and not historically determined.

The tendency to interpret semiotic systems and ideological assertions (however important and formative they are taken to be) as the unmediated and hence valid description of the reality one wishes to understand—the basic left-Hegelian procedure—is obviously difficult to resist for those of us who, like literary critics, prize the truth-value of texts. But in new historicist modes of analysis, this trend toward unmediated reading operates even in those areas where literary truth-value would seem to be of little interest. In the latter part of her analysis of "Injury and the Structure of War," Elaine Scarry wishes to deconstruct the rhetoric that represents war as a privileged event uniquely imposing the "power of enforcement" of victor over loser— that is, as requiring a decisive ending which deprives the loser of the power of contesting the outcome. As a discussion of the ubiquitous use of euphemism to describe injuries in war, and of the mystified categories of war strategists, Scarry's essay makes rather well-known points. But she begins to believe in the mystifying rhetoric she discusses. In order to show that war, as a conceptual category, not only does not entail the power of enforcement, but often deconstructs itself through the victor's rehabilitation of the loser, Scarry cites the example of Germany after the Second World War. In this way, war can be shown to hemorrhage the significance its strategists invoke. But she remains suspended in the realm of undecidable paradox precisely because she takes official rhetoric—that is, obviously ideological assertion— at its word. Thus, in order to reveal the incoherence of war as a concept, she must completely accept General George Marshall's rationale for encouraging "Germany's" economic miracle: in Marshall's words, "It is logical that the United States should do whatever it is able to do to assist the return of normal economic health in the world, without which there can be no political stability and no assured peace. Our policy is directed not against any country or doctrine but against hunger, poverty, desperation, and chaos."[58] To Scarry, economic stability also "comes to be understood" as implying "by extension" military impotence—but she in fact provides no evidence that this was the case, or that it was a "rationale" for economic assistance. Thus, she finds the "full recovery" of a former opponent's economic strength "startlingly" encouraged, the belief that economic stability would ensure military impotence surprisingly contradictory.[59] "That the western allies would have to assure themselves about the future harmlessness of Germany is unremarkable; what is remarkable is that they discovered a form of self-assurance that not only included Germany's well-being but was in fact premised on it."[60] The result, for Scarry, is that war's conceptual coherence is illusory.

But the "premise" of Germany's recovery is remarkable, and incoherent from the vantage of war strategy, only because Scarry believes what people like Marshall said. Even more "startlingly," Scarry conflates "West Germany" with "Germany": the post-war division of the country is treated as if it were insignificant to the issue. The military impotence of "Germany" is of course guaranteed mainly because it no longer exists; but, though there were clearly debates in the West over the wisdom of rearming any Germans after the war, economic aid to Europe was never intended to insure military impotence, though it was surely intended to increase the stability and security *of the Western alliance,* and to recover markets for Western capital. Somehow, Scarry believes Marshall when he talks of the economic welfare "of the world," when he insists that "our policy is not directed against any country or doctrine." But of course, why should Marshall feel it necessary to say this? Clearly, the real "opponent" in this discussion cannot be a formerly belligerent and now divided "Germany," but the Soviet Union with its new "allies"—countries which profess a "doctrine" which Marshall's plan most surely is directed against. That the West later readily accepted the Federal Republic as a trusted and staunch ally—willingly preserving its Nazi scientific elite along the way—might have made Scarry rethink her assumptions that "Germany" was the single or even the primary "opponent" of the Western allies in the closing months of the war, and that the paradoxes of recovery inevitably deconstruct the coherence of strategic assumptions. That there was no decisive victory, in Scarry's sense, hardly threatens the privileged aura of "power of enforcement" notions—it is simply, to reverse Karl von Clausewitz, that the war still goes on, by other means.

Finally, despite objections like those of Brook Thomas that new historicist theory falsely ignores the specific qualities of literary texts as opposed to other semiotic systems, there is the tendency toward a surreptitious re-validation of "Literature."[61] While this last trend is not generally evident in "corporalist," feminist, and much of the new American pragmatist criticism, it is especially evident in Renaissance and, to a lesser extent, Romantic scholarship. Thomas correctly identifies the new historicism's stated goal of demystifying the privileged status of a literary work, but his claim that "genre" is an ignored category is itself belied by much good new historicist writing—Montrose on pastoral being the most obvious example. Rather, I would claim that, while new historicism may suffer from having no theory of the "literary" per se, often it overcomes the institutional problem thus raised—"why write about literature at all?"—with a version of what I would call "de Man's paradox": the life-world is already variously textualized, and all particular socially produced texts are equal, but some are more equal than others. The result is a perspective that—contrary to its stated objectives—must eventually reconstitute the aesthetic as the dominant category of social interaction, and the aesthetic "resistances" of the literary text as the dominant mode of social opposition. Indeed, Barbara Leah Harmon deftly pointed to this kind of problem in Greenblatt several years ago:

> ... true to the methodological precautions outlined at the beginning of the book, Greenblatt also considers how selves resist incorporation. The terms in which he imagines their resistance seem surprising, however, and here, I believe, we encounter a real fissure in Greenblatt's work. In his analysis of Wyatt's poetry he suggests—as the American deconstructionists Paul de Man and J. Hillis Miller might—that literary texts have a special capacity to expose the systems of power on which they otherwise rely, and then to escape from those very systems. And in the book's final chapters, the insistence upon "play" in Marlowe, and on the power of "aesthetic pleasure" in Shakespeare, take the place of "internal distance" as descriptions of the means by which selves resist and escape the defining force of sponsoring cultures. It is important to note, moreover, that these significant instances of resistance occur in the work of the only literary figure in the first triad, and in the work of the great canonical author, Shakespeare, in the second. Resistance is most likely to occur where texts are most complex, and great literary works thus become occasions of the most serious resistance to social and ideological systems—though resistance is characteristically described in terms so muted that they lead us to question the very meaning and value of resistance.[62]

That is, the same criticism which claims to destroy the old-fashioned humanist privileging of literature, by treating it as no more than a version of ubiquitous processes of cultural semiosis, must at the same time defend the logic of its focus by constructing the literary both as a more revealing, and potentially as a more oppositional, version of cultural production. That such dilemmas have long haunted progressive styles of critique is a given. What makes much new historicist criticism less compelling in this regard, I think, than other critical perspectives—such as Theodor Adorno's, or Jameson's—is its general failure to take such a dilemma as in itself theoretically fundamental. That the specifically "literary" had less of a claim to a unique ontological status before Kant is now widely accepted, and Renaissance new historicists often emphasize the pre-Romantic, pre-organic nature of the aesthetic in their period. But to embrace de Man's paradox, or to call an entire subgenre of tragedy "radical," is to reinvent the privileged social status of the aesthetic object without confronting the hard questions earlier critical theory, indeed theory since Schiller, struggled over: Is the play of judgment and the purposelessness of pleasure in a specifically "literary" text a retreat from, or a model for, making judgments in the world at large?

To conclude, I would like to join the trajectory I have been drawing in this essay to something Louis Montrose has already noted in his own review of the new historicist enterprise: that it "is on its way to becoming the latest academic orthodoxy—not so much a critique as a subject of ideological appropriation."[63] It can of course be objected that all modern critical theories run this risk; I would in any case not agree with Montrose's corollary view that English "cultural materialism" actually escapes his censure. But the point, I would suggest, is an immanent one: within this process of "appropriation," how large is the discrepancy between what such styles of critique promise, and what they actually deliver? I would want to insist, as I have done several times already, that a great deal of important historical scholarship has been abetted by new historicist theory. But if the presence of Clifford Geertz's interpretive anthropology behind this theory reveals anything, it is that the primary political agenda of a cultural semiotics cannot be anything but conservative of the dominant, ethno-centric concerns: in Geertz, the commitment to the local expression of local relations works to negate the power of the anthropologist's culture to determine the outcome of the events he describes. In the new historicism, such a perspective induces tendencies toward a new kind of formalism, trapping the critic inside the semiotic systems he or she would wish to explain, even as the definition of such formative systems requires the assumption of a non-semiotic, non-textual outside which is to be shaped. The result is a fairly widespread trend in literary studies, not to make such studies more political or engaged, but to make them less so. That texts are often, in Edward Said's words, "a form of *impressive* human activity" is something new historicist criticism could help us to see; but of course, Said goes on to add: "they must be correlated with (not reduced to) other forms of impressive, perhaps even repressive and displacing, forms of human activity."[64] Ironically, with the new historicism, critique may be diminishing its own socio-political efficacy precisely by insisting on the semiotic powers of its object of study.[65]

Notes

1. See Jonathan Dollimore and Alan Sinfield, eds., *Political Shakespeare: New Essays in Cultural Materialism* (Manchester: Manchester Univ. Press, 1985), 10.

2. See, for example, Walter Benn Michaels's "The Gold Standard and the Logic of Naturalism," *Representations* 9 (1985), where any attempt to resist the collapse of things into their representations, to separate any degree of use value from processes of semiotic exchange— the test case is "naturalism," but this is methodologically unimportant—traps the proponents of such resistance in a mystified cultural "logic that, regardless of their own views, entailed a whole series of other commitments, and . . . it is this logic and these commitments that locate them in the discourse of naturalism" (128).

3. Clifford Geertz, *The Interpretation of Cultures* (New York: Basic Books, 1973), 361; subsequent references are to this edition, hereafter cited as *IC*.

4. Clifford Geertz, *Local Knowledge* (New York: Basic Books, 1983), 58.

5. Michel Foucault, *Discipline and Punish,* trans. Alan Sheridan (New York: Pantheon, 1977), 23.

6. John Bender, *Imagining the Penitentiary* (Chicago: Univ. of Chicago Press, 1987), 8.

7. *The New York Times,* 12 March, 1966. For a useful discussion of the role of U.S. strategy in Indonesia leading to the massacres in East Timor by the Indonesian military in 1977–78, see Richard W. Franke, "East Timor: The Responsibility of the United States," *Bulletin of Concerned Asian Scholars* 15: 2 (1983), 42–58.

8. U.S. Central Intelligence Agency, *Indonesia—1965: The Coup That Backfired* (December, 1968), 70–71. The C.I.A., however concerned it was to make the PKI fully responsible for the massive destruction of its own membership, as well as for many peasant "sympathizers" real or imagined (an "interpretation" often adopted by the U.S. media in the years following the massacres), had no more doubt about the net result of the "coup" than did the Johnson Administration, the State Department, or the Congress: beyond "a massive purge of the Communist party organization" and the toppling of the "demigod" Sukarno, the C.I.A. noted "a complete turnabout in the country's international alignment—from that of being one of Communist China's closest allies in growing estrangement from the rest of the world and one of the harshest critics of the West to a new posture of being a friend of the West, seeking the goodwill of all other nations of the world except Communist China. These developments have all come about as a direct result of the coup" (70). Though the official position was that the C.I.A. had absolutely nothing to do with Sukarno's fall, such passages come as close to an interdepartmental boast as one is likely to get; as it turns out, the C.I.A. involvement was in all probability extensive enough to warrant a little boasting, a point to which I shall return later.

9. Harold Crouch, *The Army and Politics in Indonesia* (Ithaca: Cornell Univ. Press, 1978), 153. Crouch goes on here to maintain that the army never intended the massacres to proceed much beyond crushing the PKI's leadership "at all levels," and destroying its potential for revival, and that it had no interest in the "holy war" mentality of groups like the NU. But Crouch also indicates how suspect such "intentions," at least in Java, must have been:

> Although the army usually had control of operations in the towns, religious leaders in the villages were encouraged to take their own measures. Most commonly the lead was taken by the *kiyais* (religious leaders) and *ulamas* (religious scholars) affiliated with the NU, who mobilized students from their *pesantrens* (religious schools) to drag Communists, members of pro-PKI organizations, and suspects from their homes and take them to river-banks where their throats were cut and their bodies thrown into the river. Members of the Ansor youth organization [of the NU] moved from area to area inciting Muslims to exterminate "atheists". . . . In some villages the massacre even extended to children, while in others only party activists were killed. Often the army stood by, sometimes supplying trucks to cart off the victims, although it was not uncommon for soldiers to participate more actively. (152)

10. Crouch, *The Army and Politics,* 156.

11. Amnesty International, *Indonesia* (AI, 1977), 13; cited in Noam Chomsky and Edward S. Herman, *The Washington Connection and Third-World Facism* (Boston: South End, 1979), 208.

12. Noam Chomsky, *The Chomsky Reader* (New York: Pantheon, 1987), 305.

13. See Franke, "East Timor," 48–58.

14.   See Chomsky, *Chomsky Reader,* 308.

15.   See Franke, "East Timor," 45; Chomsky and Herman, *The Washington Connection,* 206–7. See also David Wise and Thomas Ross, *The Invisible Government* (New York: Random House, 1964), 145–57.

16.   *The New York Times,* 27 April, 1966.

17.   James Reston, "A Gleam of Light in Asia," *The New York Times,* 19 June, 1966. For further discussion of C.I.A. intervention during the decade prior to the "coup," as well as the role of other "internal" pro-U.S. organizations like the Ford Foundation and the Rand Corporation, see Peter Dale Scott, "Exporting Military-Economic Development—America and the Overthrow of Sukarno, 1965–67," in Malcolm Caldwell, ed., *Ten Years' Military Terror in Indonesia* (Nottingham: Spokesman Books, 1975), 209–61.

18.   See, for example, Ralph McGehee, "The C.I.A. and the White Paper on El Salvador," *The Nation* (11 April, 1981), 423–25. McGehee's account was extensively censored by the C.I.A., though the substantive claims about C.I.A. involvement in the 1958 attempt to overthrow Sukarno, and in the 1965 massacres after the "coup" (seen here as led by "progressive" junior officers), were allowed to stand.

19.   Lucian W. Pye, "Armies in the Process of Political Modernization," in John J. Johnson, ed., *The Role of the Military in Underdeveloped Countries* (Princeton: Princeton Univ. Press, 1962), 72.

20.   Crouch, *The Army and Politics,* 22.

21.   Pye, "Armies in the Process," 87, 77, 83, and 77.

22.   Guy J. Pauker, "Southeast Asia as a Problem Area in the Next Decade," *World Politics* (April, 1959), 343. On the concept of "Tutelary Democracy," see Edward Shils, "The Military in the Political Development of the New States," in Johnson, ed., *The Role of the Military in Underdeveloped Countries,* 59–60.

23.   Guy J. Pauker, "The Role of the Military in Indonesia," in Johnson, ed., *The Role of the Military in Underdeveloped Countries,* 186.

24.   See Crouch, *The Army and Politics,* 22 and 63.

25.   Rudolf Mrázek, *The United States and the Indonesian Military 1945–1965,* vol. II (Prague: Oriental Institute, 1978), 107.

26.   *Foreign Assistance Act of 1968,* Hearings, House Committee on Foreign Affairs, 706; cited in Franke, "East Timor," 46.

27.   *Foreign Assistance and Related Agencies Appropriations* for 1976, Hearings, House Committee on Appropriations, part 2, 631; cited in Franke, "East Timor," 46.

28.   *Congressional Record,* vol. 122, part 5, Mar. 3, 1976, 5202.

29.   Franke, "East Timor," 46.

30.   Cited in Mrázek, *The United States and the Indonesian Military,* 123.

31.   *Congressional Record,* Vol. 114, part 6, Mar. 27, 1968, 7948.

32.   Franke, "East Timor," 48.

33.   See Chomsky and Herman, *The Washington Connection,* 209–15, for some of the details of the "good circle" of corruption stimulated by U.S. aid, "assistance" which has left Indonesia $6 billion in debt.

34.   Pauker, "The Role of the Military in Indonesia," in Johnson. ed., *The Role of the Military in Underdeveloped Countries,* 227.

35. See also in this regard *The New York Times* (10 July, 1965) for a report of a photocopied letter dated March 24 and published in *Al Ahram* in Cairo, from Sir Andrew Gilchrist, the British Ambassador, to the Foreign Office in London. The letter describes a conversation between Gilchrist and Howard P. Jones, the U.S. Ambassador to Indonesia at that time, which suggests that Britain and the United States were prepared to invade Indonesia. The document created a great stir in the Indonesian press, but was disavowed by Gilchrist and the U.S. charge d'affaires, Francis J. Galbraith.

36. *The New York Times,* 12 April, 1978.

37. For a particularly lurid account of the massacres, see Dan Moser, "Where the Rivers Ran Crimson," *Life,* 1 July, 1966. In spite of the rather racist tone of the piece (such as: the "coup" had "all the earmarks of a Black Mass," complete with castrated cats, and naked, drugged communist women, dancing ritually before the captured generals, and gouging out their eyes with small harvest knives; or, "the Balinese are also capable of the most exquisite cruelty"), and his stated claim that "the people" spontaneously rose up to crush the communists, Moser nevertheless provides ample evidence for the assertion that the primary struggle lay between the army and the PKI, and that the army provoked and directed the killing.

38. Chomsky and Herman, *The Washington Connection,* 216. The authors add this note to explain their last remark:

Scott [Peter Dale Scott, in his essay in *Ten Years' Military Terror in Indonesia*] cites RAND memoranda by Indonesian specialist Guy Pauker who feared in 1964 that the Indonesian anti-Communist forces "would probably lack the ruthlessness that made it possible for the Nazis to suppress the Communist Party of Germany" in 1933, since they "are weaker than the Nazis, not only in numbers and in mass support, but also in unity, discipline, and leadership." But, as he explained four years later, "The assassination of the six army generals by the September 30 Movement elicited the ruthlessness that I had not anticipated a year earlier and resulted in the death of large numbers of Communist cadres." (403, n8)

39. See, for only one example of such elucidation, *IC,* 360–411, Geertz's 1966 analysis of "Person, Time and Conduct in Bali."

40. See Clifford Geertz, "Religious Belief and Economic Behavior in a Central Javanese Town," *Economic Development and Cultural Change* 4 (1956), and *Agricultural Involution* (Berkeley: University of California, 1963); for a critique, see Jennifer Alexander and Paul Alexander, "Shared Poverty as Ideology: Agrarian Relationships in Colonial Java," *Man* 17: 4 (1982), and "Labour Demands and the 'Involution' of Javanese Agriculture," *Social Analysis* 3 (1979).

41. Benjamin White, *"Agricultural Involution* and Its Critics: Twenty Years After," *Bulletin of Concerned Asian Scholars* 15: 2 (1983), 28.

42. See Jonathan Lieberson's review of Geertz's *Local Knowledge* for a similar charge: ". . . we never really learn what Geertz thinks a symbol is, or how things acquire symbolic value, or vary in symbolic intensity, let alone how symbols (or symbolic systems) change, or are linked to broader aspects of social existence" ("Interpreting the Interpreter," *New York Review of Books,* 15 March, 1984, 43).

43. Geertz, *Local Knowledge,* 62.

44. Cited in Crouch, *The Army and Politics,* 154 n49.

45. James Clifford, "On Ethnographic Authority," *Representations* 1: 2 (1983), 119.

46. Clifford, "On Ethnographic Authority," 133. Clifford's admirable suggestion is, however, unfortunately based on a misreading of Mikhail Bakhtin which sees devices like "free indirect discourse" as the suppression of other voices by the controlling discourse of the author,

a style which Clifford sees as common in traditional ethnographic writing. For Bakhtin, "free indirect discourse" is indeed one of the expressions of the inevitability of dialogism. I would only add that, in many cases, Clifford's interpretation of the significance of this device might be the preferable one.

47.   Jonathan Goldberg, "The Politics of Renaissance Literature: A Review Essay," *ELH* 49 (1982), 527.

48.   Goldberg, "The Politics of Renissance Literature," 529.

49.   See Louis Montrose, " 'Eliza, Queen of shepheardes,' and the Pastoral of Power," *ELR* 10: 2 (1980), 153–82.

50.   For another example of this problem, see Paul Brown's emphasis on the interplay between "masterlessness" in civil society and "savagism" in alien cultures as "mutually reinforcing" categories in John Rolfe's letter from Virginia, Shakespeare's *The Tempest,* and seventeenth-century culture generally (" 'This thing of darkness I acknowledge mine': *The Tempest* and the discourse of colonialism," *Political Shakespeare,* ed. Dollimore, 48–71).

51.   Julia L. Epstein, "Writing the Unspeakable: Fanny Burney's Mastectomy and the Fictive Body," *Representations* 16 (1986), 131.

52.   Stephen Greenblatt, *Renaissance Self-Fashioning* (Chicago: Univ. of Chicago Press, 1980), 3–4.

53.   See for example Foucault's widely heeded formula in *Discipline and Punish:* ". . . there is no power relation without the correlative constitution of a field of knowledge, nor any knowledge that does not presuppose and constitute at the same time power relations" (27).

54.   Goldberg, "The Politics of Renaissance Literature," 527–28.

55.   See Louis Montrose, "The Purpose of Playing: Reflections on a Shakespearean Anthropology," *Helios* 7 (1980), 51–74.

56.   See Jonathan Dollimore, *Radical Tragedy* (Chicago: Univ. of Chicago Press, 1984), 17–19.

57.   See Dollimore, ed., *Political Shakespeare,* 10.

58.   Cited in Elaine Scarry, "Injury and the Structure of War," *Representations* 10 (1985), 49 n62.

59.   Scarry, "Injury and the Structure of War," 29.

60.   Scarry, "Injury and the Structure of War," 49 n62.

61.   See Brook Thomas, "The New Historicism and the Privileging of Literature," *Annals of Scholarship* 4: 4 (1987), 23–48.

62.   Barbara Leah Harmon, "Refashioning the Renaissance," *Diacritics* (spring, 1984), 63.

63.   Louis Montrose, "Renaissance Literary Studies and the Subject of History," *ELR* 16:1 (1986), 7 n4. See also his essay in this volume.

64.   Edward Said, "The Problem of Textuality: Two Exemplary Positions," *Critical Inquiry* 4: 4 (1978), 713.

65.   I am indebted to Luke Carson's able assistance in doing research for this essay.

18

The New Historicism: Political Commitment and the Postmodern Critic

Gayatri Chakravorty Spivak

In December, 1986, I sent some notes to Harold Veeser for my part in a forum on the topic above. In May, 1988, Veeser and I had a long telephone conversation, he in Kansas, I in California. What you read below is these two documents, edited lightly, as with this headnote. The substance of the topic announced above got worked out in between: the forum itself; my quick trip to France to hear French cultural workers—pro- and contra-Lacan psychoanalysts, Derrida, and a "deconstructive" psychoanalyst—debate Elisabeth Roudinesco's recently published *La bataille des cent ans: histoire de la psychanalyse en France* (Paris, Seuil, 1986), volume 2 (1925–1983), from the perspective of the intellectual-cultural politics of the last three decades in France; my eight months of teaching in New Delhi and Calcutta, involved in the politics of cultural identity as well as the culture of political identity as an unwillingly visible post-structuralist marxist local girl from the outside; the uncovering of de Man's juvenilia; a long seminar on a thousand pages of Marx with a group of highly motivated students at Pittsburgh; a nerve-touching quarter at Stanford which taught me in a new and more detailed way, once again, deconstruction's marxist usefulness in the construction of the "third world" (the term recuperated for me as an Asian, from the Bandung Conference of 1955) (wo)man as object of study in the classroom—we are teachers, after all. Yet the two documents printed here seem not too different from each other. Perhaps I am making a virtue out of necessity, but it seems to me appropriate that this should be so. The immediate politics of human-scientific academic movements *are* in class-rooms. The long term politics, from published and unpublished evidence, are constructed and judged by the future. The most ambitious hope of any academic would be that something like the gap I describe will stand, however obscurely, as "unpublished evidence." "Thought is . . . the blank part of the text, the necessarily indeterminate index of a future epoch of *differánce*" (Derrida, *Grammatology*, tr. Spivak, Baltimore: Hopkins, 1976, p. 93), a future that will bracket "our" thought, in "our" text, by interpreting it as that future is necessarily different from it, as that future necessarily defers it toward yet another bracketing future.

MLA Program Notes

I shall say what I always say: let us not make the immediate occasion transparent. "What are we doing here, now?" is an important question for deconstruction, so pervasive in Derrida that it's useless citing a particular passage. (The obvious problems with *saying* this are not unimportant but should perhaps be shelved on the present occasion. As far as deconstruction goes, this is the problem one has with saying anything.)

In order to come back to the question "What are we doing here, now?" I will stray into the following points:

1.   We are not discussing actual political commitment but our fear that students and colleagues will think we are old-fashioned if we produce a coherent *discourse about* political commitment after the postwar critiques of Modernism and, indeed, of Sartrean humanism. (One way of avoiding this is to follow Habermas, but no one on the present panel is doing this.)

Can one be necessarily involved in political activism by way of writing, and teaching deconstruction; or while occupying a critical position regarding Modernism and Modernization, is a different question and would be of little interest to the present occasion. The issue of "history" comes up in the larger political arena in a *situational* way and has little to do with the professed historicism of a school of literary criticism.

2.   Because of this fear or unease, we tend to conflate post-modernism and post-structuralism. (Will cite Brice Wachterhauser's *Hermeneutics and Modern Philosophy* [Albany: SUNY Press, 1986], p. 50 and title "Hermeneutics and Post-Modernism" of the last section, to show extreme case.) This is a recent and *post hoc* phenemenon. This involves conflating

Lyotard: macronarrative legitimation programs are defunct; hence "paralogy" (must be distinguished from "innovation . . . [m]orphogenesis [giving rise to new forms or moves], . . . not without rules . . ., but . . . always locally determined" (Lyotard, *Post-modern Condition*, tr. Bennington and Massumi, Minnesota, 1984, p. 61). For examples of socialism/marxism legitimized by these postmodern pragmatics, see Ernesto Laclau and Chantal Mouffe, *Hegemony and Socialist Strategy: Towards a Radical Democratic Politics* (London: Verso, 1985) and Stephen A. Resnick and Richard D. Wolff, *Knowledge and Class: A Marxian Critique of Political Economy* (Chicago: Univ. of Chicago Press, 1987)

Jameson: enthusiasm for Modernism is anachronistic; hence cognitive mapping for individual subject showing him his place and the place of cultural phenomena in geopolitics.

The Foucault of "What is An Author?" (both *The Archaeology of Knowledge* and the Foucault of the last interviews are here forgotten)

The tough semiological Barthes of the first phase (this involves ignoring the semioclastic and semiotropic Barthes).

This conflated mass is thrown into a vague old New Critical guise and we mourn the loss of history, the foregrounding of criticism and form, and the demoting of the author (often called the subject).

This then leads into Derrida, who has, in a certain way, given New Criticism renewed life. (Though the adherents of the North Atlantic Way—whether new pragmatic [Rorty] or neo-new critical [Lentricchia] would object to this.) He is also taken to have written the narrative of the dead or decentered subject, said that history is bunk, and also said that everything is language. If time allows, I would like to show (by way of citations as well as commentary) that these are not positions necessarily implied or held by a deconstructive stance. For this position paper, it will be enough to risk the following rather hermetic statement:

> One argument about the subject in deconstruction runs this way. The subject is always centered. The critic is obliged to notice persistently that this centering is an "effect," shored up within indeterminate boundaries that can only be deciphered as determining. No politics can occupy itself with only this question. But when a political analysis or program forgets this it runs the risk of declaring ruptures in place of repetition—a risk that can congeal itself into varieties of fundamentalism.

If I am asked to speak on Marxism in this context, I should be obliged to repeat a reading of certain passages in Marx that I offered at SAMLA. Not enough time has elapsed for me to have developed it any further. [The Pittsburgh seminar on Marx has changed this, but that work is brewing.] If there should be any interest in this, I might distinguish my position from Michael Ryan's in this respect, since recently both Barbara Foley and Terry Eagleton have spoken of our positions as identical.

3. In my judgment, then, 2 is produced by the fear and unease in 1. I will offer a few analytical remarks about item number 2.

 a. "Politics" here is allegorical for turf battles.
 b. "History" is a catachresis here, heavily charged with symbolic significance. [catachresis: "Improper use of words, application of a term to a thing which it does not properly denote, abuse or perversion of a trope or metaphor" (OED). My usage: a metaphor without an adequate literal referent, in the last instance a model for all metaphors, all names.]
 c. "New" historicism is a misnomer, basically in agreement with Fox-Genovese and La Capra here. "Old" idealism/materialism debate. If time offers, comments on Stephen Greenblatt, Jonathan Goldberg, Sande Cohen. [In the event, I only discussed Sande Cohen's *Historical Culture: On the Re-coding of An Academic Discipline* (Berkeley: Univ. of Calif. Press, 1986), pointing out that the political promises of its introduction, heavily indebted to Nietzsche's *Use and*

Abuse of History, can necessarily not be performed in the impressive theoretical exposures in the body of the book. Is there a parable here?]

4.   "What are we doing here, now?" A quick recap of deconstruction-bashing at the MLA, 1977–86. How it should and should not be done. In postmodernity "Knowledge is power" has shifted to information-command, and the pedagogy of the high humanities, or the appropriation of the popular into the pedagogic format of the h h's has become trivialized, or banalized. Within those sad limits, what the lowest common denominator of a specific politics of the humanist academy might be. For a "paralogy," with respect, is not feasible, or perhaps only too feasible. (There will no doubt be no time for a discussion of this last point.)

The Interview

H.V.   How would you like to position yourself in relation to the new historicism?

G.S.   Whatever I might say about deconstruction versus the NH is a sort of echo without an origin, because my point of reference is the rather elaborately stage-managed conference held at the University of California at Irvine in May 1987, where I was not present. As I believe Derrida himself surmised at the conference, the conflict between New Historicism and deconstruction can now be narrowed down to a turf battle between Berkeley and Irvine, Berkeley and Los Angeles. I do not have much of a position vis-à-vis new historicism, because willy-nilly, I am not part of that turf battle. I think this is recognized by most people who more and more think of me as an anomaly. I am not a real Marxist literary critic. Fred Jameson does that. I'm not really a deconstructionist because I can't do those meticulous yet playful (literary criticism) or scholarly yet audacious (philosophy) readings. I don't get into the representative feminist collections. There are even wings that would say that I do not reflect the ways in which the critique of materialism should be done. That's an issue too close to me, I would start to gossip if I talked about that. At any rate, since I see the *new* historicism as a sort of academic media hype mounted against deconstruction, I find it hard to position myself in its regard.

H.V.   In fact your marginality has made you a particularly central figure. As you've said in another context, the challenge has been for you to shuttle between the margins and the center. How has your work empowered or suggested for years something that has begun to take place now? I mean the insertion of history in literary critical discourse.

G.S.   As for the question of marginality, you know, the essay "Explanations of Culture" which I wrote some years ago, was written very strongly under the influence of United States academic feminism which has been very enabling for me in order for me to be able to find a place. But it wasn't a place, like most places, where I could stay very long. And now I look at the concept-metaphor of margins in a slightly different way. More and more people have found in me a very convenient marginal, capital M, and this of course I have myself found politically very troubling. Thinking about that, I looked at the concept-metaphor of margins and began to realize that in the old days, marginalia were, in fact, rather important. Textual criticism in the pre-modern period is much interested in marginalia. In the early print culture in the West it was in the margins that the so-called argument of the paragraph or set of paragraphs was written. I would like to take away the current notion of marginality, which implicitly valorizes the center. It is, for the critic, a necessarily self-appointed position which is basically an accusing position. It seems to me that I would like to re-invent this kind of marginality which I now find: exclusion from various turfs. I would like to re-invent it as simply a critical moment rather than a de-centered moment, you know what I mean. That's the way I think of the margin—as not simply opposed to the center but as an accomplice of the center—because I find it very troubling that I should be defined as a marginal. I don't see how I could possibly have that definition except in terms of people's longing to find a marginal who is locatable. And as far as the business of real margins goes one of the things that I hear more and more these days is that Bengalis (I am a Bengali) really don't like what I do with Mahasweta Devi, whose fiction I translate from the Bengali. I am not particularly troubled by Bengalis not liking what I do. But a lesson can be drawn from it. Ngugi Wa Thiong'o, in his very important book *Writers In Politics,* has called an absolute demand upon the cultural worker: that he or she break her alliance with the native bourgeoisie. The authenticity of the margins, the defining of me as the spokesperson for "the third world," is undermined by the fact that my own class in India does not particularly like what I'm doing. I'm not repesentative of the margins in that sense either. Thus I am beginning to think of the concept-metaphor of margins more and more in terms of the history of margins: the place for the argument, the place for the critical moment, the place of interests for assertions rather than a shifting of the center as I suggested in that earlier essay. Now your question concerns the insertion of history into literary criticism. It seems to me that history, like most master words, is a word without an adequate literary reference. When people talk about history, that proper name is generally not opened up. Or if it is opened up, it begins to resemble something that in common parlance is not called history. If there is an insertion of what I do into history, it is very much into history as a catachresis, in the case of decolonized space the fact that what politically it would like to lay claim to—nationhood, citizenship, all of those things—that the actual supposedly literal history of those concepts was not written in those spaces. Culturally, of course, there is talk of ethnicity which is strongly endorsed by ministries of culture. But practically speaking what these spaces want is access to proper names, for which there is in fact no adequate literal reference, whatever you might call the narrative of reproduction. So if history entered into literary criticism for me, definitely it enters as catachresis, rather than as the real nitty-gritty about materiality, if you know what I mean.

H.V.   In the specific context of Mahasweta Devi's narrative (*In Other Worlds* [Routledge], pp. 222–268) you have a section entitled "The Author's Own Reading: A Subject Position" in which she offers an allegorical reading of her own work as a story about British colonial oppression in India. You interestingly marginalize that author position as just one position among many. Does your response to Mahasweta, therefore, foreclose her own consciously intended narrative of emergence? And, if so, what advantages does your more complex reading of the same story offer to the subaltern to whom by your own scrupulous admission of interest you declare yourself to be allied?

G.S.   If Mahasweta is giving an allegorical reading which I find less than satisfactory, it is still not the reading which makes the mistake of thinking that the woman is India and her tormentors are the British. No. That is an *old* story. In fact, what she looks at is the structures of oppression within post-colonial space. The story has shifted under neo-colonialism in the greater Third World to an encounter with the indigenous elite, who are in fact caught up in the suppression of the subaltern. Then following through, Mahasweta's narrative of emergence, as you put it, of course revised in the way that I have revised it, is not in fact some kind of Indian production over against my production as a university scholar here. The point that I'm trying to make, and in fact I asked my friend, Henry Louis Gates to talk about the influence of F. R. Leavis on the formerly British African intelligentsia rather than simply of Africa as the tradition to which black Americans must look. Her production is also a colonial production, which takes shall we say a certain unwitting mixture of Leavis, A. C. Bradley, Raymond Williams, some amount of American New Criticism, perhaps all of this gathered together as the natural way of reading. Because we are after all talking about India as a place with a history, where the idea of literature and the reading of literature are also produced through the very mechanics that I am trying to critique. So it is not as if I am over against Mahasweta as the authentic voice and me as the U.S. scholarly reader. Mahasweta herself was a teacher of English so that what we're looking at is two different kinds of readerly production. One, old British colonial production transmogrified into an understanding as Indian. In her writing Mahasweta can question it; in her own production as reader, she acts it out. And quite another readerly production is critical of it.

The next item, where you say that I declare myself allied to the subaltern. I don't think that I declare myself to be allied to the subaltern. The subaltern is all that is not elite, but the trouble with those kinds of names is that if you have any kind of political interest you name it in the hope that the name will disappear. That's what class consciousness is in the interest of: the class disappearing. What politically we want to see is that the name would not be possible. So what I'm interested in is seeing ourselves as namers of the subaltern. If the subaltern can speak then, thank God, the subaltern is not a subaltern any more.

H.V. With some new historicists, the self-unmasking gesture can become a carpet under which to sweep complicities. In what way do you understand your own "scrupulous declaration of interest" to be a different sort of acknowledgment?

G.S. Most of the interest in deconstruction has been based upon the fact that at both ends of the deconstructive morphology there is a stalling, to borrow a word from Werner Hamacher. The stalling at the beginning is called *différance* and the stalling at the end is called aporia. This is a focus that one can discuss in terms of the institutional space in which the deconstruction program has been welcome.

Although I acknowledge the crucial importance of these stallings at beginnings and ends, my interest is much more in the middle, which is where something like a practice emerges by way of a mistake. "Mistake" within quotes because the possibility of this mistake cannot be derived from something that is over against it, "correct." I believe that Derrida is interested in this as well. In an interview given to *Art Papers* some years ago, he has said that he's interested in the production of truths rather than exposure of errors. And to an extent that middle ground is the production of truth, which is an act of transgression, rather than an ignoring of deconstruction, as Richard Rorty would have it. Within that space, against what would you declare your own inability since there is no model where anyone is fully able to do anything. That's the declaration of interest as far as I am concerned, it is in fact a deeply theoretical move, as there is no room there for apologizing for the limits of one's own production.

H.V. That's an important corrective at a moment when the New Historicists often seem painfully to straddle two positions: a will to the power to conduct what might be called a symptomatic reading of a Machereyan or Althusserian disclosure of what gets left out of a text and on the other side feelings of antifoundationalist guilt, causing them to disavow privileged insight and to acknowledge their own partiality and critical blindness, which disenables them; a paralyzing position to be put in. You seem to have pointed, with your conception of a middle between stallings, to a position that moves beyond stalled-out paralysis.

G.S.   At Stanford I was talking about crisis and about the enabling violation of the culture of imperialism. The students were there with me. They were looking at the words crisis and violation and integrating them into whatever it was that they were thinking of. In the last third of the course they began to see me just as they had wanted to see me right from the beginning, as a third world woman. Except by then I had changed the definition of that phrase and what I was telling them was that, if they were breaking away from ethnocentrism, they were wrong. Right? When I started talking about this at Stanford, they didn't realize it but they were actually in that crisis I was talking about. On the last day I told them, "Now I don't want to do counter transference, but look how the temperature has risen, because I've been telling you it's not so easy to construct us as an object of investigation. It hasn't been the usual kind of negative critique ('you can't know how to see our cultural systems'). I've criticized all arguments from ethnicity, all arguments from culturalism, and see now how I'm using post-structuralism and Marxism and using those tools and those which you think are contaminated. I'm telling you that your solution to enlarge the curriculum is in fact a continuation of the neocolonial production of knowledge although in practice I am with you, because on the other side are real racists. The fact that this battle should be won does not mean at all that winning it does not keep a Euroamerican centrism intact." That is the real sense of crisis, the real sense of what is involved, the production in the middle that *cannot* be endorsed by origin or end. There is no other way.

H.V.   Since you raise the question of pedagogy and crisis together, let me take that further. Minette Marcroft from a Marxist teaching collective at Syracuse University recently told me when she heard about this upcoming interview to ask you about the violence of your writing and teaching. That reminded me of your first words to me as we jogged along, "Are you a Marxist or what?" Is your pugnacious personal style a metonymy for learning to work in the crisis?

G.S.   I want to distinguish between two things here. First is my personal style which I am dissatisfied with. I would like to be able to write more sober prose.

Now that's a different problem, but if we keep that to one side I think the violence comes out of the conviction that the forces against which one is speaking are at their worst when they are most benevolent, and that they are most benevolent when embodied by the most vulnerable, that is to say, the students in class. The reason why I've been hedging the question of how do I put myself against the new historicism is that I'm profoundly uninterested in joining those battles with colleagues. This is something that goes on all over the world, wherever there are universities. But when one realizes that the real battleground is the classroom and the real focus is the benevolent young radical in the bosom of the neocolonial production of knowledge, and that one has to take away from them their conviction of where they are at their best without leaving them with nothing but a breast-beating, which is also something that is part of the neocolonial production of knowledge—"I'm only a white male," etc., and then business goes on as usual—that very uneasy predicament is I think what she is implying as the recognizable violence rather than the socratic method revamped, where anxiety is felt throughout the classroom, and you can congratulate yourself as doing correct politics. I think that's where the violence comes from. I've been fortunate over the past twenty-three years that students have been my best audience, that they have been able to see that this is a big problem—not exactly a guilt and shame trip.

H.V. Stephen Greenblatt tells a story in his essay for this volume: when he was teaching a course called "Marxist Aesthetics" at Berkeley, a student shouted at him, denouncing his politics. This experience led Greenblatt to change the title and content of his course to "Cultural Poetics," which would presumably warn the Bolsheviks off. Is your teaching confrontational in ways that Greenblatt's would not be? Could one say that new historicists tend to resolve conflicts in texts and in their classes, whereas you tend to precipitate crises?

G.S. The idea of shifting into cultural criticism for me is not a very happy response. That to me would not signify that I was moving away from confrontational to integrative. Look at Marxist texts. Especially the mature texts. They are all exhortative—to an implied reader. The division is between radical criticism of capitalism on one hand and cultural criticism on the other hand. And then comes a kind of complete trivialization of the category of class and this you see in the writings of many so-called post-Marxists. Instead of working *with* the notion of class and complicating and expanding it, it is simply rejected as an unexamined universalist notion. You know how in the 70s there were all kinds of contortions to avoid the word communist and so the use of euphemisms: are we going to call our group "radical"? What about the possibility of "socialist"? Now there has come another alibi word, which is "materialist." One is struck by the absence of any sense of what the history of materialism might be. The use of the adjective is an alibi for Marxism. I would not include Edward Said in this group but in that great critique of Said in his new book, Clifford does talk about what one can and cannot do with Foucault and one of the things that one cannot do with Foucault is turn him into a hermeneut who talks about nothing but the microphysics of power and thus make him an alibi for an alliance politics which takes for its own format the post-modern pragmatics of non-teleological and not necessarily innovative morphogenetics, giving rise to more and more moves. And it seems to me that the real story from this shift from let's say so-called Marxist interventions in literary criticism to a taking up of cultural criticism is not the story of simply a decision about one or another kind of criticism but it has a much broader social text within which it is embedded.

H.V.   You've pointed to the central difficulty of new historicism. You have said "I do not want to identify reality with the production of signs. Something else might be going on." That's an important caution that the new historicists have tended to overlook even as they pretend to negotiate it. That is, they move between this thing outside the production of signs by use of a metaphorics of their own. They refer to the traffic between these two levels as circulation. That has been the metaphor in a lot of the new historicists essays that I've received: circulation, exchange, negotiation. All of these terms are taken to describe the mediation between the cultural analysis of cultural artifacts and something else.

G.S.   What is that something else?

H.V.   That's never defined.

G.S.   Let me talk about Marx. It seems to me that the mode of production narrative in Marx is not a master narrative and the idea of class is not an inflexible idea. The mode of production narrative is a working hypothesis within the context. One should go to *Capital Volume 3* where he is talking about the law of the tendency of the rate of profit to fall and where he's talking about the counteractive process. There is a small but crucial section on foreign trade where he says that these specific analyses are no use in the area of foreign trade because these are places where the capitalist mode of exploitation has been exported without the capitalist mode of production, so if you really want to make calculations here you will have to go outside of the general equivalent—which is money—and look at value production in other ways, other codings, other inscriptions. We are literary critics. If we look at the production of Marx's own text, we see alternatives based on reading Marx's text carefully.

H.V.   In other words, you are not suggesting that Marx presents negative critique and no positive politics, but rather a limited field of alternatives.

G.S.   I am suggesting that Marx's texts are by no means univocal. The immense energy in transforming this to a univocal narrative has its own political history within our own lifetimes and one lifetime before us. You know this is not a very long story. So it seems to me that what is required of the people who would like to think that the choice between Marxism and micropolitics is the giving up of the master narrative—I think the real requirement there is to make time again to look at Marx. If one identifies Marxism with a master narrative one is conflating the history of Marxism with the texts of Marx, and the texts of Marx—I'm not a fundamentalist—the texts of Marx are precisely the place where there is no sure foundation to be found. In terms of decolonized space, if it is true that that's how Marx talks about how to analyze places where the capitalist mode of exploitation has been exported without the capitalist mode of production, then the idea that all their world literature is an allegory of nationalism becomes nonsense. Other ways of analysis can be enabled through Marx's incredible notion of that "slight, contentless thing"—Marx's way of describing value, a value that is not necessarily trapped in the circuit of the general equivalent in all possible contents.

H.V. Is Catherine Gallagher not claiming the same sort of exemption for New Historicist cultural criticism, when she says that NH doesn't entail positive politics or political ignition? How does that claim differ from the claim you're making for Marx?

G.S. That's a completely different question from global politics. So the first question has to do with what's happening in literary criticism, basically in the U.S.—its relationship to global politics is so complex. I mean what is it? Lit. Crit. next to global politics is a trivial discipline. Even if one were to look at the university system in the U.S.—we're not talking about the fight between Berkeley and Irvine—over who wins—but if we look at the four-year colleges, and the two-year colleges, and the community colleges and then relate to federal funding and Allan Bloom and the National Endowment for the Humanities, so on and so forth, there is very little resemblance to the relation between that and the third world and let's say the Monetary Fund and the World Bank, it's not even—the parallels are non-existent. Global politics is an arena in which the only way in which we can even begin to make some kind of a claim is that in the decolonized space, the indigenous bourgeoisie has a much stronger connection to the machineries that are going into state formation. In general these upwardly class-mobile people in the decolonized space go to universities which traditionally over the last 150 years have received ammunition from the metropolis, although often declaring that it doesn't do so. So perhaps the way we talk about the third world or feminism or this and that might become constructed as a simulacrum in those spaces so that the ministries of culture can be kept fed. Now that's a relationship which is not at all the kind of relationship that people who want to conflate the distinction between global politics with what is happening in the U.S. for baby boom critics would want to acknowledge because the fact is that they know very little about how systems of education operate in Japan, in some of the African states, in India, in Afghanistan, in Sri Lanka.

These things are not comparable. If you wanted really to say there was any kind of relationship between global politics and this stuff, you would have to look at the system of education and the history of the university in those places. Otherwise, to think that that is an allegory of any kind of direct political action, I think it's the way most people who are in trivial positions like to imagine that they're in control.

I am always surprised by how these battles are inevitably always given the name of political forces operating globally. It's almost like a morality play. I always ask my students: "Do you really think that in order for the world to change, everybody must learn how cognitively to map the place of a hotel in Los Angeles on the geopolitical grid?" The claims made in the U.S. and how those claims are reprocessed by the Third World elite who then begin to masquerade as the representatives of the third world—it's the most bizarre narrative of its own.

H.V.   Touché. I suppose it's difficult to return to questions of literary criticism after that comment. But let me try anyway. At the *Marxism and Interpretation of Culture* colloquy a couple of years ago, you were teaching along with Stuart Hall. Stuart Hall's Althusserianism was a topic at that time. But whereas Hall took up things like Althusser's ideas about theoretical work and theoretical production, the new historicists have seemed to take up Althusser on ideology and the Machereyan variants for symptomatic readings devoted to locating the absences in literary texts, internal distances, things not said. You rarely do that sort of reading. What is wrong with that sort of symptomatic reading in your view, and what sort of readings do you do?

G.S.   Basically I learned first from de Man and then from Derrida the importance of reading absolutely literally. And of course the word "literally" is like the word "history." Like any master word, it is a catachretical word. I should say that, perhaps my early training at the University of Calcutta in the hands of a man called Sen gave me the first impulse in this direction and then the de Man of the '60's when I was his student, between '61 and '64 was certainly very interested in reading the logic of metaphors, absolutely literally. And then what I see of Derrida's reading especially of literary texts like Blanchot, etc., is a sort of inspired literalism. So I, in fact, do not go into a text thinking to diagnose the absences because you leave a lot outside the door when you enter as a doctor. And after all, a doctor cannot read the text as the body of her mother, his wife, or her husband, or their lovers. This relationship of love, which is the deconstructive relationship—you cannot deconstruct something which is not your own language. You know that passage I quote over and over again—the reason why in a certain way every deconstruction falls prey to its own critique is because the language that it uses is borrowed structurally and in every way from that position. Now in a sense the stance of the diagnostician is one in which, if it is consciously taken almost into the first step into the text, it is suspicious of love, of one's own bound place. Even if I know how to do it I would be afraid to do it. So I hang on to my literalist reading and then the reading that develops, develops. As in the classroom I am helpless, I'm never sure. But the symptomatic thing troubles me, and I'm not really capable of locating things. I would rather think of the text as my accomplice than my patient or my analysand. Unspoken stuff does come out, but if it comes out, it comes out against the grain of my reading. When it begins to clamor for my attention, it catches my eye.

H.V. This makes me think of all the other people who have drawn on your work—Barbara Harlow and people at Texas, for example—have taken your work and moved in different directions with it. Would you comment on any of their projects or your feelings about having your work carried on in that way.

G.S. You know, I don't think of Barbara as influenced by my work. I think of her very much as an ally. But I think the sources of her inspiration are probably much more Edward Said and her contacts with West Asian politics. I think she has carved out a theory of criticism which has found support from some of what I do but I don't think she's influenced by me. I think Chandra Mohanty is someone who's working in the same area. I think Lata Mani in Santa Cruz is. My work is not really on colonial discourse. It is very much more sort of the contemporary cultural politics of neocolonialism in the U.S.—And I think Lata's work is more on colonial discourse and she is a real historian. So there's a relationship there but not an influence. I have my student, Forest Pyle, who has written on the Romantic ideology of the imagination, which is about to be published by Stanford Press. Again, I think whatever influence I might have had on him—and obviously a dissertation director has some influence—he's turned into something quite different. And then Jennifer Sharpe, who is my student, whose work is on the construction of the British university subject, again, her work is going in another direction. I have not formed disciples. That's a great thing. I am an autodidact and not a good scholar, and my teaching style is so odd that nobody in their right mind would want to imitate it—I am trying to get away from it. And therefore it protects me from actually having disciples. I feel that these people are allies. I have in no way exercised an independent influence on independent workers in the field, like Homi Bhabha, for instance. So I feel that Chandra Mohanty, Lata Mani, Mary Pratt, Barbara Harlow, all of these people, of course Edward as a sort of senior person in our midst, all of us sort of working in the same direction. In India I see connections with other people, some of whom are ahead of me, and some who have been working independently. But I don't see these people as really influenced by my work.

H.V.   Your teaching style prevents your having disciples or acolytes, perhaps, but I think also of the unusual cultural inscription of the people you name—Said growing up speaking several languages, attending the best Cairine prep schools, recreating himself at the old colonial Ghezira Club in the middle of the Nile, and you yourself, from Bengali aristocracy. Does that mean that people of the middle and lower middle classes growing up in whitebread families in the U.S. are somehow disenabled from doing this sort of work?

G.S.   No. One would have to be a complete cultural determinist in order to . . . how can I say that? No, I don't think that's true. We all transform our situations of lack into situations of excess. I mean that is the condition of impossibility, with parentheses put around "im." There are real differences between Edward and me, Barbara and me—all of us. Incidentally, my origins are solidly metropolitan middle class. How about those differences?

In fact, Said came to Pittsburgh to lecture with Romila Thapar, the other colleague I was mentioning, who is an archaeologist and a historian. She gave a brilliant talk, she totally obliterated the Aryanist argument in ancient Indian history. Said gave a talk on anthropology, and it was a wonderful talk. But at the end, some students asked about the people, and he was dismissive. I walked up to him and I said, "You really need to say this. After all, look at the two of us. We are post-colonials. We are in fact wild anthropologists." We, because of our class alliance, went out to do our field work—not only we but our parents did, not mine so much as his: my class status was lower—we went out to do field work in the West, not in the disciplinary sense, but pushed by class alliance and power lines, and we became successful, almost indistinguishable from them, unlike the disciplinary anthropologist. And we have now decided to look at the scandal of our production. So in fact, most post-colonials are not like us. Most post-colonials in fact are still quite interested either in proving that they are ethnic subjects and therefore the true marginals or that they are as good as the colonials. Barbara Harlow will tell you: she has very little in common in her early production with Edward and me. She wrote her dissertation with Eugenio Donato and then she went to Egypt because that is where she found a job and she really set about learning Arabic and so on because that's where she felt her work lay. There's nothing in her early production that would determine that she'd work there. We should not be cultural determinists. We live in a post-colonial neo-colonized world. And we should teach our students to find a toe-hold out of which they can become critical so that so-called cultural production—confessions to being a baby-boomer and therefore I'm a new historicist—that stuff is seen as simply a desire to do bio-graphy where actually the historical narrative is catachretical. If you think of the '60s, think of Czechoslovakia, not only Berkeley and France, or that the promises of devaluation didn't come true in some countries in Asia in '67. So one must not think of one's cultural production as some kind of literal determinant of what one can or cannot do.

H.V. That brings to mind another area in which you have attacked cultural bio-determinism, that is within feminism. In the essay "Discourse and the Displacement of Woman," you say that the simple alterity of women is not a notion that is going to take women very far. Would you elaborate on that a bit?

G.S. Anyone who can say "je est un autre," she's still strictly a "je." Look at the way this claim to otherness—I mean, it's becoming a scandal, I mean the damn thing is getting so institutionalized that everyone should wear T-shirts. This "je est un autre" reminds me of something else. Apparently in the book that David Morrell wrote after the filmscript of *Rambo III* there is an epigraph from Rimbaud's *A Season in Hell. Je est un autre*—"I am an Other" is also an epigraph from Rimbaud. As I was saying when you asked me, didn't I ally myself with the subaltern. I said by no means, I noticed myself as a namer of the subaltern. The subaltern is a name as "woman" in Derrida, or "power" in Foucault, and the name comes with an anxiety that if the political program gets anywhere the name will disappear. In that way I would say that women who claim alterity should see themselves—should in fact see themselves as naming rather than named. I think it's really bogus to legitimize the other side by claiming alterity. It doesn't move me at all. We've been reading from French feminism and part of the term of the class was how this kind of theory constructs third world feminism basically as an object of investigation for first world students. I was saying that reading against the grain doesn't just apply to our enemies by also to our friends so that if one reads someone like Irigaray within the history in France of the deployment of rhetoricity in a text, it becomes much more interesting than if read in this very old-fashioned way as declaring for woman's otherness. Most of the interesting people—feminists who have written about women's otherness—have also done a lot of other things, and the ones who are just repeating it as an incantation in order to justify their institutional privileges are dangerous. The dangerousness will not be noticed because they are precisely managing the crisis that the recognition of women's stratification would otherwise bring. It seems to me to be really rather obvious, no?

H.V. The question for a student of yours remains, how should one choose one's texts in the light of interests, desires, prejudgments of disempowered or marginalized groups? Ought one to choose one's texts on the basis of one's own interests, scrupulously declared, or should there be no conscious choosing of these kinds of texts at all?

G.S. It depends on who one is. If one were a student in a less than stellar institution, the ambit of one's choice is limited. If one is nontenured faculty in a less than stellar institution, one's ambit is also limited. I almost sometimes think that it is better to learn to read what one can read so well that one can be critical—rather than learn to read what one cannot hope to discern because there isn't an institution to support one's learning of languages, etc., and to read simply in order to say, "my conscience is clear." I was quite interested in Catherine Gallagher's use of Houston Baker's astute remark that those kids were really trying to free themselves of racism rather than help the black. Perhaps that's why I'm interested in not conflating that with what's going on in the general third world vis-à-vis institutions of learning. It's not supposed to clear one's own conscience—coming back to the Bloomsbury fraction—the social conscience in the end is supposed to protect the private consciousness. I don't think we should give it sanction as somehow adjudicating a freedom of choice.

H.V.   What about the formal determination of those two essays, "Draupadi" and "Stanadayini?" These seem to be entirely unexpected, unscheduled formal achievements on your part. And yet that is the kind of claim you now hear Joel Fineman and some of the others making about new historicist work. Do you see your intervention in the form of the narrative as somehow related to theirs?

G.S.   I don't really know if there is a relationship. I wrote the "Draupadi" piece in 1981 because I was absolutely shocked by the fact that I had become the spokeswoman for French feminism for *Yale French Studies* and *Critical Inquiry*. That was for me a moment of awakening. What the hell happened that I had become this? So I wrote "French Feminism in an International Frame" for *Yale French Studies* and I told *Critical Inquiry* that I was going to translate a piece of fiction—and it was interesting that it immediately changed to "on spec" rather than "commission" and so that was that. So in fact, all of the little paragraphs about deconstruction are there because Elizabeth Abel asked me, "How does all this relate to deconstruction?" And that's how that came about—by happenstance. "Breast Giver" was because I went to the Subaltern Studies Conference. They're all historians and they said that the paper should be based on something empirical. And I told them, look, I'm a literary critic: the only thing empirical for me would be a short story. What I produced was quite unlike the essay as you see it now. The essay as you see it now is a response to the response of the indigenous Leftist bourgeois intellectual in Calcutta up in arms against what I seemed to have perpetrated. And so the audience there is very definitely that person. So if it looks like new historicism, well, I'm glad, though I wasn't trying.

19

New Historicism: A Comment

Hayden White

New Historicists present their project as little more than an attempt to restore a historical dimension to American literary studies. On the face of it, they wish only to supplement prevailing formalist practices by extending attention to the historical contexts in which literary texts originate. Thus, according to Louis Montrose, New Historicism represents an effort merely to *refigure* "the socio-cultural field within which canonical . . . literary and dramatic works were originally produced" and to *situate* such works "not only in relationship to other genres and modes of discourse but also in relationship to contemporaneous social institutions and non-discursive practices . . ."

There is very little here to which other critics, whether traditional literary scholars, "cultural materialists," feminists, or "social historians," could reasonably take exception. In the process of elaborating the theory, methods, techniques, and aims of this project, however, the New Historicists have, inadvertently or by design, run afoul of some reigning orthodoxies in both literary and historical studies.

Thus, for example, Louis Montrose, after setting forth the New Historicist program in relatively conventional terms, goes on to say: "In effect, this project *reorients* the axis of intertextuality, substituting for the diachronic text of an autonomous literary history the synchronic text of a cultural system . . ." Here Montrose has shifted the interests and grounds of New Historicism considerably. First, it is now "a cultural system," rather than "contemporaneous social institutions and non-discursive practices," to which literary works are to be related. Second, it is now the "synchronic" rather than the "diachronic" aspects of the relationship between literature and the "cultural system" that become the preferred focus of the New Historicists' attention. Third, in his characterization of the New Historicist "project" as a "reorientation" of "the axis of intertextuality," Montrose implicitly effects a shift from the notion that "literature" consists of a body of "works" to the notion that it consists of a set of "texts," with all that the term "texts" implies in contemporary Post-structuralist discussions of language, discourse, and culture. And, fourth, the idea of "text" has now been explicitly constituted as a *tertium comparationis* by which to characterize the differences and to mediate between an older, formalist notion of an "autonomous literary history" and a newer, historicist notion of literature as a function of the "cultural system." It is the "text" of "a cultural system" that is to be substituted for the "text" of "an autonomous literary history." Consequently, what was originally represented as an interest in studying the relation between literary works and their socio-cultural contexts is suddenly revealed as a radical reconceptualization of literary works, their socio-cultural contexts, the relations between them, and therefore of "history" itself—all are now to be considered as kinds of "texts."

A formulation such as this offends against a number of orthodoxies in both literary and historical studies. First, by suggesting that literary texts can be illuminated by the study of their relations to their historical contexts, the New Historicists offend against the formalist tenets of an older but still powerful New Criticism. New Historicists appear to be returning to the older philological approach to the study of literary texts and in the process committing what New Critics called the "genetic fallacy." Second, by suggesting that it is possible to distinguish between text and context, they offend against the newer, Post-structuralist versions of formalism. According to Post-structuralist theory, there is nothing "outside" of texts, and consequently the efforts of the New Historicists to distinguish between text and context lead to the commission of the "referential fallacy." Third, the ways in which they construe the nature of the historical context give offense to historians in general. For the New Historicists, the historical context is the "cultural system." Social institutions and practices, including politics, are construed as functions of this system, rather than the reverse. Thus, New Historicism appears to be based on what might be called the "culturalist fallacy," which marks it as a brand of historical idealism. And, fourth, the way the New Historicists construe the relations between literary texts and the cultural system gives offense to historians and traditional literary scholars alike. This relationship is conceived to be "intertextual" in nature. It is a relationship between two kinds of "texts": "literary" on the one side, "cultural" on the other. Whence the charge that New Historicism is reductionist in a double sense: it reduces the social to the status of a function of the cultural, and then further reduces the cultural to the status of a text. All of which adds up to the commission of what might be called the "textualist fallacy."

As thus envisaged, New Historicism is anything but a synthesis of formalist and historical approaches to the study of literature. On the contrary, it appears rather more as an attempt to combine what *some* historians regard as "formalist" fallacies (culturalism and textualism) in the study of history with what *some* formalist literary theorists regard as "historicist" fallacies (geneticism and referentiality) in the study of literature. Thus, for Fox-Genovese, speaking as representative of a properly "historical" approach to the study of cultural phenomena, the New Historicists are not geneticist or referential enough. Their culturalogical ("literary theory") approach and textualist ("Post-structuralist") biases blind them to the "social structural" and "political" nature of history.

So, too, it is less the formalism of New Historicist approaches to the study of literary texts and their contexts than the peculiar kind of formalism (Geertzian, de Manian, Derridean, Foucauldian) that offends the various "cultural materialists" represented in this volume: Newton, Thomas, Klancher, Pecora. For these critics, the New Historicists are simply not "materialist" enough in their formalism. Thus, it would seem, the New Historicists are both too historical and not historical enough; they are too formalist and not formalist enough, depending upon which variety of historical theory or of literary theory is taken as the basis for criticizing them.

Now, there are many good reasons for criticizing a textualist approach to the study of culture, society, or a given period of history, but the contention that textualism is inherently a- or anti-historical is not one of them. For whether "history" is considered simply as "the past," the documentary record of this past, or the body of reliable information about the past established by professional historians, there is no such thing as a distinctively "historical" method by which to study this "history." Indeed, the history of historical studies displays ample evidence of the necessity of importing conceptual models, analytical methods, and representational strategies from other disciplines for the analysis of structures and processes considered to be generally historical in nature. In principle, therefore, there is nothing inherently a- or anti-historical in importing models, methods, and strategies borrowed from Geertzian cultural anthropology, Foucauldian discourse theory, Derridean or de Manian deconstructionism, Sausurrian semiotics, Lacanian psychoanalytical theory, or Jakobsonian poetics into historical studies. The version of history that you will get by employing such models, methods, and strategies will certainly look different from that composed on the basis of other principles, such as those of Marxist dialectics or the methods of what used to be called "the new social history." But it will be a "historical" history nonetheless if it takes as its object of study any aspect of "the past," distinguishes between that object and its various contexts, periodizes the processes of change governing the relationships between them, posits specific causal forces as governing these processes, and represents the part of history thus marked out for study as a complex structure of relationships at once integrated at any given moment and developing and changing across any sequence of such moments.

To be sure, the use of a culturalogical as against a sociological model for orienting an approach to the study of history carries with it implications of a decidedly ideological order. These implications are specified by Vincent Pecora, Brook Thomas, Betsy Fox-Genovese, Jon Klancher, and Frank Lentricchia, with greater or lesser relevance to the actual critical practices of the New Historicists themselves. But both the identification of these implications and the grounds for condemning them as ahistorical are themselves functions of the ideological positions of these critics. And indeed the specific criticisms directed against the New Historicists by these critics turn for the most part on political and ethical issues. But it has to be said that a preference for a sociological over a culturalogical approach to the study of history cannot be justified by an appeal to the "facts" of history, since it is precisely the nature of these facts and the determination of what they are facts *of* that are at issue in the conflict between the two approaches.

So, obviously, it is less the culturalogical approach to the study of history, than the specific culturalogy employed by the New Historicists that offends their critics. Whether it is Geertzian culturalogy, with its technique of "thick description," alleged blindness to political realities, and conservative ethnocentrism (Pecora); Foucauldian culturalogy, with its theory of epistemes, reduction of social and cultural processes to "discursive practices," political pessimism, and ethical "egotism" (Lentricchia), it is the *kind* of culturalogy used by the New Historicists to study history that gives offense. And here it is the shared "textualism" of both Geertzian and Foucauldian culturalogy, whatever the other differences between them, that is the sticking point.

Is there anything inherently a-historical in the use of "text" as a model for construing, first, the cultural system conceived as the primary unit of historical study and, secondly, the elements or aspects of the unit thus construed? Every approach to the study of history presupposes some model for construing its object of study, for the simple reason that since "history" comprises everything that ever happened in "the past," it requires some *tertium comparationis* by which to distinguish between what is "historical" and what is not and, beyond that, between what is "significant" and what is relatively insignificant, within this "past." This is the function of the model of the "social structure" appealed to by Professor Fox-Genovese in her critique of the "literary theoretical" bias of the New Historicists. And this is also the function of the model of the Base-Superstructure relationship appealed to more or less openly by "cultural materialist" critics of New Historicism, such as Thomas and Pecora. For the New Historicists, apparently, it is language in general, specifically discursive language, and particularly textualized discursive language that serves as the *tertium comparationis* without which it cannot do its work or play its game of historical study. So, the question at issue is whether the concept of "text" can legitimately be used as a viable *tertium comparationis* by which to identify a specifically historical phenomenon and whether, if it can be so used, it can yield any significant knowledge about the relative historical significance and insignificance of the events, structures, and processes of history.

First, it should be said that every approach to the study of the past presupposes or entails some version of a textualist theory of historical reality of some kind. This is because, primarily, the historical past is, as Fredric Jameson has argued, accessible to study "only by way of its prior textualizations," whether these be in the form of the documentary record or in the form of accounts of what happened in the past written up by historians themselves on the basis of their research into the record. Secondly, historical accounts of the past are themselves based upon the presumed adequacy of a written representation or textualization of the events of the past to the reality of those events themselves. Historical events, whatever else they may be, are events which really happened or are believed really to have happened, but which are no longer directly accessible to perception. As such, in order to be constituted as objects of reflection, they must be described, and described in some kind of natural or technical language. The analysis or explanation, whether nomological or narrativistic, that is subsequently provided of the events is always an analysis or explanation of the events as previously *described*. The description is a product of processes of linguistic condensation, displacement, symbolization, and secondary revision of the kind that inform the production of texts. On this basis alone, one is justified in speaking of history as a text.

This is, to be sure, a metaphor, but it is no more metaphorical than Marx's statement that "all previous history is the history of class struggle" or the statement by Fox-Genovese that "History, at least good history, is inescapably structural." More importantly, the statement "History is a text" is in no way inconsistent with these other statements about the nature of history. On the contrary, it is or at least can be so considered for methodological purposes, if anything, a qualification of these other statements. As thus envisaged, the textualism of the New Historicists, like the textualisms of Structuralists and Post-structuralists, of Geertz and Foucault, has the advantage of making explicit and therefore subject to criticism the textualist element in any approach to the study of history. And beyond that it permits us to see that the conflict between the New Historicists and their critics, especially those of them who come from literary studies or cultural studies in general, is a conflict between different theories of textuality.

It is worth recalling that, for the New Historicists, the principal problem for which their brand of historicism was to be a solution was less formalism than the brand of literary history which formalism produced. The older formalist treatment of literary works presupposed both the "autonomy" of literature with respect to its historical contexts and the incomparability of individual works with one another except insofar as they manifest the same or similar "stylistic" features. Consequently, the "history" of literature could only be conceived as a sequence of unique stylistic moments, each of which could be grasped as a paradigmatic structure but the relations among which, due to the uniqueness of each, had to remain in principle indeterminable. New Historicism, if I understand Montrose correctly, wishes to continue to honor this conception of literary history as a sequence of unique moments, each of which can be grasped as a discrete structure of relationships paradigmatically organized, but also wishes to extend the principle of paradigmatic structuration to include non-literary texts, on the one hand, and the social institutions and practices that comprise historical contexts, on the other.

The result of all this is a view of history as a sequence of integral "cultural systems" of which both literature and social institutions and practices are to be regarded as manifestations or expressions and the relations among which are to be regarded as mutually determining and determined. Whence Montrose's suggestion that:

> We might . . . entertain the propositions that the interdependent processes of subjectification and structuration are both ineluctably social and historical; that social systems are produced and reproduced in the interactive social practices of individuals and groups; that collective structures may enable as well as constrain individual agency; that the possibilities and patterns for action are always socially and historically situated, always limited and limiting; and that there is no necessary relationship between the intentions of actors and the outcomes of their actions.

It seems to me that there is nothing here—or very little—that might give offense to Professor Fox-Genovese or the cohort of "structural" social historians for which she speaks. There is plenty of room for what Fox-Genovese represents as the properly historical view, that literary texts are a "function, or articulation of context," rather than the reverse, namely, that the context is a function and articulation of literary texts—a view which she attributes to the New Historicists. To be sure, it is the nature of this "function, or articulation" that is at issue. Is the literary text to be accorded any special status as a "function, or articulation" of its context? Does the literary text "function" as an especially privileged historical datum, not only yielding insight into the nature of its context but also providing a model for the study of that context as well? Montrose thinks it does, Fox-Genovese thinks it doesn't.

But the crucial differences between them turn upon the question of the nature of that context of which the literary text is to be considered a "function, or articulation." Montrose explicitly rejects the view that literature is "an autonomous aesthetic order that transcends the shifting pressures and particularities of material needs and interests." And while he also rejects the notion that it is either "a collection of inert discursive records of 'real' events" or merely "a superstructural reflexion of an economic base," I presume, on the basis of her own remarks, that these are views that Fox-Genovese could share without too much difficulty. If literary texts are "functions, or articulations" of their historical contexts, it does not follow that they are nothing but "records" or "reflexions" of such contexts. In fact, Montrose argues only for the "relative autonomy" of literary works, their status as evidence of the human capacity to respond, and not merely react, to the social and cultural conditions of the time and place of their production.

Montrose's propositions are perfectly compatible with Fox-Genovese's contention that "History, at least good history, is inescapably structural." And I take this to be true as well of both the principles and practices of New Historicism as represented in the work of Catherine Gallagher and Stephen Greenblatt. New Historicism in general argues only for what Montrose calls "the relative autonomy" of literature, which can hardly be objectionable even to Marxist historians and social theorists, since it is the "relative autonomy" of human consciousness and action and of the cultural superstructure, which includes literature, that constitutes a main problematic of their historical studies and authorizes the employment of a "dialectical" method for the analysis of all specifically historical phenomena. If the agents and agencies of historical reality were not "relatively autonomous" with respect to the dominant structures prevailing at a given time and place, such structures would undergo no changes of a specifically "historical," as against a generally "natural," kind at all.

All of which suggests that, if New Historicism retains residues of the formalism that it seeks to supplement or revise, this is true of Marxist historicism as well. Marxism and New Historicism alike are committed to some notion of a paradigmatic relationship between cultural forms, on the one side, and social relations of production, on the other, in discrete periods of history. And for Left critics, including "cultural materialists," or various oppositionalist critics, including feminists and ethno-critics, to pillory New Historicism for the formalist and therefore anti-historical nature of its theory, methods, or practices amounts to no more than a denial of those aspects of their own theories, methods, and practices which they share with the New Historicists themselves.

But there is another aspect of the New Historicism over which there exists a possibility of genuinely principled disagreement with both traditional "bourgeois" historians and their Marxist counterparts. This has to do with the manner in which the New Historicists, as represented in this instance by Montrose, conceptualize the *syntagmatic* dimension of the history of literature and by extension the history of both culture and society as well.

Recall that Montrose speaks of "substituting for the *diachronic* text of an autonomous literary history the *synchronic* text of a cultural system . . ." Recall, too, that it is this substitution that is to provide the desired "historical" supplement to the formalist manner of construing the history of literature as a diachronic sequence of unique moments of literarity. The formulation appears strange, because conventionally "diachronic" is taken to be synonymous with a specifically "historical," and "synchronic" with a generally "ahistorical" treatment of phenomena. So, how could one possibly redress the balance of a predominantly formalist approach to the study of literary history by substituting for it or supplementing it with a specifically "synchronic" treatment?

Here it might be helpful to recall Roman Jakobson's famous characterization of the similarities and differences between the "poetic" and the "metalinguistic" functions of language. According to Jakobson, *"The poetic function projects the principle of equivalence from the axis of selection* [i.e., the paradigmatic axis] *to the axis of combination* [i.e., the syntagmatic axis]." The principle of equivalence thus comes to serve as the device constitutive of the patterns and periodicities of a distinctively poetic sequentiality. The metalinguistic function of language, by contrast, refers to and specifies the "code" in which an uterrance is cast. It, too, "makes a sequential use of equivalent units when combining synonymic expressions into an equational sentence: A = A (*'Mare* is *the female of the horse'*)." But, Jakobson argues, "Poetry and metalanguage . . . are in diametrical opposition to each other: in metalanguage the sequence is used to build an equation, whereas in poetry the equation is used to build a sequence" ("Closing Statement: Linguistics and Poetics," in Thomas Sebeok, ed., *Style in Language* [Cambridge: MIT Press, 1960], pp. 357–58).

Something like this formulation of the relationship between the poetic and the metalinguistic functions of language might lie behind and inform Montrose's notion of the differences between "the diachronic text of an autonomous literary history" and "the synchronic text of a cultural system." As thus envisaged, what appears at first sight to be a conflict between "diachronic" and "synchronic" conceptualizations of historical processes could be seen upon further reflection to involve contrasting notions of the nature of *historical sequentiality.* In the former, formalist instance, the sequence of literary periods, authors, works, corpora, genres, and so on is used to build a series of equations (A = A ["Shakespeare is a classic," "The Elizabethan Renaissance was an apex of English literature," *"Hamlet* is a tragedy," "Wordsworth was the quintessential British Romantic lyricist," etc.]). The explanatory effect of the series thus built is a function of the progressive classification of historical entities (Shakespeare, Wordsworth, *Hamlet,* the Elizabethan Renaissance) as instantiations or exemplifications of the categories constituting the "code" of English literary history ("classic," "tragedy," "Renaissance," "Romantic," "lyric," etc.). Although each instance or exemplification might be treated as a unique moment in the sequence, it is its status as a "function, or articulation" of the fundamental structure (or code) of English literary history that reveals its meaning.

In the latter, New Historicist instance, by contrast, an equation ("Literature is a relatively autonomous medium of cultural production and exchange, the forms and functions of which vary with changes in the cultural system at large"—something like that) is used to build a sequence of discrete moments, the pattern of which would be retrodictively discernible but not prospectively predictable from within any given moment of the sequence itself. This would not imply that no fundamental structure or code is discernible in the production of the sequence, only that the code cannot be appealed to in order to account for the unique features of specific moments in the series that comprises the sequence. As thus construed, a historical sequence would have to be envisaged as a complex interaction between two kinds of syntagmatic processes: one corresponding to the "metalinguistic" dimension of Jakobson's linguistic model, the other corresponding to the "poetic" dimension thereof.

It seems evident that the principal criticisms leveled against the New Historicists are advanced on the presumption that historical sequences are to be comprehended as functions of forces more "code-like" than "poetic" in nature. Moreover, the general gist of these criticisms is that the New Historicists share this presumption but have simply mis-identified the nature of the code or codes that actually determine the structures and processes of historical sequences, seeking to substitute a cultural, literary, discursive, or "poetic" code for others more primary—political, social, class, ethnic, gender, and so on.

But, on my understanding of the matter at least, the New Historicists have advanced the notion of a "cultural poetics" and by extension a "historical poetics" as a means of identifying those aspects of historical sequences that conduce to the breaking, revision, or weakening of the dominant codes— social, political, cultural, psychological, and so on—prevailing at specific times and places in history. Whence their interest in what appears to be the episodic, anecdotal, contingent, exotic, abjected, or simply uncanny aspects of the historical record. These aspects of history can be deemed "poetic"— in the sense of "creative" (rather than that of "fanciful" or "imaginary")— in that they appear to escape, transcend, contravene, undermine, or contest the rules, laws, and principles of the modes of social organization, structures of political superordination and subordination, and cultural codes predominating at the time of their appearance. In this respect, they can be said to resemble poetic speech which, even though it may contravene the rules of both grammar and logic, not only *has* meaning, but also always implicitly challenges the canonical rules of linguistic expression prevailing at the time of its utterance. It is not that such "poetic" aspects of history are its sole content. Nor is it that history displays no evidence of being informed by processes more logical than poetical in kind. It is just that, as Vico argued in the *New Science,* the "logic" of history is as much "poetical" as it is "grammatical" in kind.

Practitioners of established fields of studies in the human and social sciences, such as sociology, economics, politics, linguistics or literary studies, go to history for a variety of reasons and in a variety of ways. When they do so, they are usually looking for information about some aspect of the specific object of interest that their discipline has been established to study: social structures, economic practices, political institutions, language use, literary works. Often, however, students of an established discipline may turn to history, less for information about their own specialized objects of interest than for the kind of knowledge a specifically "historical" approach to the study of those objects is supposed to be able to provide. In this case, they are compelled to make specific claims about the nature of "history," whether considered simply as "the past," the documentary record of the past, or what historians have established as reliable information about the past, and to make explicit what they understand to be the specifically "historical approach" they are using for the study of their own special objects of interest. And it is here that they run the risk of offending both professional historians, practitioners of the one discipline in the human sciences which takes "history" as *its* special object of interest, and other practitioners of their own field of studies who either have their own versions of what "history" consists of or view their special objects of interest as intractable by the methods used in other disciplines, history included.

So it is with the New Historicists. On the evidence presented in this volume, they appear to have turned to history, less for information about that literature of which they are students, than for the kind of knowledge that a specifically historical approach to its study might yield. What they have discovered, however, is that there is no such thing as a specifically historical approach to the study of history, but a variety of such approaches, at least as many as there are positions on the current ideological spectrum; that, in fact, to embrace a historical approach to the study of anything entails or implies a distinctive philosophy of history; and that, finally, one's philosophy of history is a function as much of the way one construes one's own special object of scholarly interest as it is of one's knowledge of "history" itself.

Commentary: The Young and the Restless

Stanley Fish

As a privileged first reader of these essays I want to comment on the many and varied pleasures they provide. Whatever the New Historicism is or isn't, the energies mounted on its behalf or in opposition to its (supposed) agenda, are impressive and galvanizing. In a brief afterword, as this is intended to be, I cannot do justice to the arguments and demonstrations of more than twenty pieces, but some things, while perhaps obvious, should at least be noted. The footnotes to some of the essays (see particularly Newton, Klancher, Pecora, Montrose, Marcus, and Fineman) are alone worth the price of admission; they illustrate even more than the essays themselves the richness and diversity of concerns that cluster around the questions raised by the banner of a New Historicism. One is grateful also for the glimpse into new (and at least for this literary scholar) uncharted territories—the politics of modern Indonesia (Pecora), the political emplotment of Latin American narrative (Franco), the fortunes of feminism in the First World War (Marcus), the history of art's efforts to be historical (Bann). These, however, are pleasures along the way, and even when they are provided, they are more often than not ancillary to whatever pleasure is to be derived from polemical debate, which is to say, from theory. For the most part (and this is a distinction to which I shall return) these essays are not doing New Historicism, but talking about doing New Historicism, about the claims made in its names and the problems those claims give rise to; and ungenerous though it may be, those problems will be the focus of my discussion.

The chief problem is both enacted and commented on in more than a few essays: it is the problem of reconciling the assertion of "wall to wall" textuality—the denial that the writing of history could find its foundation in a substratum of unmediated fact—with the desire to say something specific and normative. How is it (the words are Newton's) that one can "recognize the provisionality and multiplicity of local knowledge" and yet "maintain that it is possible to give truer accounts of a 'real' world"?* On what basis

---

*The quoted passages appear in a longer version: Judith Newton, "History as Usual," *Cultural Critique* 9 (Spring 1988), 98.

would such a claim be made if one has just been arguing that all claims are radically contingent and therefore vulnerable to a deconstructive analysis of the assumptions on which they rest, assumptions that must be suppressed if the illusion of objectivity and veracity is to be maintained? One can see this "dilemma" with Brook Thomas as a tension between the frankly political agenda of much New Historicist work and the poststructuralist polemic which often introduces and frames that same work. Thomas notes the tendency of many New Historicists to insist that any representation "is structurally dependent on misrepresentation" (184), on exclusions and forgettings that render it suspect, and wonders how their own representations can be proffered in the face of an insight so corrosive: "If all acts of representation are structurally dependent on misrepresentation, these new histories inevitably create their own canons and exclusions" (185).[1] Thomas's chief exhibit is Jane Tompkins who, he says, switches from asking the metacritical question, "Is there a text in this classroom" to asking the political and normative question, "What text should we have in the classroom?" and thereby "abandons her up-to-date poststructuralist pose and returns to old-fashioned assumptions about literature and historical analysis" (185). It would seem, he concludes, that "the very post-structuralist assumptions that help to attack past histories seem necessarily forgotten in efforts to create new ones" (186). We shall return to the idea of "forgetting" which appears more than once in this collection, and I shall suggest that as an action of the mind it is less culpable than Thomas seems to suggest; but for the time being, I shall let his formulation stand since it clearly sets out a problematic to which many in this volume are responding.

One response to this problematic is to refuse it by denying either of its poles. Thus Elizabeth Fox-Genovese, Vincent Pecora, Jane Marcus, and (less vehemently) Jon Klancher simply reject the post-structuralist textualization of history and insist on a material reality in relation to which texts are secondary. For these authors the "dance" of New Historicism substitutes the ingenuity and cobbled-up learning of the critic for the "history" he or she supposedly serves: "When New Historicism plays with history to enhance the text," objects Marcus, "its enhancement is like the coloring of old movies for present consumption. . . . To learn political lessons from the past we need to have it in black and white" (133). Her effort is to remove from the history of literary women in the First World War the coloring imposed by Sandra Gilbert; she wants, she says, to do "justice to women's history" (144). In a similar vein Pecora contrasts "the kinds of symbolic significance Geertzian anthropology creates" (264) in its so called "thick descriptions" of Indonesian life to the "complex and polymorphous internecine struggles of the Indonesian people for self-determination" and finds that in his analyses Geertz reduces historical experience to "a well-known Western myth" (262), to "anthropological abstraction in spite of [his] claim to greater specificity"

(266). "What, for many historians, would be . . . 'basic' categories such as material want and material struggle . . . lose their privileged position" in Geertzian New Historicism and become, like everything else, "merely culturally constructed sign systems" (244). New Historicist accounts, Pecora concludes, "are theoretically and anthropologically given and not historically determined" (269).

Fox-Genovese is even more blunt. History, she declares, is not simply "a body of texts and a strategy of reading or interpreting them"; rather, "history must also be recognized as what did happen in the past—of the social relations and, yes, 'events' of which our records offer only imperfect clues." It may be possible "to classify price series or . . . hog weights . . . as texts— possible, but ultimately useful only as an abstraction that flattens historically and theoretically significant distinctions" (216). "Distinctions" is a key word in this sentence and in many of the essays, and indeed it names a place of emphasis for both New Historicists and their materialist critics, finally reducing the difference between them in a shared devotion to difference. I shall return to this point, but for the moment I want simply to note the materialist position and to observe that its large vulnerability is one of the subjects of Hayden White's essay. While the materialist critics of New Historicism criticize the ideological program of its practitioners and declare that program to be ahistorical, the grounds for this condemnation "are themselves functions of the ideological positions of these critics" (296). The implicit claim of the materialists to be more immediately in touch with the particulars of history cannot be maintained, because all accounts of the past (and, I might add, of the present) come to us through "some kind of natural or technical language" (297) and that language must itself proceed from some ideological vision. "Every approach to the study of history presupposes some model for construing its object of study"; and it is from the perspective of that model, whatever it is, that one distinguishes "between what is 'historical' and what is not" (296). What this means is that "the conflict between the New Historicists and their critics" is not a conflict between textualists and true historians, but "between different theories of textuality" (297). Thus everyone's history is textual—"there is no such thing as a specifically historical approach to the study of history" (302)—and while one can always lodge objections to the histories offered by one's opponents, one cannot (at least legitimately) label them as non-historical. In the words of Lynn Hunt, herself a respected historian, "there is no such thing as history in the sense of a referential ground of knowledge."[2]

Of course, such remarks return us to the dilemma with which we began and invite the familiar question, "but if you think *that* about history, how can you, without contradictions, make historical assertions?" How, in other words, can you theorize your own position in a way that escapes the critique you want to make of those who have been historians before you? It would seem that one must either give up the textualist thesis as the materialists urge (which leaves them open to the charge of being positivist at a time when it is a capital offense to be such) or stand ready to be accused of the sin of contradiction. Some New Historicists outflank this accusation by making it first, and then confessing to it with an unseemly eagerness. In this way they transform what would be embarrassing if it were pointed out by another into a sign of honesty and methodological self-consciousness.

In this mode Louis Montrose may be thought a virtuoso. His now familiar formula, "the textuality of history, the historicity of texts," is a succinct expression of the (supposed) problem. By the textuality of history Montrose means "that we can have no access to a full and authentic past, a lived material existence, unmediated by the surviving textual traces of the society in question, . . . traces . . . that . . . are themselves subject to subsequent textual mediations when they are construed as the 'documents' upon which historians ground their own texts, called 'histories' " (20). By the historicity of texts, Montrose means "the cultural specificity, the social embedment, of all modes of writing" (20). The problem is to get from the quotation marks put around "documents" and "histories" to the specificities, or more point-edly, to the strong assertion of the specificities that have now, it would seem, dissolved into a fluid and protean textuality. Once you have negotiated the shift, as Montrose puts it later, from "history to histories," that is, to multiple stories and constructions no one of which can claim privilege, how do you get back?

At one point Montrose seems to say "no problem," as he simply declares the passage easy. "We may simultaneously acknowledge the theoretical indeterminacy of the signifying process and the historical specificity of discursive practices" (23). More often, however, he allows the dilemma to play itself out as he tacks back and forth between the usual claims for the special powers of the New Historicist methodology and the admission that his own epistemology seems to leave no room for those special powers. The climax of this drama late in his essay finds Montrose bringing these two directions of his argument together in a moment of high pathos. In one sentence he asserts that by foregrounding "issues such as politics and gender" in his readings of Spenser and Shakespeare, he is participating both in the "re-invention of Elizabethan culture" and in the "re-formation" of the constraints now operating in our own; and in the next, he acknowledges that his work is "also a vehicle for my partly unconscious and partly calculating negotiation of disciplinary, institutional and societal demands" and that therefore "his pursuit of knowledge and virtue is necessarily impure" (30). The conclusion, which seems inescapable, is that you cannot "escape from ideology," but this insight is itself immediately converted into an escape when the act of having achieved it is said to have endowed the agent (in this case Montrose) with a special consciousness of the conditions within which he lives:

> However, the very process of subjectively *living* the confrontations or contradictions within or among ideologies makes it possible to experience facets of our own subjection at shifting internal distances—to read as in a refracted light, one fragment of our own ideological inscription by means of another. A reflexive knowledge so partial and unstable may, nevertheless, provide subjects with a means of empowerment as agents. (30)

Partiality and instability—the very impediments to achieving any distance from our situation—become the way to that distance when one becomes reflexively aware of them. The questions one might ask of this reflexivity—what is its content, where does it come from?—are never asked. Montrose is content to solve his dilemma by producing (but not recognizing) another version of it in the claim that while he, like all the rest of us, is embedded and impure, he and some of his friends *know* it, and thus gain a perspective on their impurity which mitigates it.

Elsewhere I have named this move antifoundationalist-theory-hope and declared it illegitimate,[3] but here I am interested in it largely as one response to the dilemma New Historicists and materialists negotiate in different (and sometimes opposing) ways. What I want to say in the rest of this essay is that it is a false dilemma ("no problem" is the right answer) that is generated by the conflation and confusion of two different questions:

1.   Can you at once assert the textuality of history and make specific and positive historical arguments?
2.   Can you make specific and positive historical arguments that follow from— have the form they do as a consequence of—the assertion that history is textual?

The answer to the first question is "yes," and yes without contradiction (whether it is a contradiction one castigates or wallows in) because the two actions— asserting the textuality of history and making specific historical argument—have nothing to do with one another. They are actions in different practices, moves in different games. The first is an action in the practice of producing general (i.e. metacritical) accounts of history, the practice of answering such questions as "where does historical knowledge come from?" or "what is the nature of historical fact?" The second is an action in the practice of writing historical accounts (as opposed to writing an account of how historical accounts get written), the practice of answering questions such as "what happened" or "what is the significance of this event?" If you are asked a question like "what happened" and you answer "the determination of what happened will always be a function of the ideological vision of the observer; there are no unmediated historical perceptions," you will have answered a question from one practice in the terms of another and your interlocutor will be justifiably annoyed. But isn't it the case, one might object, that the two are intimately related, that you will answer the question "what happened" differently if you believe that events are constructed rather than found? The answer to that question is no. The belief that facts are constructed is a *general* one and is not held with reference to any facts in particular; particular facts are firm or in question insofar as the perspective (of some enterprise or discipline or area of inquiry) within which they emerge is firmly in place, settled; and should that perspective be dislodged (always a possibility) the result will not be an indeterminacy of fact, but a new shape of factual firmness underwritten by a newly, if temporarily, settled perspective. No matter how strongly I believe in the constructed nature of fact, the facts that are perspicuous for me within constructions not presently under challenge (and there must always be some for perception even to occur) will remain so. The conviction of the textuality of fact is logically independent of the firmness with which any particular fact is experienced.

I would not be read as flatly denying a relationship between general convictions and the way facts are experienced. If one is convinced of the truth of, say, Marxism or psychoanalysis, that conviction might well have the effect of producing one's sense of what the facts in a particular case are[4]; but a conviction that all facts rest finally on shifting or provisional grounds will not produce shifting and provisional facts because the grounds on which facts rest are themselves particular, having to do with traditions of inquiry, divisions of labor among the disciplines, acknowledged and unacknowledged assumptions (about what is valuable, pertinent, weighty). Of course, these grounds are open to challenge and disestablishment, but the challenge, in order to be effective, will have to be as particular as they are; the work of challenging the grounds will not be done by the demonstration (however persuasive) that they are generally challengeable. The conclusion may seem paradoxical, but it is not: although a conviction strongly held can affect perception and the experience of fact, the one exception to this generality is the conviction that all convictions are tentative and revisable. The only context in which holding (or being held by) *that* conviction will alter one's sense of fact is the context in which the fact in question is the nature and status of conviction. In any other context the conviction of general revisability—the conviction that things have been otherwise and could be otherwise again—will be of no consequence whatsoever.

You may have noticed that by answering my first question—can you at once profess a textual view of history and make strong historical assertions?—in the affirmative, I have at the same time answered my second question—can you do history in a way that follows from your conviction of history's textuality?—in the negative. The fact that the textualist views of the New Historicists do not prevent them from making specific and polemic points means that those points will be made just as everyone else's are—with reference to evidence marshalled in support of hypotheses that will in the end be more or less convincing to a body of professional peers. In short, in my argument New Historicists buy their freedom to do history (as opposed to meta-accounts of it) at the expense of their claim to be doing it—or anything else—differently. But of course that is a price the New Historicists will not be willing to pay, for, like their materialist critics, they have a great deal invested in being different, and, again like their materialist critics, the difference they would claim is the difference of being truly sensitive to difference, that is, to the way in which orthodox historical narratives suppress the realities whose acknowledgement would unsettle and deauthorize them. Whatever their disagreements on other matters, both New Historicists and materialists are united in their conviction that current modes of historiography are (wittingly or unwittingly) extensions of oppressive social and political agendas, and this conviction brings with it an agenda: what has been marginalized must be brought to the center; what has been forgotten or left out must be brought to consciousness; what has been assumed must be exposed to the corrosive operation of critique. The materialists believe that the New Historicists default on this program by aestheticizing it; the New Historicists respond by claiming, as Montrose does, that by producing readings of Shakespeare that foreground the politics of gender and the contestation of cultural constraints they participate in the redrawing of the lines of authority and power. Both camps are committed to cultural reformation, and both believe that cultural reformation can be effected by opening up the seams and fissures that a homogenized history attempts to deny.

The idea, although it is never stated in quite this way, is not to allow prevailing schemes of thought and organization to filter out what might be embarrassing to the interests they sustain. The byword or watchword is "complexity," a value that is always being slighted by the stories currently being told. Jane Marcus makes the point with the notion of "forgetting." She quotes Milan Kundera to the effect that "the struggle of man against power is the struggle of memory against forgetting. . . .[M]an has always harbored the desire to . . . change the past, to wipe out tracks, both his own and others" (133). Of course, what tracks are wiped out by are other tracks; for it is the nature of assertion to be selective and the path it lays down will always have the result of obscuring other paths one might have taken. This is what Richard Terdiman means when he observes that "classification always entails symbolic violence" (228). "It is not only that the class you take determines what class you get into. It is that *in classes we learn to class*"

(227), that is, learn to draw lines, establish boundaries, set up hierarchies. Classification in all of its forms, says Terdiman (following Bourdieu), "forcefully excludes what it does not embrace" (227).

This is no doubt true, and indeed it is so true that one wonders whether there is anything one can do about it. "Symbolic violence" seems to be just a fancy phrase for what consciousness inevitably does in the act of seeing distinctions, whether they be social, political, moral, or whatever. However, several writers in this volume think that there is something to be done, something that will counter the violence of "received evaluations of fundamental social operators" (Terdiman, 229). Montrose counsels a "refusal to observe strict boundaries between 'literary' and other texts" (26); we should instead "render problematic the connections between literary and other discourses, the dialectic between the text and the world" (24). Newton would have us behave in a manner appropriate to a self that is now thought to be not stable, but "multiple, contradictory and in process," and she praises those feminist theorists who "have embraced multiplicity and provisionality."* These and other contributors urge us to the same course of action: We should reject the exclusionary discourses that presently delimit our perceptions and abrogate our freedom of action in favor of the more flexible and multi-directional mode of being that seems called for by everything we have recently learned about the historicity of our situatedness; we should classify less, remember more, refuse less, and be forever open in a manner befitting a creature always in process.

The trouble with this advice is that it is impossible to follow. While openness to revision and transformation may characterize a human history in which firmly drawn boundaries can be shown to have been repeatedly blurred and abandoned, openness to revision and transformation are not methodological programs any individual can determinedly and self-consciously enact. One cannot wake up in the morning and decide, "today I am going to be open,"—as opposed to deciding that today I am going to eat less or pay more attention to my children or get my finances in order. Someone who declares "today I am going to be more open" is in turn open to the question, "open with respect to what?" That is an answerable question and the answer can make sense, as in, "with respect to my habit of dismissing relevant student comments I am going to be open" or "where up to now I have refused to consider sex and race as a criteria for admission to this program, I am henceforth going to be open." But of course *that* kind of openness is nothing more (or less) than a resolution to be differently closed, to rearrange the categories and distinctions within which some actions seem to be desirable and others less so; whereas the openness (apparently) desired

*The quoted passage appears in a longer version of Newton's essay in *Cultural Critique* 8 (Spring 1988), note 33, p. 99.

by several of the contributors to this volume is something very much more, a *general* faculty, a distinct muscle of the spirit or mind whose exercise leads not to an alternative plan of directed action but to a plan (if that is the word) to be directionless, to refuse direction, to resist the drawing of lines, to perform multiplicity and provisionality.

This is not a new goal. It is, as Catherine Gallagher points out, a familiar component of the left radical agenda, at least since the sixties. She calls it "indeterminate negativity" (interestingly Roberto Unger's name for it is "negative capability"),[5] and characterizes it correctly as the attempt "to live a radical culture" (41), an attempt in which Montrose thinks we partially succeed when we live—that is, consciously employ as part of our equipment—"the contradictions . . . of our own subjection" (30). What I am saying is that radical culture—understood as the culture of oppositional action, not opposition in particular contexts, but just *opposition* as a principle—cannot be lived, and it cannot be lived for the same reason that the textualist view of history cannot yield an historical method: it demands from a wholly situated creature a mode of action or thought (or writing) that is free from the entanglements of situations and the lines of demarcation they declare; it demands that a consciousness that has shape only by virtue of the distinctions and boundary lines that are its content float free of those lines and boundaries and remain forever unsettled. The curious thing about this demand, especially curious as a component of something that calls itself the New Historicism, is that what it asks us to be is unhistorical, detached at some crucial level from the very structures of society and politics to which the New Historicism pledges allegiance. My point again is that the demand cannot be met; you cannot not forget; you cannot not exclude; you cannot refuse boundaries and distinctions; you cannot live the radical or indeterminate or provisional or textualist life.

What you can do is write sentences like this:

> English Romantic writings were staged within an unstable ensemble of older institutions in crisis (state and church) and emerging institutional events that pressured any act of cultural production—the marketplace and its industrializing, the new media and their reading audiences, the alternative institutions of radical dissent, shifting modes of social hierarchy. (Klancher, 80)

It is tempting (and it is a temptation many of my generation would feel) to mount a full-scale close reading of this sentence, but I will content myself with pointing out the efforts of the prose to keep itself from settling anywhere: English Romantic writings are barely mentioned before they are said to be "staged," i.e. not there for our empirical observation, but visible only against a set of background circumstances that must be the new object of our attention; but before those circumstances are enumerated they are declared to be "unstable" and also an "ensemble" (not one particular thing); and then this instability itself is said to be "in crisis," but in a crisis that is only "emerging" (not yet palpable); and this entire staged, unstable, emerging and "ensembling" crisis is said to put pressure on "any act of cultural production." At this point it looks, alarmingly, as if there is actually going to be a reference to such an act, but anything so specific quickly disappears under a list of the "institutional events" through which "it" is mediated; and finally, lest we carry away too precise a sense of those events (even from such large formulas as "the new media" and "radical dissent") they are given one more kaleidoscopic turn by the phrase "shifting modes." The question is, how long can one go on in *this* shifting mode? Not for many sentences and certainly not for entire essays. Klancher himself touches down to tell a quite linear (and fascinating) story of the institution of Romantic criticism, and indeed no one of the authors in this volume is able to sustain the indeterminacy of discourse that seems called for by the New Historicist creed.

The problem, if there is one, is illustrated by Jean Franco's criticism of allegorical or homogenizing stories. Repeatedly in her essay Franco opposes allegorical readings to enactments of contradiction and difference (see 208, 210). The last few pages of the piece resound with the praise of that which "def[ies] categorization," of the "uneasy and unfinished," of that which "generic boundaries cannot really contain," of the "unclassifiable," of "pluralism," of clashing styles, of the "kaleidoscope [that] constantly shifts to form different and unreconcilable patterns." "We need," she says in conclusion, "density of specification in order to understand the questions to which literary texts are an imaginary response" (212). But while she opposes "density of specification" to allegorical reading, in her own reading of Latin American novels this same insistence on density and the deferral of assertion becomes an allegory of its own. If density of specification is put forward as an end in itself, it is an allegory as totalizing as any, an allegory of discontinuities and overlappings; and if it is urged as a way to flesh out some positive polemical point, it is an allegory of the more familiar kind. Not that I am faulting Franco for falling into the trap of being discursive and linear; she could not do otherwise and still have as an aim (in her terms an allegorical aim) the *understanding*—the bringing into discursive comprehension—of anything. In the end you can't "defy categorization," you can only categorize in a different way. (Itself no small accomplishment.)

Where then does this leave us? Precisely where we have always been, making cases for the significance and shape of historical events with the help of whatever evidence appears to us to be relevant or weighty. The reasons that a piece of evidence will seem weighty or relevant will have to do with the way in which we are situated as historians and·observers, that is, with what we *see* as evidence from whatever angle or perspective we inhabit. Of course, not everyone will see the same thing, and in the (certain) event of disputes, the disputing parties will point to their evidence and attempt to educe more. They will not brandish fancy accounts of how evidence comes to be evidence or invoke theories that declare all evidence suspect and ideological, because, as I have already said, that would be another practice, the practice not of giving historical accounts, but the practice of theorizing their possibility. If you set out to determine what happened in 1649, you will look to the materials that recommend themselves to you as the likely repositories of historical knowledge and go from there. In short, you and those who dispute your findings (a word precisely intended) will be engaged in empirical work, and as Howard Horwitz has recently said, arguments about history "are not finally epistemological but empirical, involving disputes about the contents of knowledge, about evidence and its significance" ("I Can't Remember: Skepticism, Synthetic Histories, Critical Action," *South Atlantic Quarterly* 87: 4 [Fall 1988]: 798).

Another way to put this is to say what others have said before me: the New Historicism is not new. But whereas that observation is usually offered as a criticism—it should be new and it's not—I offer it as something that could not be otherwise. The only way the New or any other kind of historicism could be new is by asserting a new truth about something in opposition to, or correction of, or modification of, a truth previously asserted by someone else; but that newness—always a possible achievement—will not be *methodologically* new, will not be a new (non-allegorical, non-excluding, non-forgetting, non-boundary-drawing) way of doing history, but merely another move in the practice of history as it has always been done.

If New Historicist methodology (as opposed to the answers it might give to thoroughly traditional questions) is finally not different from any other, the claim of the New Historicism to be politically engaged in a way that other historicisms are not cannot be maintained. The methodological difference claimed by New Historicism is the difference of not being constrained in its gestures by narrow disciplinary and professional boundaries. The reasoning is that since New Historicists are aware of those boundaries and aware, too, of their source in ultimately revisable societal (and even global) structures, they can angle their actions (or interventions as they prefer to call them) in such a way as to put pressure on those structures and so perform politically both in the little world of their institutional situation and the larger world of POLITICS. Now in essence this picture of the radiating or widening out effects of institutional action is an accurate one; for since all activities are interrelated and none enables itself, what is done in one (temporarily demarcated) sphere will ultimately have ramifications for what goes on in others. The question is can one perform institutionally with an eye on that radiating effect? Can one grasp the political constructedness and relatedness of all things in order to do one thing in a different and more capacious way? Given that disciplinary performance depends on the in-place force of innumerable and enabling connections and affiliations (both of complicity and opposition), can I *focus* on those connections in such a way as to make my performance self-consciously larger than its institutional situation would seem to allow?[6]

The answer to all these questions is "no," and for the same reason that it is not possible to practice openness of a general rather than a context specific kind. The hope that you can play a particular game in a way that directly affects the entire matrix in which it is embedded depends on there being a style of playing that exceeds the game's constitutive rules (I am not claiming that those rules are fixed or inflexible, just that even in their provisional and revisable form they define the range of activities—including activities of extension and revision—that will be recognized as appropriate, i.e. in the game); depends, that is, on there being a form of destabilization that is not specific to particular practices, but is simply DESTABILIZATION writ large. If there is no such form—no destabilizing act that does not leave more in place than it disturbs— the effects of your practice will be internal to that practice and will only impinge on larger structures in an indirect and etiolated way.

In short, there is no road, royal or otherwise, from the insight that all activities are political to a special or different way of engaging in any particular activity, no politics that derives from the truth that everything is politically embedded. Interrelatedness may be a fact about disciplines and enterprises as seen from a vantage point uninvolved in any one of them (the vantage point of another, philosophical, enterprise), but it cannot be the motor of one's performance. Practices may *be* interrelated but you cannot *do* interrelatedness—simultaneously stand within a practice and reflectively survey the supports you stand on. One often hears it said that once you have become aware of the political and constructed nature of all actions, this awareness can be put to methodological use in the practices (history, literary criticism, law) you find yourself performing; but (and this is the argument about openness, provisionality, and interrelatedness all over again) insofar as awareness is something that can be put into play in a situation it will be awareness relative to the demarcated concerns of that situation, and not some separate capacity that you carry with you from one situation to another.

I not do mean to deny that New Historicist practice may be involved in a politics, only that it could not be involved in the (impossible) politics that has as its goal the refusing of boundaries as in "I refuse to think of literature as a discrete activity" (sometimes you do, sometimes you don't) or "I refuse to think in terms of national or regional identities" (it depends on what you're thinking about), and the exclusion of exclusions, as in "I will remember everything" (which means you will be unable to think of anything) or "I close my ears to no voice" (which means that no voice will be heard by you). Nor am I saying that New Historicist practice has no global implications;

only that the global implications of New Historicist practice cannot be operated by its practitioners. Of course, this is not true of all practices. The actions, say, of members of Congress or of officials of the national administration will have far-reaching and immediate consequences and those consequences can be held in mind as those actions are taken; moreover, it is not impossible that literary criticism could in time become a practice with similarly far-reaching effects.

One can imagine general political conditions such that the appearance on Monday of a new reading of *The Scarlet Letter* would be the occasion on Tuesday of discussion, debate, and proposed legislation on the floor of Congress; but before that can happen (if we really want it to happen) there will have to be a general restructuring of the lines of influence and power in our culture; and while such a restructuring is not unthinkable, it will not be brought about by declarations of revolutionary intent by New Historicists or materialists or anyone else. So long as literary studies are situated as they are now, the most one can hope for (at least with respect to aims that are realistic) is that your work will make a difference in the institutional setting that gives it a home.

And that, as Catherine Gallagher points out, is quite a lot. She observes that New Historicist and allied practices have already altered the institutional landscape by influencing "the curricula in the literature department, introducing non-canonical texts into the classroom . . . making students more aware of the history and significance of . . . imperialism, slavery and gender differentiation" (44–5). She also notes that for many on the left these changes are insufficient, and there is evidence in the present volume that in the minds of some they are downright suspicious. Montrose, as we have seen, is uneasy at the thought that the successes of New Historicism may be merely professional, and that his own labors may be "a vehicle for . . . partly unconscious and partly calculating negotiation of disciplinary, institutional and societal demands and expectations." He is nervous, that is, at the thought that his career may be going well. Vincent Pecora is distressed at the alacrity at which the New Historicism has turned into a "new kind of formalism" (272), and he complains that cultural semiotics for all its pretensions remains determinedly literary and that its effect has been to make our activities not "more political . . . but . . . less so." It is hard to know whether such anxieties are a sign of large ambitions that have been frustrated—do these critics want to be the acknowledged legislators of the world?—or a sign of the familiar academic longing for failure—we must be doing something wrong because people are listening to us and offering us high salaries. But whatever the source of the malaise, I urge that it be abandoned and that New Historicists sit back and enjoy the fruits of their professional success, wishing neither for more nor for less.[7] In the words of the old Alka-Seltzer commercial, "try it, you'll like it."

Notes

1.   I would reply that histories create their own exlusions not because they are misrepresentations—a word that requires for its intelligibility the possibility of a representation that is not one—but because as narratives that tell one story rather than all stories they will always seem partial and inaccurate from the vantage point of other narratives, themselves no less, but differently, exclusionary.

2.   From a talk delivered at a meeting of the English Institute, August 27, 1988.

3.   See my "Consequences," *Critical Inquiry*, vol. 11, (March, 1985), 440–41.

4.   But one could be strongly committed to Marxism or psychoanalysis at one level and still practice history (or literary criticism or pedagogy) in a way that was free of Marxist or psychoanalytic assumptions (although the practice would flow from some other assumptions). This might hold true even if in answer to a direct question about your practice you declared that it was Marxist or psychoanalytic. Your theory of what you do is logically independent of what you in fact do (although, as I acknowledge above, a relationship, at least in some cases, is always possible). Thus someone might reasonably disagree with your account of your practice and agree wholeheartedly with its assertions. To demand a perfect homology between practice and theory and between theory and politics is, as Catherine Gallagher says, to surrender "to the myth of a self-consistent subject impervious to divisions of disciplinary boundaries and outside the constraints of disciplinary standards" (46).

5.   See Roberto Unger, "The Critical Legal Studies Movement, 96 *Harvard Law Review* (1983), and see my "Unger and Milton," in *Doing What Comes Naturally: Change, Rhetoric, and the Practice of Theory in Legal and Literary Studies* (Durham: Duke University Press, 1989).

6.   In fact, were I to adopt such a focus I would no longer be doing literary criticism, I would be doing something else, sociology or anthropology or systems analysis, etc. It is once again a question of forgetting and remembering: one cannot keep in mind everything at once and still perform specific tasks (except perhaps the specific—and impossible—task of fully enumerating everything). The very possibility of performing a specific task depends on *not* attending to (i.e. forgetting) concerns that would, if they were given their due, involve one in the performing of a different specific task.

7.   Cf. Gallagher: "There may be no political impulse whatsoever behind [the] desire to historicize literature. This is not to claim that the desire for historical knowledge is itself historically unplaced or 'objective'; it is, rather, to insist that the impulse, norms, and standards of a discipline called history, which has achieved a high level of autonomy in the late twentieth century, are a profound part of the subjectivity of some scholars and do not in all cases require political ignition" (46). I would only add that the anti-professionalism displayed by Pecora and Montrose is yet another indication of the idealizing and ahistorical vision that generates their complaints and anxieties.

Notes on Contributors

H. Aram Veeser is Assistant Professor of English at The Wichita State University.

Jonathan Arac is Professor of English and Comparative Literature at Columbia University.

Stephen Bann is Professor of Modern Cultural Studies in Rutherford College, The University of Kent at Canterbury.

Joel Fineman is Associate Professor of English at The University of California, Berkeley.

Stanley Fish is Arts and Sciences Distinguished Professor of English and Law and Chairman of the English Department at Duke University.

Elizabeth Fox-Genovese is Professor of History and Director of Women's Studies at Emory University.

Jean Franco is Professor of Spanish at Columbia University.

Catherine Gallagher is Associate Professor of English at The University of California, Berkeley and a founding member of the editorial board of *Representations*.

Gerald Graff is John C. Shaffer Professor of English at Northwestern University and director of Northwestern University Press.

Stephen Greenblatt is Class of 1932 Professor of English at The University of California, Berkeley.

Jon Klancher is Assistant Professor of English at Boston University.

Frank Lentricchia is Professor of English at Duke University and general editor of the Wisconsin Project on American Writers.

Jane Marcus is Professor of English at the Graduate Center of the City University of New York.

Louis A. Montrose is Professor of English at The University of California, San Diego.

Judith Lowder Newton is Associate Professor of English at La Salle University and editor of *Feminist Studies*.

Vincent P. Pecora is Assistant Professor of English at The University of California, Los Angeles.

John D. Schaeffer is Associate Professor of English at Columbus College.

Gayatri Chakravorty Spivak is Professor of English at the University of Pittsburgh.

Richard Terdiman is Professor of French Literature and History of Consciousness at the University of California, Santa Cruz.

Brook Thomas is Professor of English and Comparative Literature at The University of California, Irvine.

Hayden White is Presidential Professor of Historical Studies at The University of California, Santa Cruz.